ON ISLAND TIME

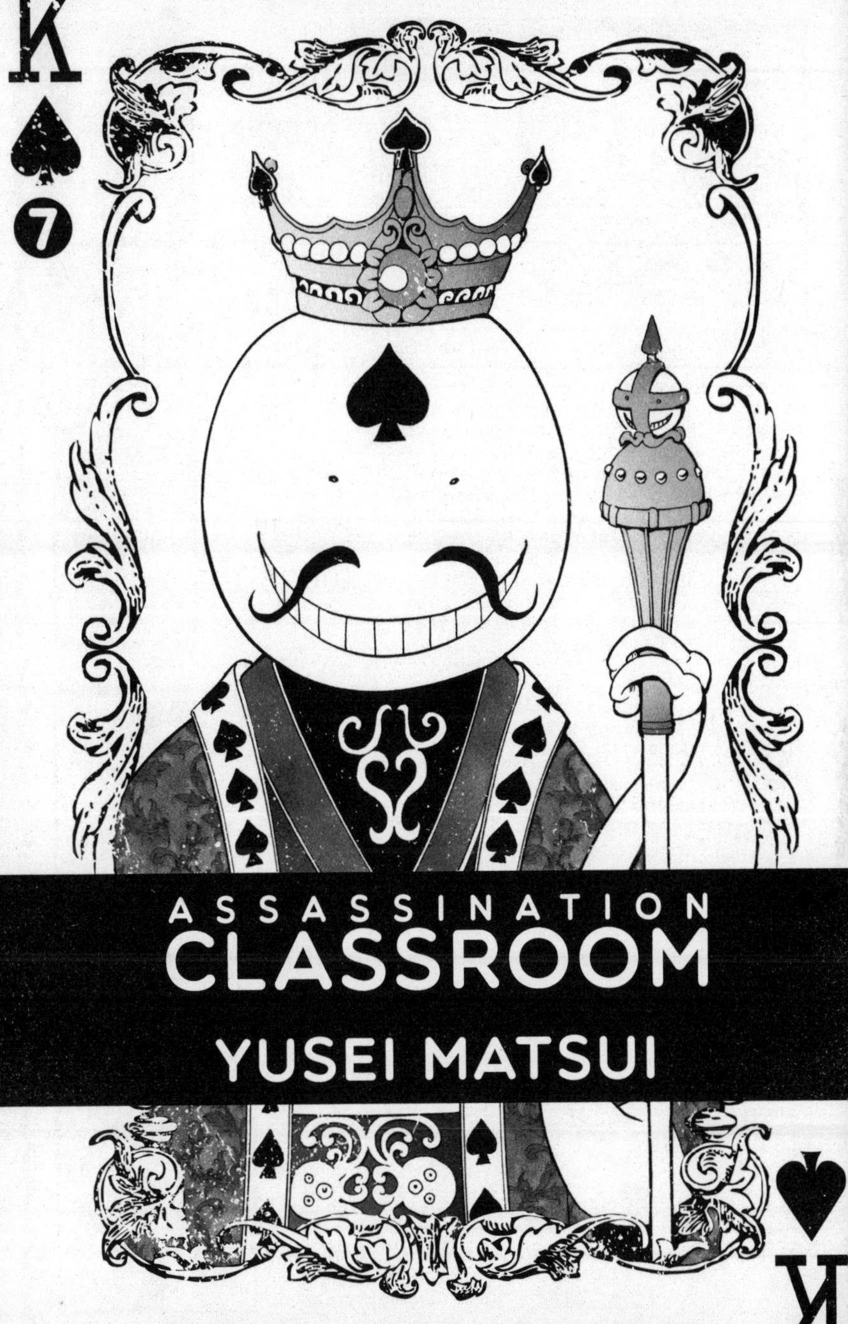
K
7
K

ASSASSINATION CLASSROOM

YUSEI MATSUI

SHONEN JUMP ADVANCED

Koro Tribune

July Issue

Published by: Class 3-E Newspaper Staff

Our new teacher is a creature who plans to destroy the world...?!

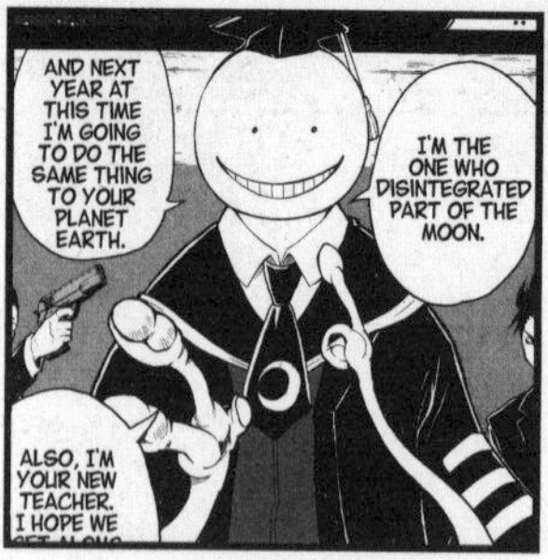
I'M THE ONE WHO DISINTEGRATED PART OF THE MOON.
AND NEXT YEAR AT THIS TIME I'M GOING TO DO THE SAME THING TO YOUR PLANET EARTH.
ALSO, I'M YOUR NEW TEACHER. I HOPE WE

Story Thus Far

One day, something destroyed 70% of the moon.

A mysterious creature showed up in our junior high classroom claiming that he had attacked the moon and promising to destroy the earth next March. And then...he took over as our teacher. What the—?! Faced with a creature beyond human understanding that no army could kill, the leaders of the world had no choice but to rely on the students of Kunugigaoka Junior High, Class 3-E, to do the job. For a reward of ten million dollars... SIGN ME UP!! Will the students of the so-called End Class, filled with losers and rejects, be able to kill their target Koro Sensei by graduation...?!

Koro Sensei

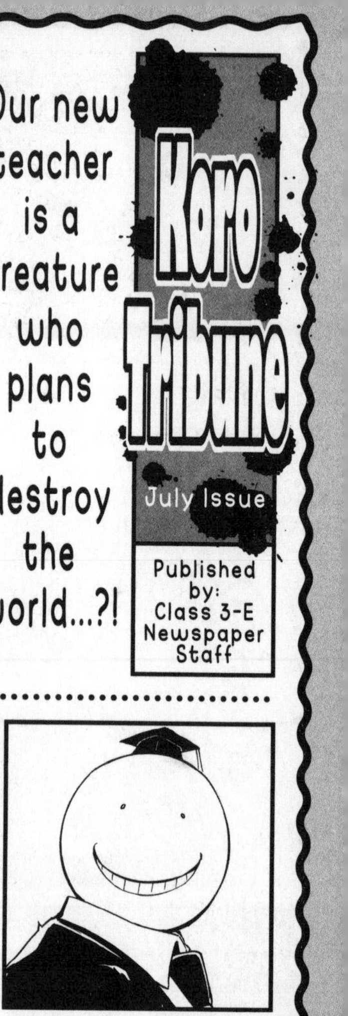

A mysterious octopus-like creature whose nickname is a play on the words "koro senai," which means "can't be killed." He is capable of flying at Mach 20 and his versatile tentacles protect him from attacks and aid him in everyday activities. Nobody knows why he wants to teach Class 3-E, but he has proven to be an extremely capable teacher.

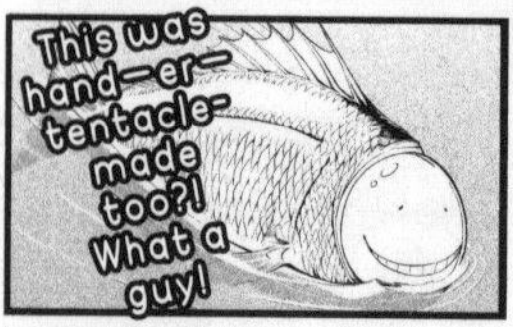
This was hand—er—tentacle-made too?! What a guy!

Kaede Kayano

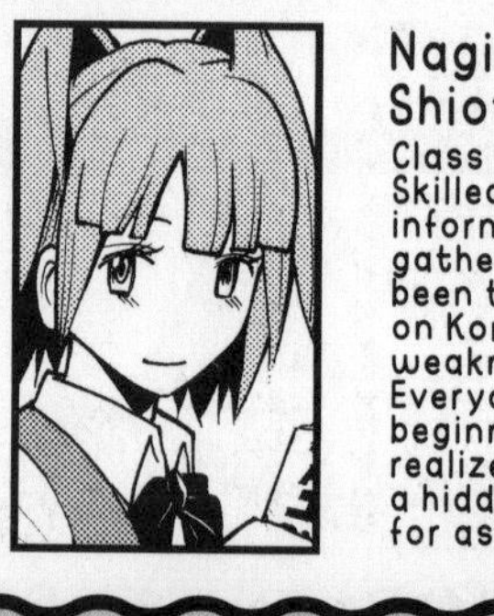

Class E student. She's the one who named Koro Sensei. Sits at the desk next to Nagisa, and they seem to get along well.

Nagisa Shiota

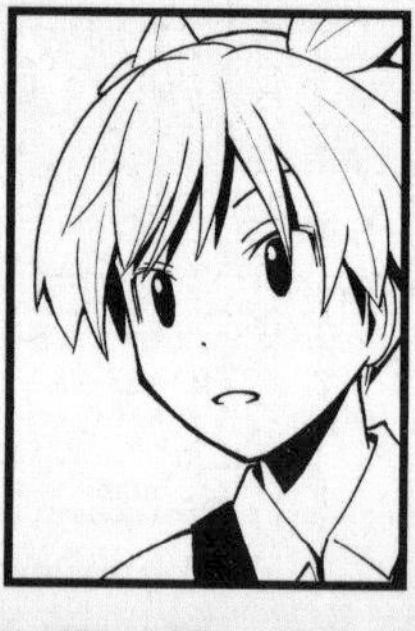

Class E student. Skilled at information gathering, he has been taking notes on Koro Sensei's weaknesses. Everyone is beginning to realize that he has a hidden talent for assassination.

pick up!

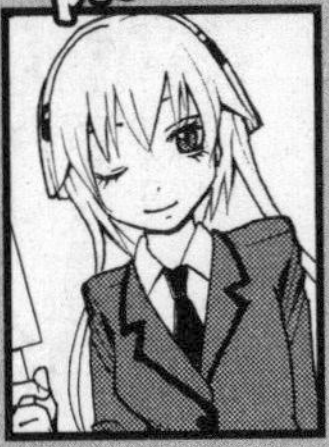

Ritsu

She took the exams as an experiment and ended up getting perfect scores on every test, except for failing the Modern Literature exam. "Human minds are far more difficult than assassinations," she said with a sad smile upon her face.

Karma Akabane

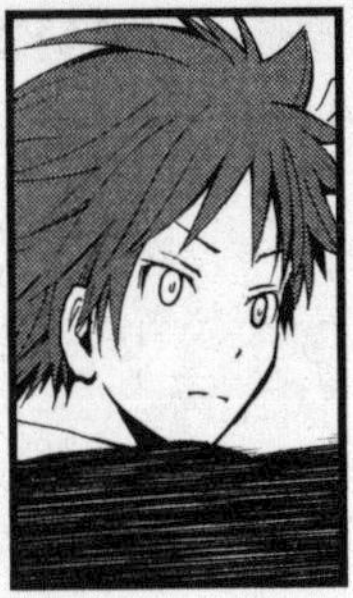

Class E student. A quick thinker skilled at surprise attacks. Succeeded in injuring Koro Sensei a few times.

The Big Five

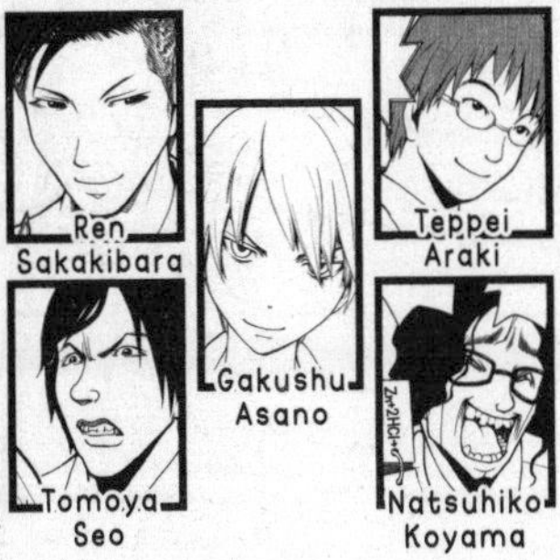

Ren Sakakibara
Gakushu Asano
Teppei Araki
Tomoya Seo
Natsuhiko Koyama

Araki, Sakakibara, Koyama, and Seo are among the top academic scorers at the academy, receiving second, third, fifth, and sixth place respectively on the midterm. Their leader Asano (the principal's son) took first place on the midterm as well as in the national practice exams. "The Big Five" are revered by the other students. Class E is competing with them for first place on the final exam in the five major subjects! How will they fare...?!

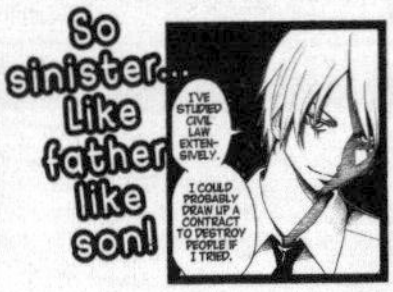

So sinister... Like father like son!
I'VE STUDIED CIVIL LAW EXTENSIVELY.
I COULD PROBABLY DRAW UP A CONTRACT TO DESTROY PEOPLE IF I TRIED.

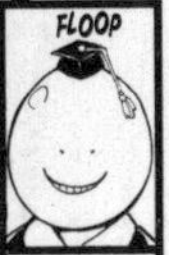

FLOOP

Water Balloon

Filled With 100% Slime

Irina Jelavich

A sexy assassin hired as an English teacher. She's known for using her "womanly charms" to get close to a target but has failed to kill Koro Sensei—yet.

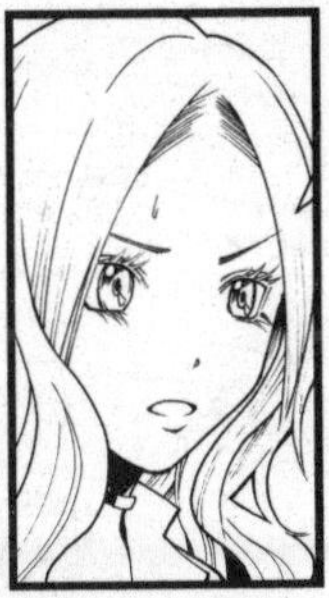

Tadaomi Karasuma

Member of the Ministry of Defense and the Class E students' P.E. teacher. Also in charge of managing visiting assassins.

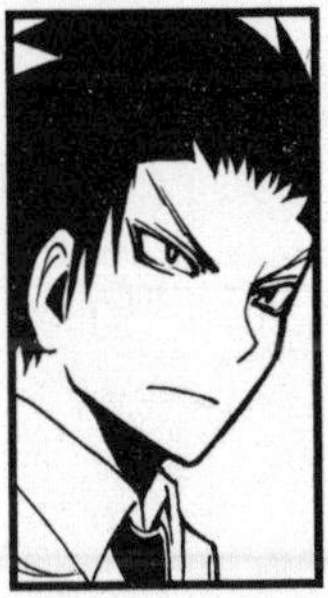

Koro Sensei Rebuilds the swimming pool!

He even added an eye-wash station. The students told him no one uses those anymore, so now it's just a drinking fountain that's really hard to use.

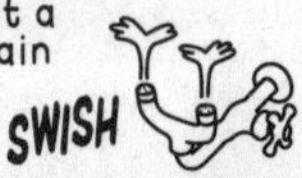

SWISH

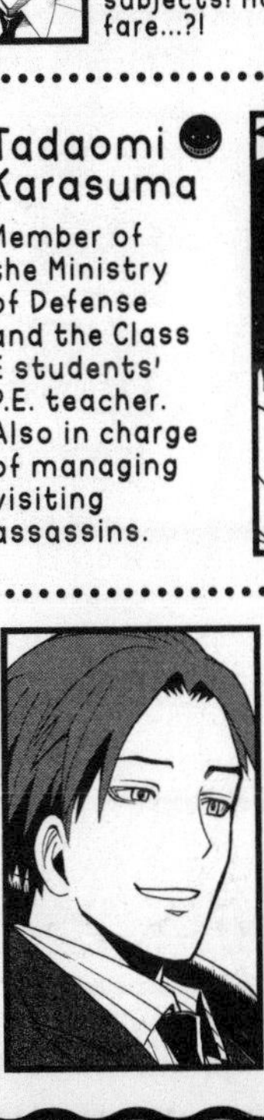

Gakuho Asano

The principal of Kunugigaoka Academy, who built this academically competitive school based on his faith in rationality and hierarchy.

ASSASSINATION CLASSROOM ❼ CONTENTS

(ANSWER SHEET)

Grade 3	Class E	Name	CONTENTS	Score

(Question
Choose

(1) 1 Leave
2 Go to
3 Go to t
4 Take a

(Question 2.)
Which of the
out of 1, 2, 3,

(1) **Kaede:** Tod

Nagisa: No,

I'll be

1 Shall I help

3 Have you fini

)**Irina:** Would you

Karasuma: (

1 Yes, please.

3 All right.

estion 3.)

d the following paragraph and choose the best answer from
, 4 to answer questions (1) and (2) to complete the sentence.

ssassin Contest

tudents of Kunugigaoka Junior High! Assassination Classroom TV is coming to our

hold an audition for the next assassination contest show. Come to the audition if

at assassination and want to b

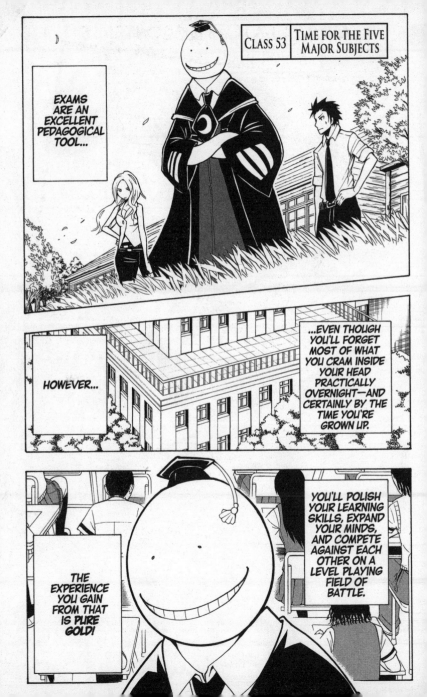

CLASS 53 | TIME FOR THE FIVE MAJOR SUBJECTS

EXAMS ARE AN EXCELLENT PEDAGOGICAL TOOL...

...EVEN THOUGH YOU'LL FORGET MOST OF WHAT YOU CRAM INSIDE YOUR HEAD PRACTICALLY OVERNIGHT—AND CERTAINLY BY THE TIME YOU'RE GROWN UP.

HOWEVER...

YOU'LL POLISH YOUR LEARNING SKILLS, EXPAND YOUR MINDS, AND COMPETE AGAINST EACH OTHER ON A LEVEL PLAYING FIELD OF BATTLE.

THE EXPERIENCE YOU GAIN FROM THAT IS PURE GOLD!

CLASS 53 TIME FOR THE FIVE MAJOR SUBJECTS

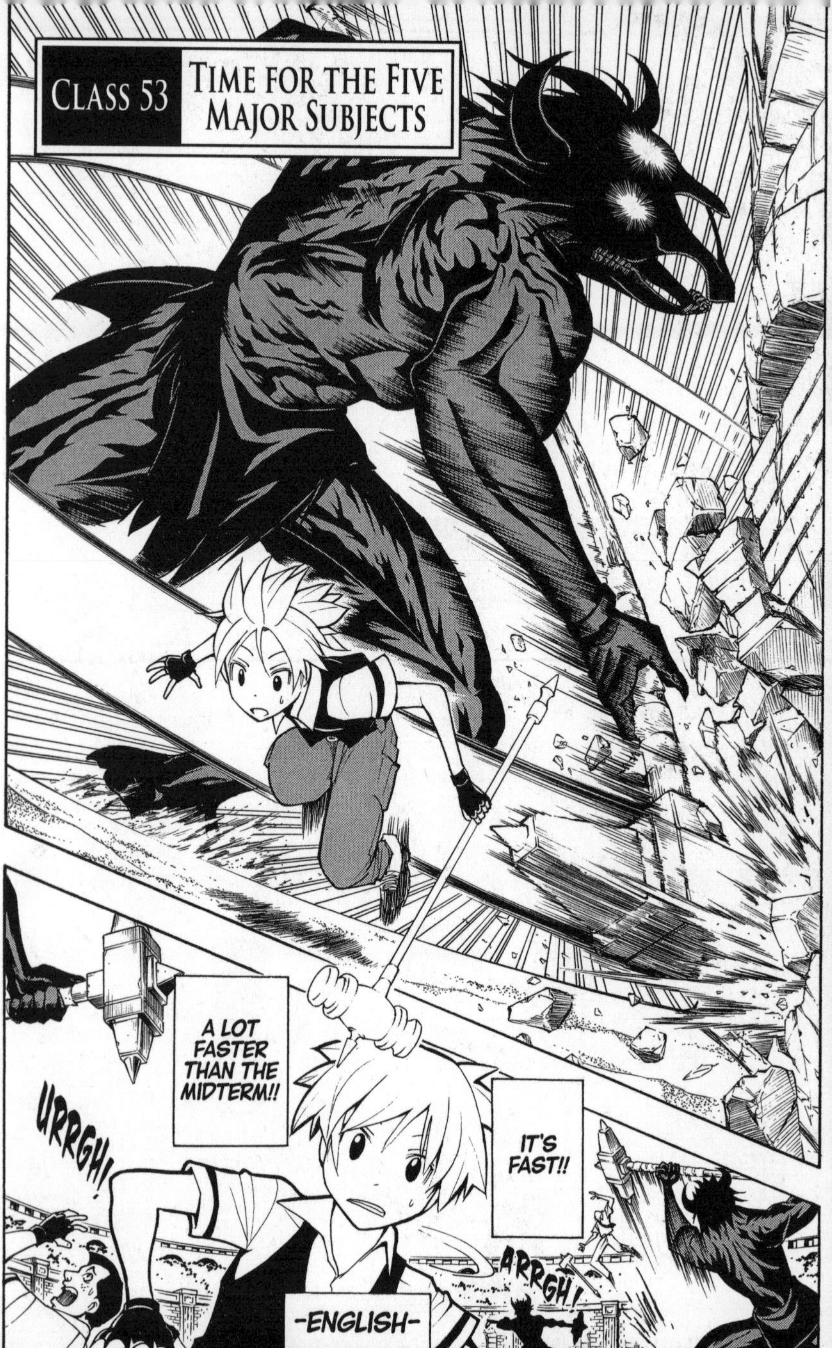
IT'S FAST!!
A LOT FASTER THAN THE MIDTERM!!
ARRGH!
URRGH!
-ENGLISH-

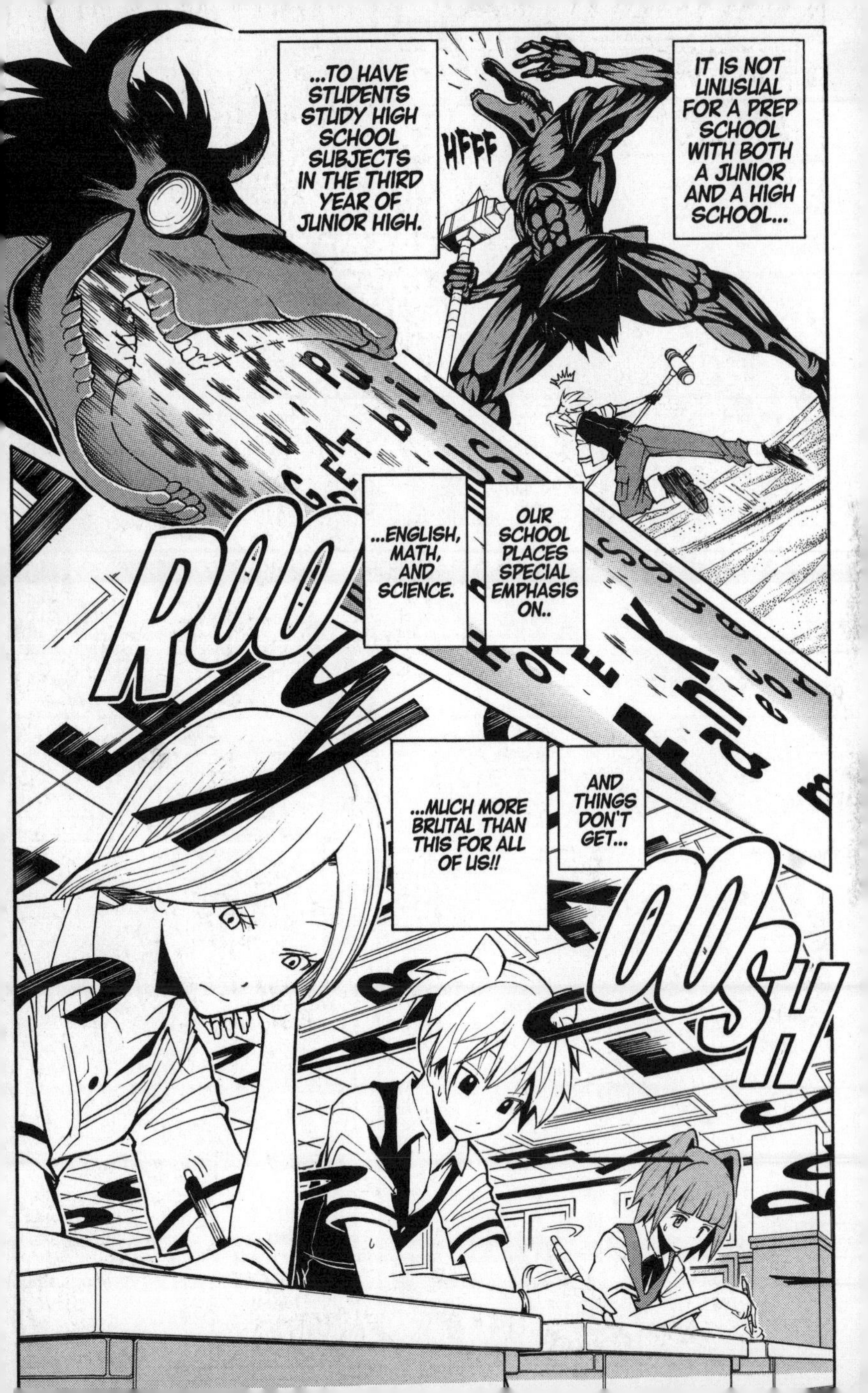
IT IS NOT UNUSUAL FOR A PREP SCHOOL WITH BOTH A JUNIOR AND A HIGH SCHOOL...
...TO HAVE STUDENTS STUDY HIGH SCHOOL SUBJECTS IN THE THIRD YEAR OF JUNIOR HIGH.
HFFF
OUR SCHOOL PLACES SPECIAL EMPHASIS ON..
...ENGLISH, MATH, AND SCIENCE.
ROO
AND THINGS DON'T GET...
...MUCH MORE BRUTAL THAN THIS FOR ALL OF US!!
OOSH

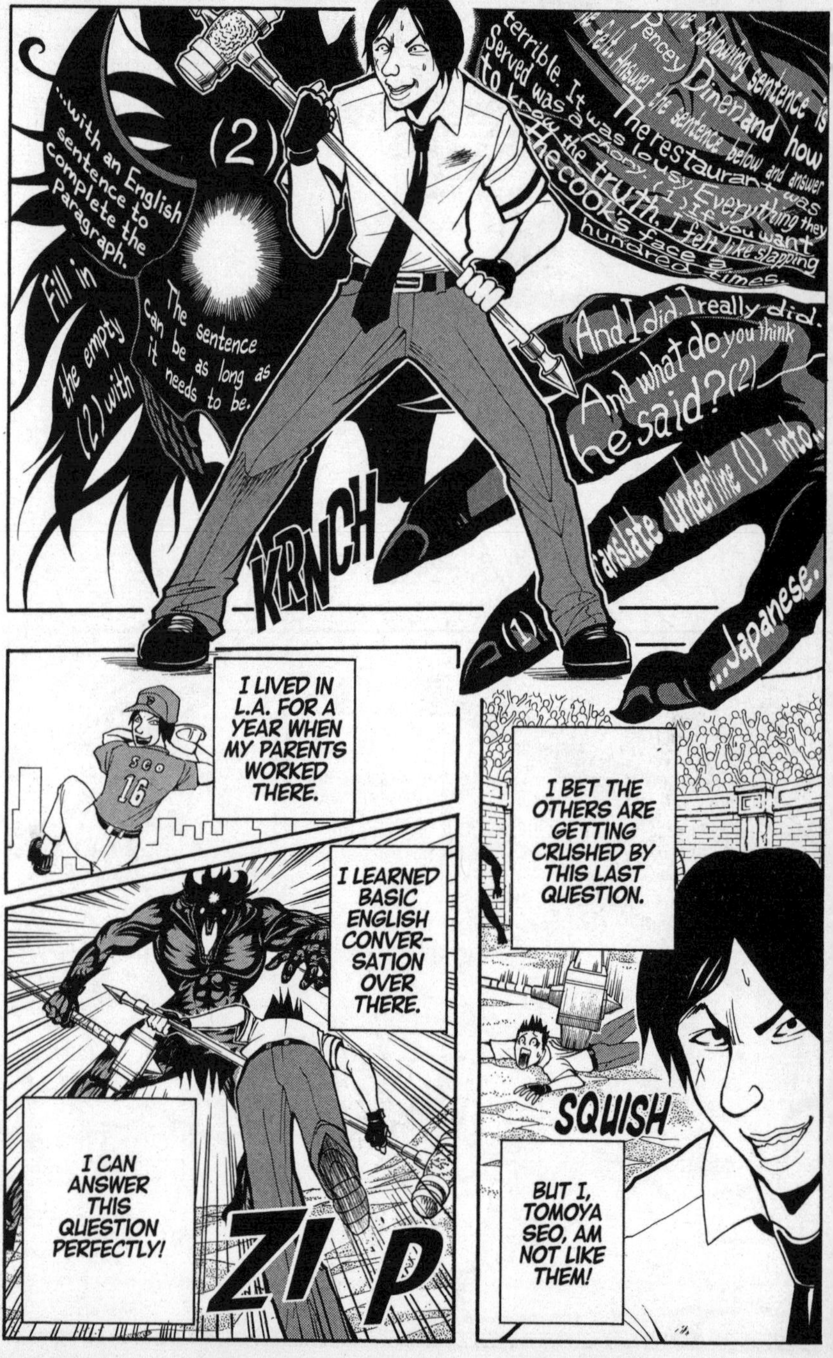

Pencey Diner and how
he felt. Answer the sentence below and answer
The restaurant was terrible. It was lousy. Everything they served was a phony. (1) If you want to know the truth. I felt like slapping the cook's face a hundred times.
And I did. I really did.
And what do you think he said? (2)
translate underline (1) into...
...Japanese.
(1)
(2)
...with an English sentence to complete the paragraph.
Fill in the empty (2) with
The sentence can be as long as it needs to be.
KRNCH
I BET THE OTHERS ARE GETTING CRUSHED BY THIS LAST QUESTION.
SQUISH
BUT I, TOMOYA SEO, AM NOT LIKE THEM!
I LIVED IN L.A. FOR A YEAR WHEN MY PARENTS WORKED THERE.
SEO
16
I LEARNED BASIC ENGLISH CONVER-SATION OVER THERE.
I CAN ANSWER THIS QUESTION PERFECTLY!
ZIP

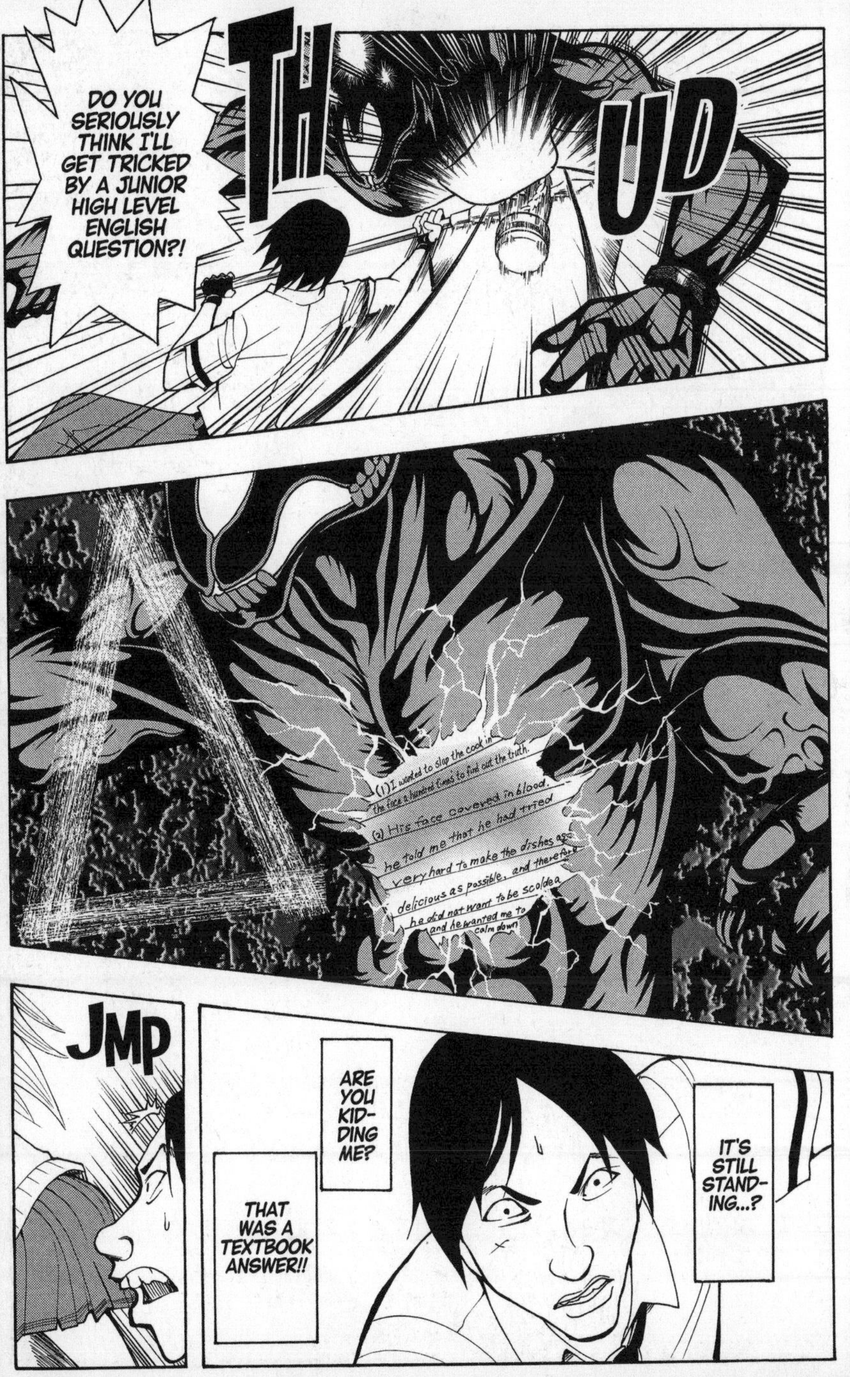
THUD
DO YOU SERIOUSLY THINK I'LL GET TRICKED BY A JUNIOR HIGH LEVEL ENGLISH QUESTION?!
(1) I wanted to slap the cook in the face a hundred times to find out the truth.
(2) His face covered in blood.
he told me that he had tried
very hard to make the dishes as
delicious as possible, and therefore
he did not want to be scolded
and he wanted me to
calm down
IT'S STILL STANDING...?
ARE YOU KIDDING ME?
THAT WAS A TEXTBOOK ANSWER!!
JMP

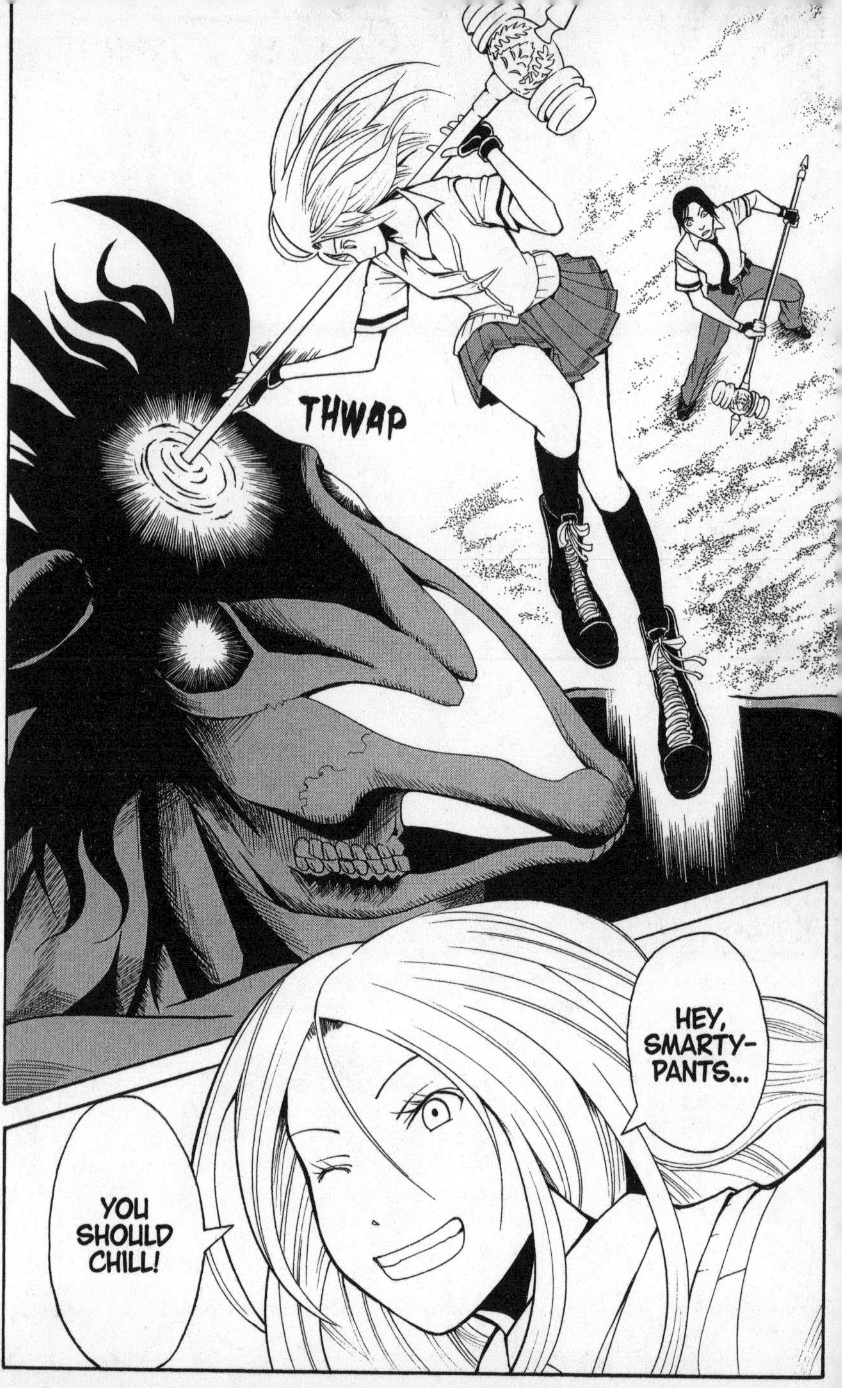
THWAP
HEY, SMARTY-PANTS...
YOU SHOULD CHILL!

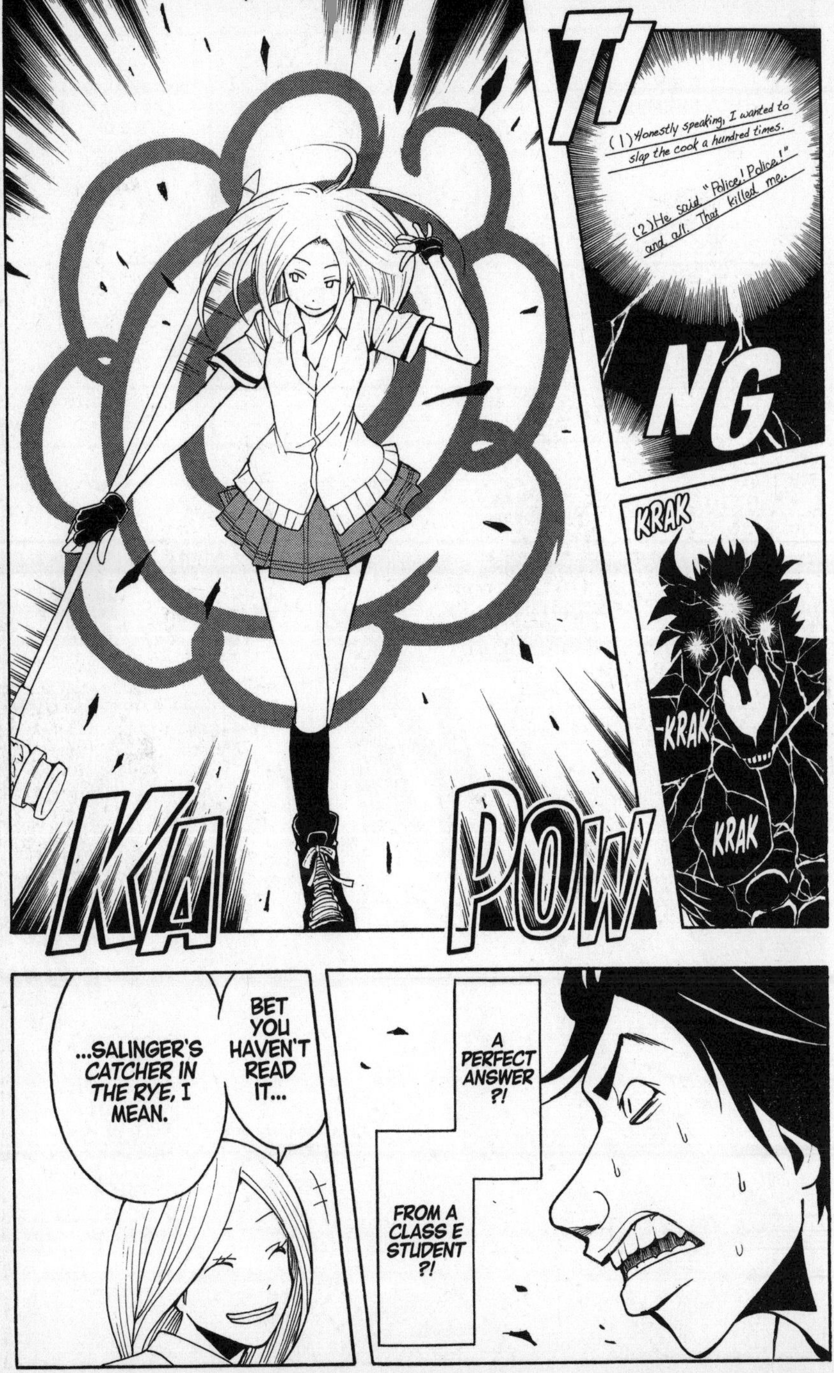
TI
(1) Honestly speaking, I wanted to slap the cook a hundred times.
(2) He said "Police! Police!" and all. That killed me.
NG
KRAK
KRAK
KRAK
KA
POW
A PERFECT ANSWER ?!
FROM A CLASS E STUDENT ?!
BET YOU HAVEN'T READ IT...
...SALINGER'S CATCHER IN THE RYE, I MEAN.

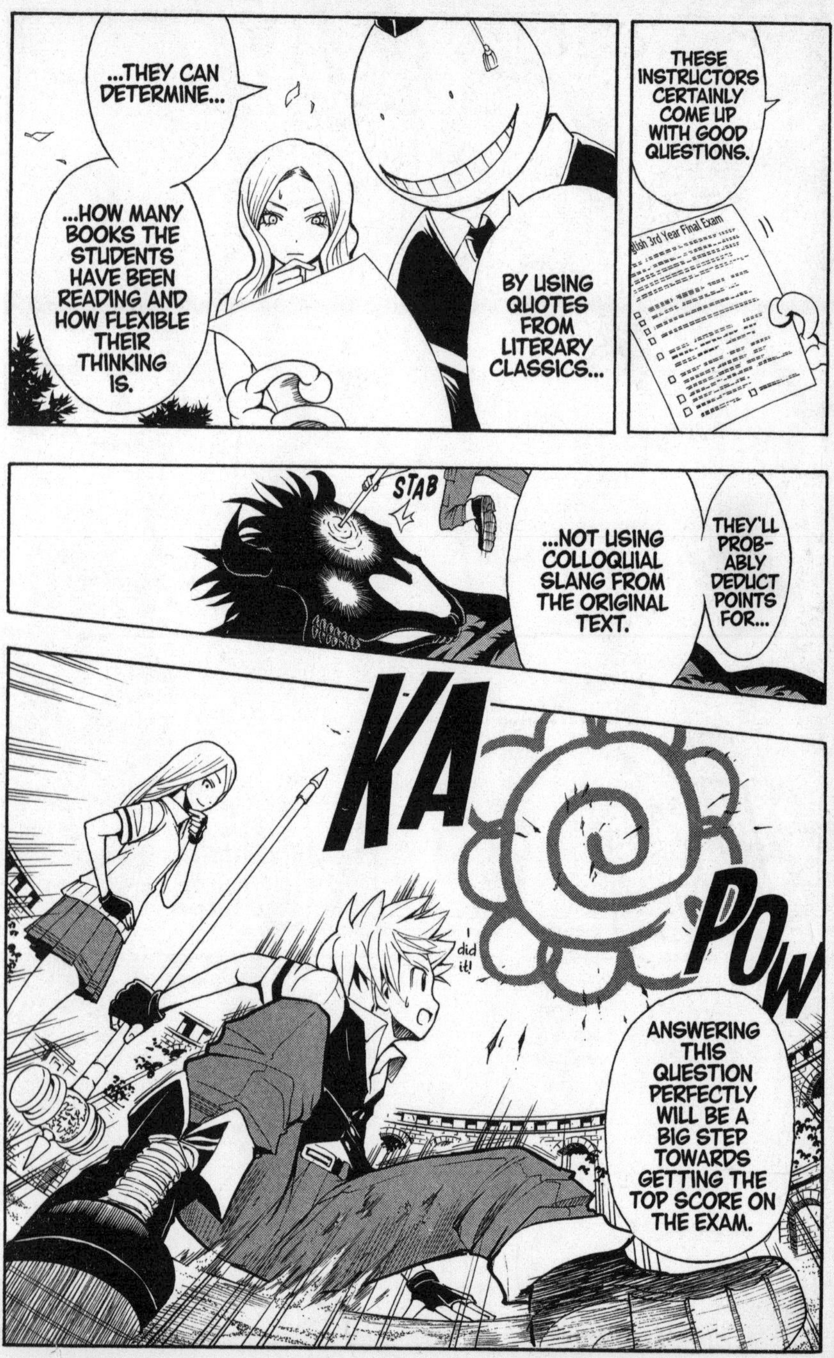
THESE INSTRUCTORS CERTAINLY COME UP WITH GOOD QUESTIONS.
glish 3rd Year Final Exam
BY USING QUOTES FROM LITERARY CLASSICS...
...THEY CAN DETERMINE...
...HOW MANY BOOKS THE STUDENTS HAVE BEEN READING AND HOW FLEXIBLE THEIR THINKING IS.
THEY'LL PROB-ABLY DEDUCT POINTS FOR...
...NOT USING COLLOQUIAL SLANG FROM THE ORIGINAL TEXT.
STAB
KA
POW
ANSWERING THIS QUESTION PERFECTLY WILL BE A BIG STEP TOWARDS GETTING THE TOP SCORE ON THE EXAM.
I did it!

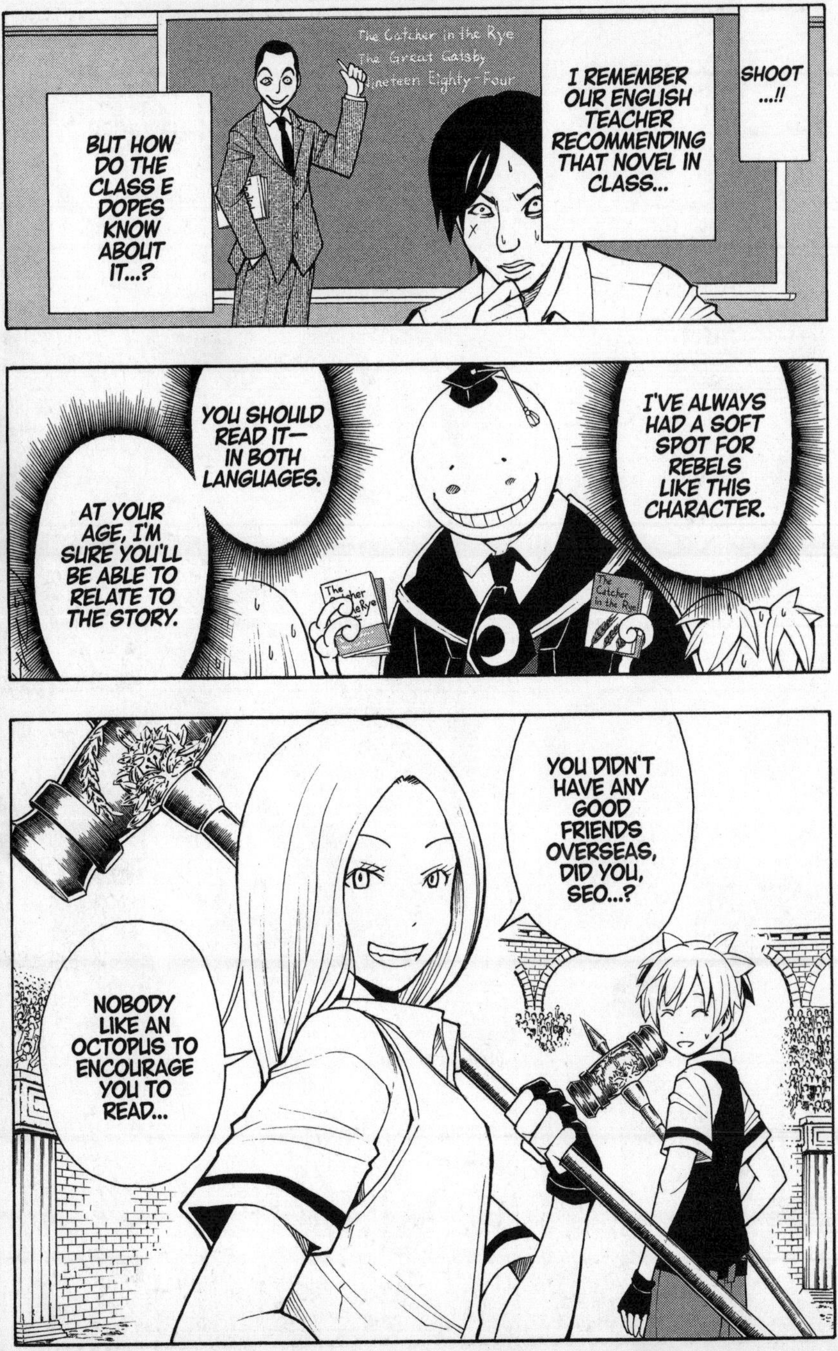
The Catcher in the Rye
The Great Gatsby
Nineteen Eighty-Four
SHOOT ...!!
I REMEMBER OUR ENGLISH TEACHER RECOMMENDING THAT NOVEL IN CLASS...
BUT HOW DO THE CLASS E DOPES KNOW ABOUT IT...?
I'VE ALWAYS HAD A SOFT SPOT FOR REBELS LIKE THIS CHARACTER.
YOU SHOULD READ IT—IN BOTH LANGUAGES.
AT YOUR AGE, I'M SURE YOU'LL BE ABLE TO RELATE TO THE STORY.
The Catcher in the Rye
YOU DIDN'T HAVE ANY GOOD FRIENDS OVERSEAS, DID YOU, SEO...?
NOBODY LIKE AN OCTOPUS TO ENCOURAGE YOU TO READ...

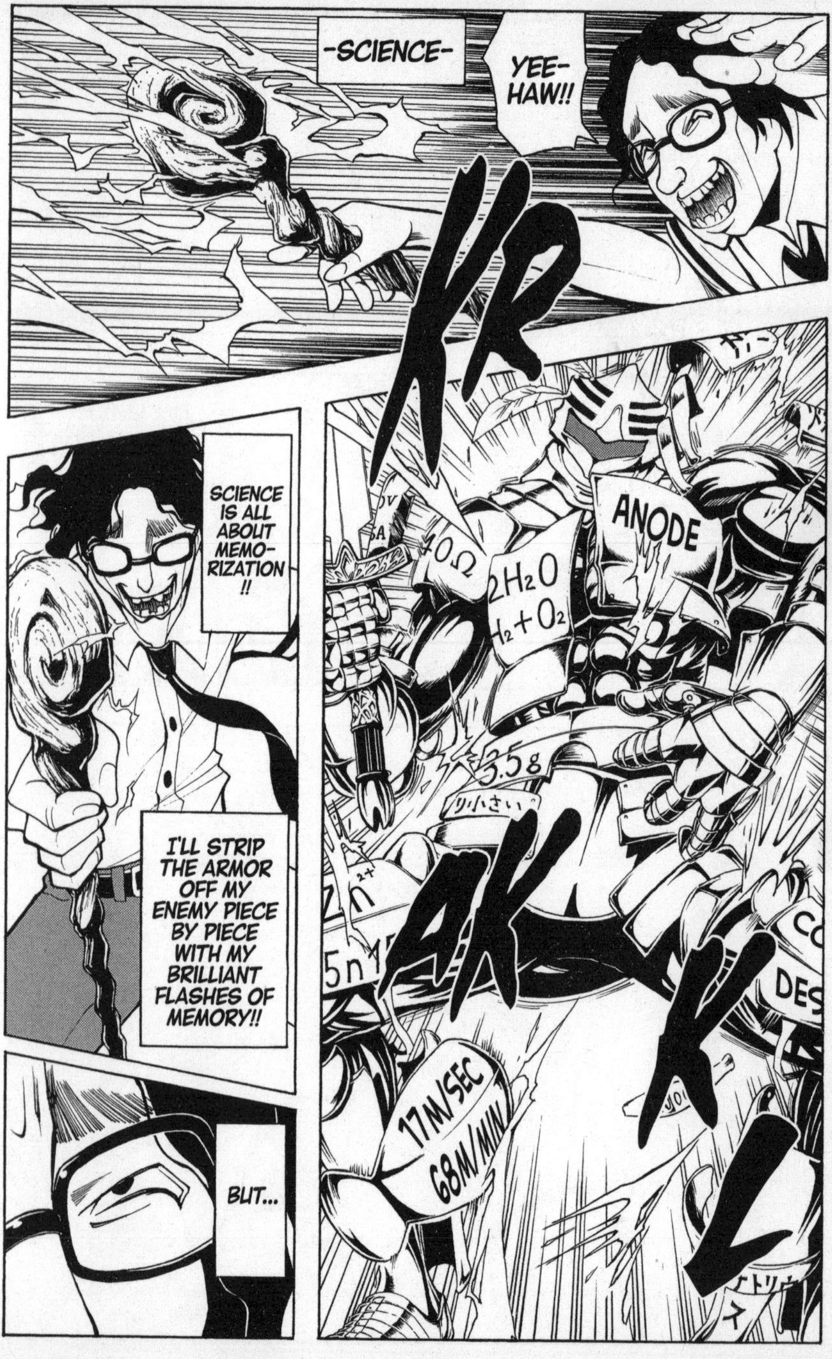

YEE-HAW!!
-SCIENCE-
KR
AK
KL
ANODE
40Ω
2H2O
H2+O2
3.5g
17M/SEC
68M/MIN
SCIENCE IS ALL ABOUT MEMORIZATION!!
I'LL STRIP THE ARMOR OFF MY ENEMY PIECE BY PIECE WITH MY BRILLIANT FLASHES OF MEMORY!!
BUT...

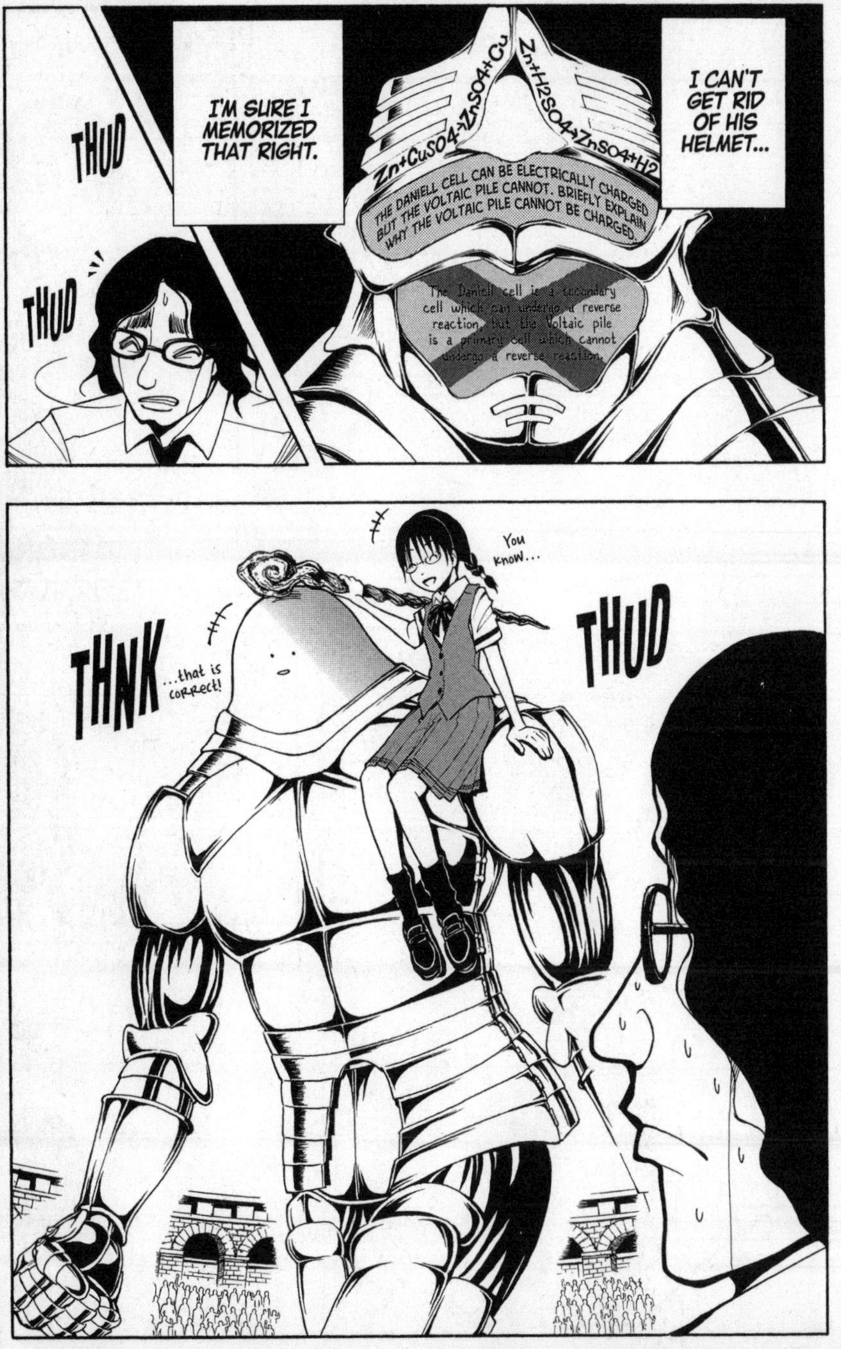
I CAN'T GET RID OF HIS HELMET...
Zn+H2SO4→ZnSO4+H2
Zn+CuSO4→ZnSO4+Cu
THE DANIELL CELL CAN BE ELECTRICALLY CHARGED BUT THE VOLTAIC PILE CANNOT. BRIEFLY EXPLAIN WHY THE VOLTAIC PILE CANNOT BE CHARGED.
The Daniell cell is a secondary cell which can undergo a reverse reaction, but the Voltaic pile is a primary cell which cannot undergo a reverse reaction.
I'M SURE I MEMORIZED THAT RIGHT.
THUD
THUD
THUD
You know...
...that is correct!
THNK

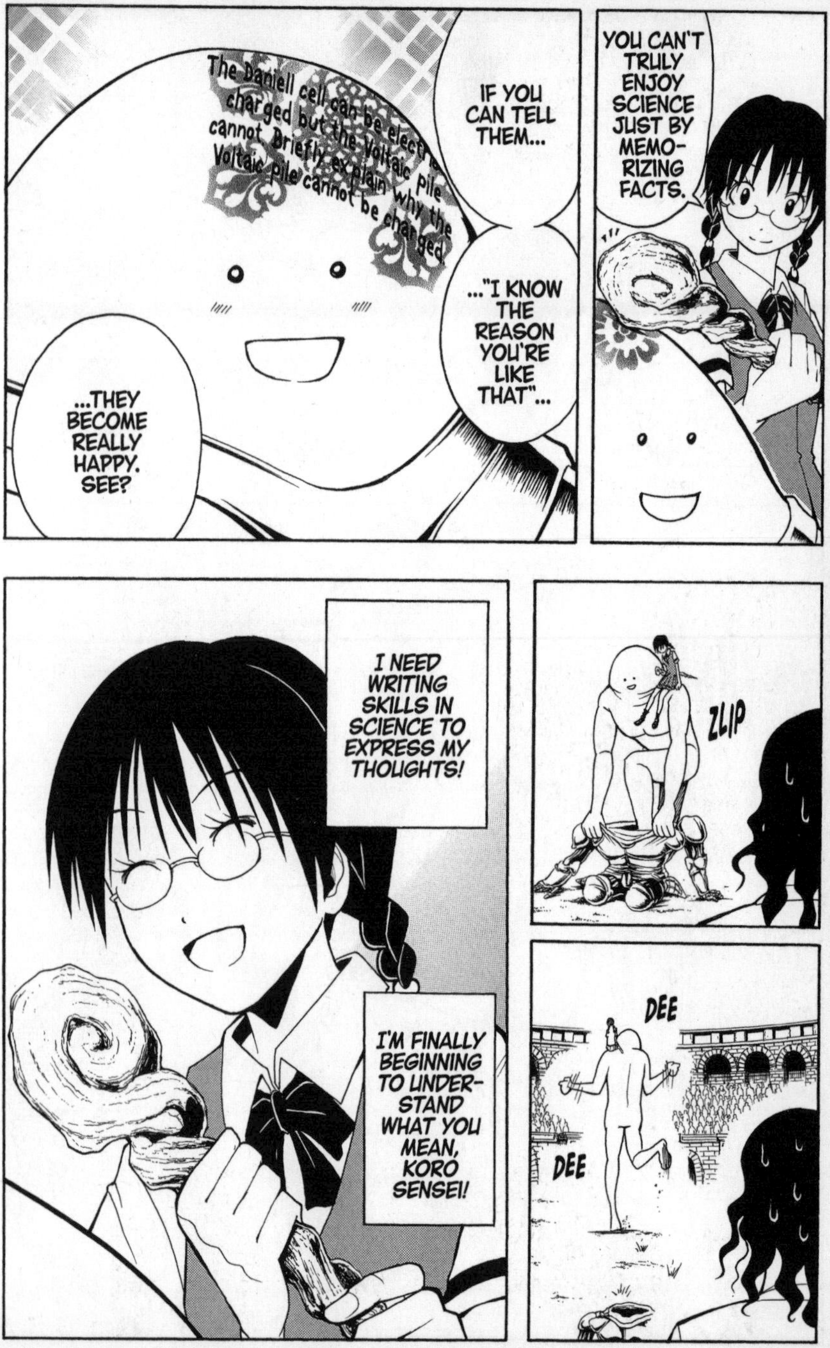
YOU CAN'T TRULY ENJOY SCIENCE JUST BY MEMO-RIZING FACTS.
IF YOU CAN TELL THEM...
..."I KNOW THE REASON YOU'RE LIKE THAT"...
The Daniell cell can be electri charged but the Voltaic pile cannot. Briefly explain why the Voltaic pile cannot be charged.
...THEY BECOME REALLY HAPPY. SEE?
ZLIP
DEE
DEE
I NEED WRITING SKILLS IN SCIENCE TO EXPRESS MY THOUGHTS!
I'M FINALLY BEGINNING TO UNDER-STAND WHAT YOU MEAN, KORO SENSEI!

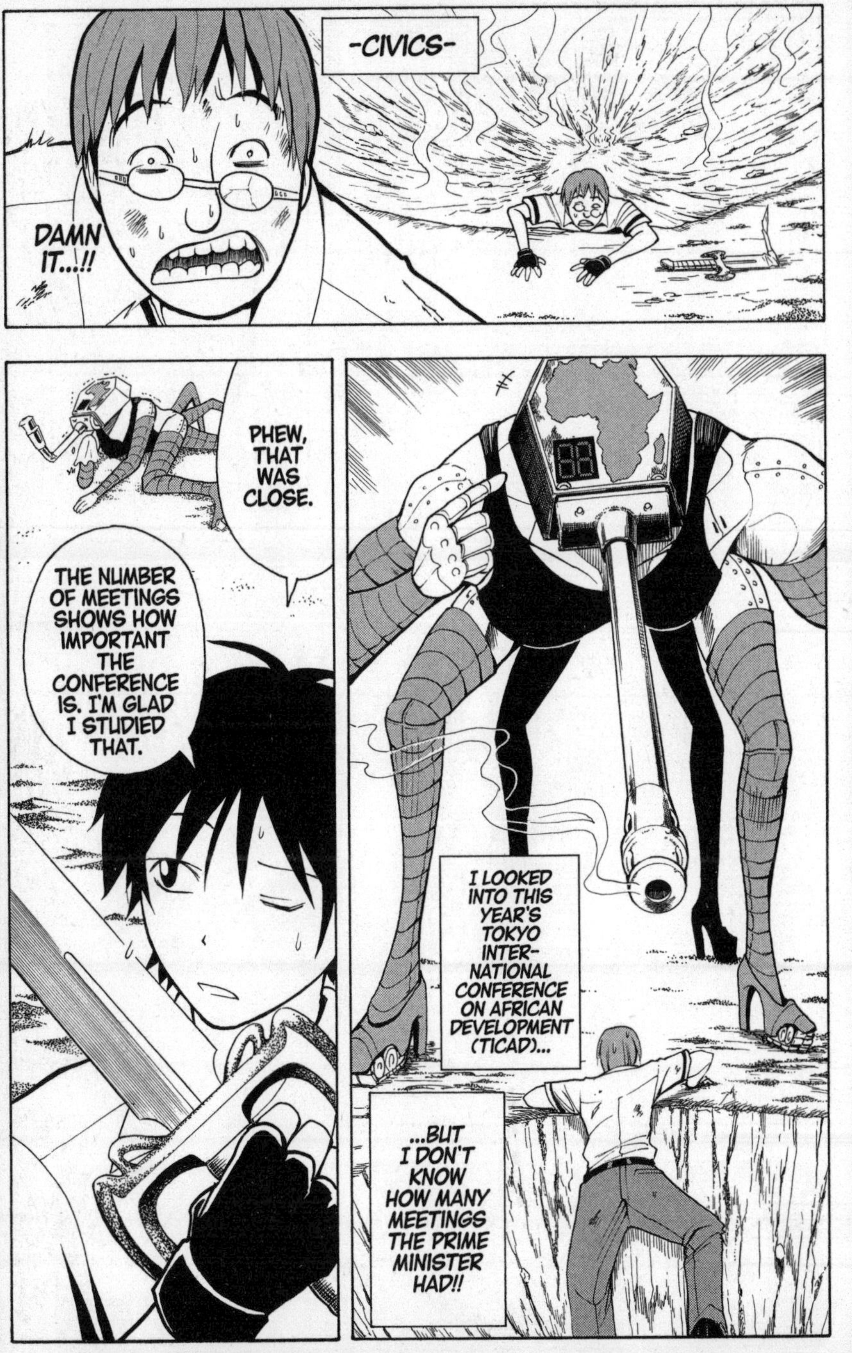
-CIVICS-
DAMN IT...!!
I LOOKED INTO THIS YEAR'S TOKYO INTER-NATIONAL CONFERENCE ON AFRICAN DEVELOPMENT (TICAD)...
...BUT I DON'T KNOW HOW MANY MEETINGS THE PRIME MINISTER HAD!!
PHEW, THAT WAS CLOSE.
THE NUMBER OF MEETINGS SHOWS HOW IMPORTANT THE CONFERENCE IS. I'M GLAD I STUDIED THAT.

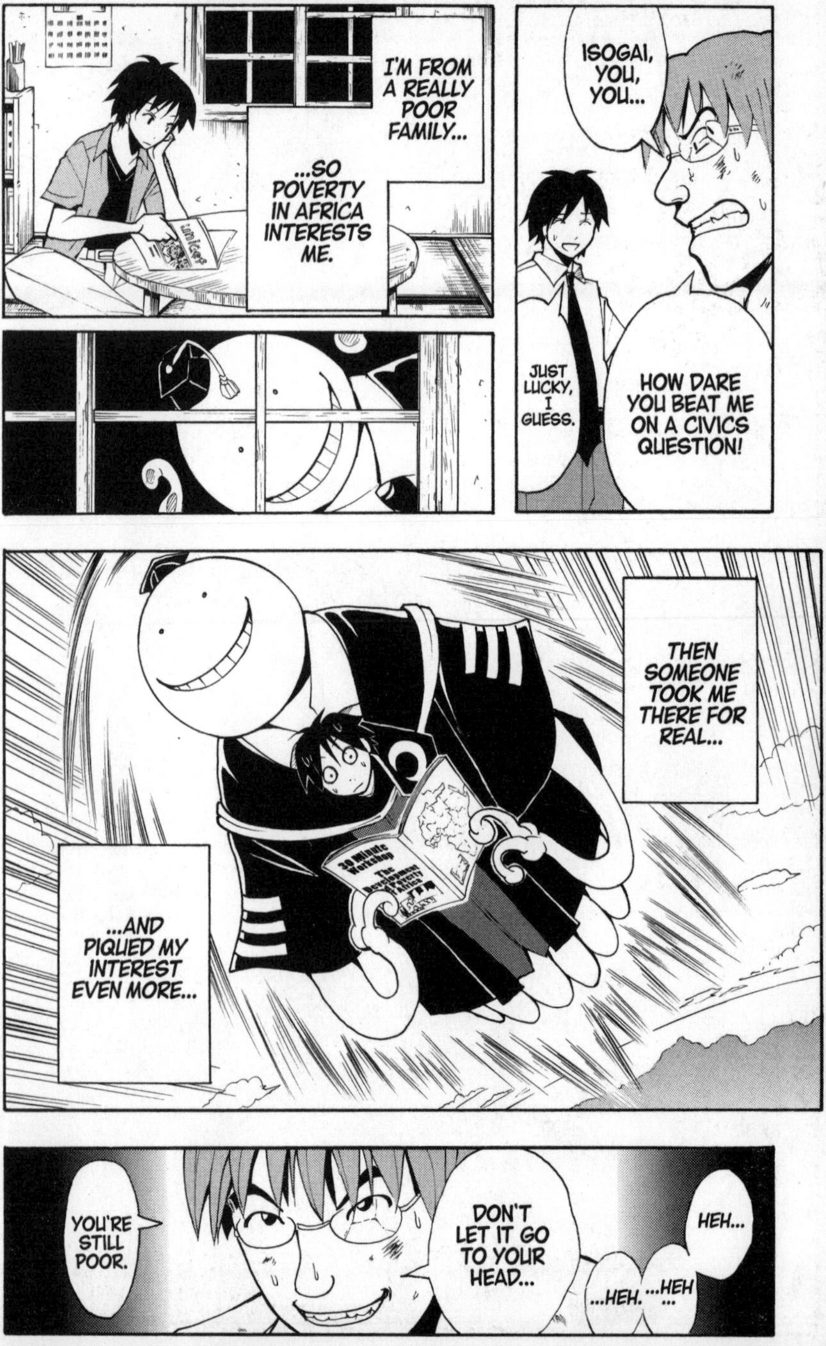
ISOGAI, YOU, YOU...
HOW DARE YOU BEAT ME ON A CIVICS QUESTION!
JUST LUCKY, I GUESS.
I'M FROM A REALLY POOR FAMILY...
...SO POVERTY IN AFRICA INTERESTS ME.
THEN SOMEONE TOOK ME THERE FOR REAL...
...AND PIQUED MY INTEREST EVEN MORE...
HEH...
...HEH ...
...HEH.
DON'T LET IT GO TO YOUR HEAD...
YOU'RE STILL POOR.

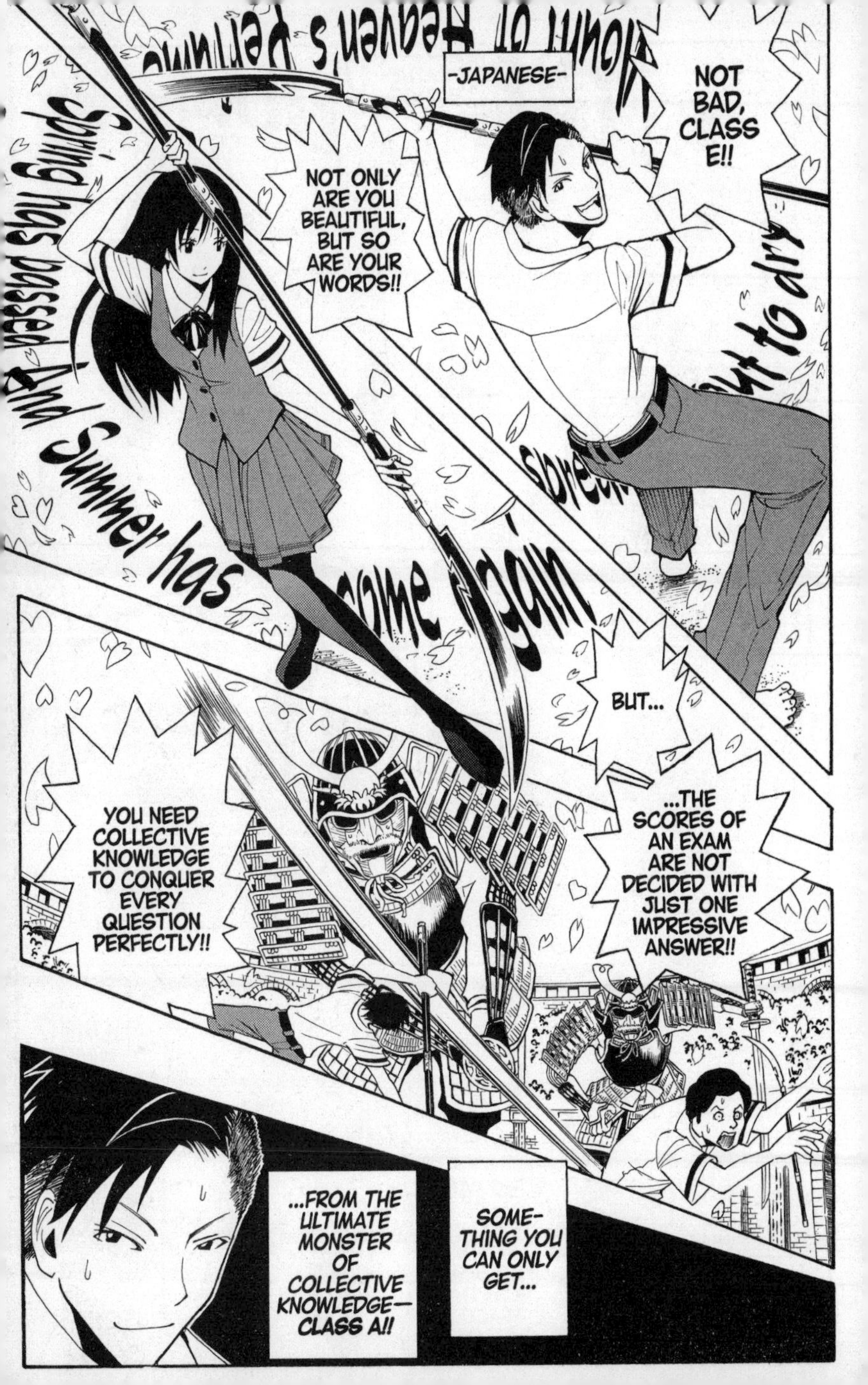
-JAPANESE-
Mount of Heaven's Perfume
NOT BAD, CLASS E!!
out to dry
NOT ONLY ARE YOU BEAUTIFUL, BUT SO ARE YOUR WORDS!!
Spring has passed And Summer has come again
BUT...
...THE SCORES OF AN EXAM ARE NOT DECIDED WITH JUST ONE IMPRESSIVE ANSWER!!
YOU NEED COLLECTIVE KNOWLEDGE TO CONQUER EVERY QUESTION PERFECTLY!!
SOME-THING YOU CAN ONLY GET...
...FROM THE ULTIMATE MONSTER OF COLLECTIVE KNOWLEDGE—CLASS A!!

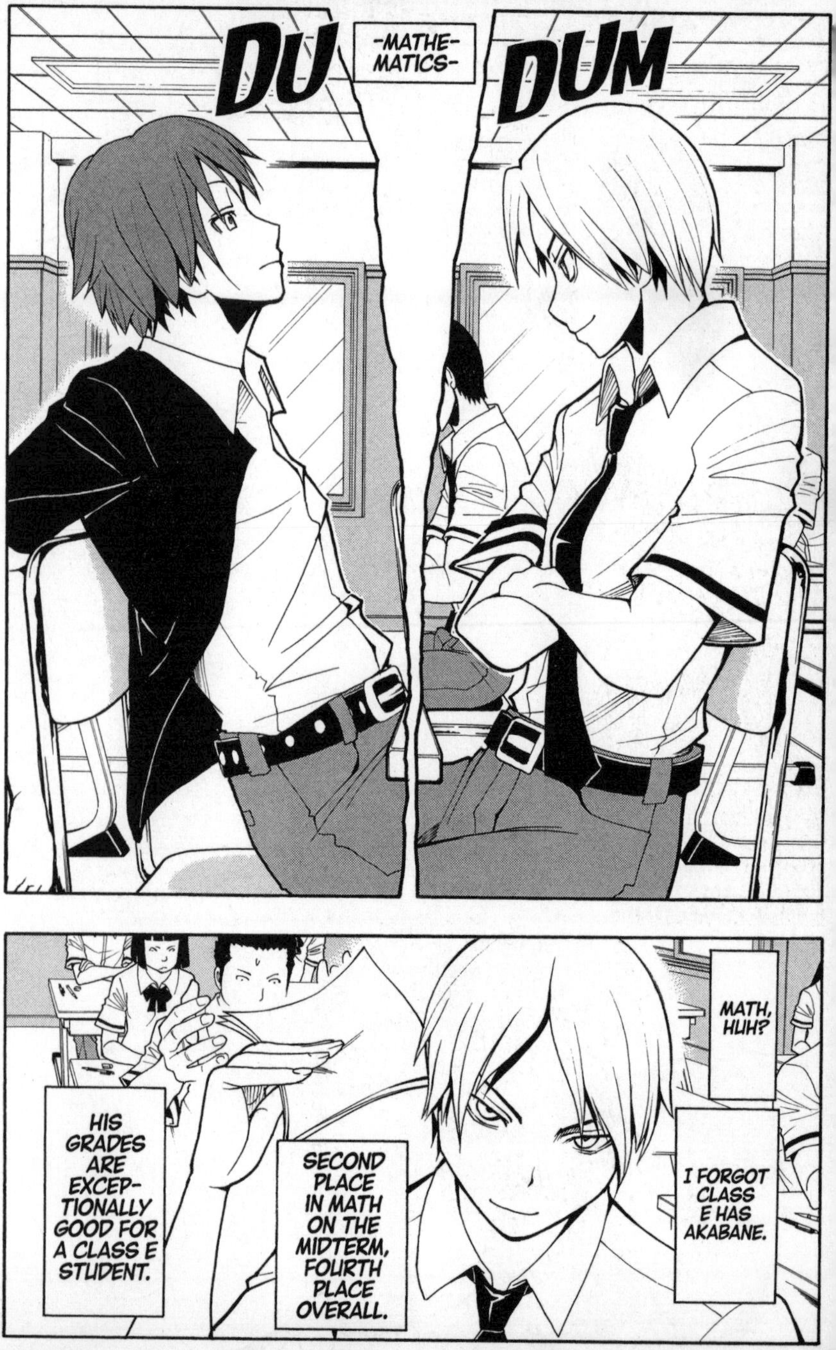
DU DUM
-MATHEMATICS-
MATH, HUH?
I FORGOT CLASS E HAS AKABANE.
SECOND PLACE IN MATH ON THE MIDTERM, FOURTH PLACE OVERALL.
HIS GRADES ARE EXCEPTIONALLY GOOD FOR A CLASS E STUDENT.

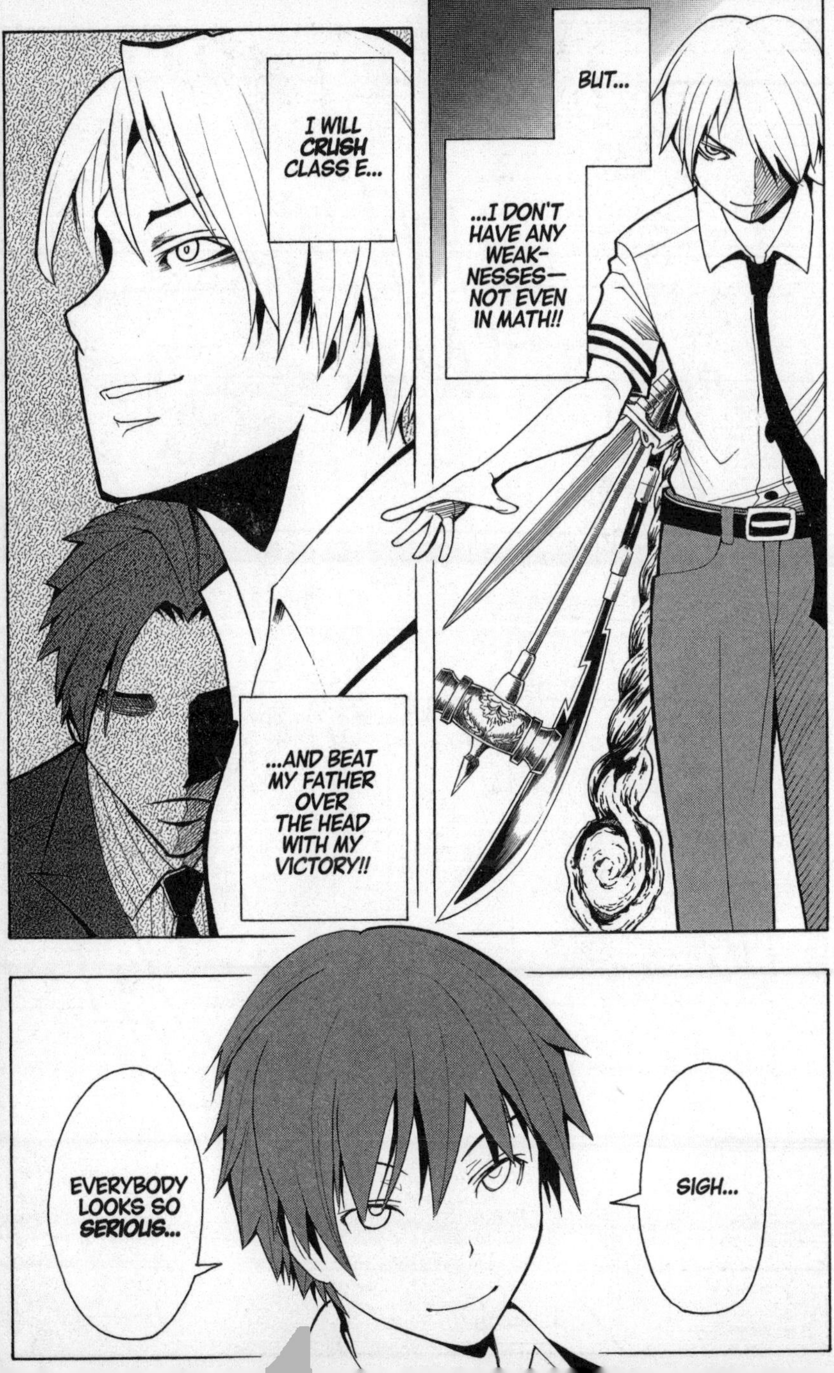
BUT...
...I DON'T HAVE ANY WEAKNESSES—NOT EVEN IN MATH!!
I WILL CRUSH CLASS E...
...AND BEAT MY FATHER OVER THE HEAD WITH MY VICTORY!!
SIGH...
EVERYBODY LOOKS SO SERIOUS...

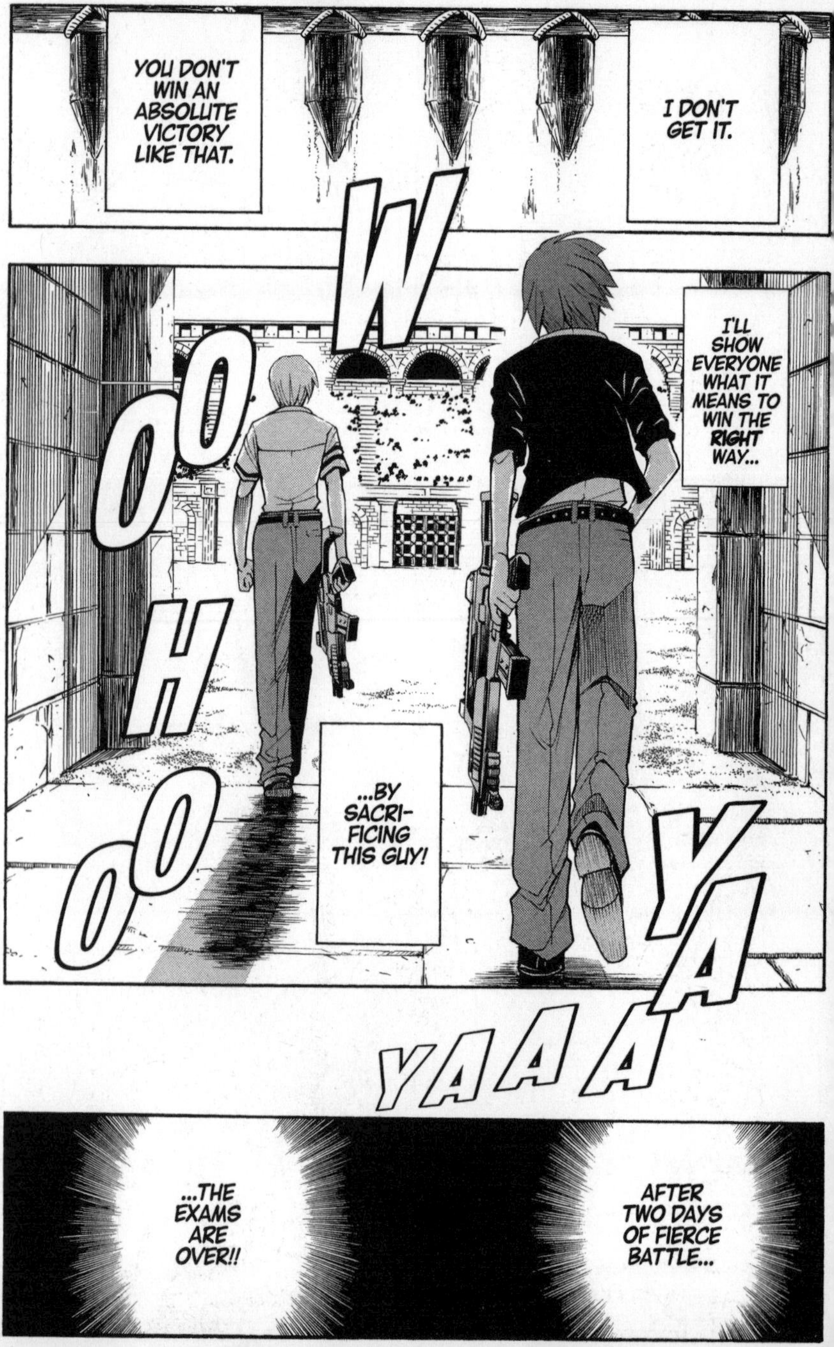
I DON'T GET IT.
YOU DON'T WIN AN ABSOLUTE VICTORY LIKE THAT.
WOOHOO
I'LL SHOW EVERYONE WHAT IT MEANS TO WIN THE RIGHT WAY...
...BY SACRI-FICING THIS GUY!
YAAAAAY
AFTER TWO DAYS OF FIERCE BATTLE...
...THE EXAMS ARE OVER!!

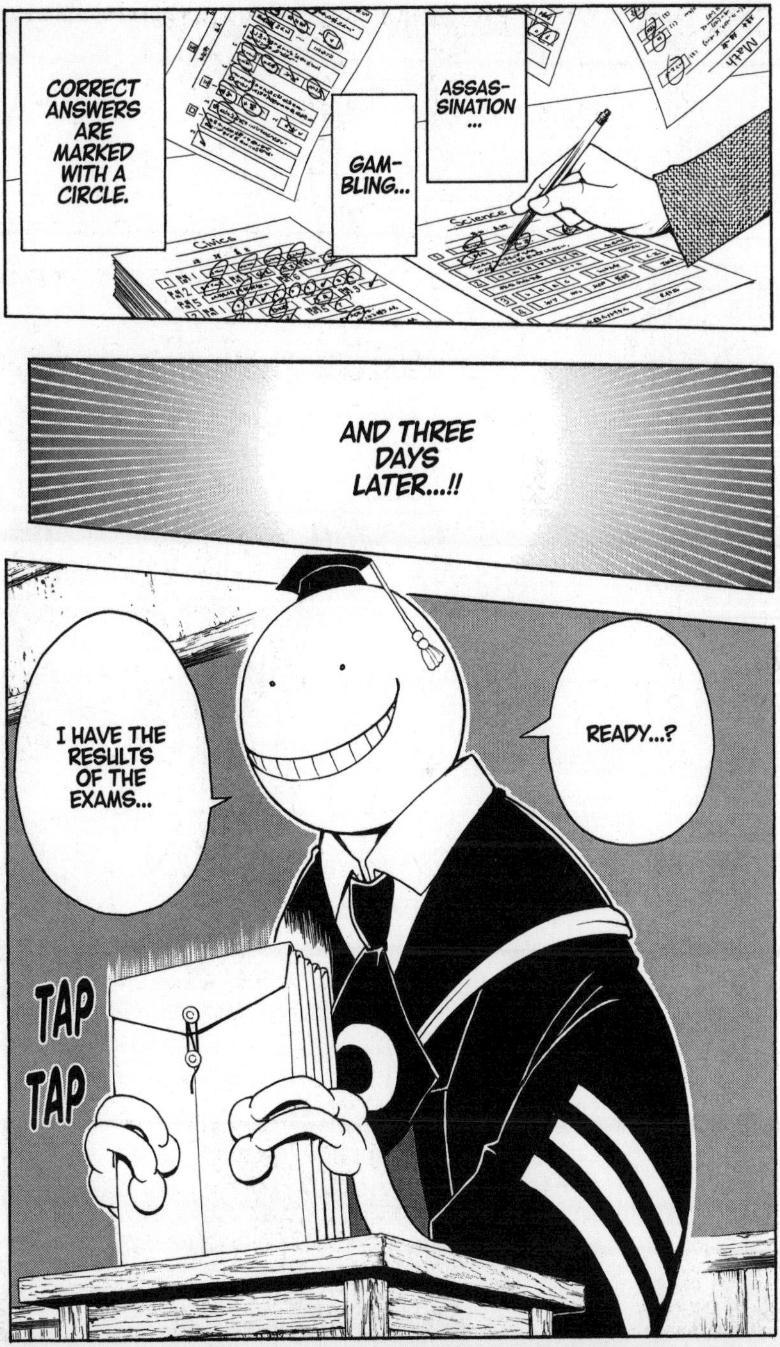
ASSAS-SINATION...
GAM-BLING...
CORRECT ANSWERS ARE MARKED WITH A CIRCLE.
AND THREE DAYS LATER...!!
READY...?
I HAVE THE RESULTS OF THE EXAMS...
TAP TAP

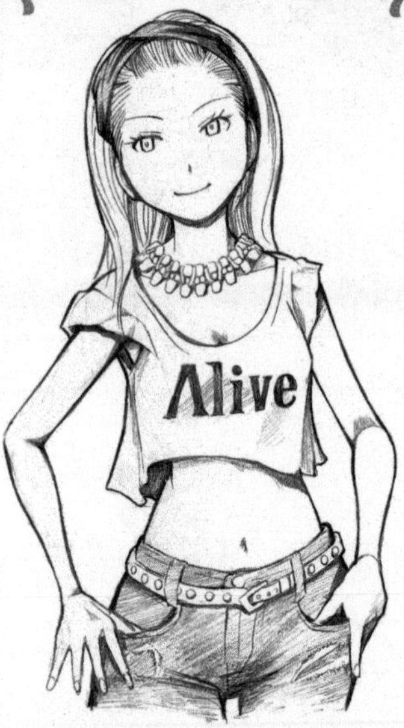
Alive

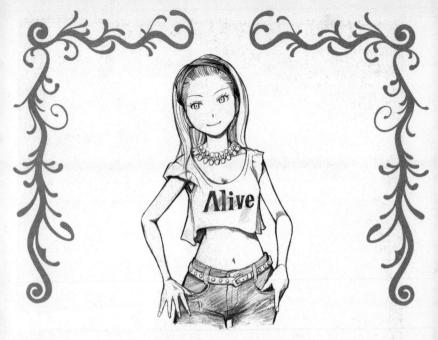

E-17 Rio Nakamura

- Birthday: August 24
- Height: 5' 4"
- Weight: 106 lbs.
- Favorite Subject: English
- Least Favorite Subject: Civics
- Hobby/Skill: Dirty jokes, sexually harassing Nagisa
- Future Goal: Diplomat
- Old Nickname: Elementary School Prodigy
- Current Nickname: Middle-Aged Junior High School Kid

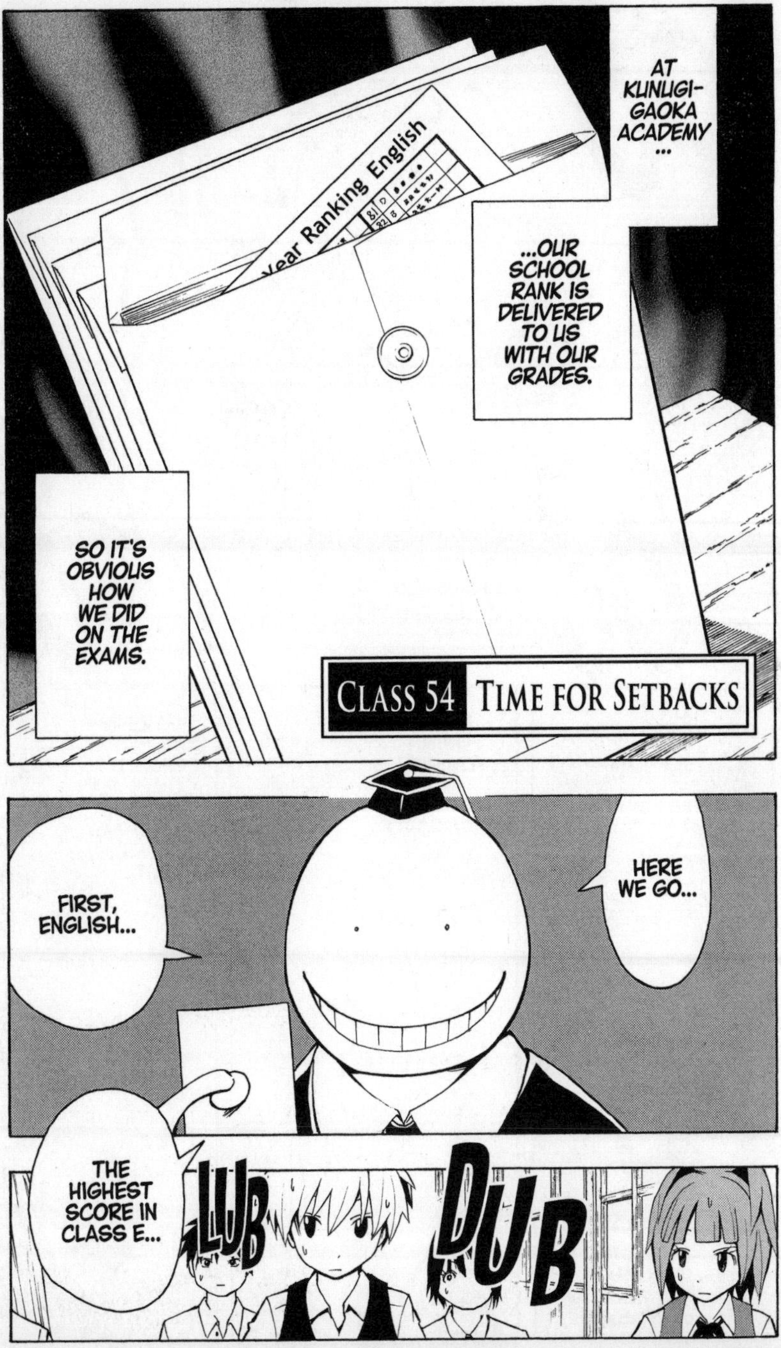
AT KUNUGI-GAOKA ACADEMY...
...OUR SCHOOL RANK IS DELIVERED TO US WITH OUR GRADES.
Year Ranking English
SO IT'S OBVIOUS HOW WE DID ON THE EXAMS.
CLASS 54 TIME FOR SETBACKS
HERE WE GO...
FIRST, ENGLISH...
THE HIGHEST SCORE IN CLASS E...
LUB
DUB

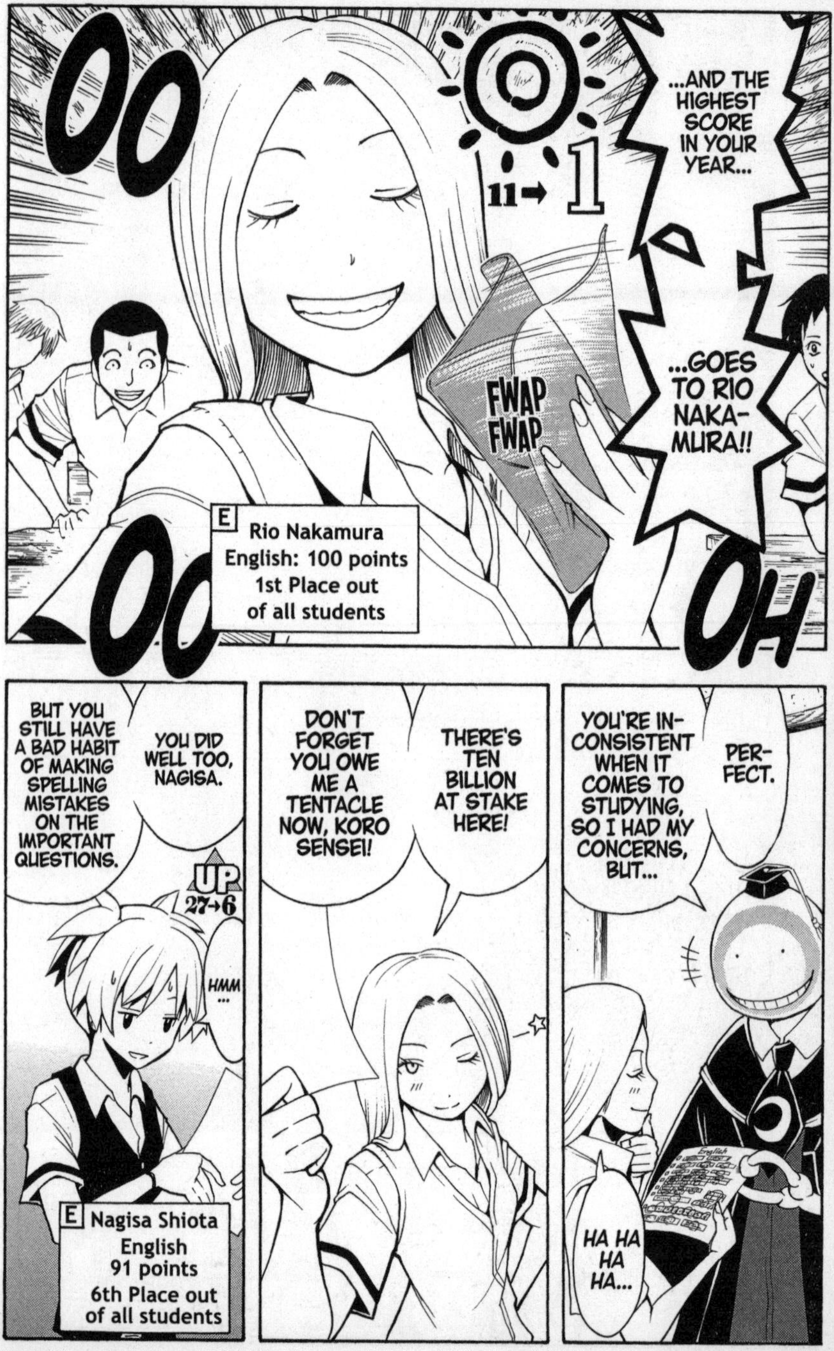
...AND THE HIGHEST SCORE IN YOUR YEAR...
11→1
...GOES TO RIO NAKA-MURA!!
FWAP FWAP
OOOOOH
E
Rio Nakamura
English: 100 points
1st Place out of all students
PER-FECT.
YOU'RE IN-CONSISTENT WHEN IT COMES TO STUDYING, SO I HAD MY CONCERNS, BUT...
HA HA HA HA...
THERE'S TEN BILLION AT STAKE HERE!
DON'T FORGET YOU OWE ME A TENTACLE NOW, KORO SENSEI!
YOU DID WELL TOO, NAGISA.
BUT YOU STILL HAVE A BAD HABIT OF MAKING SPELLING MISTAKES ON THE IMPORTANT QUESTIONS.
UP 27→6
HMM...
E
Nagisa Shiota
English
91 points
6th Place out of all students

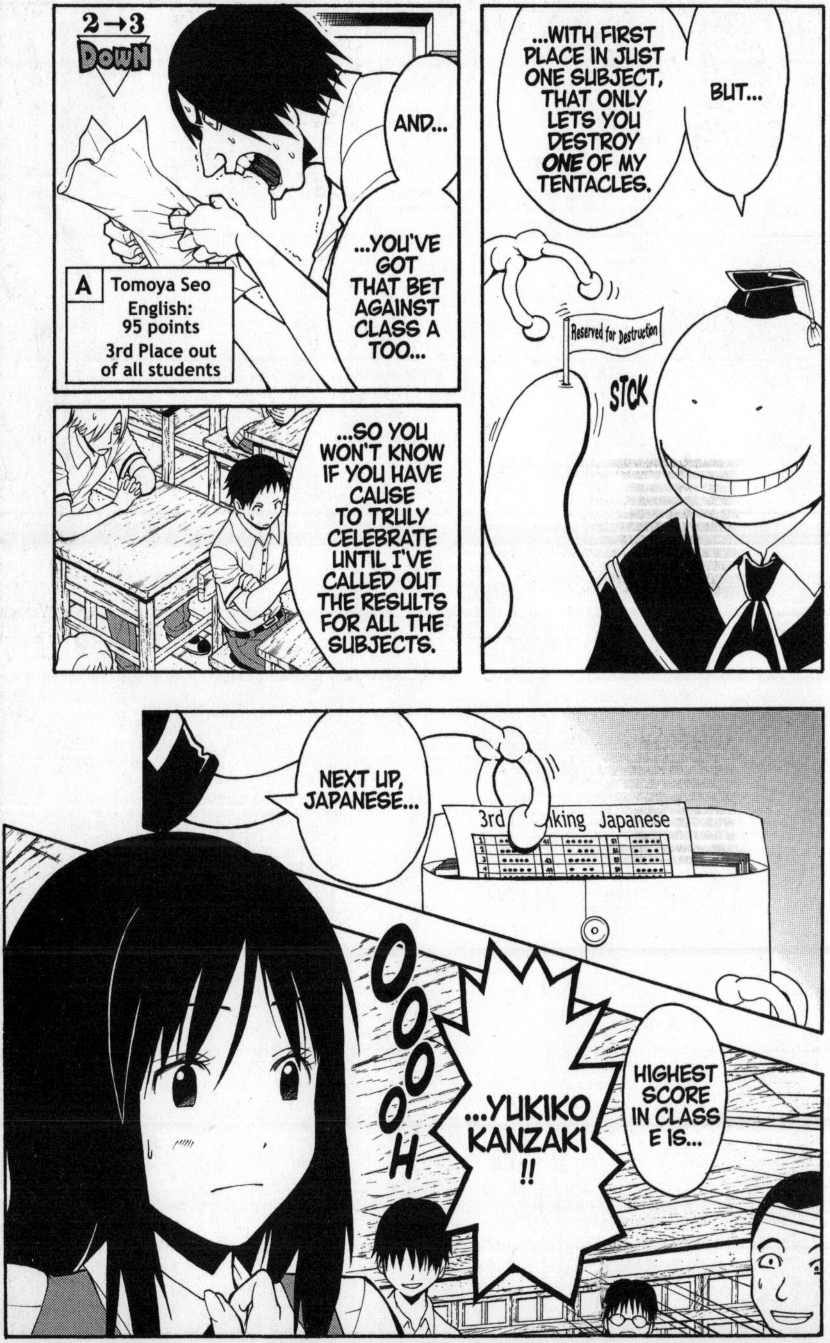
BUT...
...WITH FIRST PLACE IN JUST ONE SUBJECT, THAT ONLY LETS YOU DESTROY ONE OF MY TENTACLES.
Reserved for Destruction
STCK
2→3
DOWN
AND...
...YOU'VE GOT THAT BET AGAINST CLASS A TOO...
A
Tomoya Seo
English: 95 points
3rd Place out of all students
...SO YOU WON'T KNOW IF YOU HAVE CAUSE TO TRULY CELEBRATE UNTIL I'VE CALLED OUT THE RESULTS FOR ALL THE SUBJECTS.
NEXT UP, JAPANESE...
3rd
Japanese
HIGHEST SCORE IN CLASS E IS...
...YUKIKO KANZAKI!!
OOOOOH

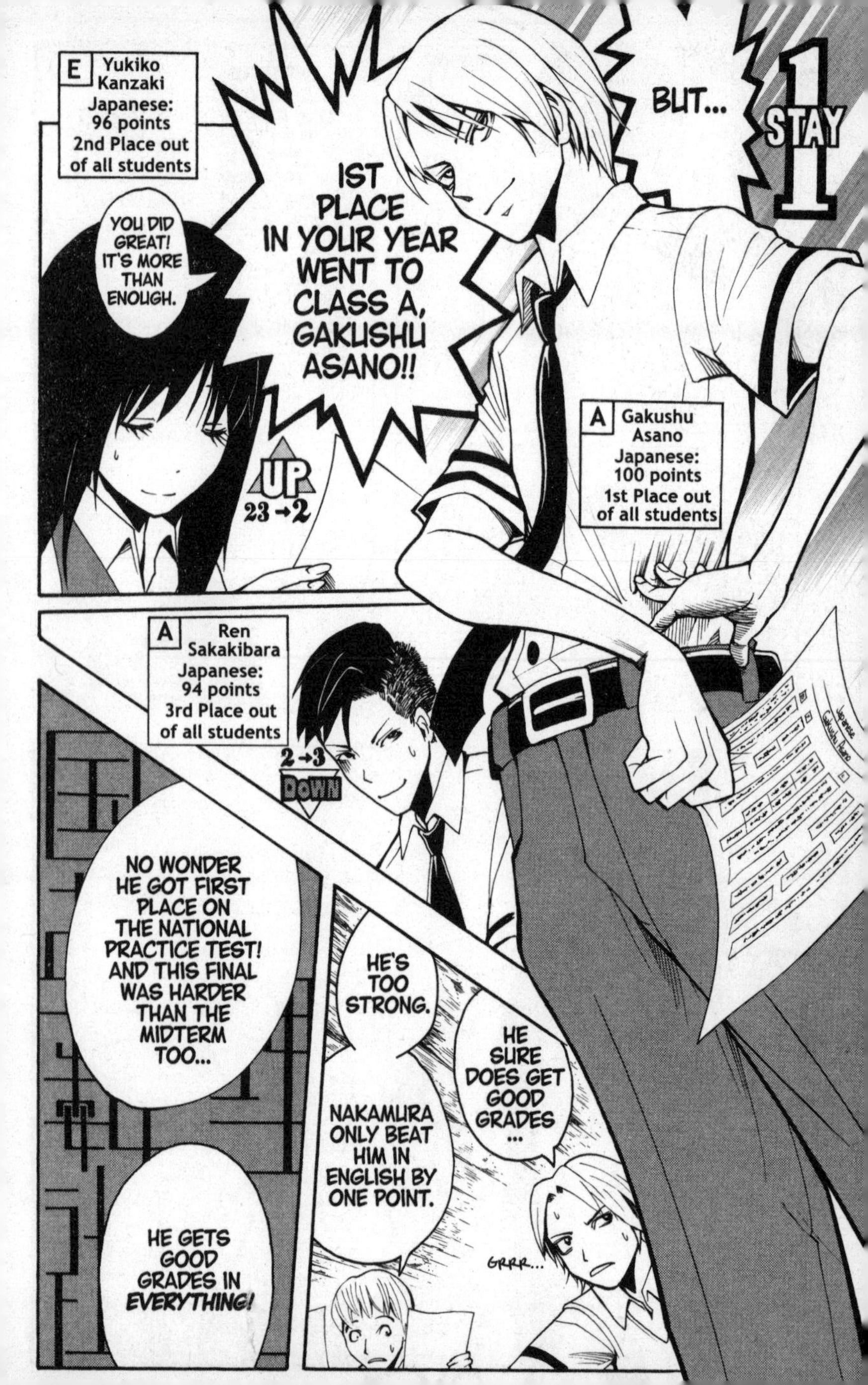
STAY 1
BUT...
1ST PLACE IN YOUR YEAR WENT TO CLASS A, GAKUSHU ASANO!!
A Gakushu Asano Japanese: 100 points 1st Place out of all students
Japanese Gakushu Asano
E Yukiko Kanzaki Japanese: 96 points 2nd Place out of all students
YOU DID GREAT! IT'S MORE THAN ENOUGH.
UP 23→2
A Ren Sakakibara Japanese: 94 points 3rd Place out of all students
2→3 DOWN
HE SURE DOES GET GOOD GRADES ...
HE'S TOO STRONG.
NAKAMURA ONLY BEAT HIM IN ENGLISH BY ONE POINT.
GRRR...
NO WONDER HE GOT FIRST PLACE ON THE NATIONAL PRACTICE TEST! AND THIS FINAL WAS HARDER THAN THE MIDTERM TOO...
HE GETS GOOD GRADES IN *EVERYTHING!*

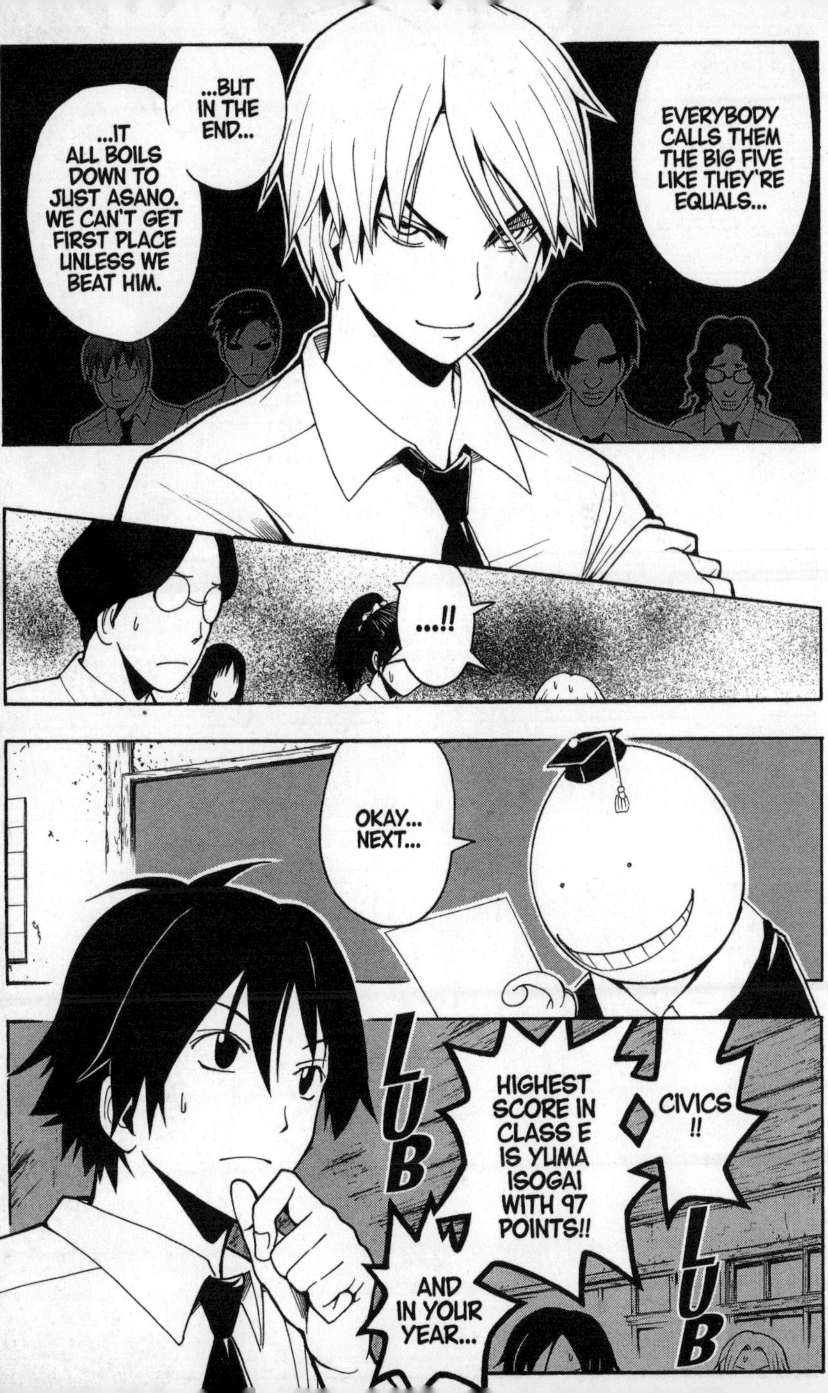
EVERYBODY CALLS THEM THE BIG FIVE LIKE THEY'RE EQUALS...
...BUT IN THE END...
...IT ALL BOILS DOWN TO JUST ASANO. WE CAN'T GET FIRST PLACE UNLESS WE BEAT HIM.
...!!
OKAY... NEXT...
CIVICS!!
HIGHEST SCORE IN CLASS E IS YUMA ISOGAI WITH 97 POINTS!!
LUB
LUB
AND IN YOUR YEAR...

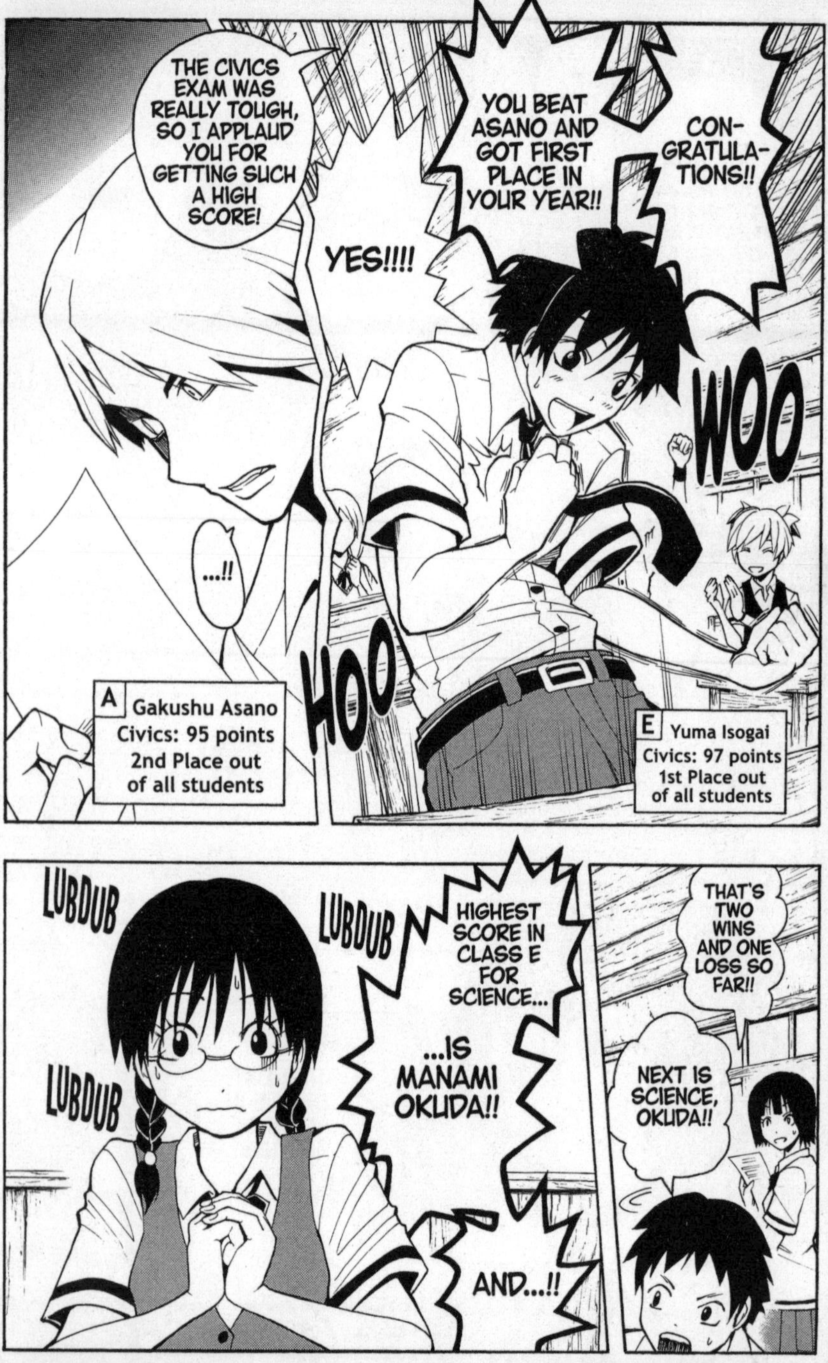
CON-GRATULA-TIONS!!
YOU BEAT ASANO AND GOT FIRST PLACE IN YOUR YEAR!!
YES!!!!
WOO
HOO
E Yuma Isogai Civics: 97 points 1st Place out of all students
THE CIVICS EXAM WAS REALLY TOUGH, SO I APPLAUD YOU FOR GETTING SUCH A HIGH SCORE!
...!!
A Gakushu Asano Civics: 95 points 2nd Place out of all students
THAT'S TWO WINS AND ONE LOSS SO FAR!!
NEXT IS SCIENCE, OKUDA!!
HIGHEST SCORE IN CLASS E FOR SCIENCE...
...IS MANAMI OKUDA!!
AND...!!
LUBDUB
LUBDUB
LUBDUB

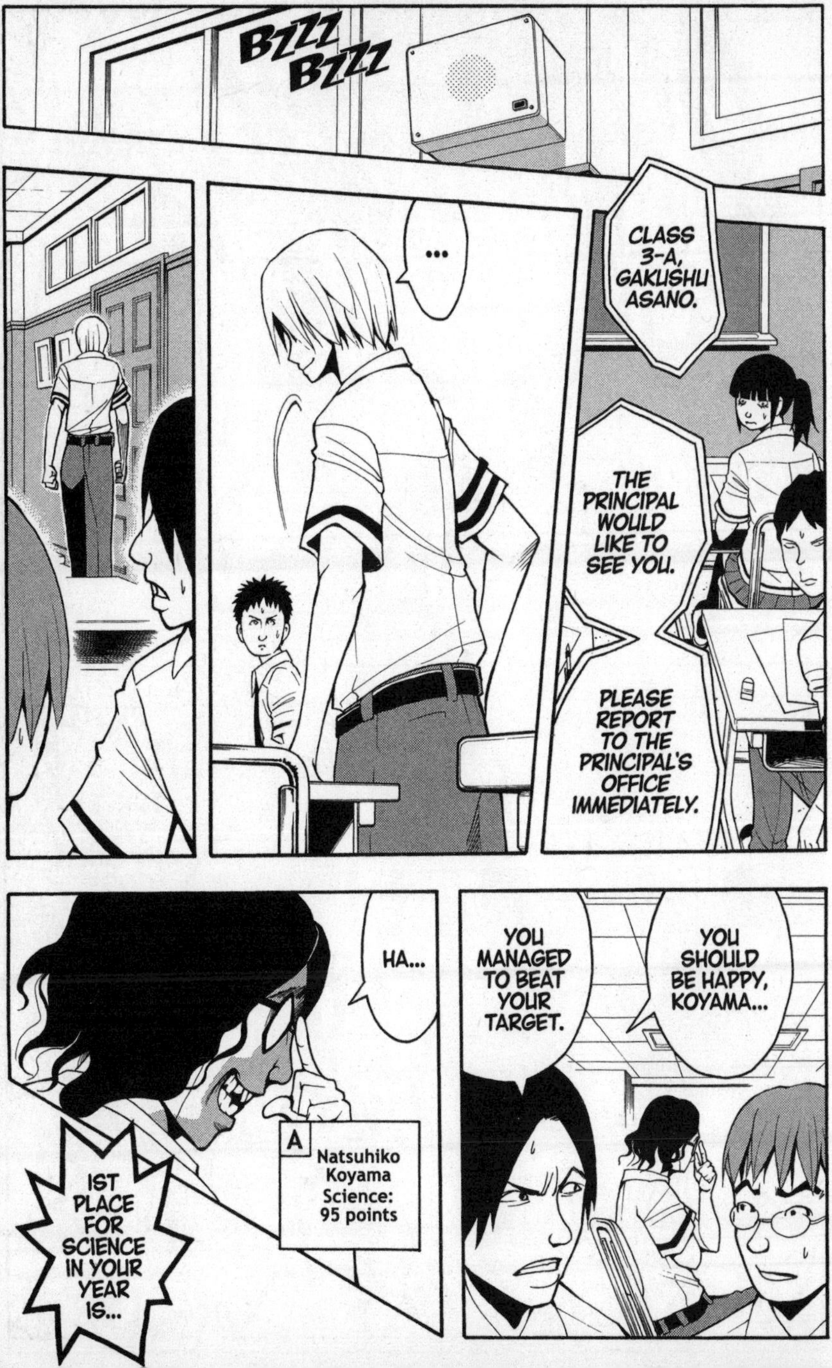
BZZZ BZZZ
CLASS 3-A, GAKUSHU ASANO.
THE PRINCIPAL WOULD LIKE TO SEE YOU.
PLEASE REPORT TO THE PRINCIPAL'S OFFICE IMMEDIATELY.
...
YOU SHOULD BE HAPPY, KOYAMA...
YOU MANAGED TO BEAT YOUR TARGET.
HA...
A
Natsuhiko Koyama Science: 95 points
1ST PLACE FOR SCIENCE IN YOUR YEAR IS...

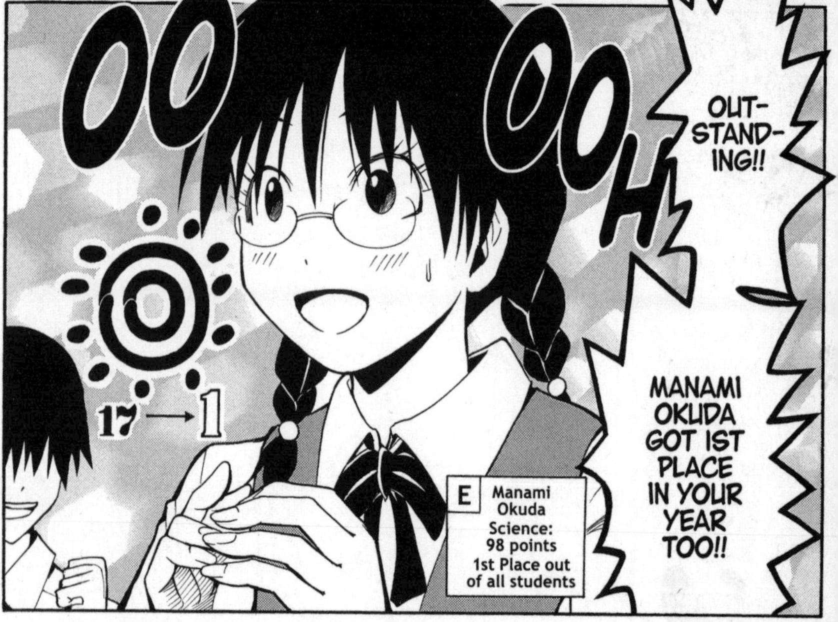
OUT-STANDING!!
MANAMI OKUDA GOT 1ST PLACE IN YOUR YEAR TOO!!
OOOOH
E Manami Okuda Science: 98 points 1st Place out of all students
17 → 1

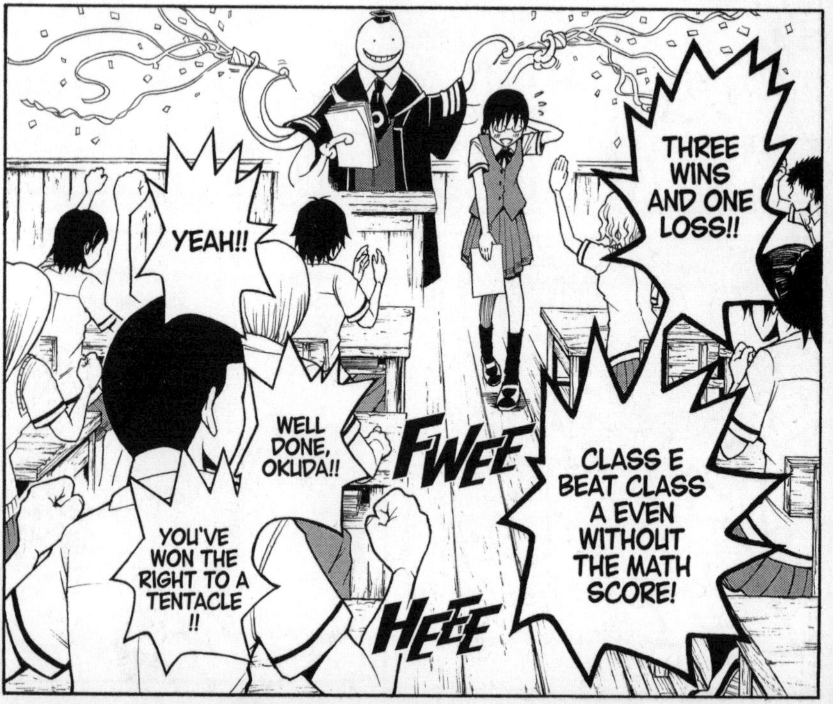
THREE WINS AND ONE LOSS!!
CLASS E BEAT CLASS A EVEN WITHOUT THE MATH SCORE!
FWEE
HEEE
WELL DONE, OKUDA!!
YEAH!!
YOU'VE WON THE RIGHT TO A TENTACLE !!

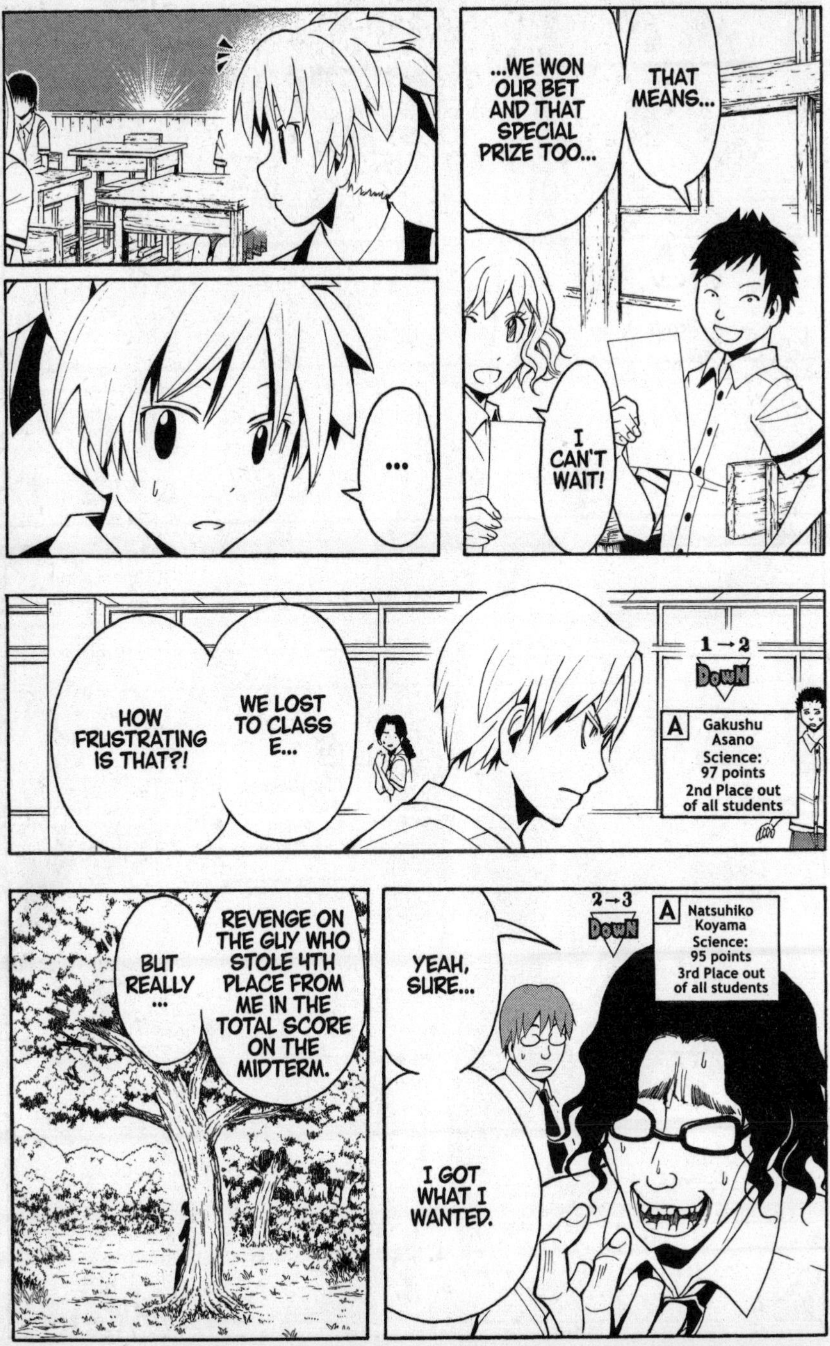
THAT MEANS...
...WE WON OUR BET AND THAT SPECIAL PRIZE TOO...
I CAN'T WAIT!
...
1→2 DOWN
A Gakushu Asano Science: 97 points 2nd Place out of all students
WE LOST TO CLASS E...
HOW FRUSTRATING IS THAT?!
2→3 DOWN
A Natsuhiko Koyama Science: 95 points 3rd Place out of all students
YEAH, SURE...
I GOT WHAT I WANTED.
REVENGE ON THE GUY WHO STOLE 4TH PLACE FROM ME IN THE TOTAL SCORE ON THE MIDTERM.
BUT REALLY ...

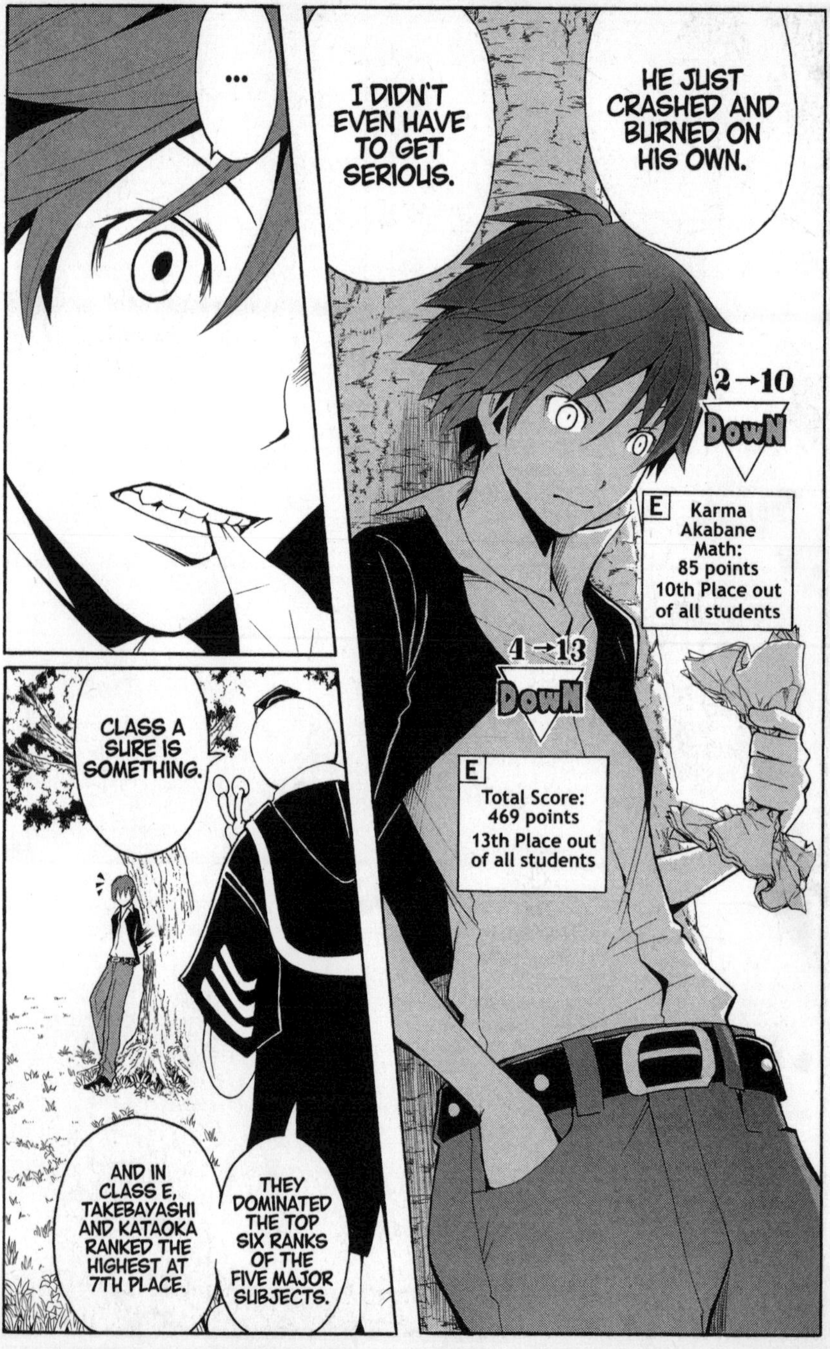
HE JUST CRASHED AND BURNED ON HIS OWN.
I DIDN'T EVEN HAVE TO GET SERIOUS.
2→10
DOWN
E Karma Akabane Math: 85 points 10th Place out of all students
4→13
DOWN
E Total Score: 469 points 13th Place out of all students
...
CLASS A SURE IS SOMETHING.
THEY DOMINATED THE TOP SIX RANKS OF THE FIVE MAJOR SUBJECTS.
AND IN CLASS E, TAKEBAYASHI AND KATAOKA RANKED THE HIGHEST AT 7TH PLACE.

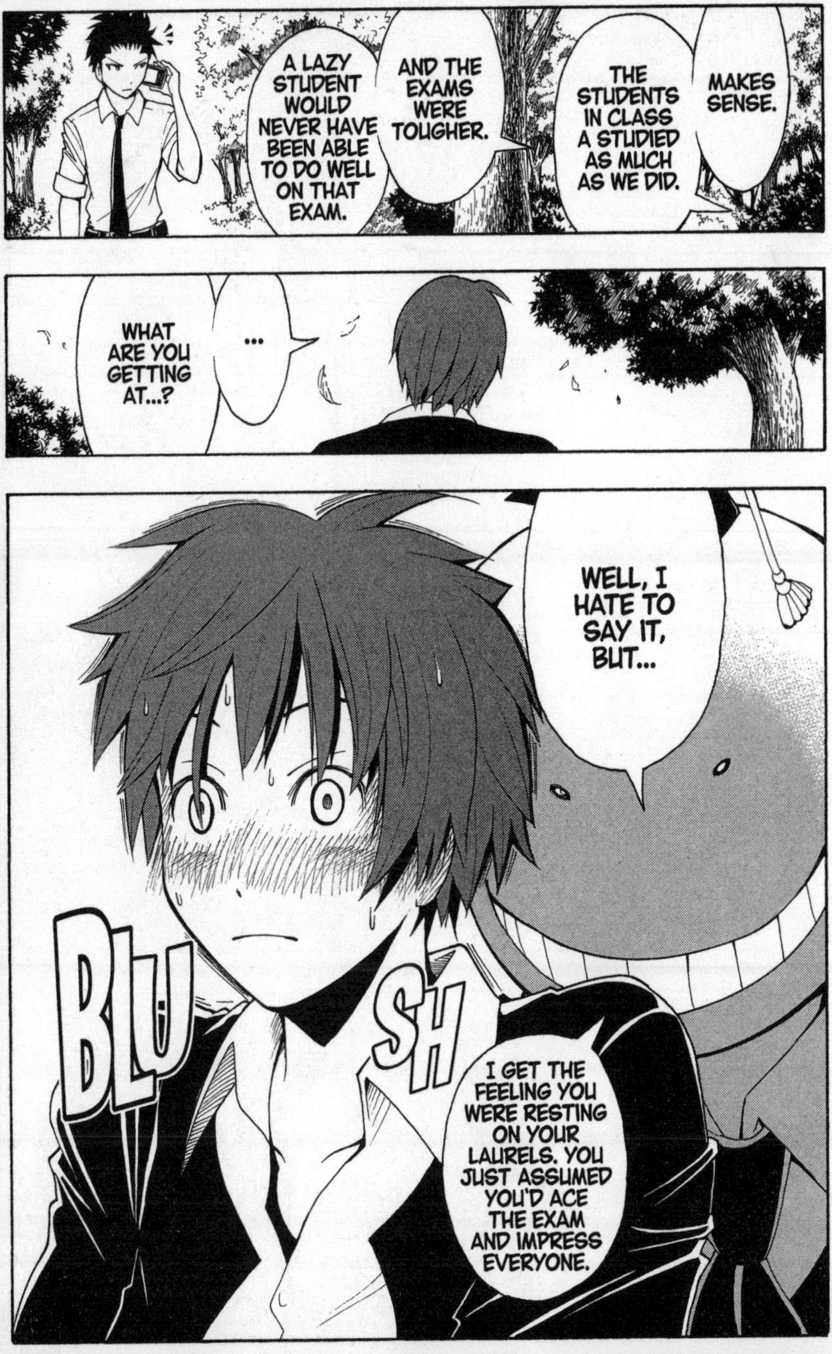
MAKES SENSE.
THE STUDENTS IN CLASS A STUDIED AS MUCH AS WE DID.
AND THE EXAMS WERE TOUGHER.
A LAZY STUDENT WOULD NEVER HAVE BEEN ABLE TO DO WELL ON THAT EXAM.
...
WHAT ARE YOU GETTING AT...?
WELL, I HATE TO SAY IT, BUT...
BLUSH
I GET THE FEELING YOU WERE RESTING ON YOUR LAURELS. YOU JUST ASSUMED YOU'D ACE THE EXAM AND IMPRESS EVERYONE.

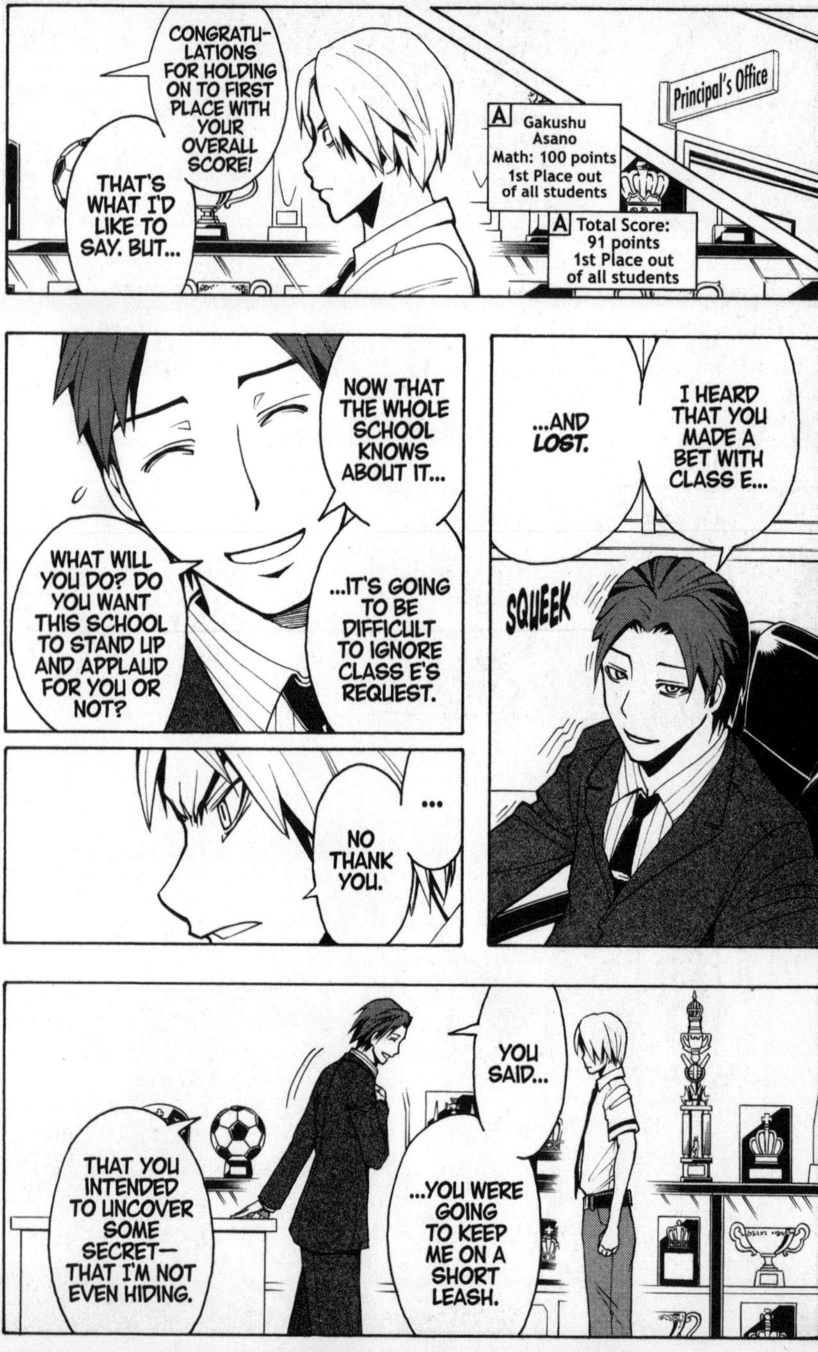
Principal's Office
CONGRATULATIONS FOR HOLDING ON TO FIRST PLACE WITH YOUR OVERALL SCORE!
A Gakushu Asano Math: 100 points 1st Place out of all students
A Total Score: 91 points 1st Place out of all students
THAT'S WHAT I'D LIKE TO SAY. BUT...
I HEARD THAT YOU MADE A BET WITH CLASS E...
...AND LOST.
SQUEEK
NOW THAT THE WHOLE SCHOOL KNOWS ABOUT IT...
...IT'S GOING TO BE DIFFICULT TO IGNORE CLASS E'S REQUEST.
WHAT WILL YOU DO? DO YOU WANT THIS SCHOOL TO STAND UP AND APPLAUD FOR YOU OR NOT?
...
NO THANK YOU.
YOU SAID...
...YOU WERE GOING TO KEEP ME ON A SHORT LEASH.
THAT YOU INTENDED TO UNCOVER SOME SECRET—THAT I'M NOT EVEN HIDING.

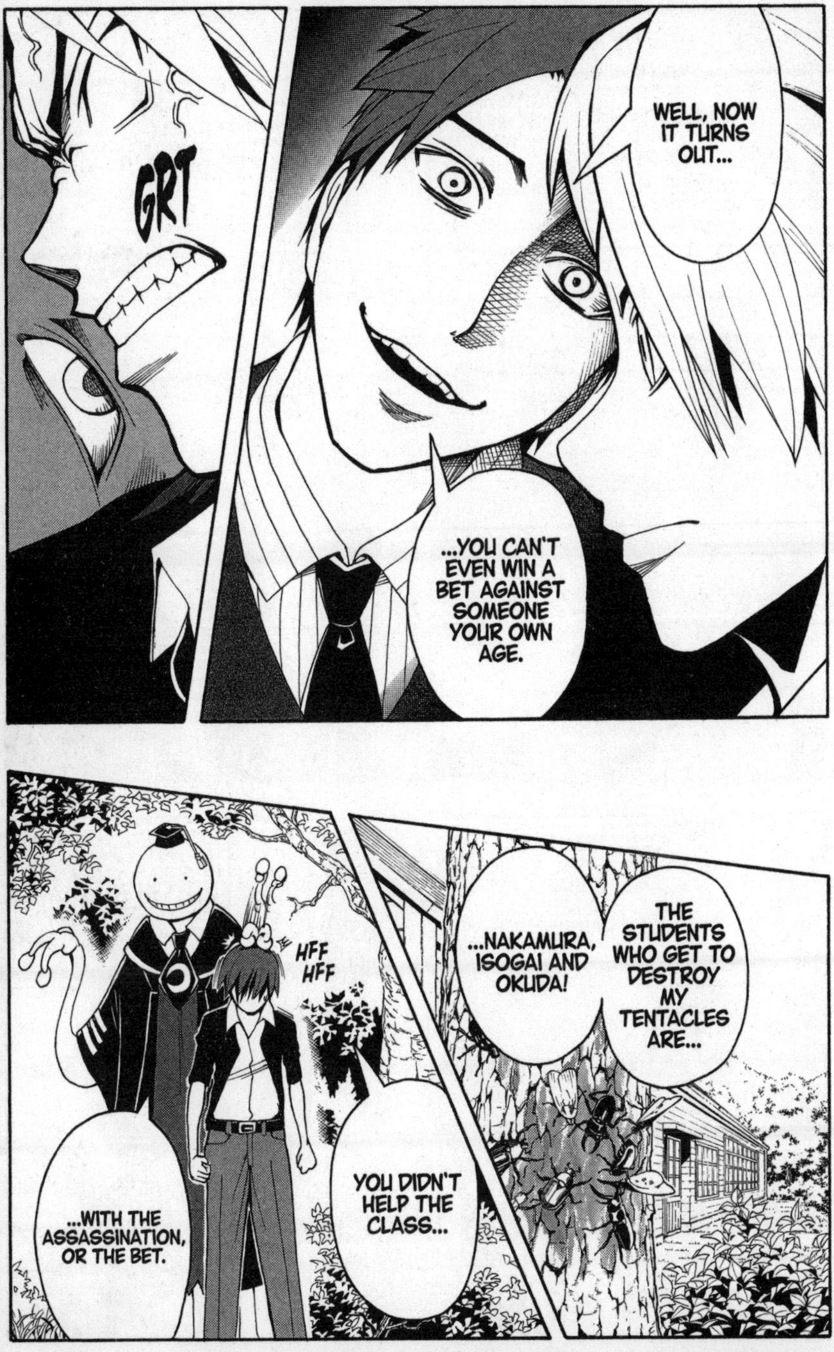
WELL, NOW IT TURNS OUT...
...YOU CAN'T EVEN WIN A BET AGAINST SOMEONE YOUR OWN AGE.
GRT
THE STUDENTS WHO GET TO DESTROY MY TENTACLES ARE...
...NAKAMURA, ISOGAI AND OKUDA!
HFF HFF
YOU DIDN'T HELP THE CLASS...
...WITH THE ASSASSINATION, OR THE BET.

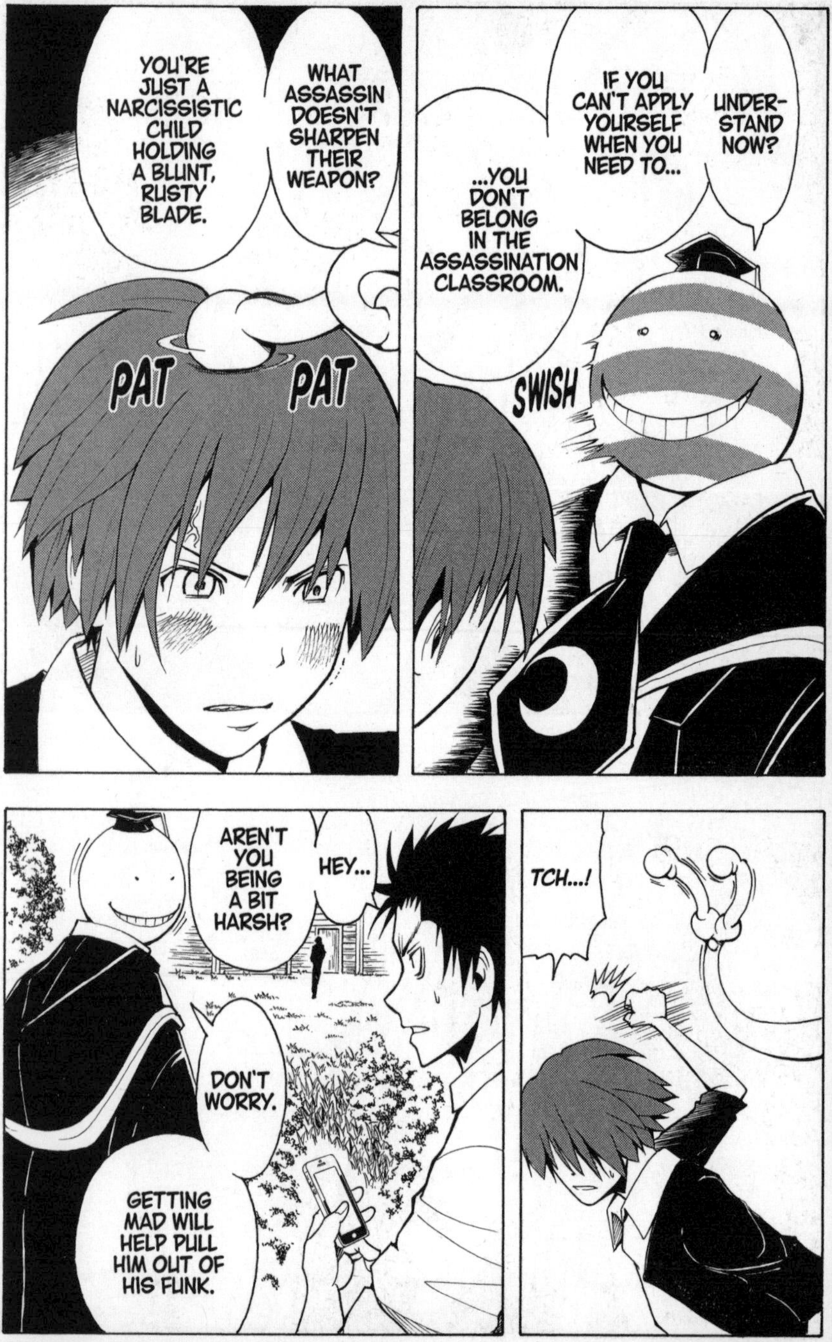
UNDER-STAND NOW?
IF YOU CAN'T APPLY YOURSELF WHEN YOU NEED TO...
...YOU DON'T BELONG IN THE ASSASSINATION CLASSROOM.
SWISH
WHAT ASSASSIN DOESN'T SHARPEN THEIR WEAPON?
YOU'RE JUST A NARCISSISTIC CHILD HOLDING A BLUNT, RUSTY BLADE.
PAT
PAT
TCH...!
HEY...
AREN'T YOU BEING A BIT HARSH?
DON'T WORRY.
GETTING MAD WILL HELP PULL HIM OUT OF HIS FUNK.

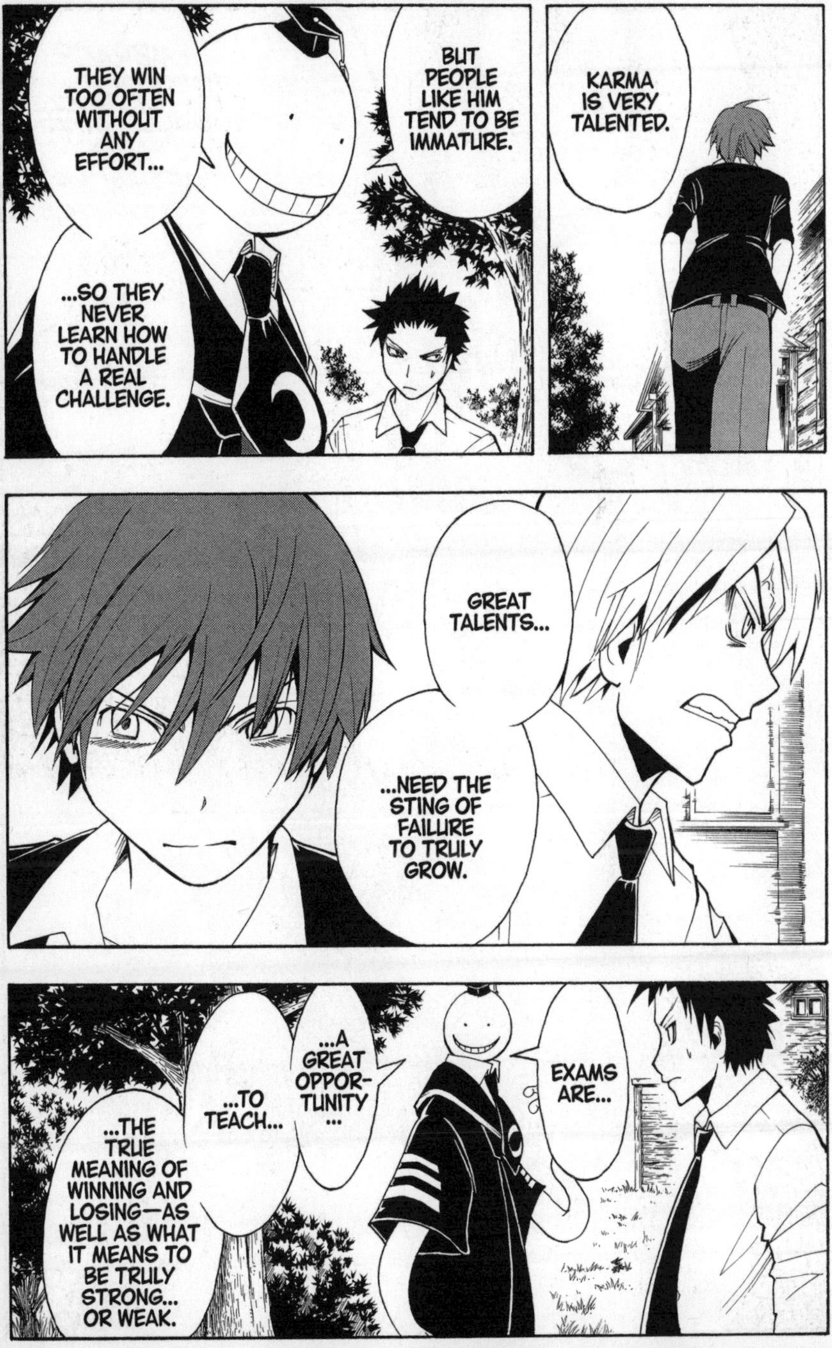
KARMA IS VERY TALENTED.
BUT PEOPLE LIKE HIM TEND TO BE IMMATURE.
THEY WIN TOO OFTEN WITHOUT ANY EFFORT...
...SO THEY NEVER LEARN HOW TO HANDLE A REAL CHALLENGE.
GREAT TALENTS...
...NEED THE STING OF FAILURE TO TRULY GROW.
EXAMS ARE...
...A GREAT OPPORTUNITY...
...TO TEACH...
...THE TRUE MEANING OF WINNING AND LOSING—AS WELL AS WHAT IT MEANS TO BE TRULY STRONG... OR WEAK.

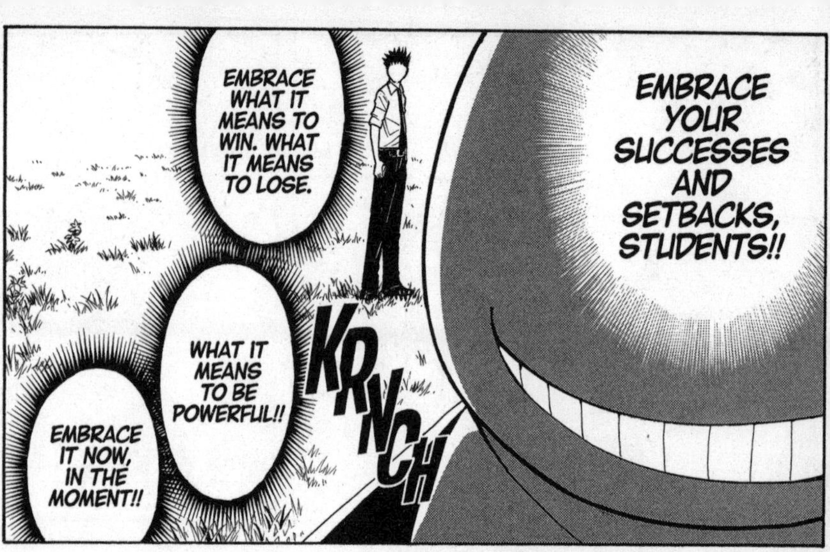
EMBRACE YOUR SUCCESSES AND SETBACKS, STUDENTS!!
EMBRACE WHAT IT MEANS TO WIN. WHAT IT MEANS TO LOSE.
KRNCH
WHAT IT MEANS TO BE POWERFUL!!
EMBRACE IT NOW, IN THE MOMENT!!

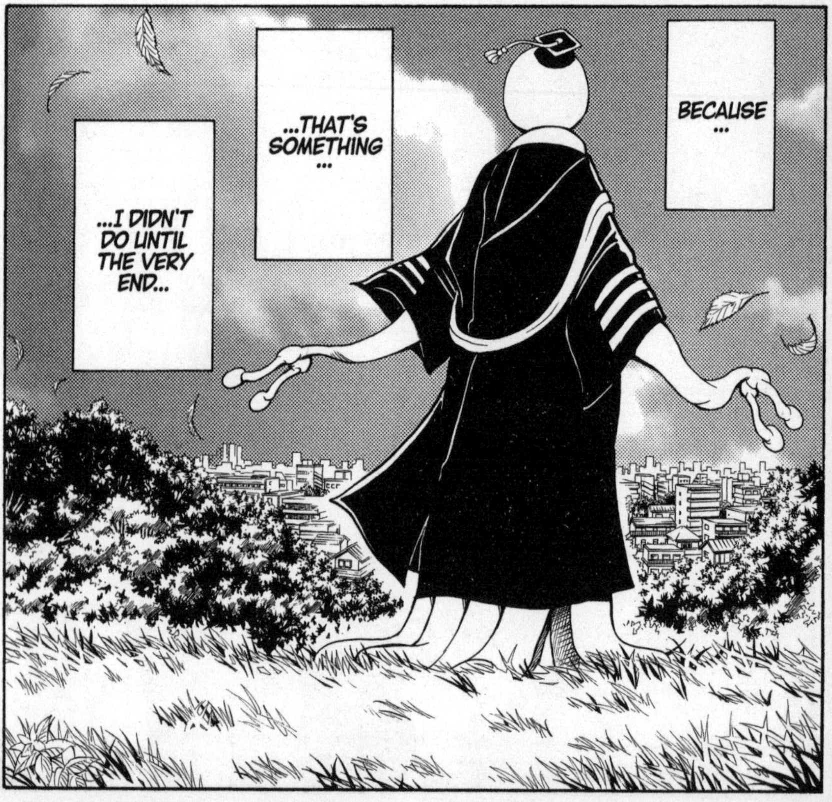
BECAUSE ...
...THAT'S SOMETHING ...
...I DIDN'T DO UNTIL THE VERY END...

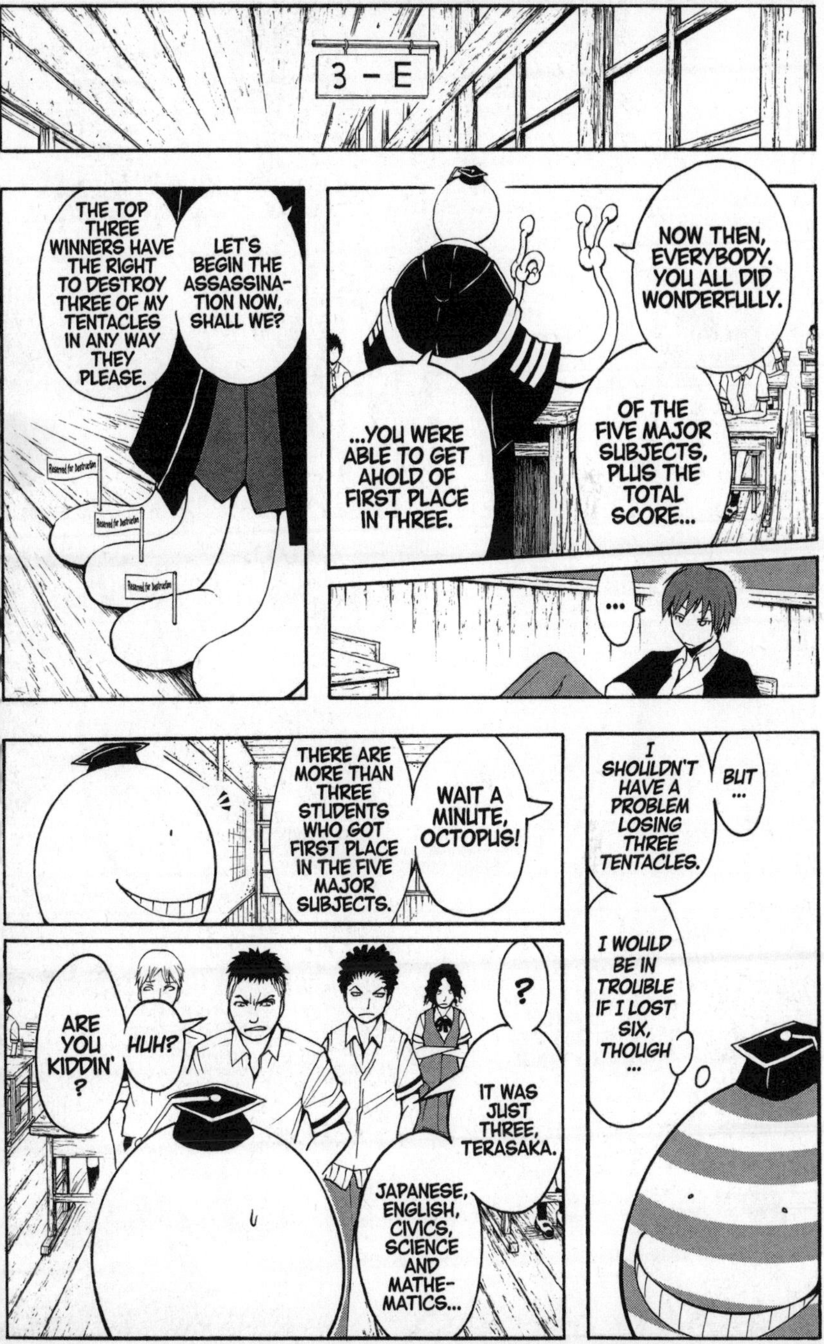
3 - E
NOW THEN, EVERYBODY. YOU ALL DID WONDERFULLY.
OF THE FIVE MAJOR SUBJECTS, PLUS THE TOTAL SCORE...
...YOU WERE ABLE TO GET AHOLD OF FIRST PLACE IN THREE.
...
THE TOP THREE WINNERS HAVE THE RIGHT TO DESTROY THREE OF MY TENTACLES IN ANY WAY THEY PLEASE.
LET'S BEGIN THE ASSASSINATION NOW, SHALL WE?
Reserved for Destruction
Reserved for Destruction
Reserved for Destruction
I SHOULDN'T HAVE A PROBLEM LOSING THREE TENTACLES.
BUT...
I WOULD BE IN TROUBLE IF I LOST SIX, THOUGH...
WAIT A MINUTE, OCTOPUS!
THERE ARE MORE THAN THREE STUDENTS WHO GOT FIRST PLACE IN THE FIVE MAJOR SUBJECTS.
?
IT WAS JUST THREE, TERASAKA.
JAPANESE, ENGLISH, CIVICS, SCIENCE AND MATHEMATICS...
HUH?
ARE YOU KIDDIN'?

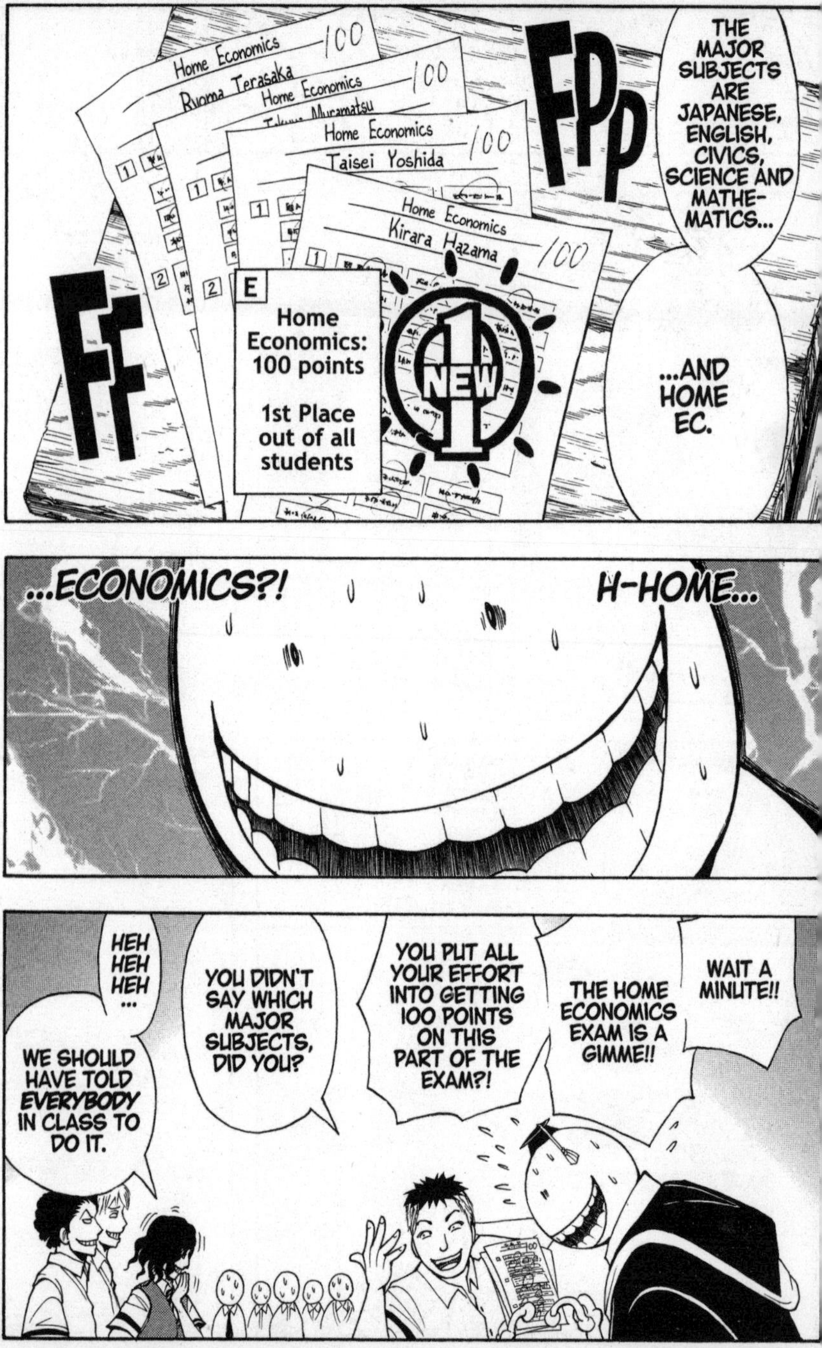
THE MAJOR SUBJECTS ARE JAPANESE, ENGLISH, CIVICS, SCIENCE AND MATHEMATICS...
...AND HOME EC.
FPP
Home Economics 100 Ryoma Terasaka
Home Economics 100
Home Economics 100 Taisei Yoshida
Home Economics Kirara Hazama 100
NEW 1
E Home Economics: 100 points
1st Place out of all students
FF
H-HOME...
...ECONOMICS?!
WAIT A MINUTE!!
THE HOME ECONOMICS EXAM IS A GIMME!!
YOU PUT ALL YOUR EFFORT INTO GETTING 100 POINTS ON THIS PART OF THE EXAM?!
YOU DIDN'T SAY WHICH MAJOR SUBJECTS, DID YOU?
HEH HEH HEH...
WE SHOULD HAVE TOLD EVERYBODY IN CLASS TO DO IT.

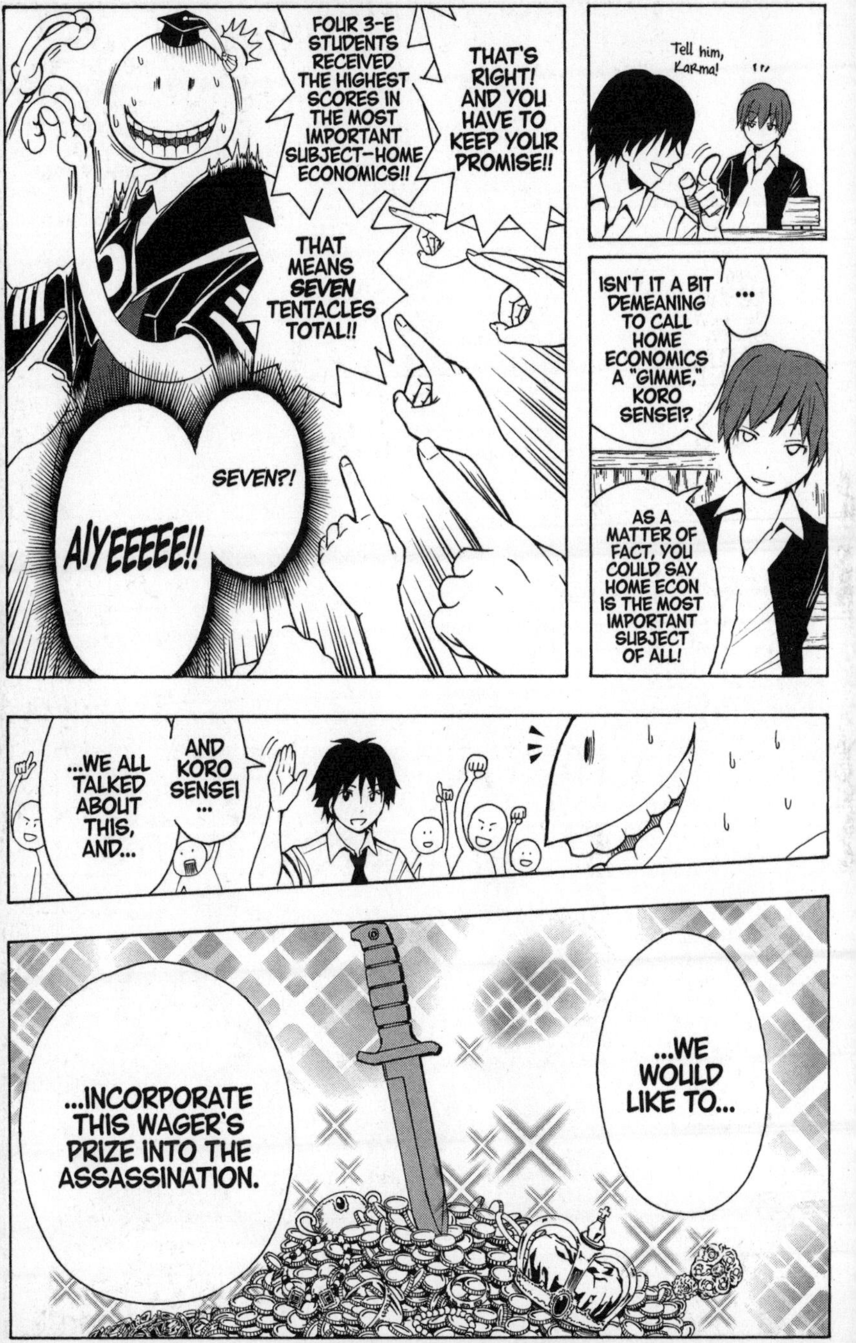
Tell him, Karma!
...
...
ISN'T IT A BIT DEMEANING TO CALL HOME ECONOMICS A "GIMME," KORO SENSEI?
AS A MATTER OF FACT, YOU COULD SAY HOME ECON IS THE MOST IMPORTANT SUBJECT OF ALL!
FOUR 3-E STUDENTS RECEIVED THE HIGHEST SCORES IN THE MOST IMPORTANT SUBJECT—HOME ECONOMICS!!
THAT'S RIGHT! AND YOU HAVE TO KEEP YOUR PROMISE!!
THAT MEANS SEVEN TENTACLES TOTAL!!
SEVEN?!
AIYEEEEE!!
AND KORO SENSEI ...
...WE ALL TALKED ABOUT THIS, AND...
...WE WOULD LIKE TO...
...INCORPORATE THIS WAGER'S PRIZE INTO THE ASSASSINATION.

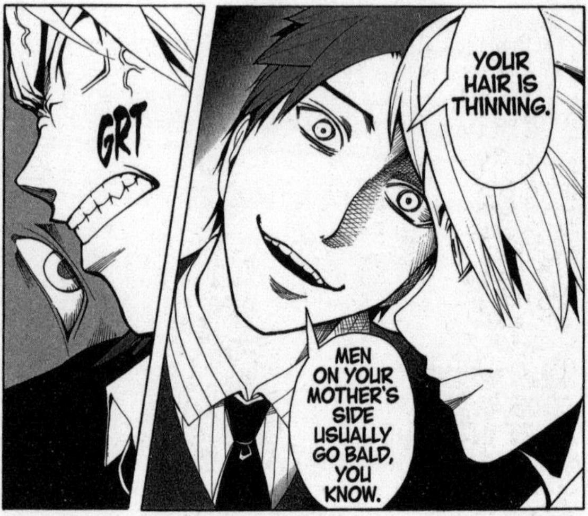
YOUR HAIR IS THINNING.
MEN ON YOUR MOTHER'S SIDE USUALLY GO BALD, YOU KNOW.
GRT

Insult to Injury

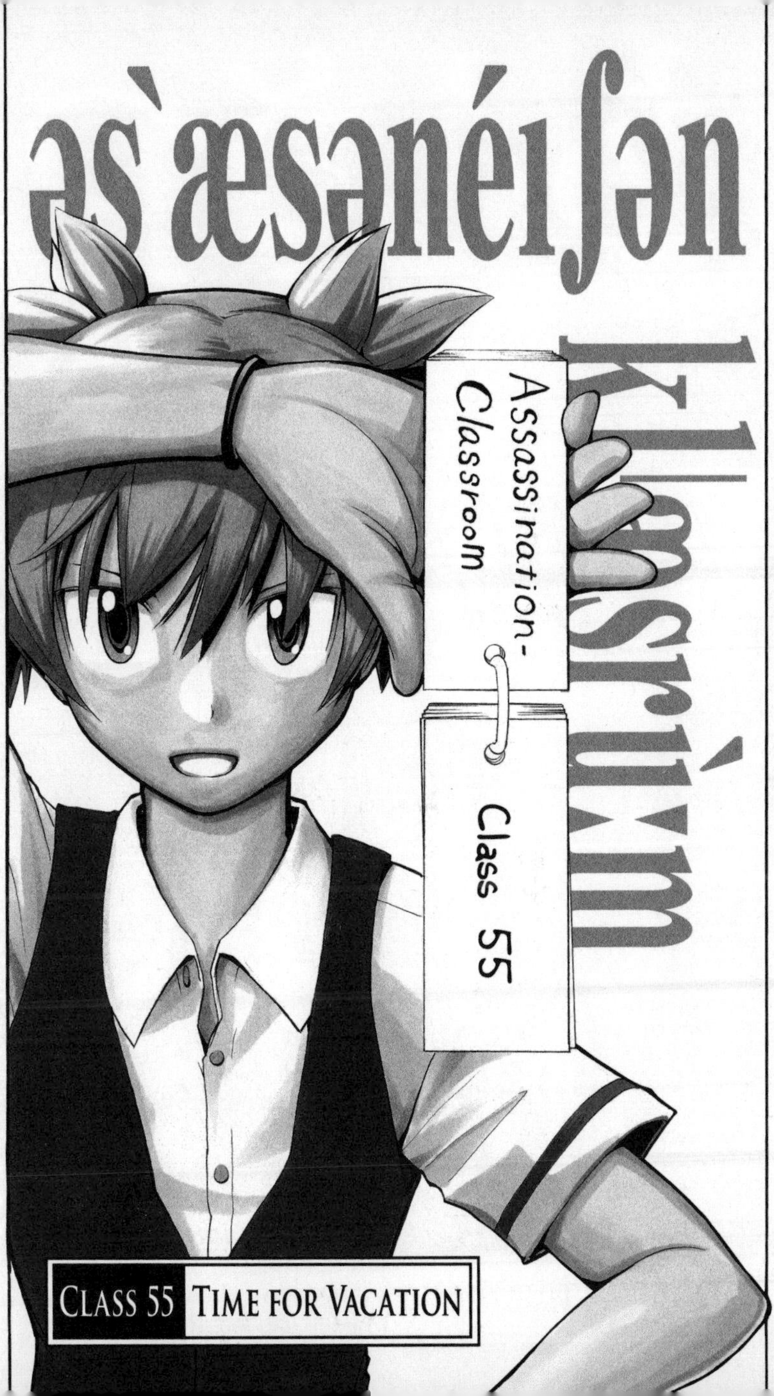
əs`æsənéiʃən
klæsrúːm
Assassination-Classroom
Class 55

Class 55 Time for Vacation

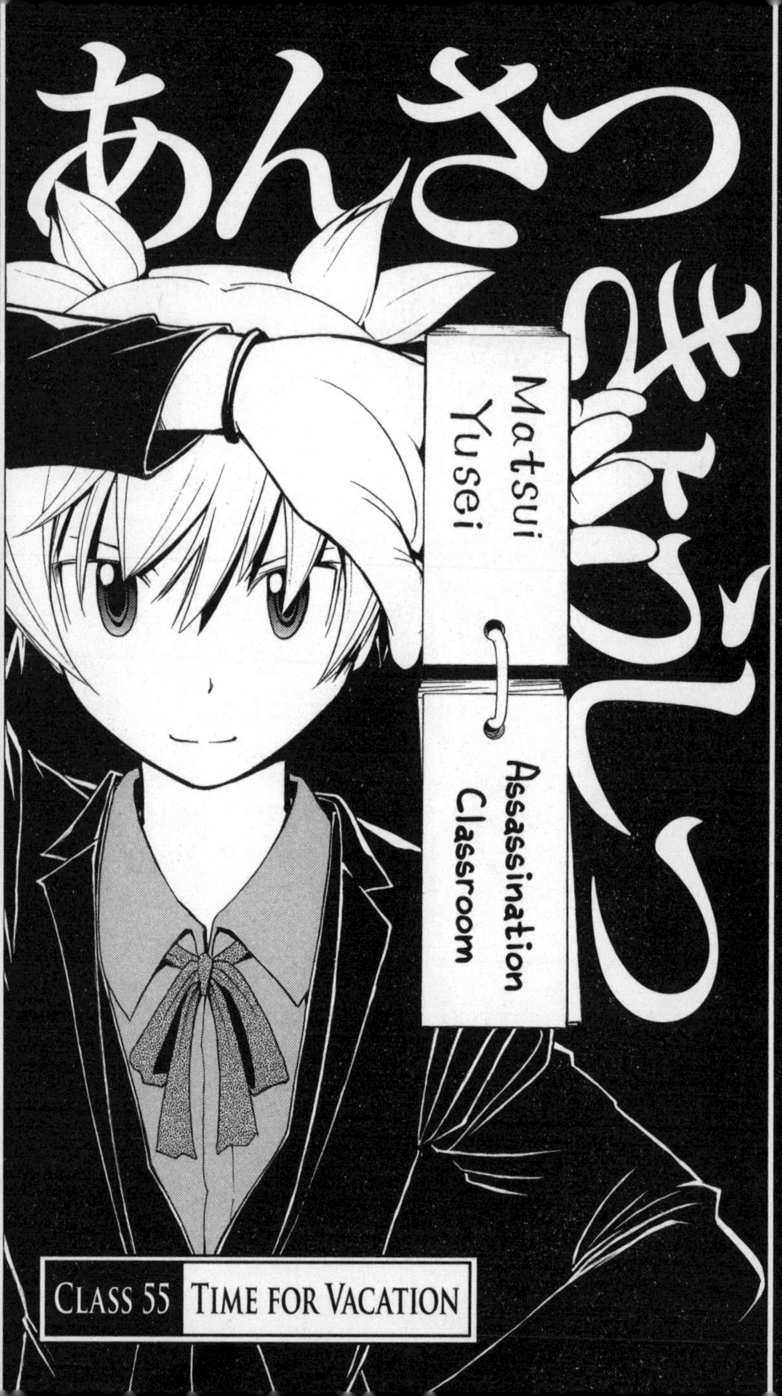
あんさつきょうしつ
Matsui Yusei
Assassination Classroom

Class 55 Time for Vacation

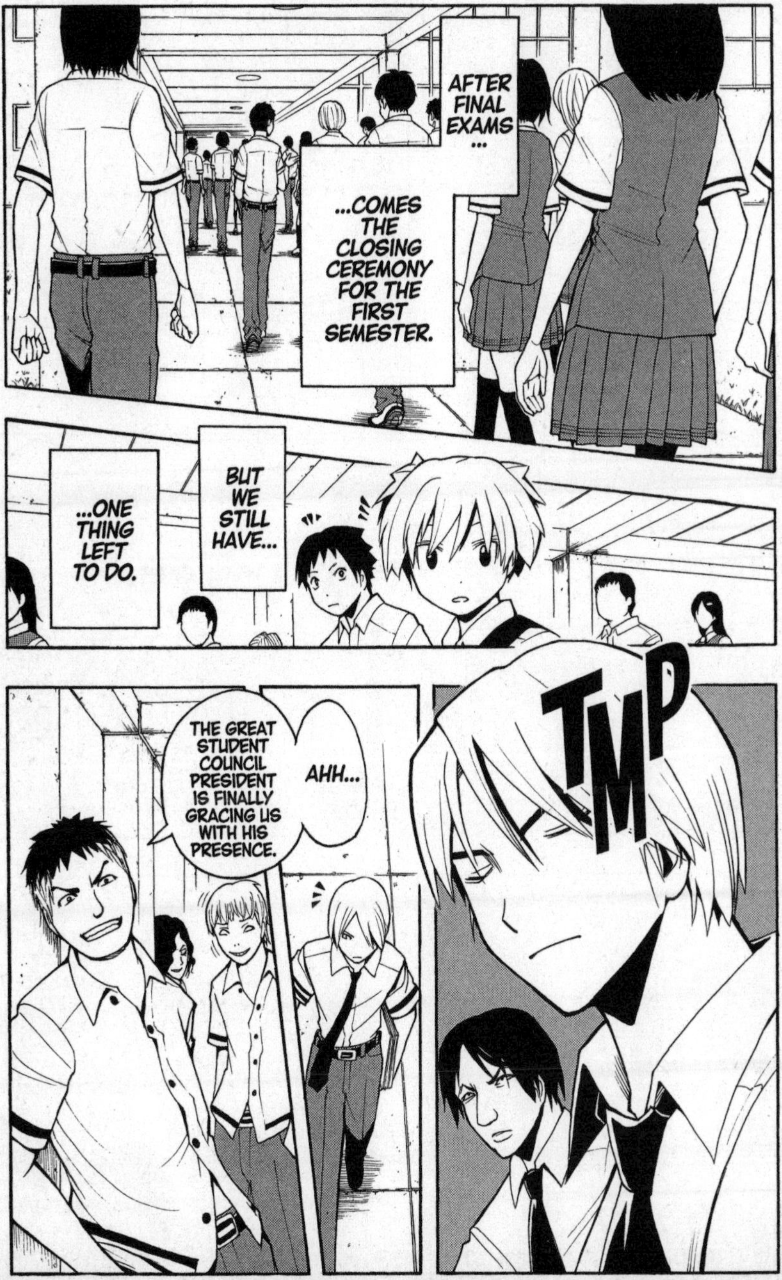
AFTER FINAL EXAMS...
...COMES THE CLOSING CEREMONY FOR THE FIRST SEMESTER.
BUT WE STILL HAVE...
...ONE THING LEFT TO DO.
TMP
AHH...
THE GREAT STUDENT COUNCIL PRESIDENT IS FINALLY GRACING US WITH HIS PRESENCE.

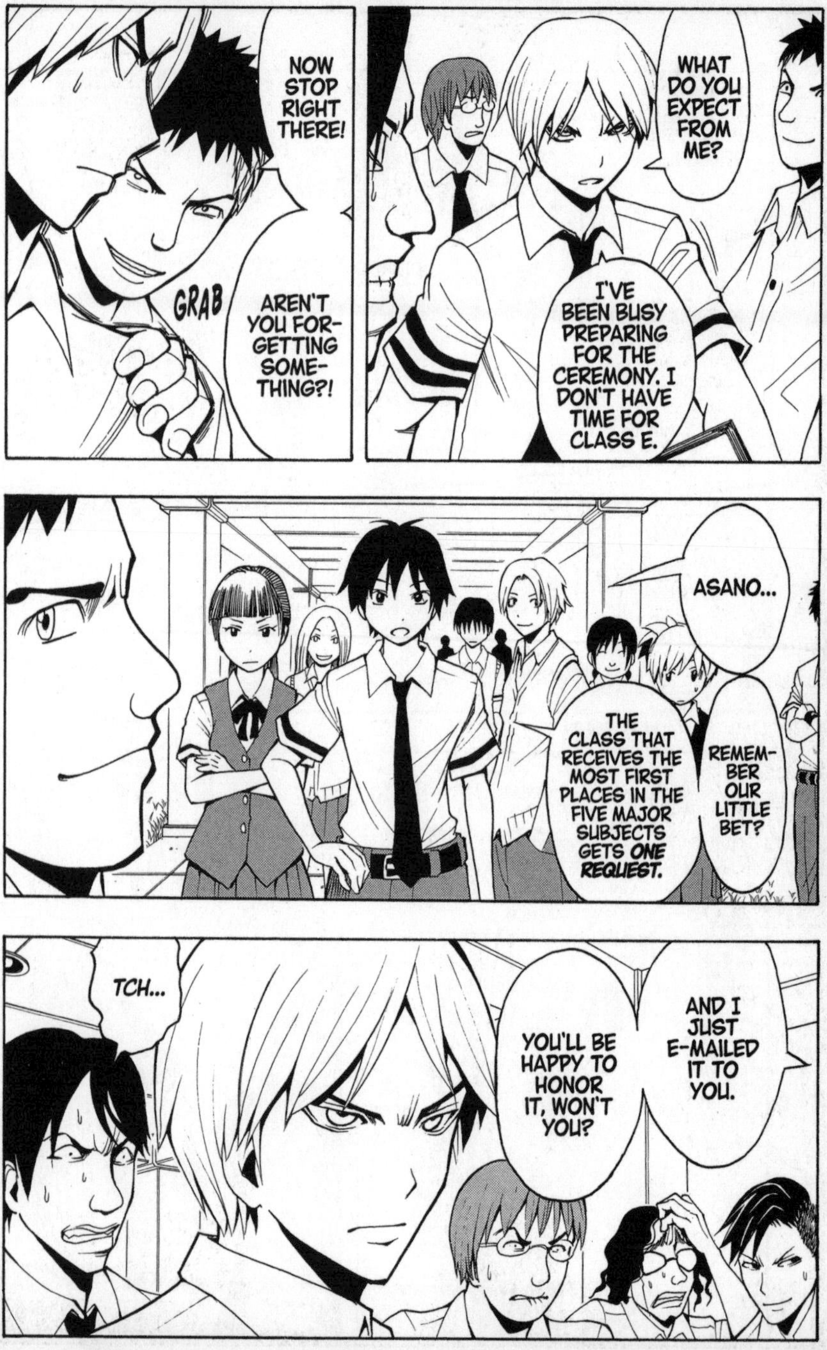
WHAT DO YOU EXPECT FROM ME?
I'VE BEEN BUSY PREPARING FOR THE CEREMONY. I DON'T HAVE TIME FOR CLASS E.
NOW STOP RIGHT THERE!
GRAB
AREN'T YOU FOR-GETTING SOME-THING?!
ASANO...
REMEM-BER OUR LITTLE BET?
THE CLASS THAT RECEIVES THE MOST FIRST PLACES IN THE FIVE MAJOR SUBJECTS GETS *ONE REQUEST.*
AND I JUST E-MAILED IT TO YOU.
YOU'LL BE HAPPY TO HONOR IT, WON'T YOU?
TCH...

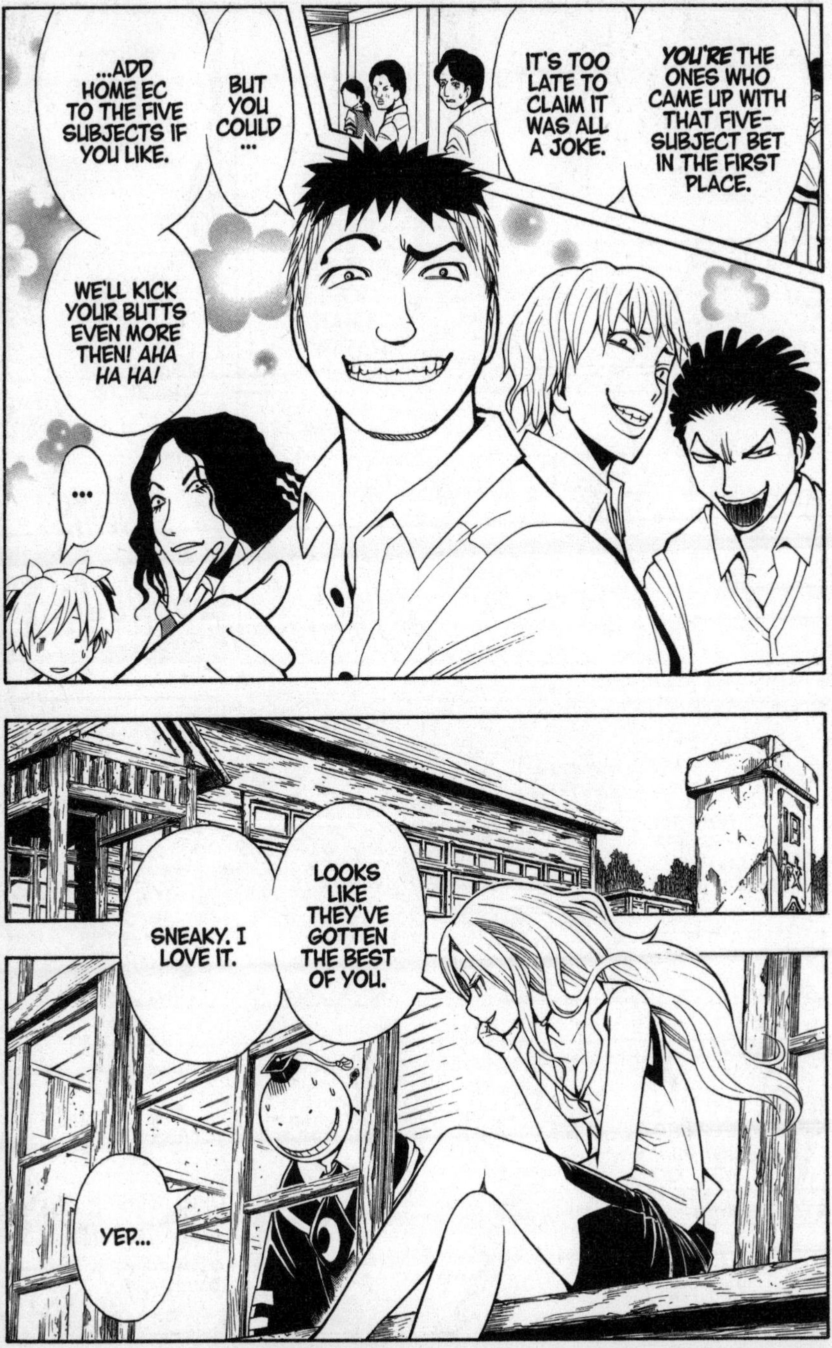
YOU'RE THE ONES WHO CAME UP WITH THAT FIVE-SUBJECT BET IN THE FIRST PLACE.
IT'S TOO LATE TO CLAIM IT WAS ALL A JOKE.
BUT YOU COULD...
...ADD HOME EC TO THE FIVE SUBJECTS IF YOU LIKE.
WE'LL KICK YOUR BUTTS EVEN MORE THEN! AHA HA HA!
...
LOOKS LIKE THEY'VE GOTTEN THE BEST OF YOU.
SNEAKY. I LOVE IT.
YEP...

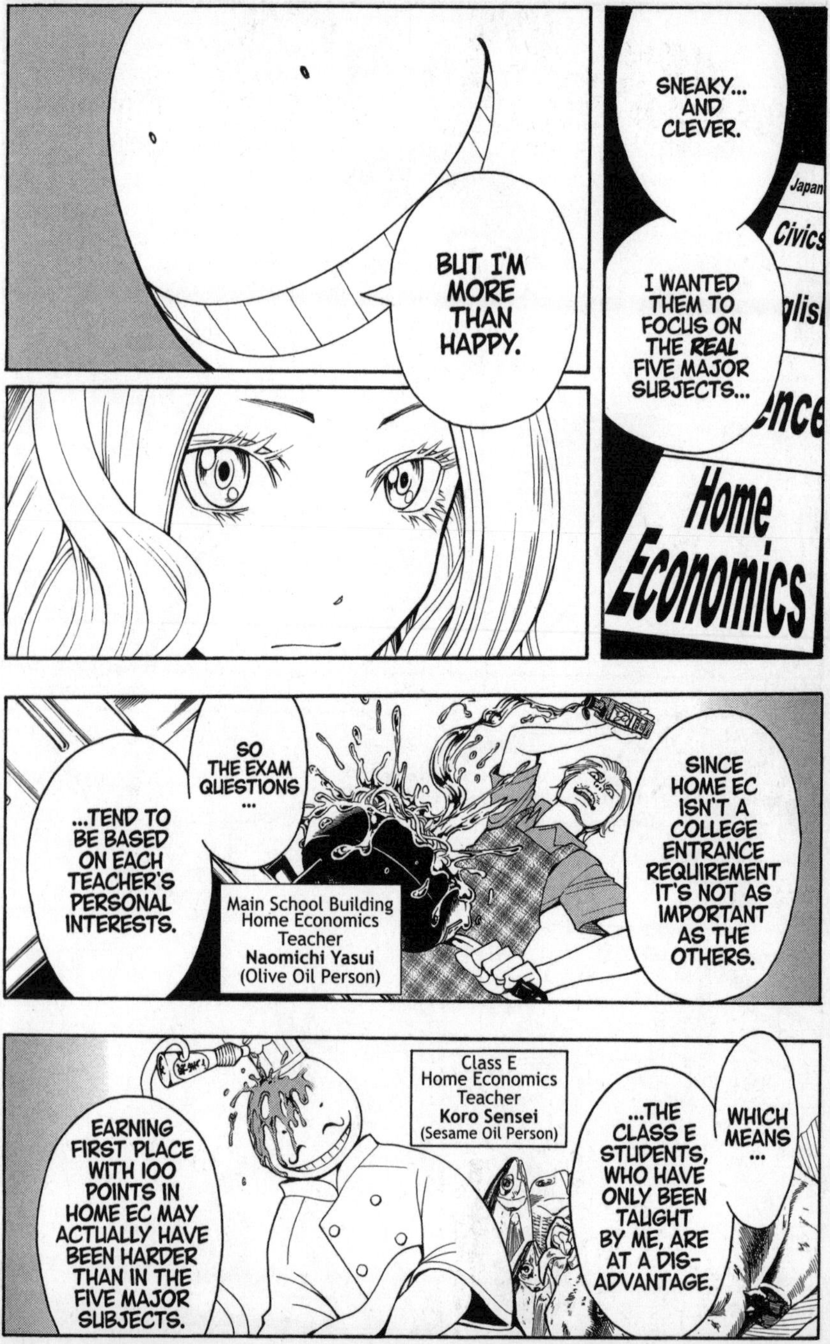
SNEAKY... AND CLEVER.
Japan
Civics
Home Economics
I WANTED THEM TO FOCUS ON THE REAL FIVE MAJOR SUBJECTS...
BUT I'M MORE THAN HAPPY.
SINCE HOME EC ISN'T A COLLEGE ENTRANCE REQUIREMENT IT'S NOT AS IMPORTANT AS THE OTHERS.
SO THE EXAM QUESTIONS...
...TEND TO BE BASED ON EACH TEACHER'S PERSONAL INTERESTS.
Main School Building Home Economics Teacher Naomichi Yasui (Olive Oil Person)
WHICH MEANS...
...THE CLASS E STUDENTS, WHO HAVE ONLY BEEN TAUGHT BY ME, ARE AT A DIS-ADVANTAGE.
Class E Home Economics Teacher Koro Sensei (Sesame Oil Person)
EARNING FIRST PLACE WITH 100 POINTS IN HOME EC MAY ACTUALLY HAVE BEEN HARDER THAN IN THE FIVE MAJOR SUBJECTS.

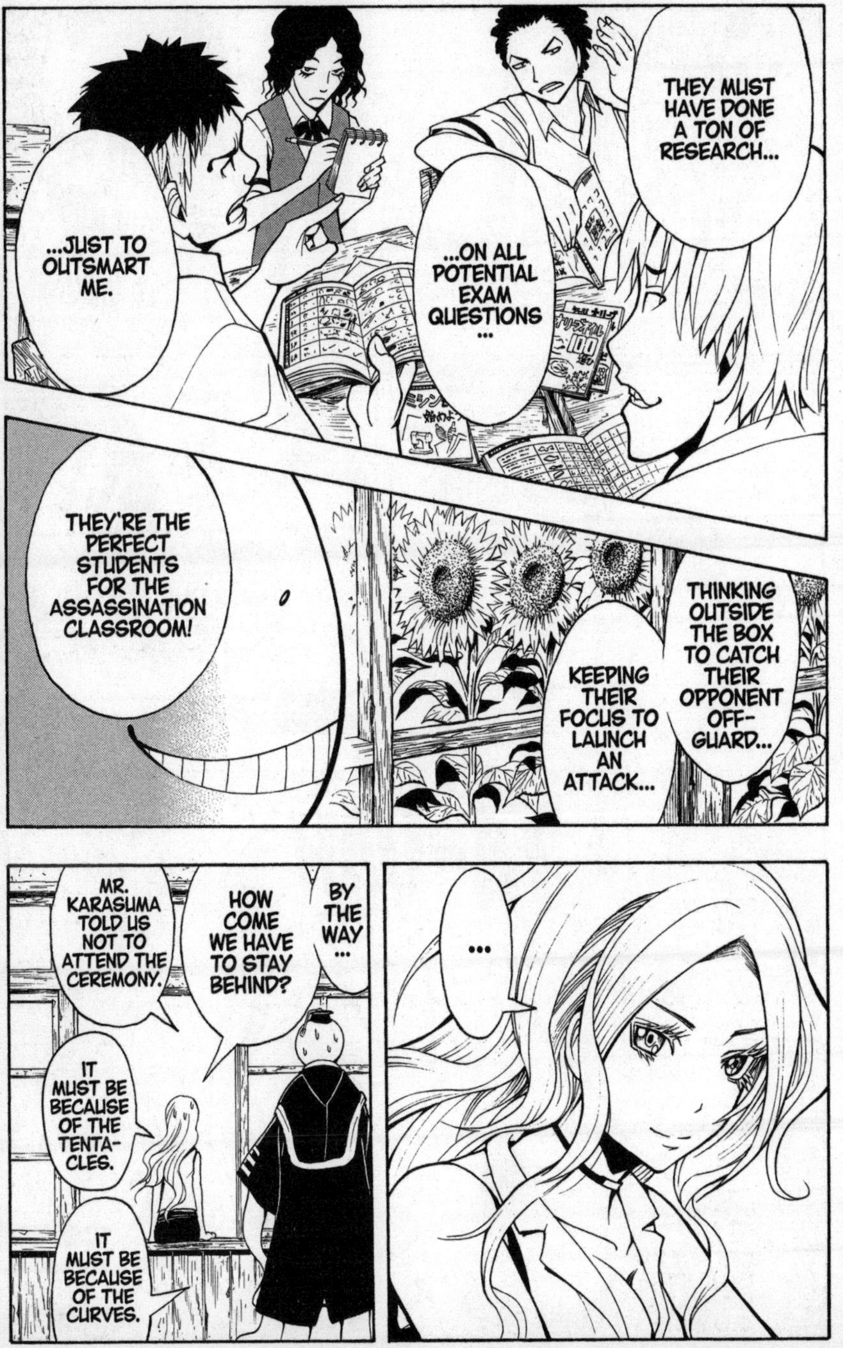
THEY MUST HAVE DONE A TON OF RESEARCH...
...ON ALL POTENTIAL EXAM QUESTIONS ...
...JUST TO OUTSMART ME.
THINKING OUTSIDE THE BOX TO CATCH THEIR OPPONENT OFF-GUARD...
KEEPING THEIR FOCUS TO LAUNCH AN ATTACK...
THEY'RE THE PERFECT STUDENTS FOR THE ASSASSINATION CLASSROOM!
...
BY THE WAY ...
HOW COME WE HAVE TO STAY BEHIND?
MR. KARASUMA TOLD US NOT TO ATTEND THE CEREMONY.
IT MUST BE BECAUSE OF THE TENTACLES.
IT MUST BE BECAUSE OF THE CURVES.

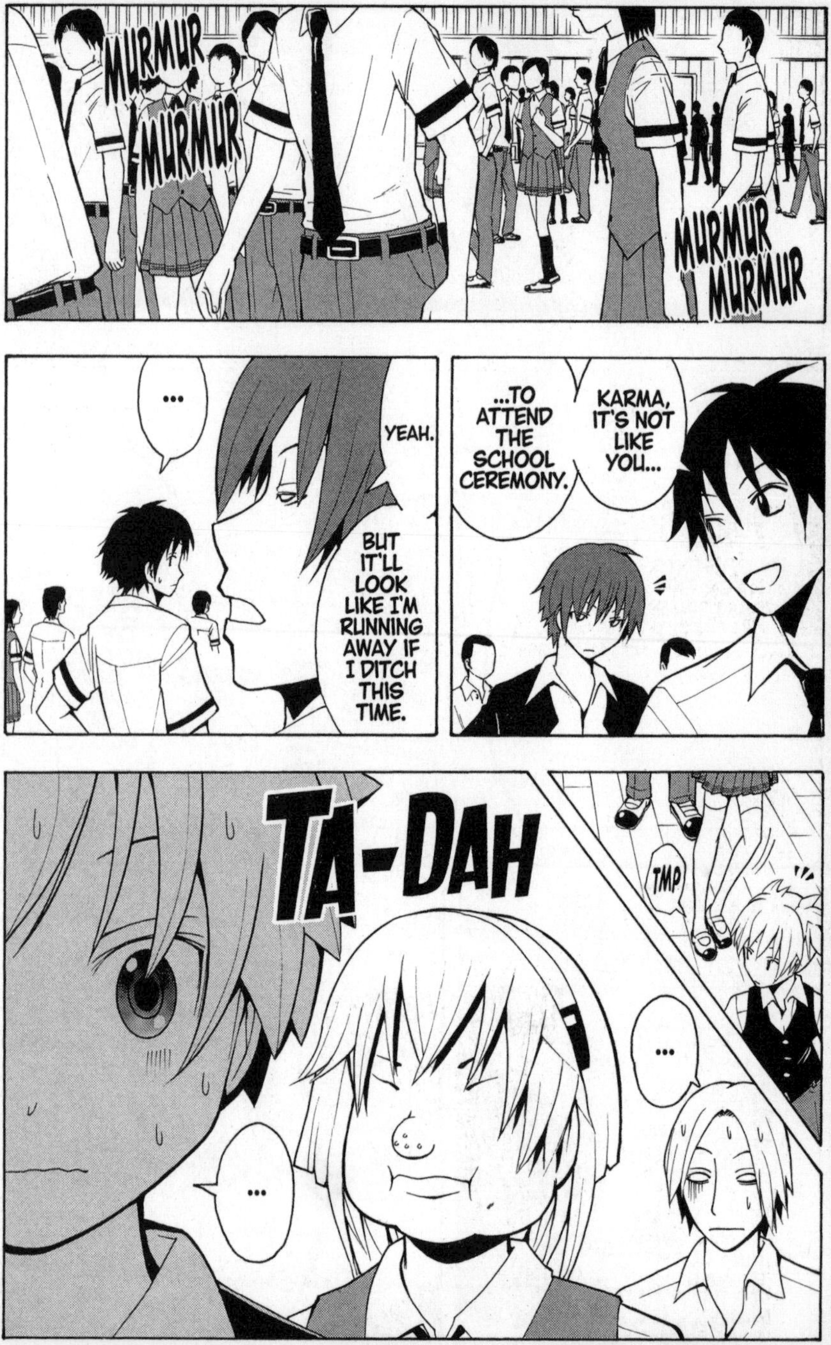
MURMUR MURMUR
MURMUR MURMUR
KARMA, IT'S NOT LIKE YOU...
...TO ATTEND THE SCHOOL CEREMONY.
YEAH.
BUT IT'LL LOOK LIKE I'M RUNNING AWAY IF I DITCH THIS TIME.
...
TMP
...
TA-DAH
...

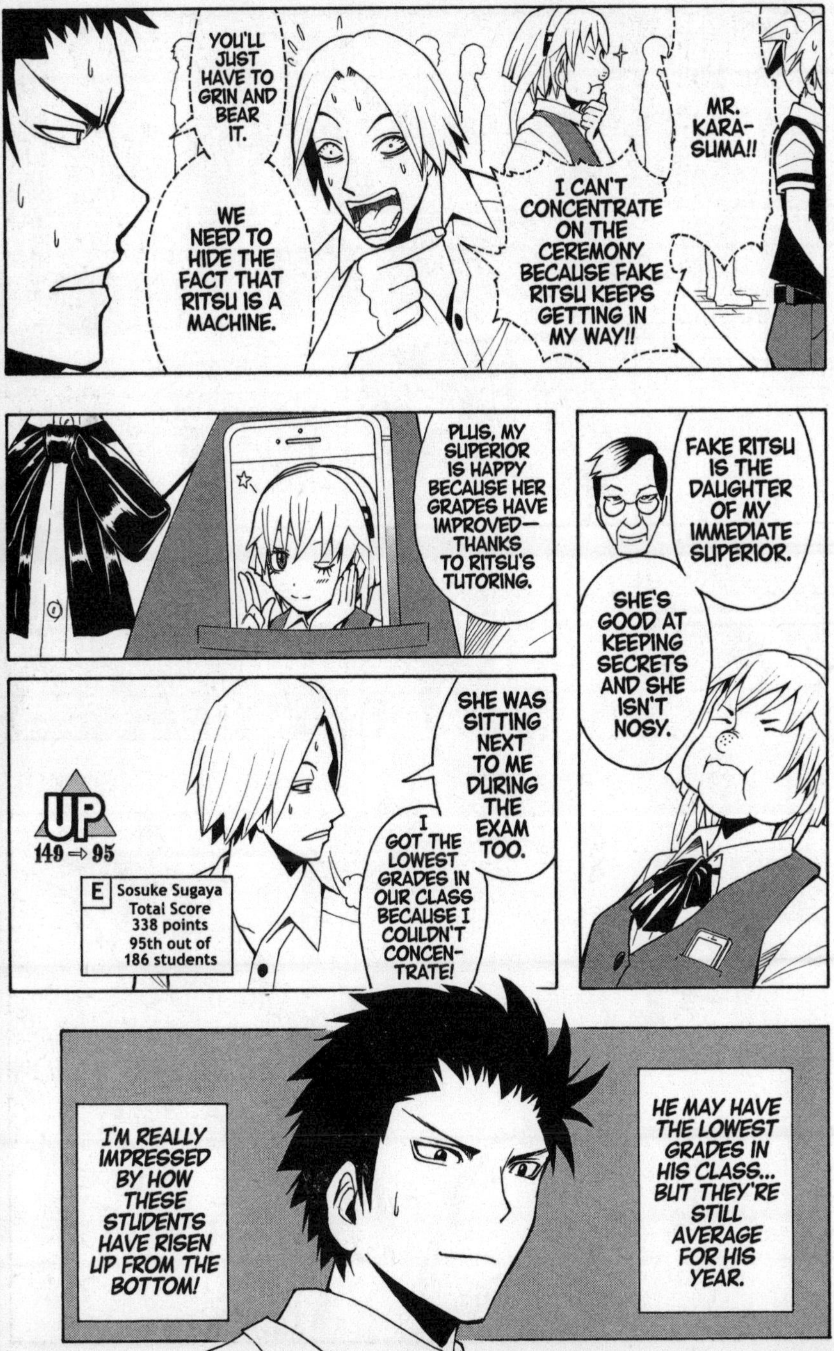
MR. KARA-SUMA!!
I CAN'T CONCENTRATE ON THE CEREMONY BECAUSE FAKE RITSU KEEPS GETTING IN MY WAY!!
YOU'LL JUST HAVE TO GRIN AND BEAR IT.
WE NEED TO HIDE THE FACT THAT RITSU IS A MACHINE.
FAKE RITSU IS THE DAUGHTER OF MY IMMEDIATE SUPERIOR.
SHE'S GOOD AT KEEPING SECRETS AND SHE ISN'T NOSY.
PLUS, MY SUPERIOR IS HAPPY BECAUSE HER GRADES HAVE IMPROVED—THANKS TO RITSU'S TUTORING.
SHE WAS SITTING NEXT TO ME DURING THE EXAM TOO.
I GOT THE LOWEST GRADES IN OUR CLASS BECAUSE I COULDN'T CONCENTRATE!
UP
149 ⇒ 95
E Sosuke Sugaya Total Score 338 points 95th out of 186 students
HE MAY HAVE THE LOWEST GRADES IN HIS CLASS... BUT THEY'RE STILL AVERAGE FOR HIS YEAR.
I'M REALLY IMPRESSED BY HOW THESE STUDENTS HAVE RISEN UP FROM THE BOTTOM!

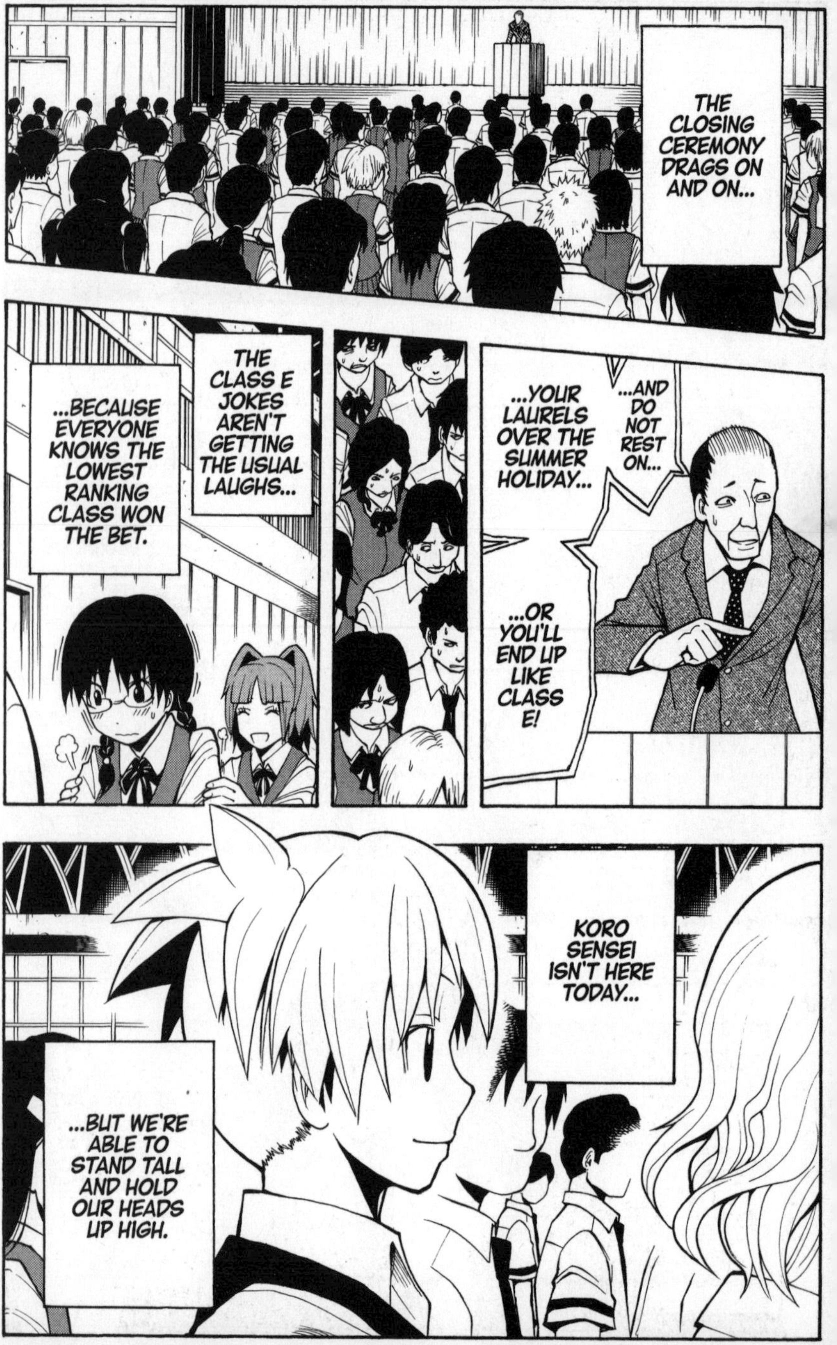
THE CLOSING CEREMONY DRAGS ON AND ON...
...AND DO NOT REST ON...
...YOUR LAURELS OVER THE SUMMER HOLIDAY...
...OR YOU'LL END UP LIKE CLASS E!
THE CLASS E JOKES AREN'T GETTING THE USUAL LAUGHS...
...BECAUSE EVERYONE KNOWS THE LOWEST RANKING CLASS WON THE BET.
KORO SENSEI ISN'T HERE TODAY...
...BUT WE'RE ABLE TO STAND TALL AND HOLD OUR HEADS UP HIGH.

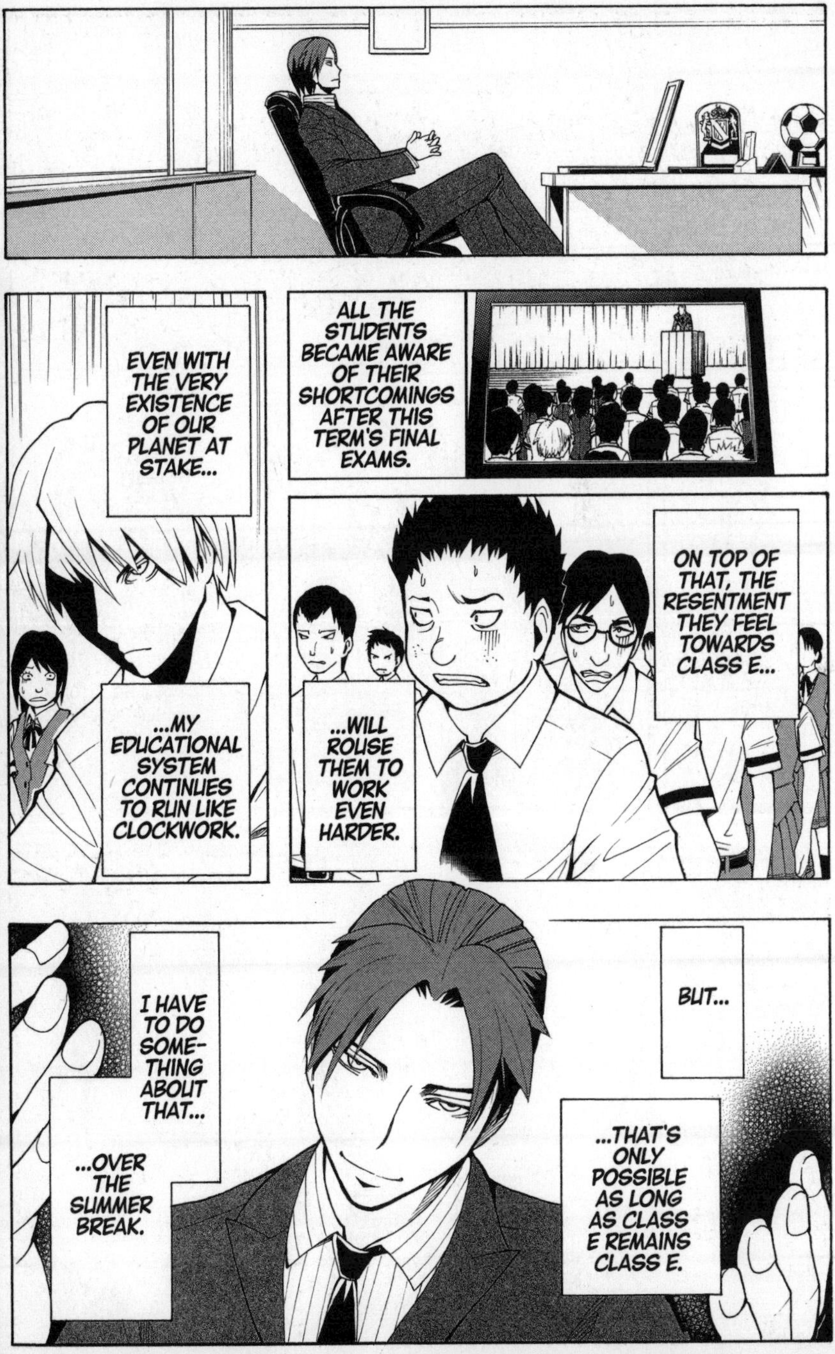
ALL THE STUDENTS BECAME AWARE OF THEIR SHORTCOMINGS AFTER THIS TERM'S FINAL EXAMS.
ON TOP OF THAT, THE RESENTMENT THEY FEEL TOWARDS CLASS E...
...WILL ROUSE THEM TO WORK EVEN HARDER.
EVEN WITH THE VERY EXISTENCE OF OUR PLANET AT STAKE...
...MY EDUCATIONAL SYSTEM CONTINUES TO RUN LIKE CLOCKWORK.
BUT...
...THAT'S ONLY POSSIBLE AS LONG AS CLASS E REMAINS CLASS E.
I HAVE TO DO SOME-THING ABOUT THAT...
...OVER THE SUMMER BREAK.

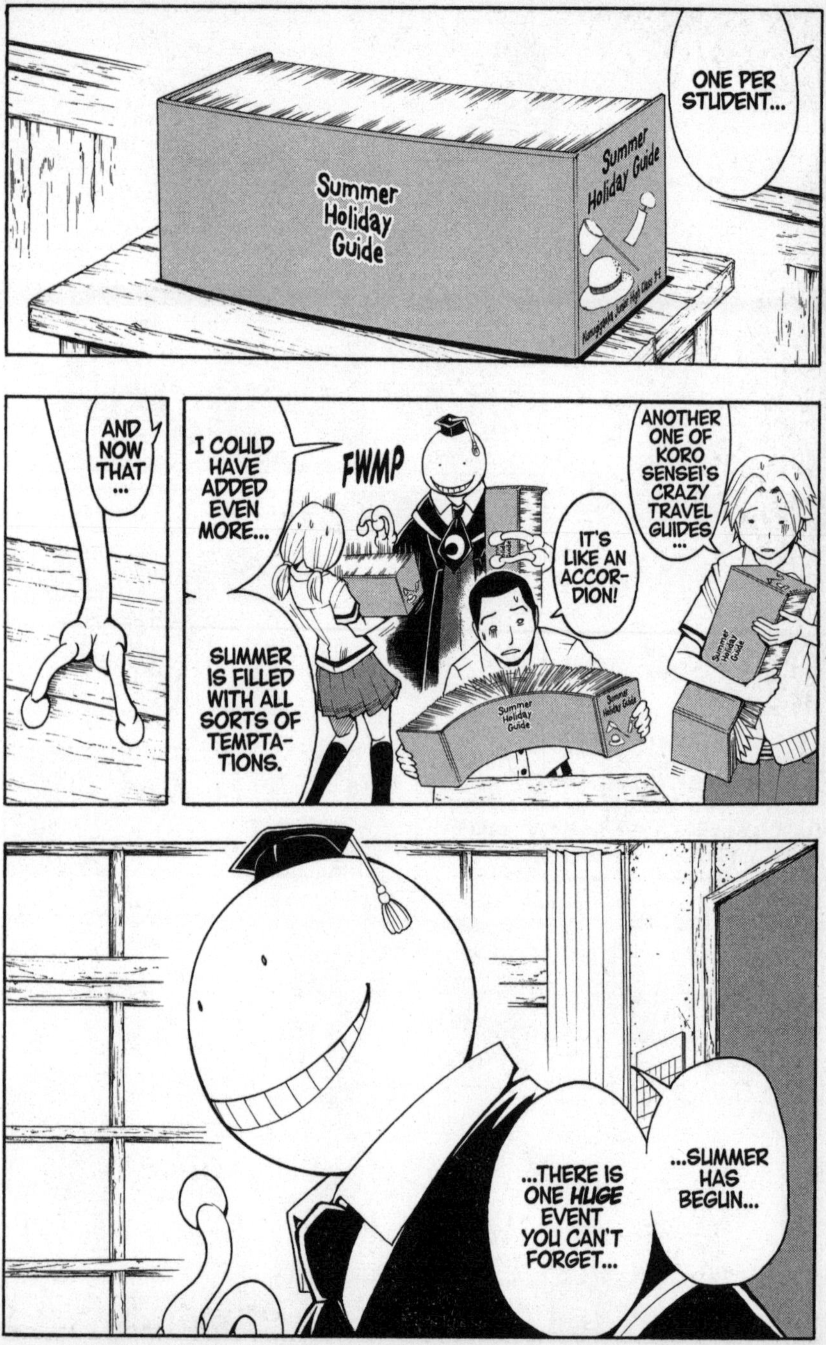

ONE PER STUDENT...
Summer Holiday Guide
Summer Holiday Guide
ANOTHER ONE OF KORO SENSEI'S CRAZY TRAVEL GUIDES...
IT'S LIKE AN ACCORDION!
Summer Holiday Guide
FWMP
I COULD HAVE ADDED EVEN MORE...
SUMMER IS FILLED WITH ALL SORTS OF TEMPTATIONS.
AND NOW THAT...
...SUMMER HAS BEGUN...
...THERE IS ONE HUGE EVENT YOU CAN'T FORGET...

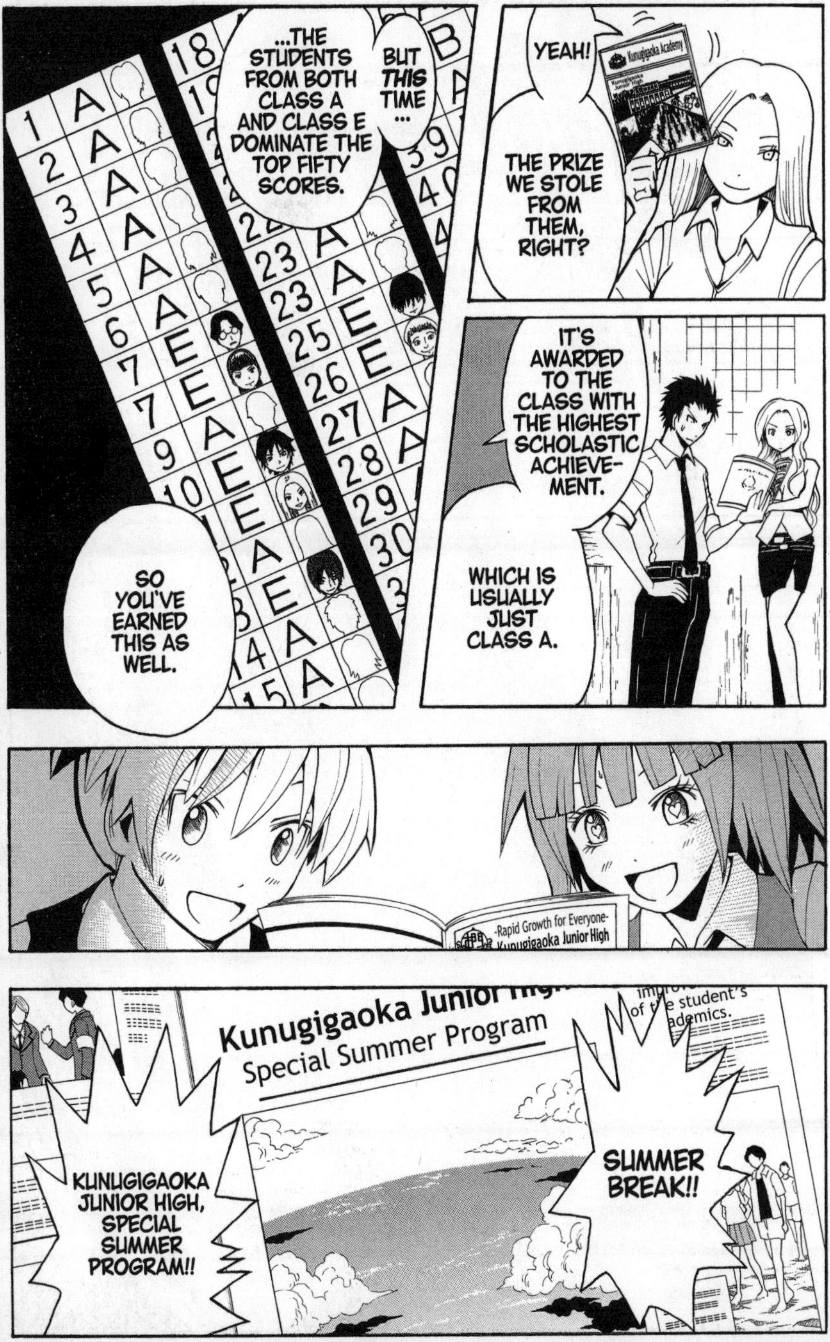
YEAH!
Kunugigaoka Academy
THE PRIZE WE STOLE FROM THEM, RIGHT?
IT'S AWARDED TO THE CLASS WITH THE HIGHEST SCHOLASTIC ACHIEVE-MENT.
WHICH IS USUALLY JUST CLASS A.
BUT *THIS* TIME...
...THE STUDENTS FROM BOTH CLASS A AND CLASS E DOMINATE THE TOP FIFTY SCORES.
SO YOU'VE EARNED THIS AS WELL.
-Rapid Growth for Everyone-
Kunugigaoka Junior High
SUMMER BREAK!!
Kunugigaoka Junior High
Special Summer Program
KUNUGIGAOKA JUNIOR HIGH, SPECIAL SUMMER PROGRAM!!

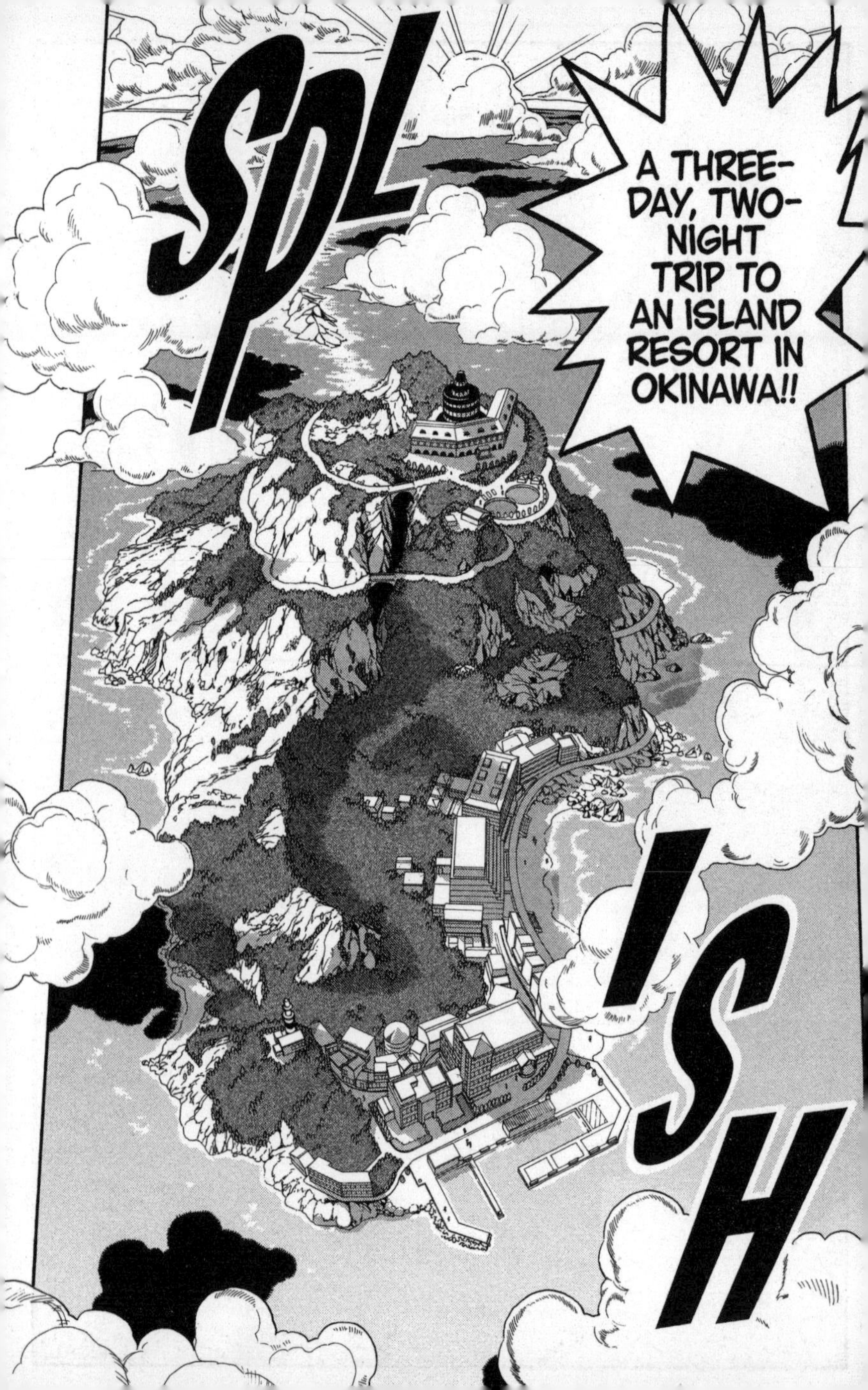
SPL
A THREE-DAY, TWO-NIGHT TRIP TO AN ISLAND RESORT IN OKINAWA!!
ISH

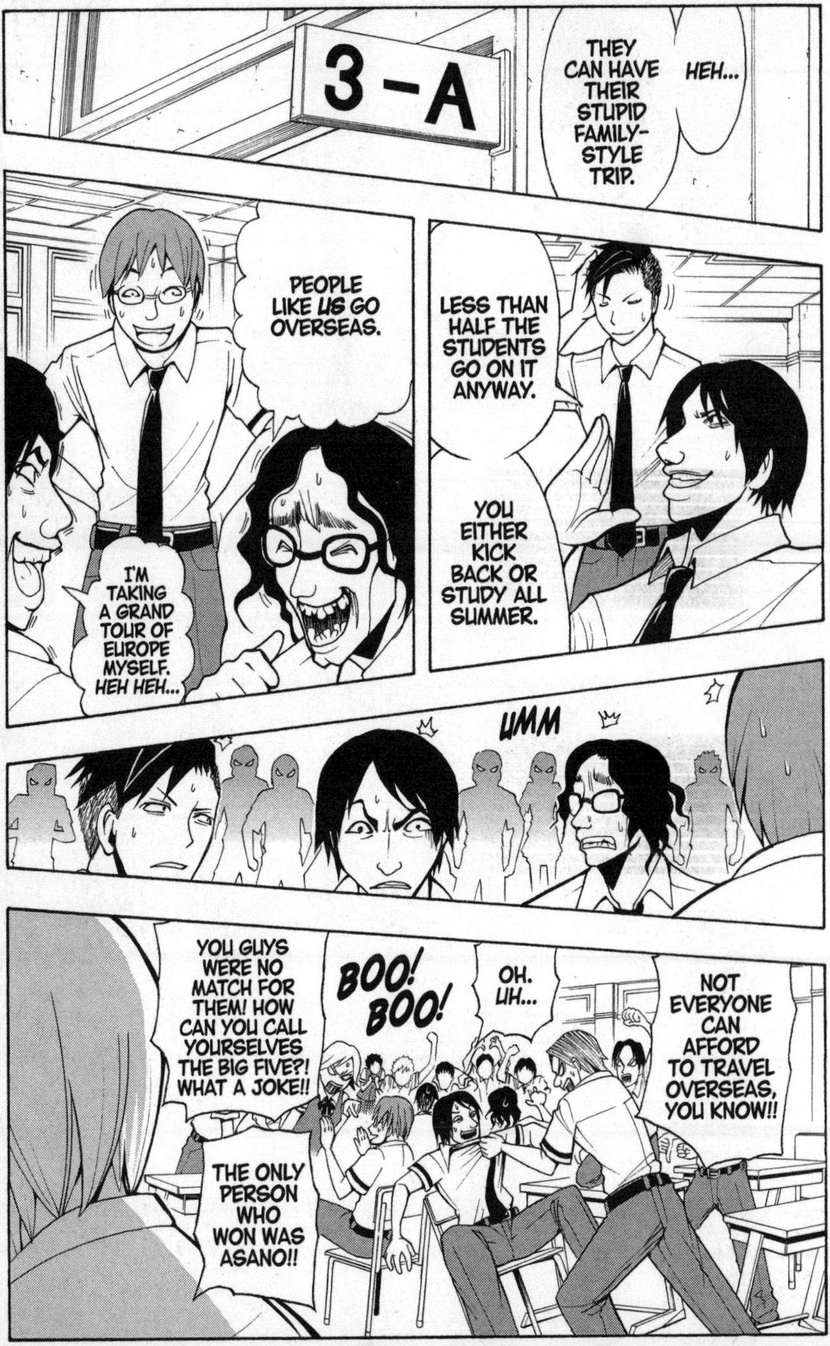
HEH...
THEY CAN HAVE THEIR STUPID FAMILY-STYLE TRIP.
3-A
LESS THAN HALF THE STUDENTS GO ON IT ANYWAY.
YOU EITHER KICK BACK OR STUDY ALL SUMMER.
PEOPLE LIKE US GO OVERSEAS.
I'M TAKING A GRAND TOUR OF EUROPE MYSELF. HEH HEH...
UMM
NOT EVERYONE CAN AFFORD TO TRAVEL OVERSEAS, YOU KNOW!!
OH. UH...
BOO! BOO!
YOU GUYS WERE NO MATCH FOR THEM! HOW CAN YOU CALL YOURSELVES THE BIG FIVE?! WHAT A JOKE!!
THE ONLY PERSON WHO WON WAS ASANO!!

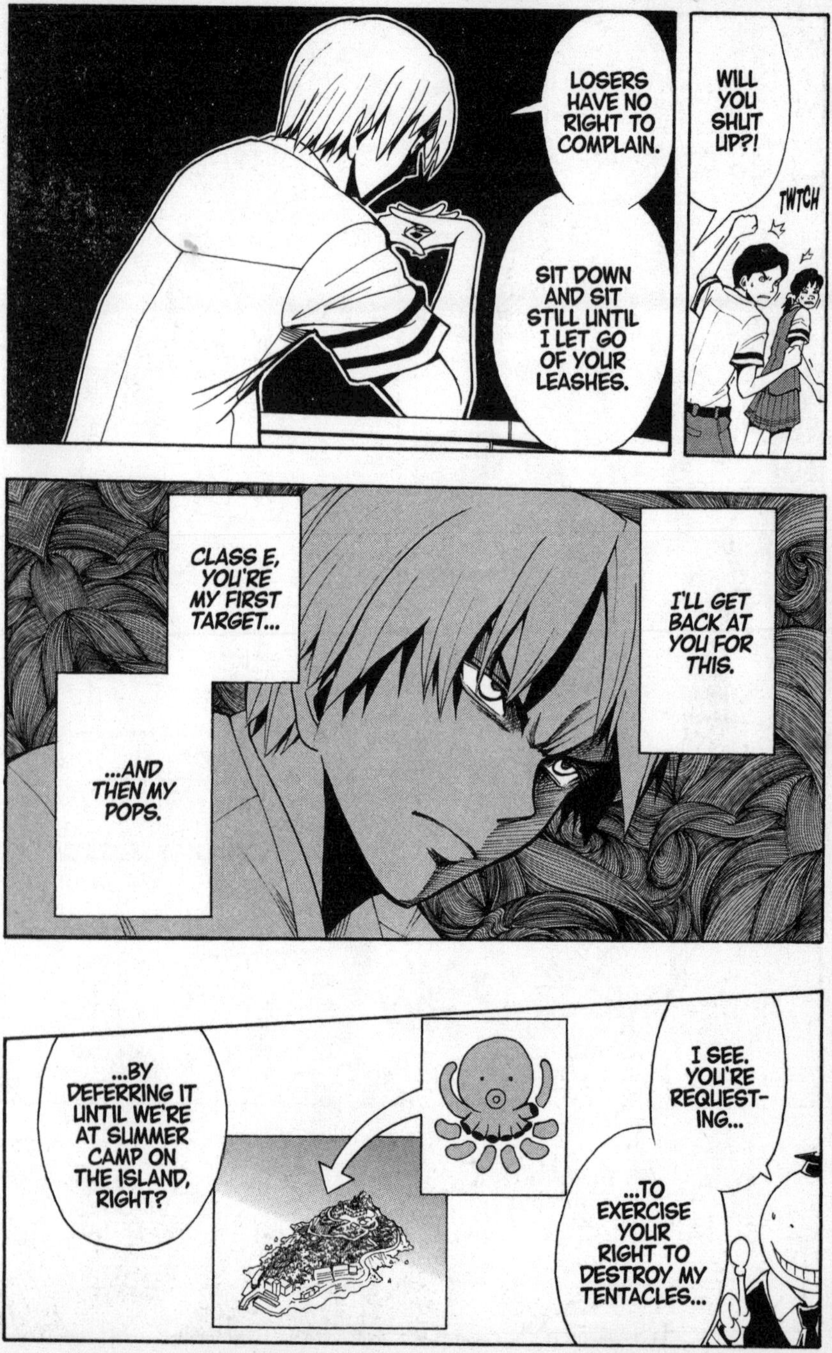
WILL YOU SHUT UP?!
TWTCH
LOSERS HAVE NO RIGHT TO COMPLAIN.
SIT DOWN AND SIT STILL UNTIL I LET GO OF YOUR LEASHES.
I'LL GET BACK AT YOU FOR THIS.
CLASS E, YOU'RE MY FIRST TARGET...
...AND THEN MY POPS.
I SEE. YOU'RE REQUEST-ING...
...TO EXERCISE YOUR RIGHT TO DESTROY MY TENTACLES...
...BY DEFERRING IT UNTIL WE'RE AT SUMMER CAMP ON THE ISLAND, RIGHT?

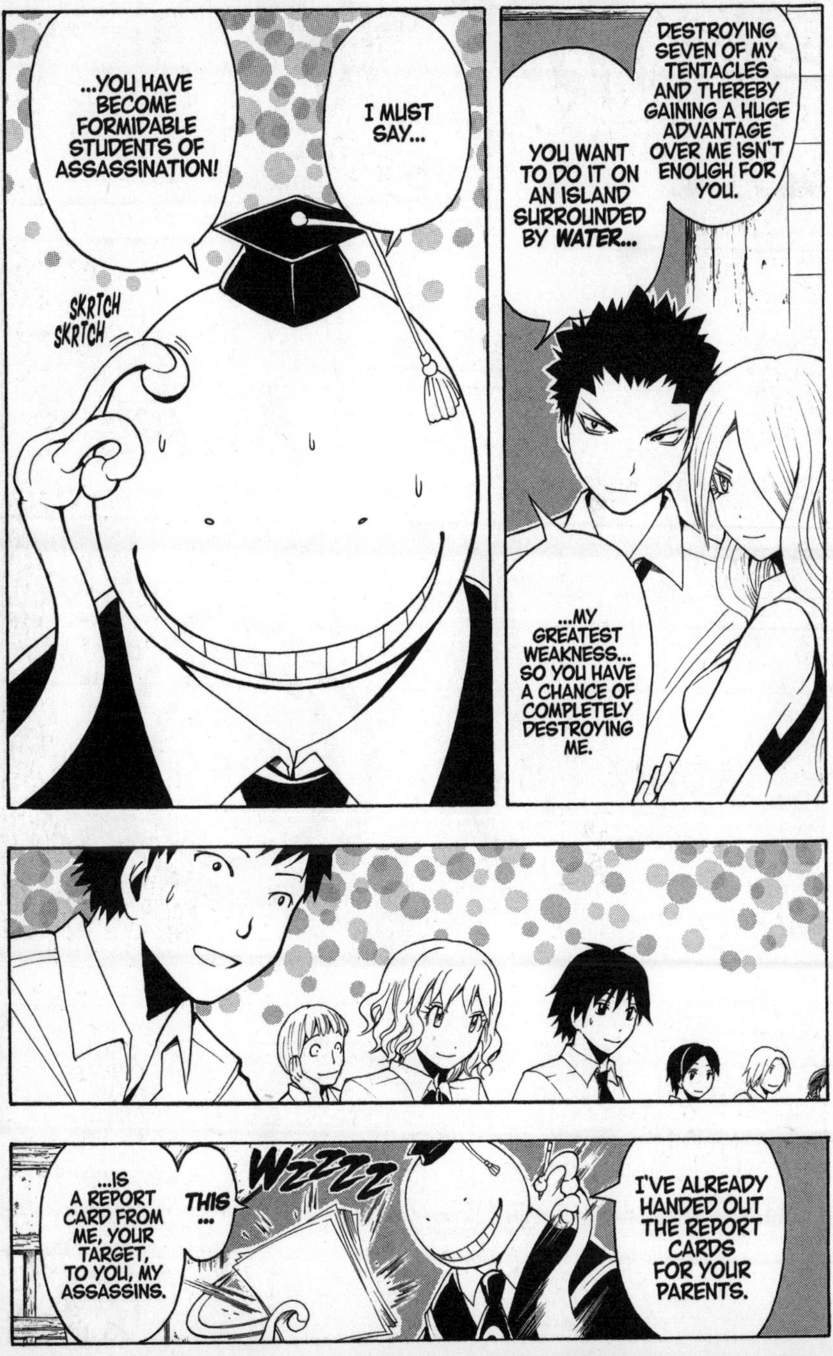
DESTROYING SEVEN OF MY TENTACLES AND THEREBY GAINING A HUGE ADVANTAGE OVER ME ISN'T ENOUGH FOR YOU.
YOU WANT TO DO IT ON AN ISLAND SURROUNDED BY WATER...
...MY GREATEST WEAKNESS... SO YOU HAVE A CHANCE OF COMPLETELY DESTROYING ME.
I MUST SAY...
...YOU HAVE BECOME FORMIDABLE STUDENTS OF ASSASSINATION!
SKRTCH SKRTCH
I'VE ALREADY HANDED OUT THE REPORT CARDS FOR YOUR PARENTS.
WZZZZ
THIS...
...IS A REPORT CARD FROM ME, YOUR TARGET, TO YOU, MY ASSASSINS.

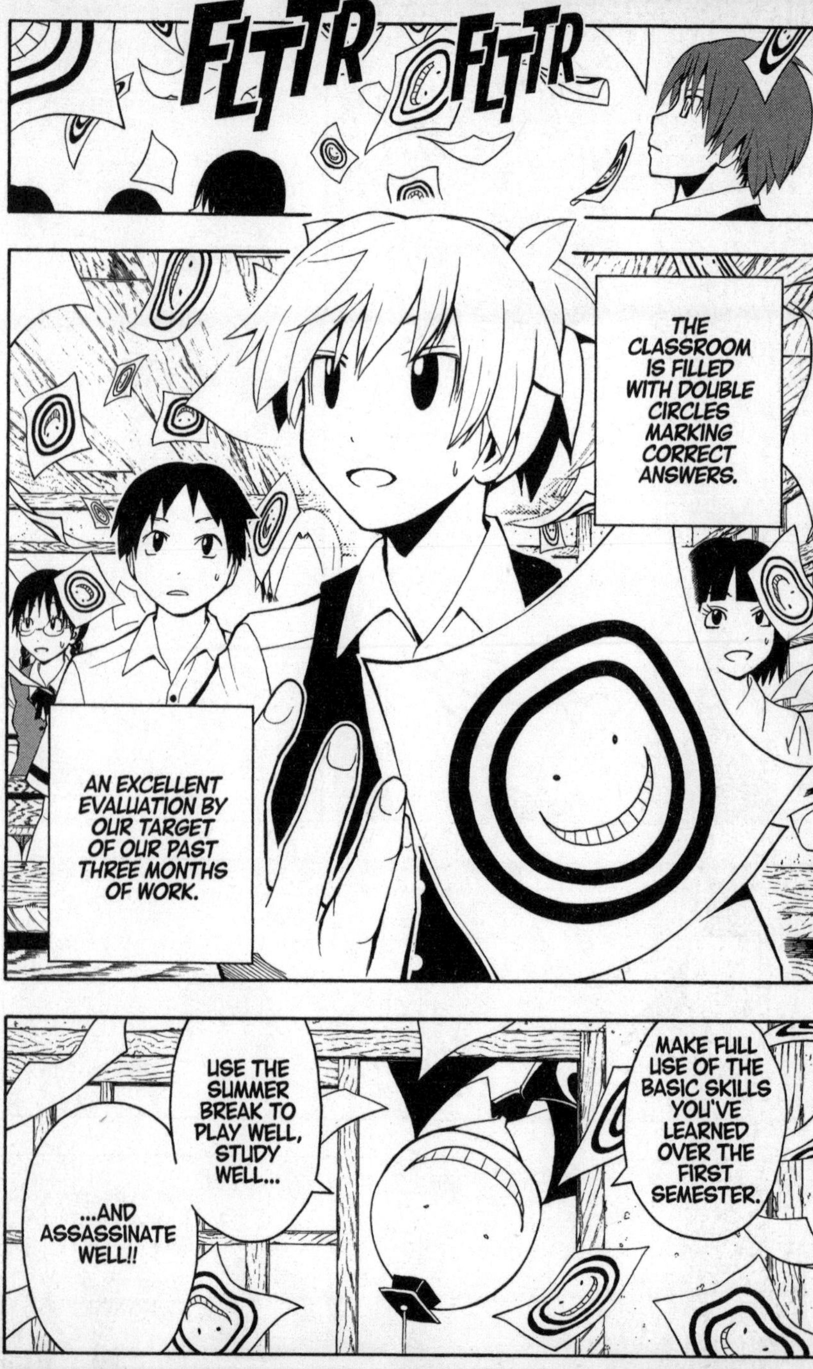
FLTTR FLTTR
THE CLASSROOM IS FILLED WITH DOUBLE CIRCLES MARKING CORRECT ANSWERS.
AN EXCELLENT EVALUATION BY OUR TARGET OF OUR PAST THREE MONTHS OF WORK.
MAKE FULL USE OF THE BASIC SKILLS YOU'VE LEARNED OVER THE FIRST SEMESTER.
USE THE SUMMER BREAK TO PLAY WELL, STUDY WELL...
...AND ASSASSINATE WELL!!

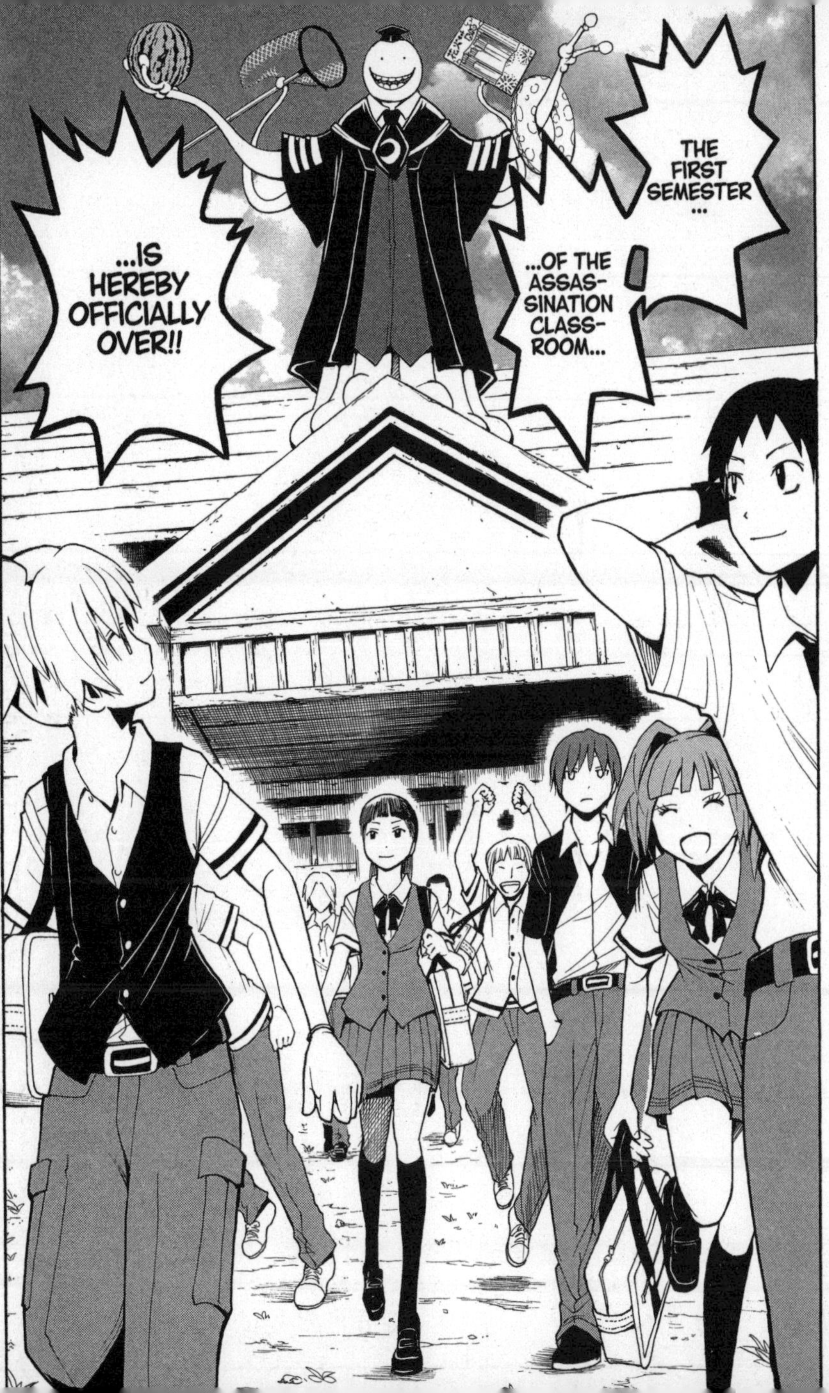
THE FIRST SEMESTER ...
...OF THE ASSAS-SINATION CLASS-ROOM...
...IS HEREBY OFFICIALLY OVER!!

They left the guide books behind.
(He personally delivered them later.)

Class 56 Spending Time in Nature

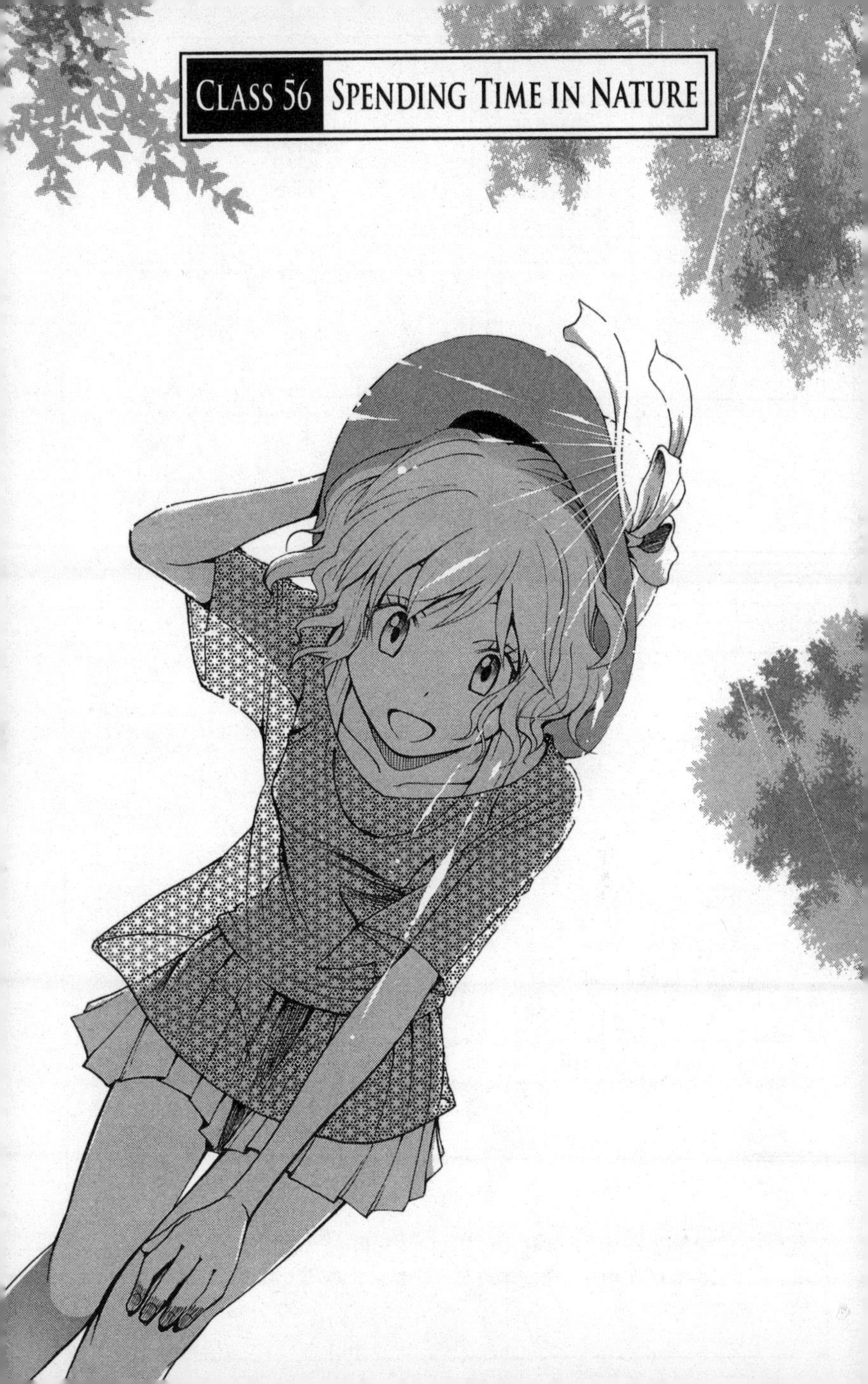

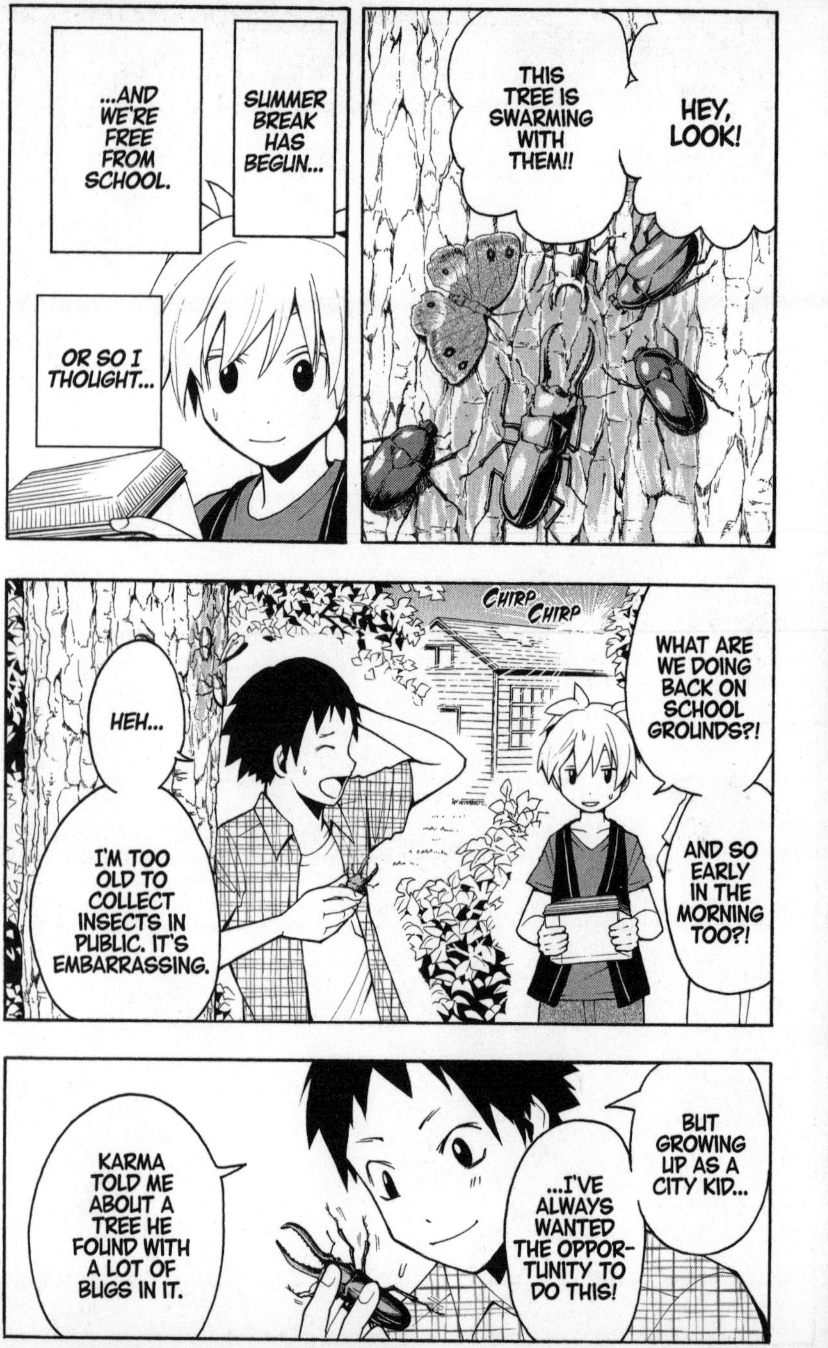
HEY, LOOK!
THIS TREE IS SWARMING WITH THEM!!
SUMMER BREAK HAS BEGUN...
...AND WE'RE FREE FROM SCHOOL.
OR SO I THOUGHT...
CHIRP CHIRP
WHAT ARE WE DOING BACK ON SCHOOL GROUNDS?!
AND SO EARLY IN THE MORNING TOO?!
HEH...
I'M TOO OLD TO COLLECT INSECTS IN PUBLIC. IT'S EMBARRASSING.
BUT GROWING UP AS A CITY KID...
...I'VE ALWAYS WANTED THE OPPOR-TUNITY TO DO THIS!
KARMA TOLD ME ABOUT A TREE HE FOUND WITH A LOT OF BUGS IN IT.

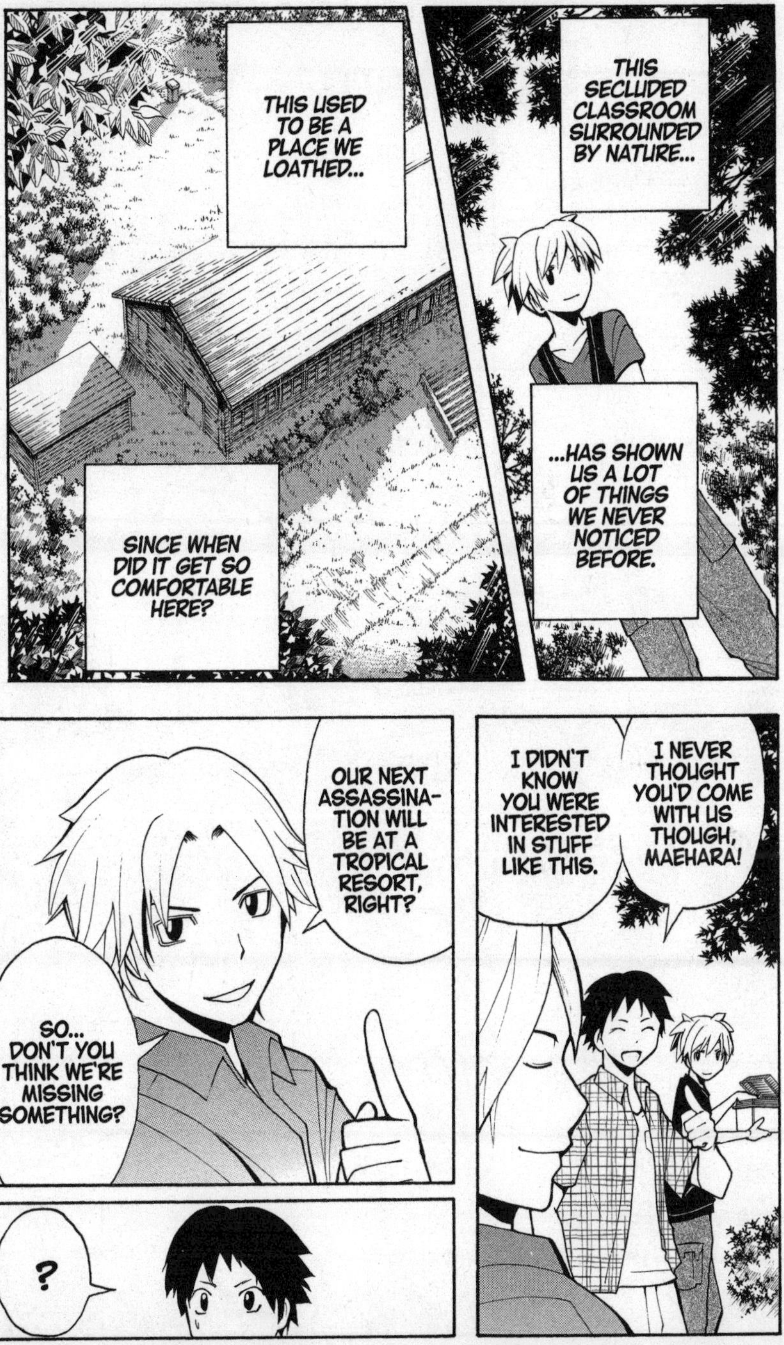
THIS SECLUDED CLASSROOM SURROUNDED BY NATURE...
...HAS SHOWN US A LOT OF THINGS WE NEVER NOTICED BEFORE.
THIS USED TO BE A PLACE WE LOATHED...
SINCE WHEN DID IT GET SO COMFORTABLE HERE?
I NEVER THOUGHT YOU'D COME WITH US THOUGH, MAEHARA!
I DIDN'T KNOW YOU WERE INTERESTED IN STUFF LIKE THIS.
OUR NEXT ASSASSINA-TION WILL BE AT A TROPICAL RESORT, RIGHT?
SO... DON'T YOU THINK WE'RE MISSING SOMETHING?
?

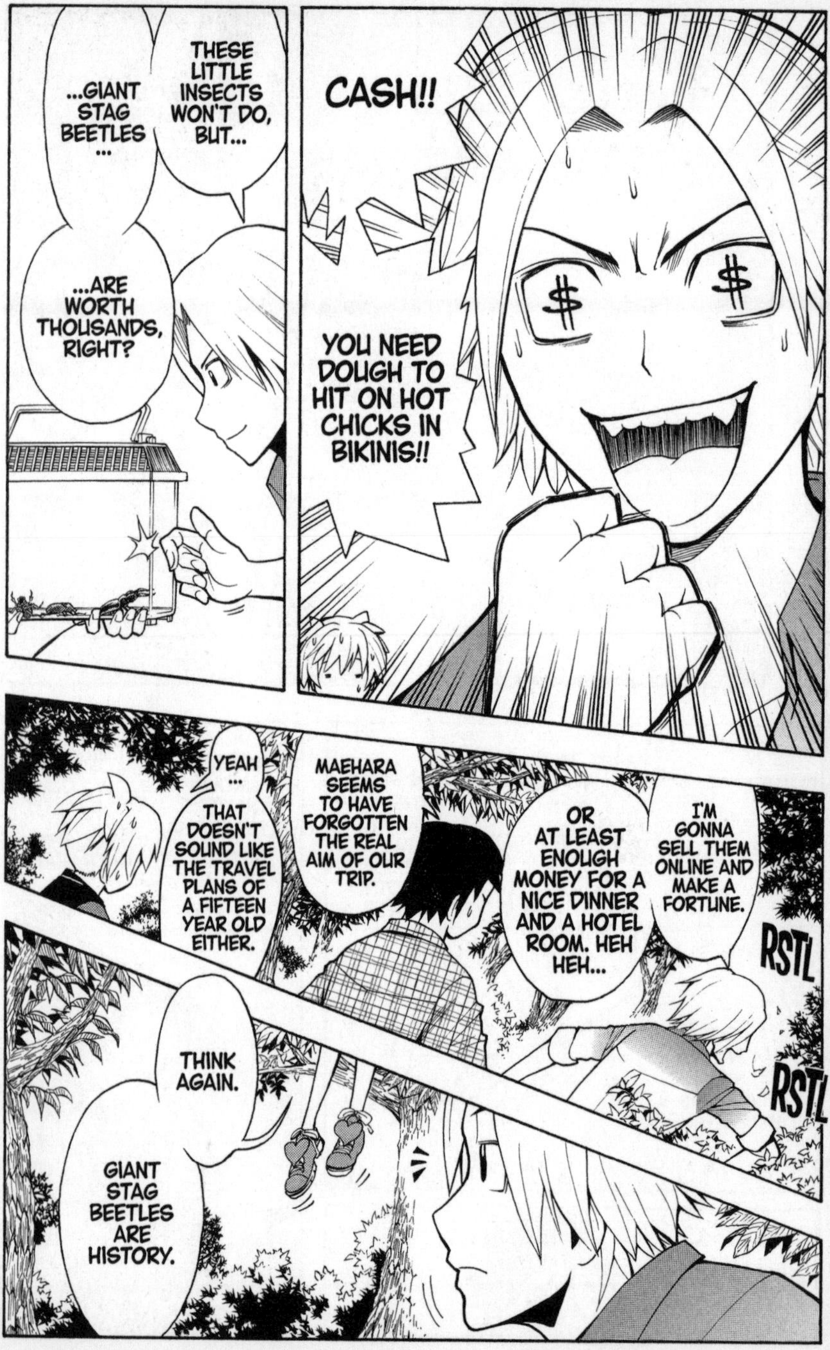
CASH!!
YOU NEED DOUGH TO HIT ON HOT CHICKS IN BIKINIS!!
THESE LITTLE INSECTS WON'T DO, BUT...
...GIANT STAG BEETLES ...
...ARE WORTH THOUSANDS, RIGHT?
I'M GONNA SELL THEM ONLINE AND MAKE A FORTUNE.
OR AT LEAST ENOUGH MONEY FOR A NICE DINNER AND A HOTEL ROOM. HEH HEH...
MAEHARA SEEMS TO HAVE FORGOTTEN THE REAL AIM OF OUR TRIP.
YEAH ...
THAT DOESN'T SOUND LIKE THE TRAVEL PLANS OF A FIFTEEN YEAR OLD EITHER.
RSTL
RSTL
THINK AGAIN.
GIANT STAG BEETLES ARE HISTORY.

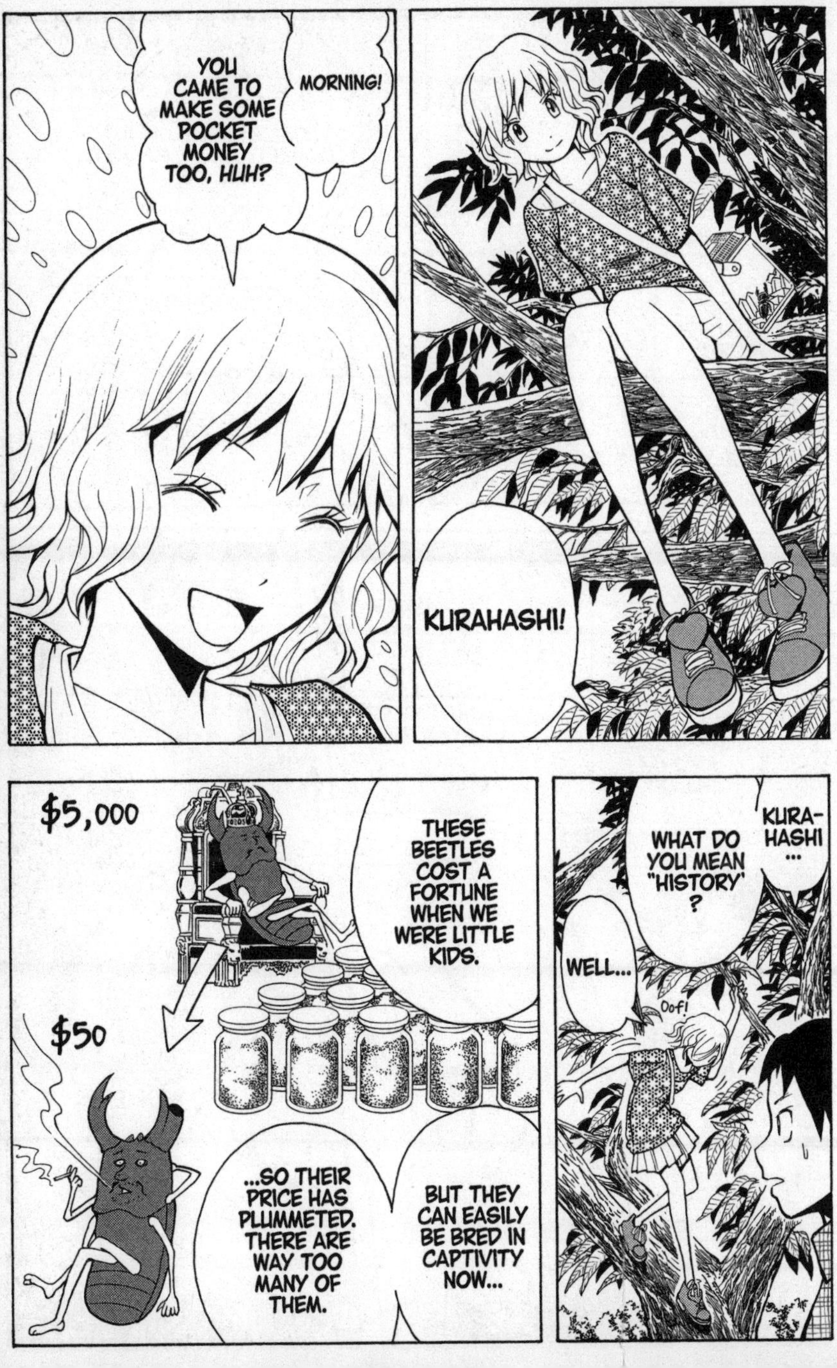
KURAHASHI!
MORNING!
YOU CAME TO MAKE SOME POCKET MONEY TOO, HUH?
KURA-HASHI ...
WHAT DO YOU MEAN "HISTORY" ?
WELL...
Oof!
THESE BEETLES COST A FORTUNE WHEN WE WERE LITTLE KIDS.
$5,000
BUT THEY CAN EASILY BE BRED IN CAPTIVITY NOW...
...SO THEIR PRICE HAS PLUMMETED. THERE ARE WAY TOO MANY OF THEM.
$50

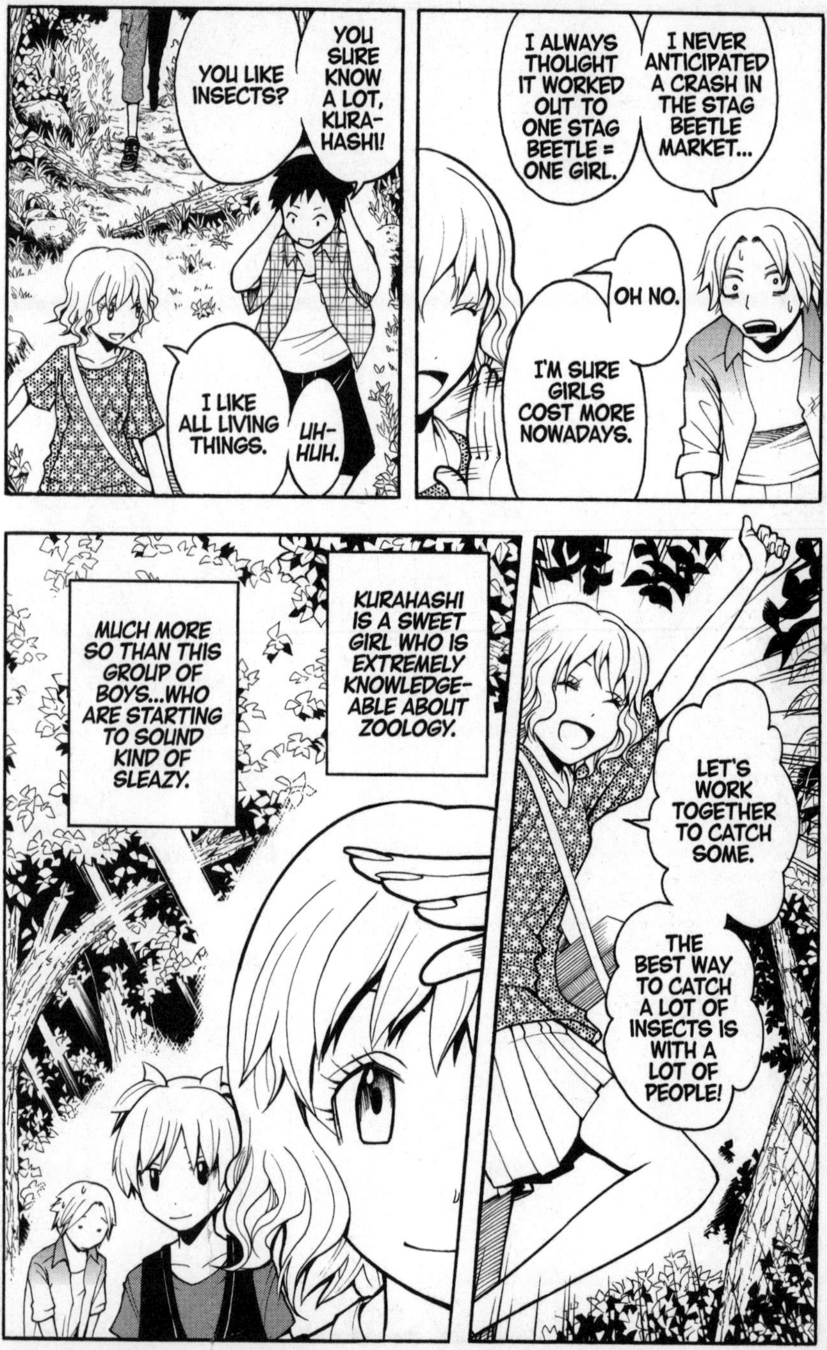
I NEVER ANTICIPATED A CRASH IN THE STAG BEETLE MARKET...
I ALWAYS THOUGHT IT WORKED OUT TO ONE STAG BEETLE = ONE GIRL.
OH NO.
I'M SURE GIRLS COST MORE NOWADAYS.
YOU SURE KNOW A LOT, KURAHASHI!
YOU LIKE INSECTS?
UH-HUH.
I LIKE ALL LIVING THINGS.
LET'S WORK TOGETHER TO CATCH SOME.
THE BEST WAY TO CATCH A LOT OF INSECTS IS WITH A LOT OF PEOPLE!
KURAHASHI IS A SWEET GIRL WHO IS EXTREMELY KNOWLEDGE-ABLE ABOUT ZOOLOGY.
MUCH MORE SO THAN THIS GROUP OF BOYS...WHO ARE STARTING TO SOUND KIND OF SLEAZY.

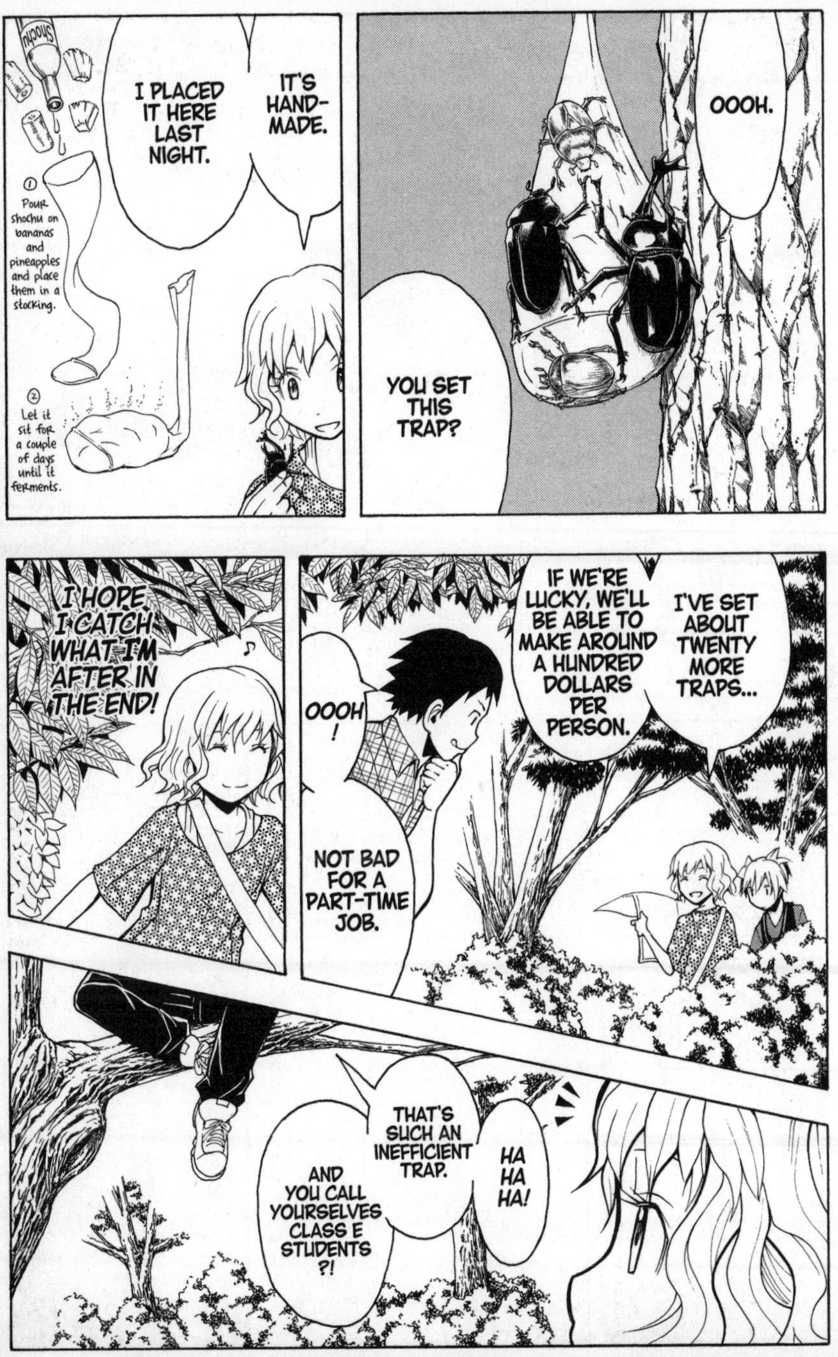
OOOH.
YOU SET THIS TRAP?
IT'S HAND-MADE.
I PLACED IT HERE LAST NIGHT.
Shochu
① Pour shochu on bananas and pineapples and place them in a stocking.
② Let it sit for a couple of days until it ferments.
I'VE SET ABOUT TWENTY MORE TRAPS...
IF WE'RE LUCKY, WE'LL BE ABLE TO MAKE AROUND A HUNDRED DOLLARS PER PERSON.
OOOH!
NOT BAD FOR A PART-TIME JOB.
I HOPE I CATCH WHAT I'M AFTER IN THE END!
HA HA HA!
THAT'S SUCH AN INEFFICIENT TRAP.
AND YOU CALL YOURSELVES CLASS E STUDENTS?!

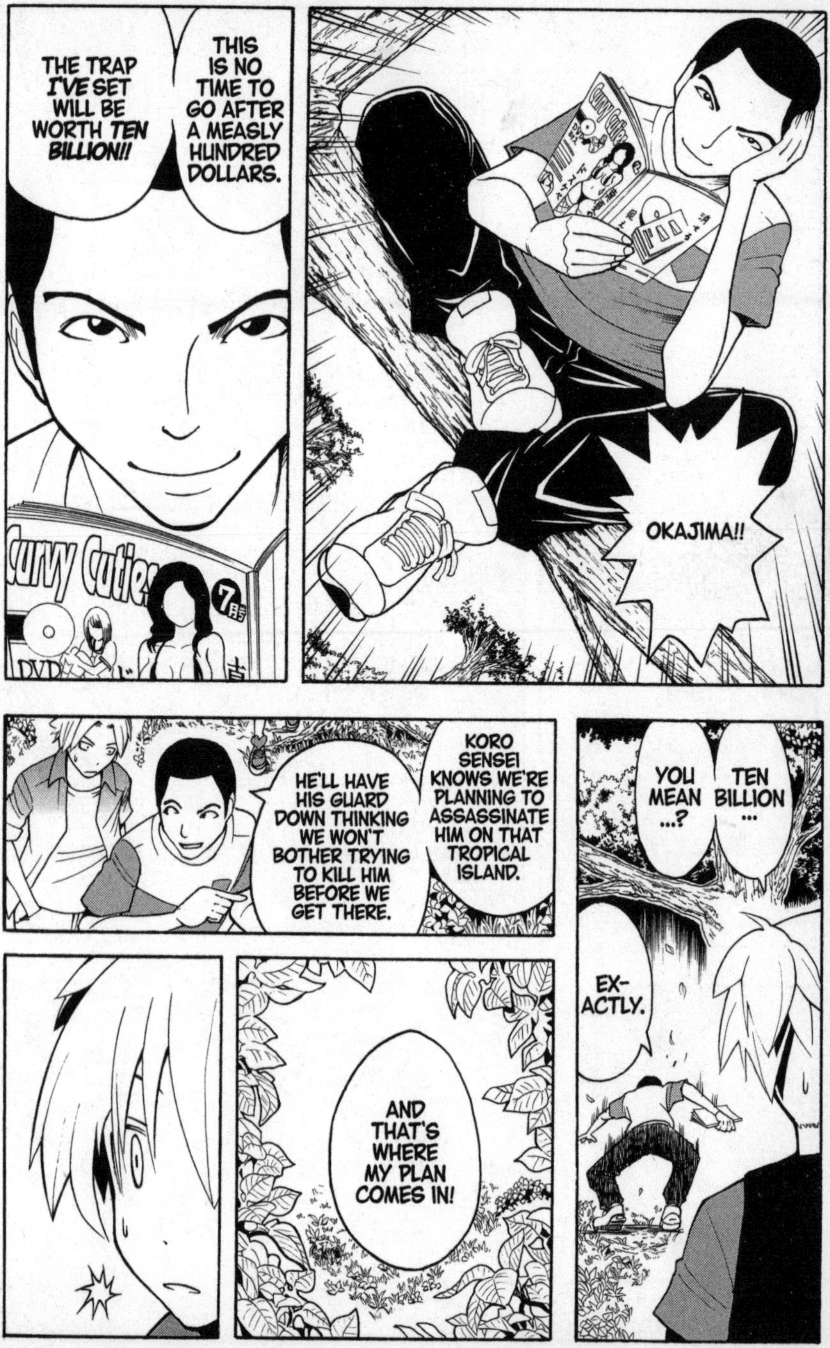
OKAJIMA!!
THIS IS NO TIME TO GO AFTER A MEASLY HUNDRED DOLLARS.
THE TRAP I'VE SET WILL BE WORTH TEN BILLION!!
Curvy Cuties
TEN BILLION ...
YOU MEAN ...?
EX-ACTLY.
KORO SENSEI KNOWS WE'RE PLANNING TO ASSASSINATE HIM ON THAT TROPICAL ISLAND.
HE'LL HAVE HIS GUARD DOWN THINKING WE WON'T BOTHER TRYING TO KILL HIM BEFORE WE GET THERE.
AND THAT'S WHERE MY PLAN COMES IN!

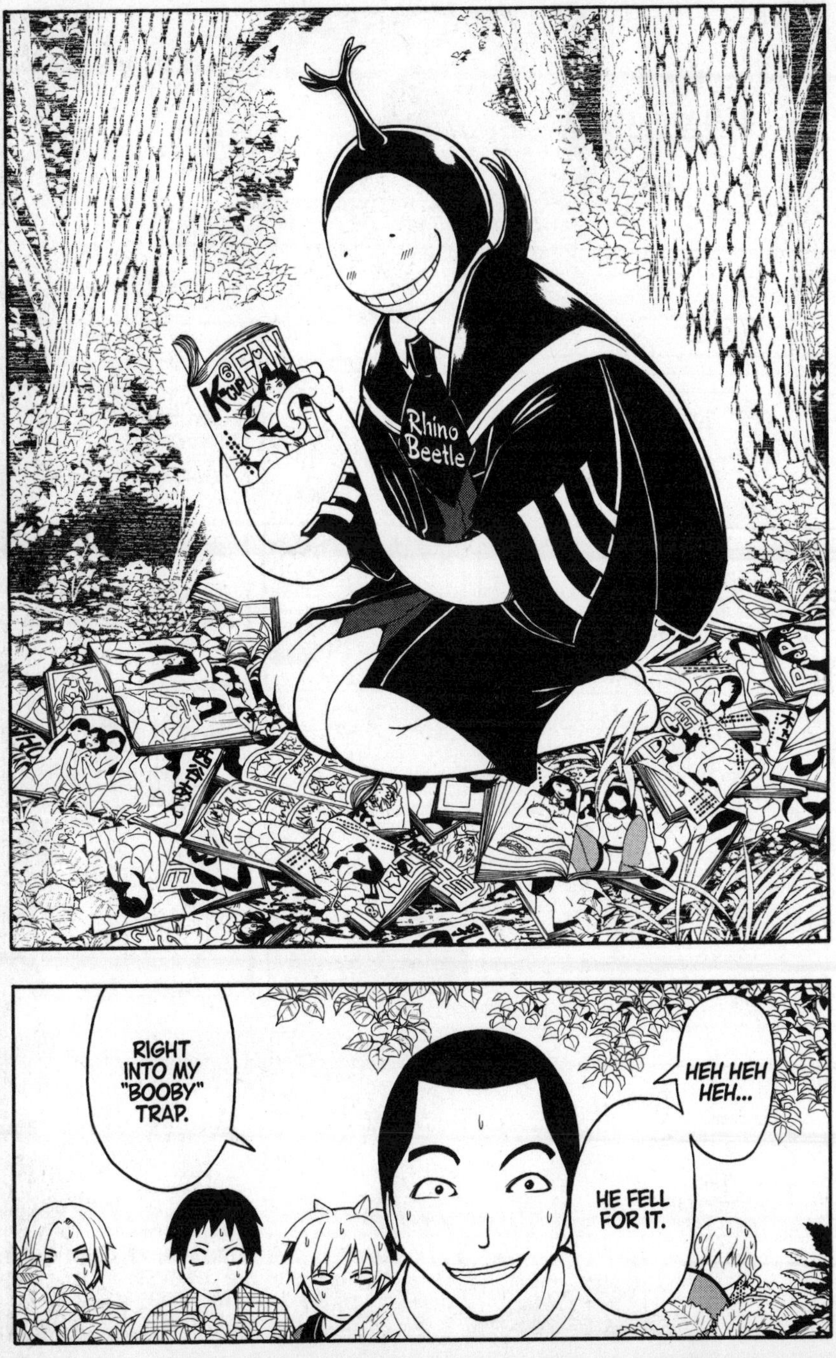
Rhino Beetle
HEH HEH HEH...
HE FELL FOR IT.
RIGHT INTO MY "BOOBY" TRAP.

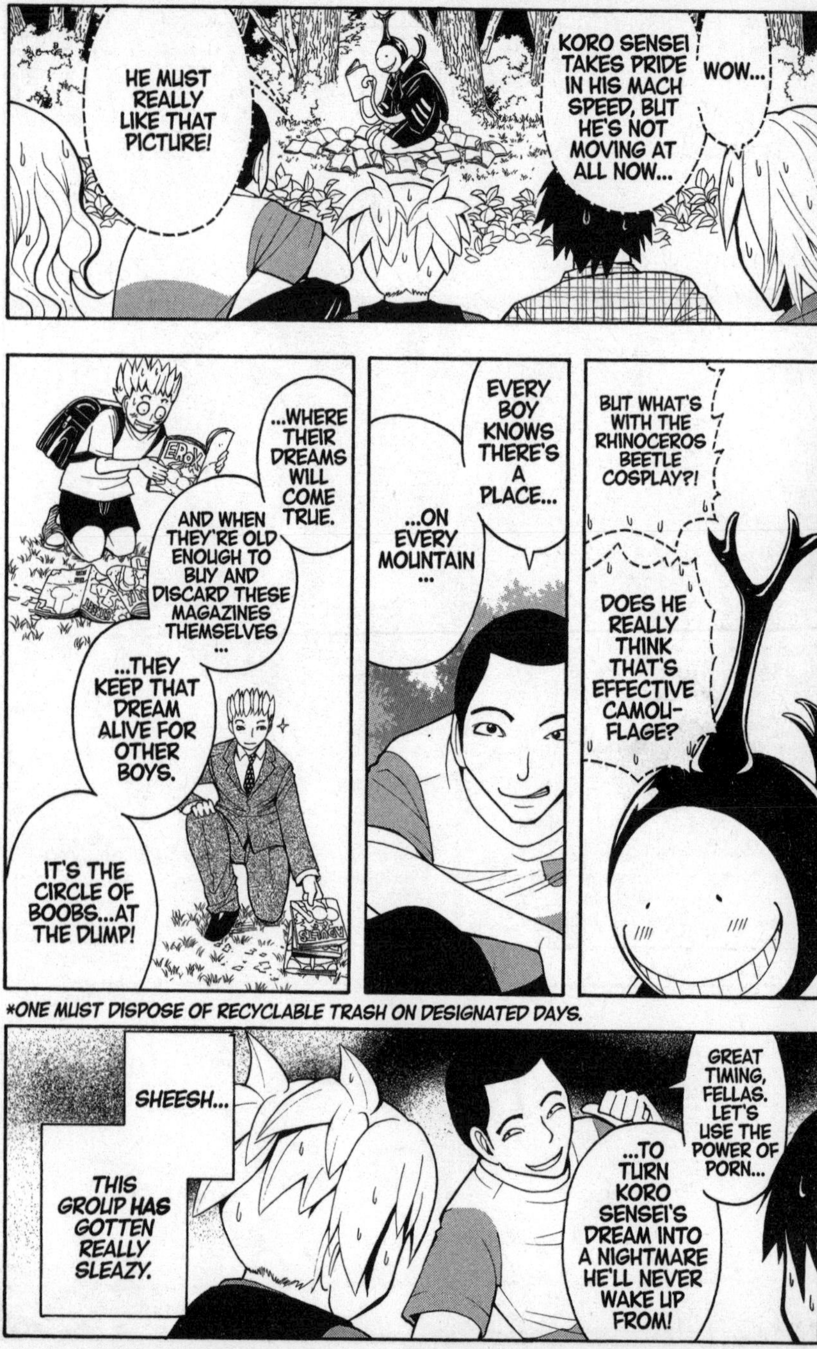
WOW...
KORO SENSEI TAKES PRIDE IN HIS MACH SPEED, BUT HE'S NOT MOVING AT ALL NOW...
HE MUST REALLY LIKE THAT PICTURE!
BUT WHAT'S WITH THE RHINOCEROS BEETLE COSPLAY?!
DOES HE REALLY THINK THAT'S EFFECTIVE CAMOU-FLAGE?
EVERY BOY KNOWS THERE'S A PLACE...
...ON EVERY MOUNTAIN...
...WHERE THEIR DREAMS WILL COME TRUE.
AND WHEN THEY'RE OLD ENOUGH TO BUY AND DISCARD THESE MAGAZINES THEMSELVES...
...THEY KEEP THAT DREAM ALIVE FOR OTHER BOYS.
IT'S THE CIRCLE OF BOOBS...AT THE DUMP!
*ONE MUST DISPOSE OF RECYCLABLE TRASH ON DESIGNATED DAYS.
GREAT TIMING, FELLAS. LET'S USE THE POWER OF PORN...
...TO TURN KORO SENSEI'S DREAM INTO A NIGHTMARE HE'LL NEVER WAKE UP FROM!
SHEESH...
THIS GROUP HAS GOTTEN REALLY SLEAZY.

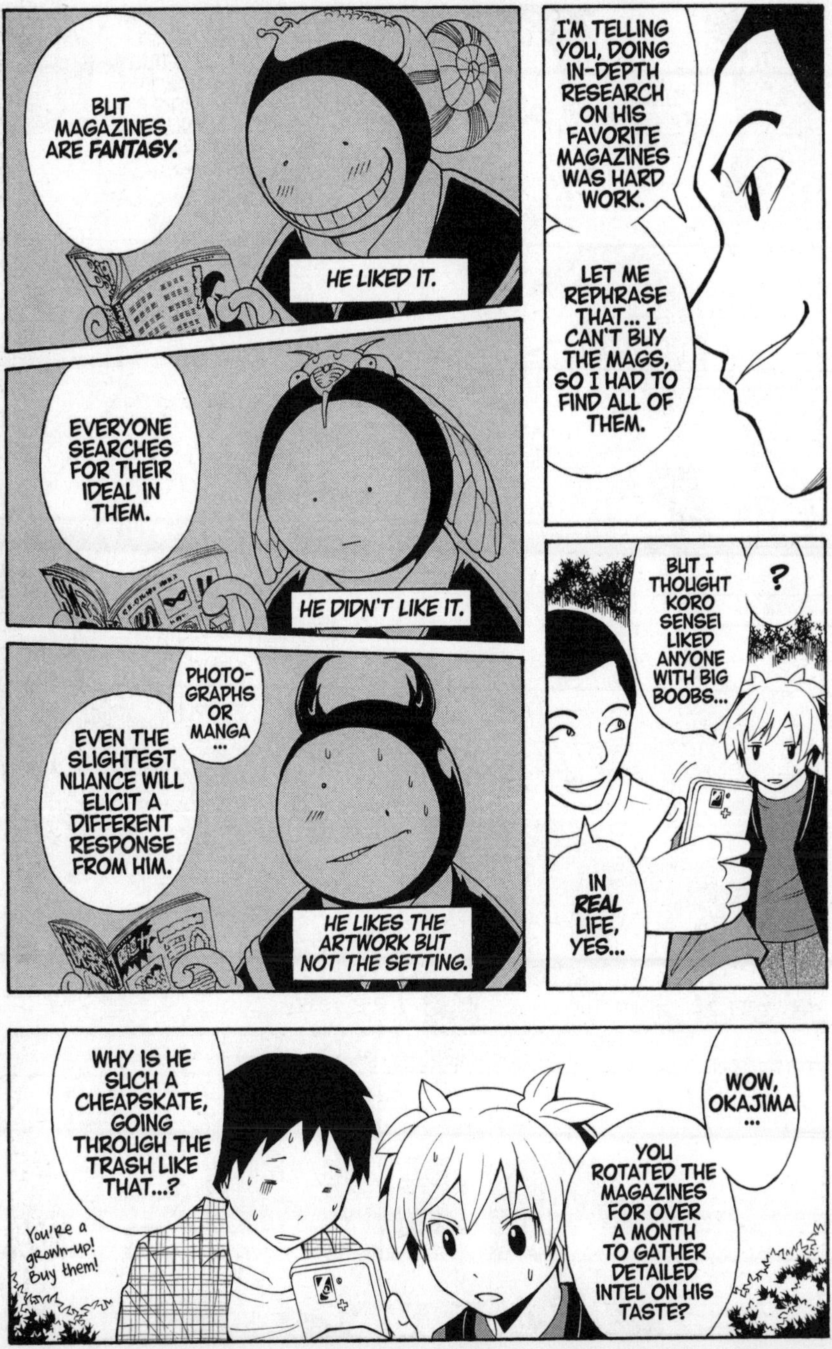
I'M TELLING YOU, DOING IN-DEPTH RESEARCH ON HIS FAVORITE MAGAZINES WAS HARD WORK.
LET ME REPHRASE THAT... I CAN'T BUY THE MAGS, SO I HAD TO FIND ALL OF THEM.
?
BUT I THOUGHT KORO SENSEI LIKED ANYONE WITH BIG BOOBS...
IN REAL LIFE, YES...
BUT MAGAZINES ARE FANTASY.
HE LIKED IT.
EVERYONE SEARCHES FOR THEIR IDEAL IN THEM.
HE DIDN'T LIKE IT.
PHOTOGRAPHS OR MANGA...
EVEN THE SLIGHTEST NUANCE WILL ELICIT A DIFFERENT RESPONSE FROM HIM.
HE LIKES THE ARTWORK BUT NOT THE SETTING.
WOW, OKAJIMA...
YOU ROTATED THE MAGAZINES FOR OVER A MONTH TO GATHER DETAILED INTEL ON HIS TASTE?
WHY IS HE SUCH A CHEAPSKATE, GOING THROUGH THE TRASH LIKE THAT...?
You're a grown-up! Buy them!

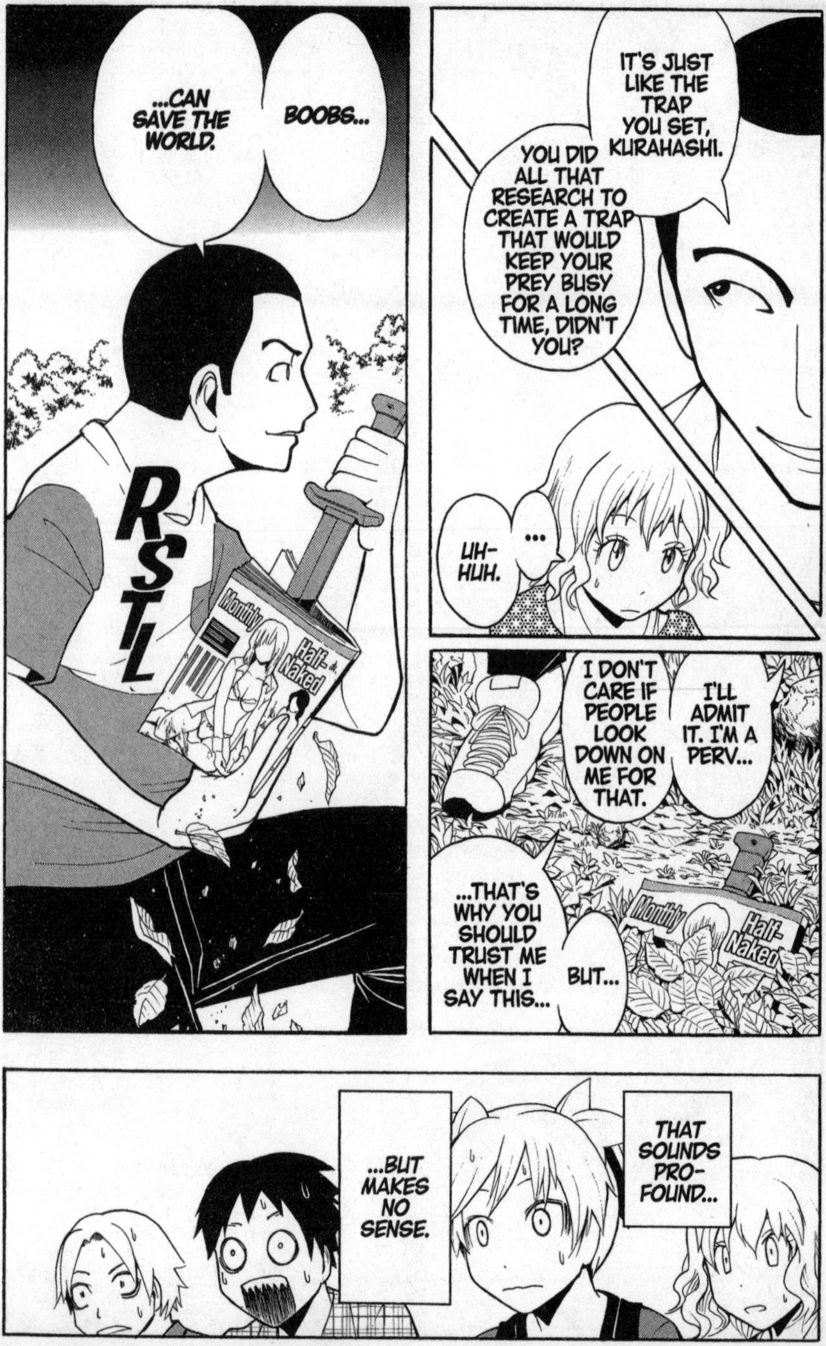
IT'S JUST LIKE THE TRAP YOU SET, KURAHASHI.
YOU DID ALL THAT RESEARCH TO CREATE A TRAP THAT WOULD KEEP YOUR PREY BUSY FOR A LONG TIME, DIDN'T YOU?
...
UH-HUH.
I'LL ADMIT IT. I'M A PERV...
I DON'T CARE IF PEOPLE LOOK DOWN ON ME FOR THAT.
Monthly Half-Naked
BUT...
...THAT'S WHY YOU SHOULD TRUST ME WHEN I SAY THIS...
BOOBS...
...CAN SAVE THE WORLD.
RSTL
Monthly Half-Naked
THAT SOUNDS PRO-FOUND...
...BUT MAKES NO SENSE.

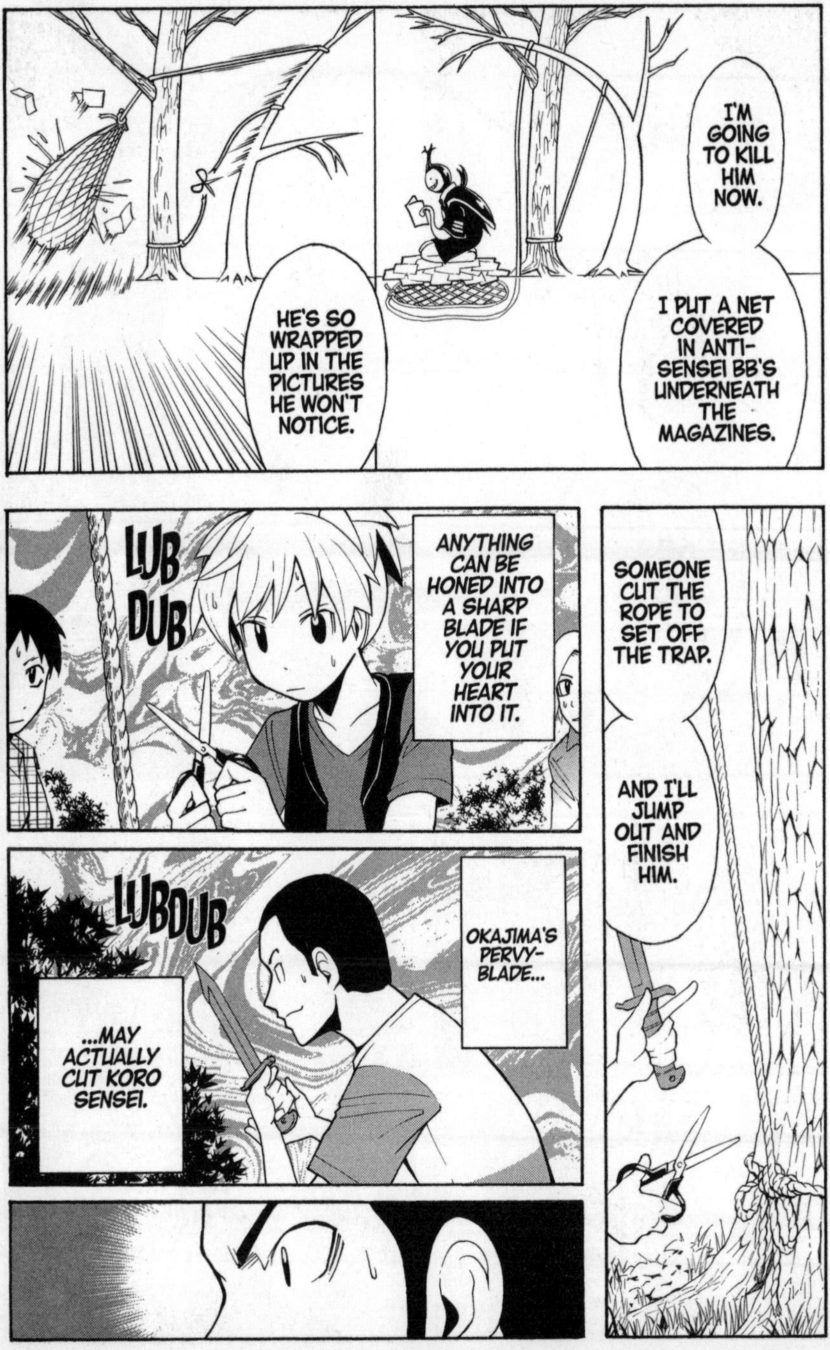
I'M GOING TO KILL HIM NOW.
I PUT A NET COVERED IN ANTI-SENSEI BB'S UNDERNEATH THE MAGAZINES.
HE'S SO WRAPPED UP IN THE PICTURES HE WON'T NOTICE.
SOMEONE CUT THE ROPE TO SET OFF THE TRAP.
AND I'LL JUMP OUT AND FINISH HIM.
ANYTHING CAN BE HONED INTO A SHARP BLADE IF YOU PUT YOUR HEART INTO IT.
LUB DUB
OKAJIMA'S PERVY-BLADE...
LUBDUB
...MAY ACTUALLY CUT KORO SENSEI.

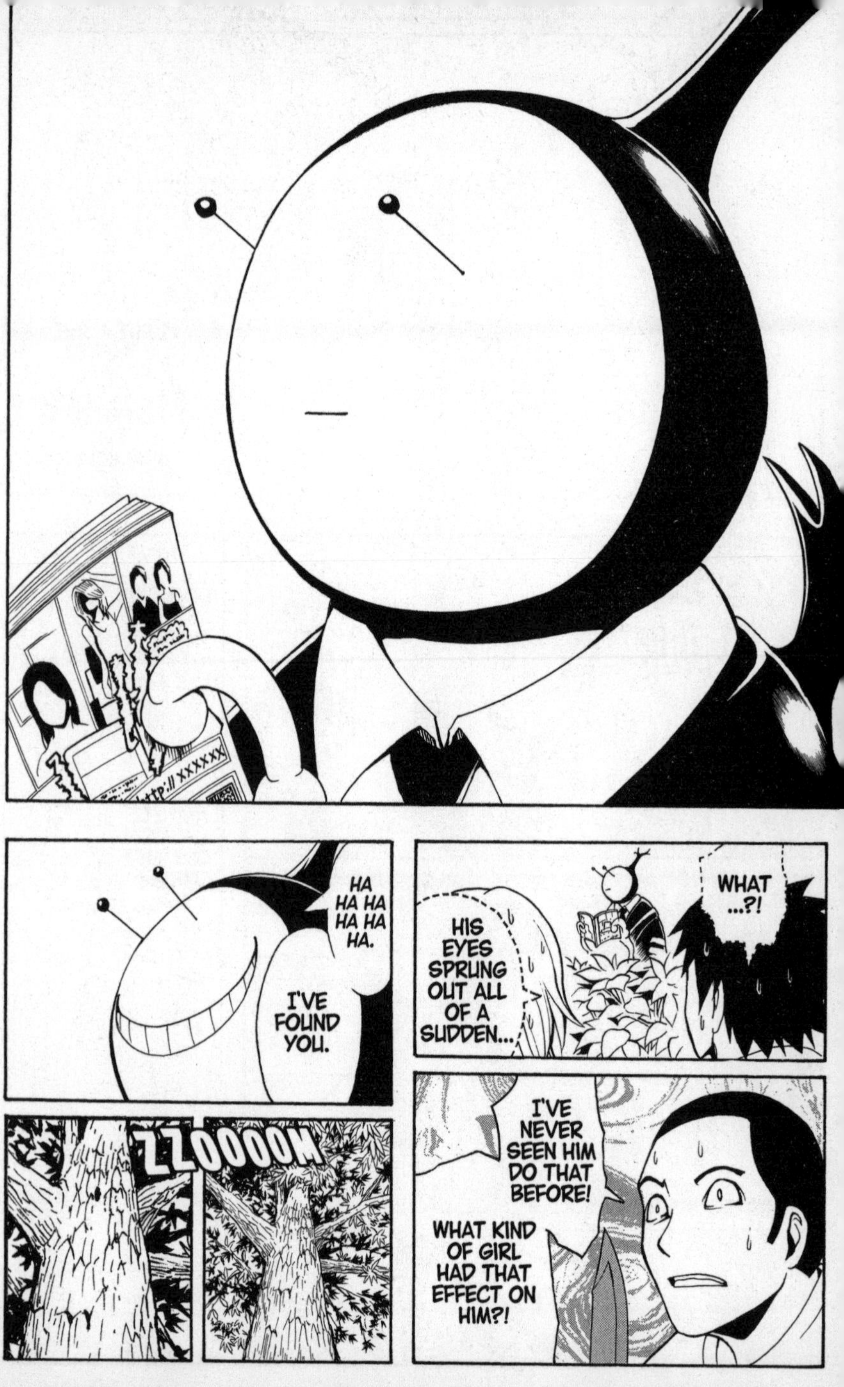
WHAT ...?!
HIS EYES SPRUNG OUT ALL OF A SUDDEN...
HA HA HA HA HA HA.
I'VE FOUND YOU.
I'VE NEVER SEEN HIM DO THAT BEFORE!
WHAT KIND OF GIRL HAD THAT EFFECT ON HIM?!
ZZOOOOM

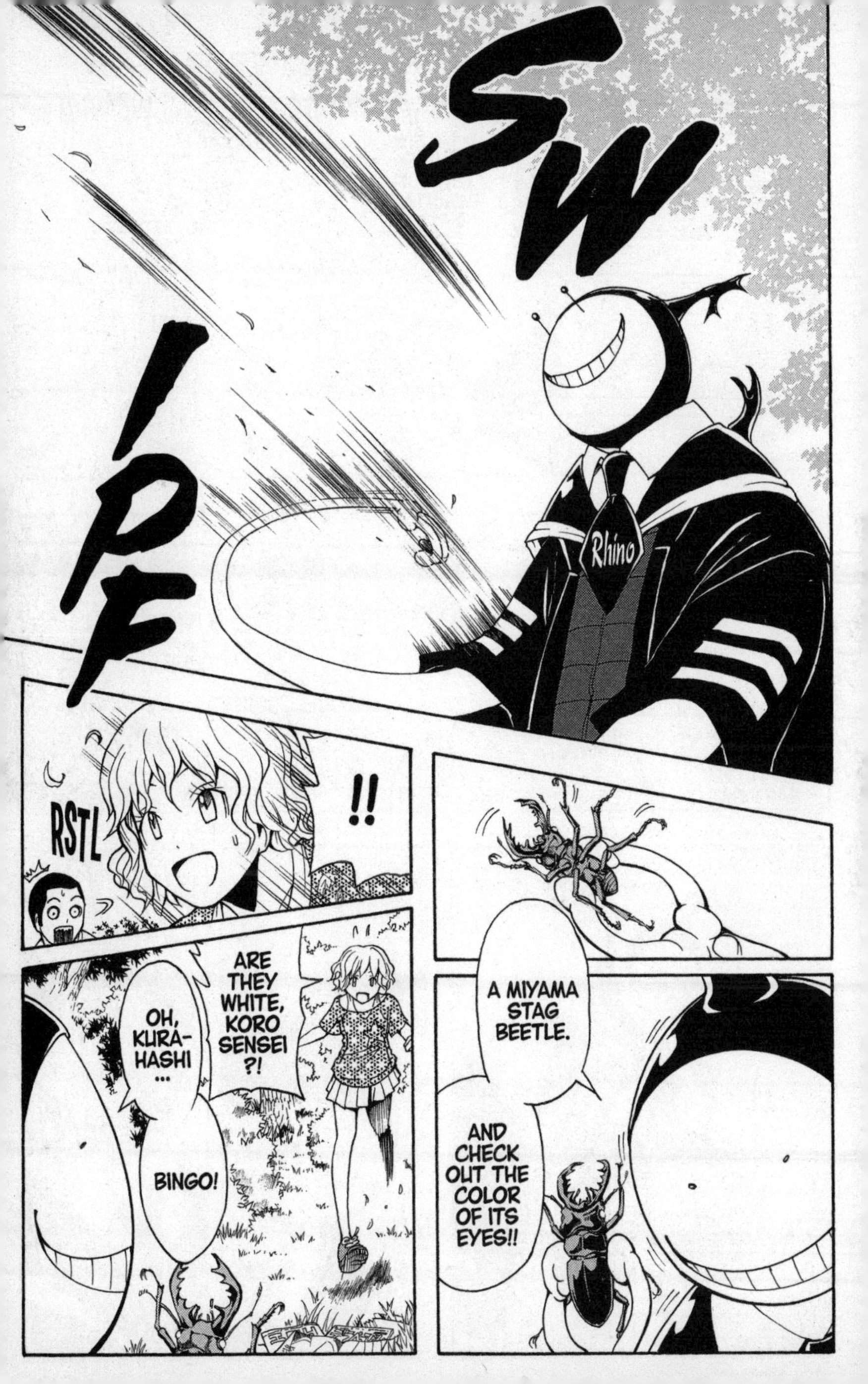
SWIPF
Rhino
RSTL
!!
A MIYAMA STAG BEETLE.
AND CHECK OUT THE COLOR OF ITS EYES!!
ARE THEY WHITE, KORO SENSEI?!
OH, KURA-HASHI...
BINGO!

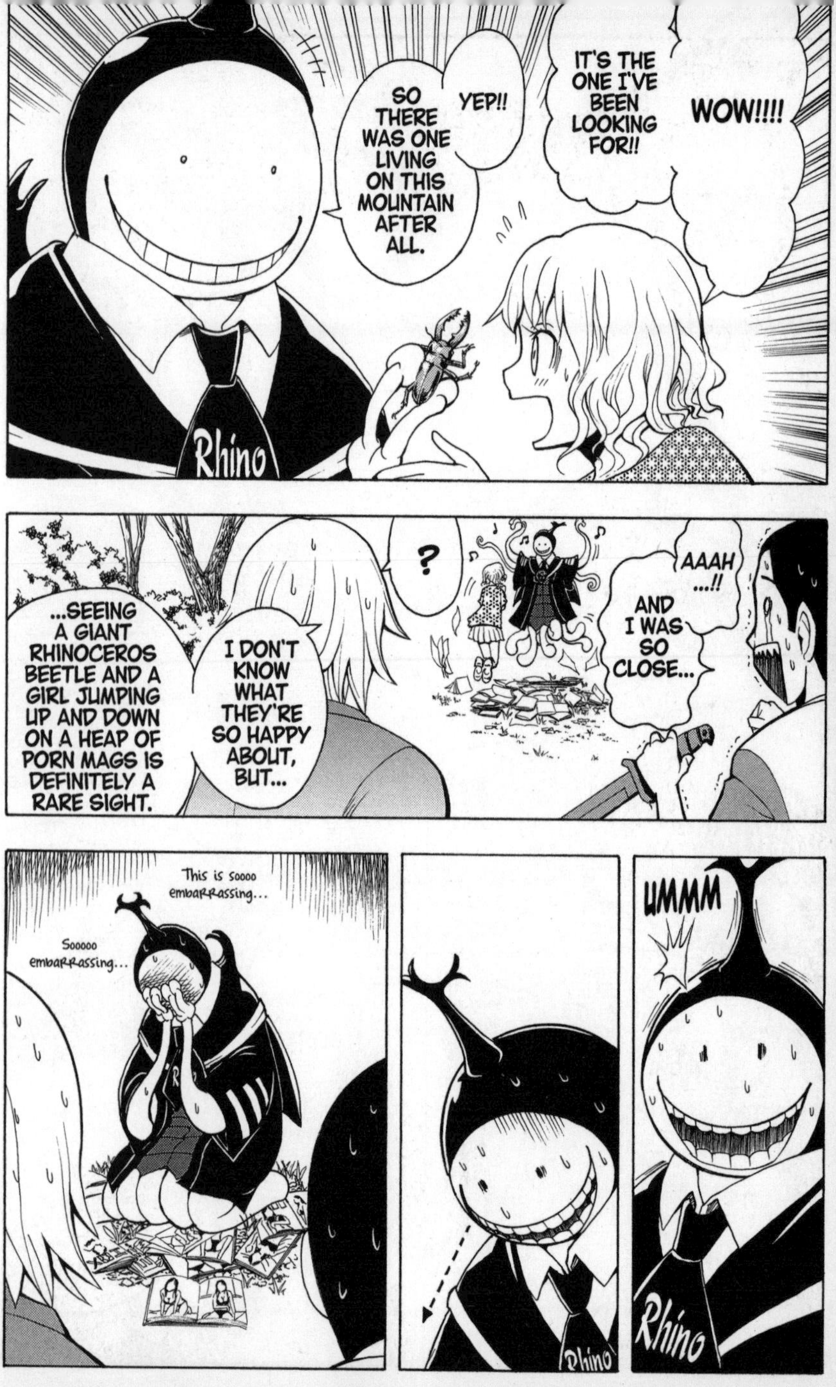
WOW!!!!
IT'S THE ONE I'VE BEEN LOOKING FOR!!
YEP!!
SO THERE WAS ONE LIVING ON THIS MOUNTAIN AFTER ALL.
Rhino
AAAH ...!!
AND I WAS SO CLOSE...
?
I DON'T KNOW WHAT THEY'RE SO HAPPY ABOUT, BUT...
...SEEING A GIANT RHINOCEROS BEETLE AND A GIRL JUMPING UP AND DOWN ON A HEAP OF PORN MAGS IS DEFINITELY A RARE SIGHT.
UMMM
Rhino
Rhino
This is soooo embarrassing...
Sooooo embarrassing...

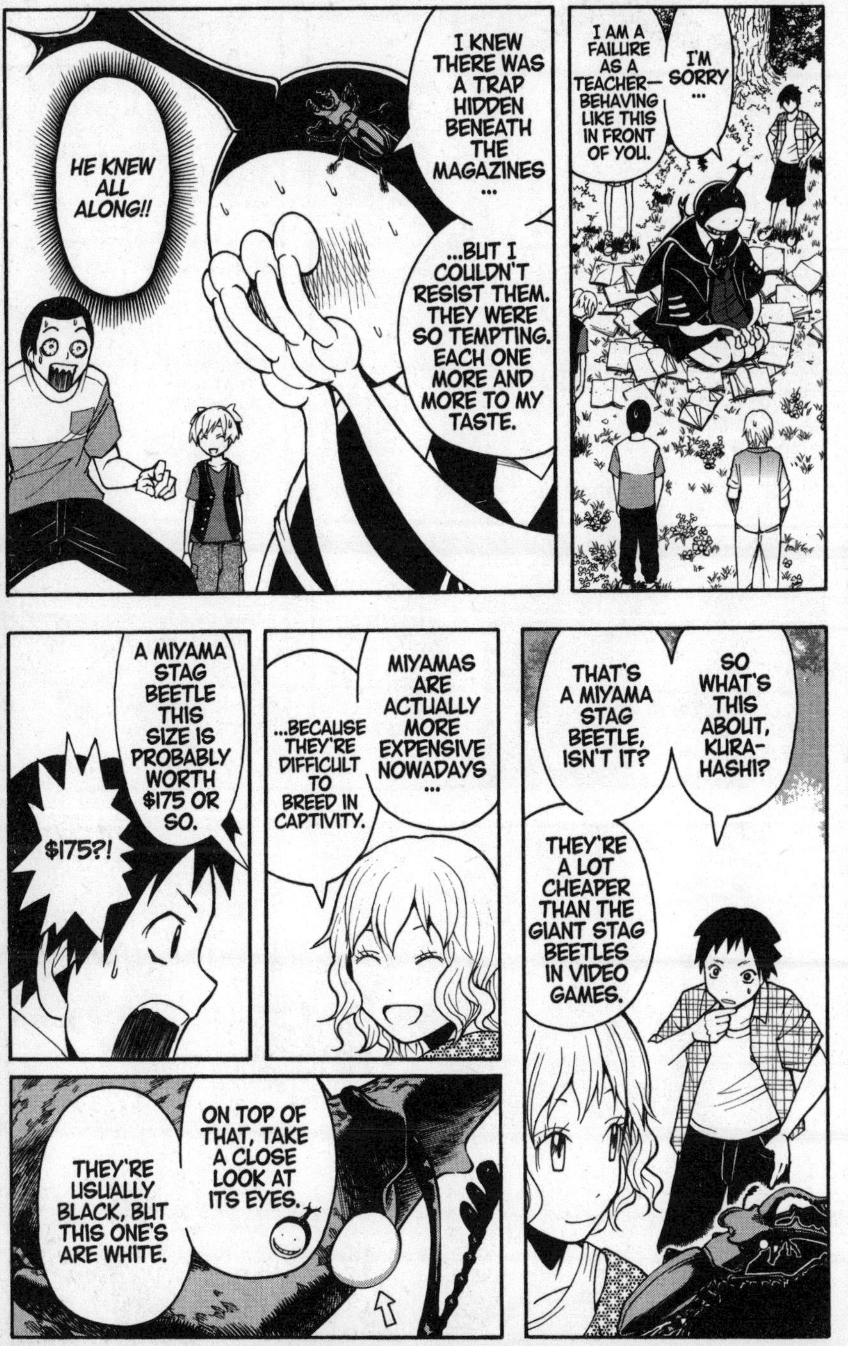
I'M SORRY ...
I AM A FAILURE AS A TEACHER—BEHAVING LIKE THIS IN FRONT OF YOU.
I KNEW THERE WAS A TRAP HIDDEN BENEATH THE MAGAZINES ...
...BUT I COULDN'T RESIST THEM. THEY WERE SO TEMPTING. EACH ONE MORE AND MORE TO MY TASTE.
HE KNEW ALL ALONG!!
SO WHAT'S THIS ABOUT, KURA-HASHI?
THAT'S A MIYAMA STAG BEETLE, ISN'T IT?
THEY'RE A LOT CHEAPER THAN THE GIANT STAG BEETLES IN VIDEO GAMES.
MIYAMAS ARE ACTUALLY MORE EXPENSIVE NOWADAYS ...
...BECAUSE THEY'RE DIFFICULT TO BREED IN CAPTIVITY.
A MIYAMA STAG BEETLE THIS SIZE IS PROBABLY WORTH $175 OR SO.
$175?!
ON TOP OF THAT, TAKE A CLOSE LOOK AT ITS EYES.
THEY'RE USUALLY BLACK, BUT THIS ONE'S ARE WHITE.

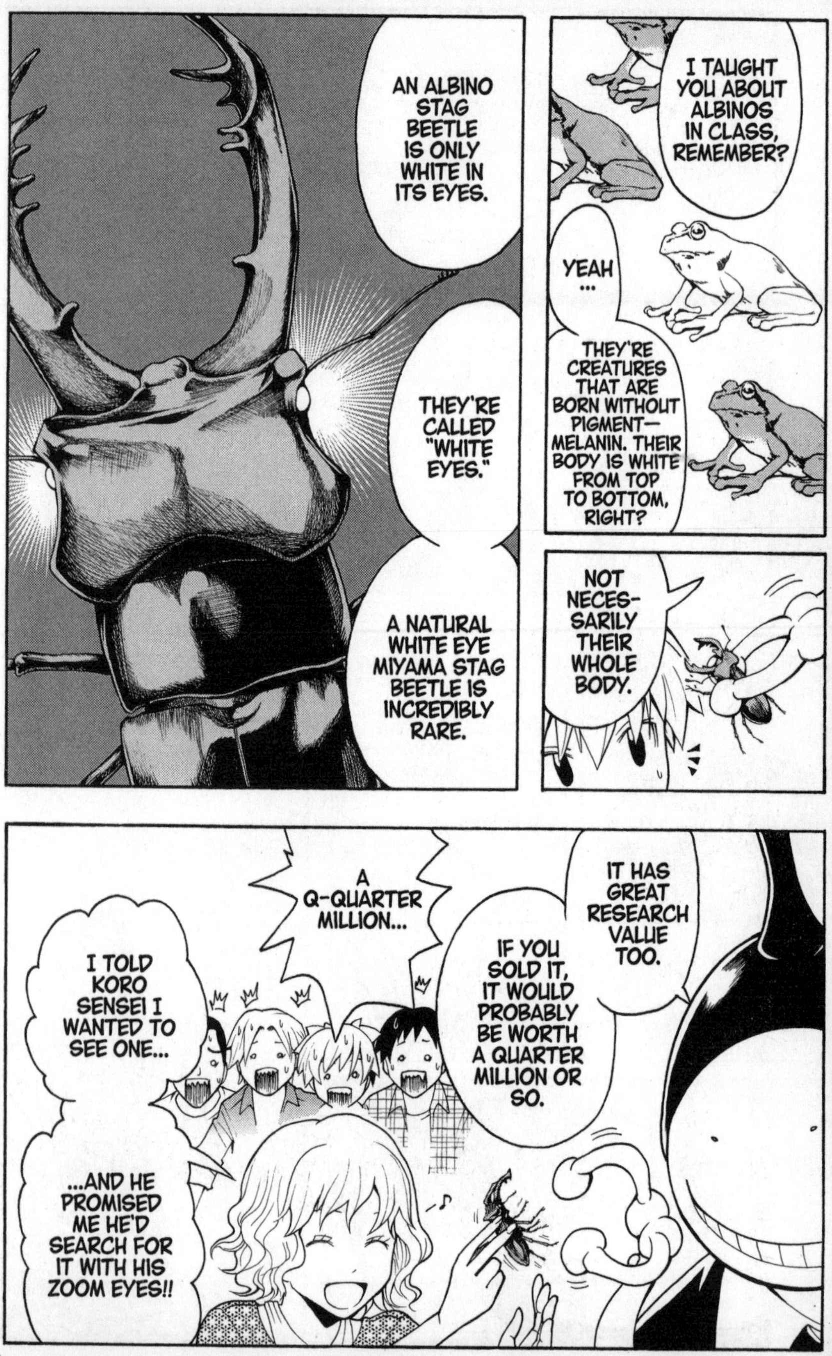
I TAUGHT YOU ABOUT ALBINOS IN CLASS, REMEMBER?
YEAH...
THEY'RE CREATURES THAT ARE BORN WITHOUT PIGMENT—MELANIN. THEIR BODY IS WHITE FROM TOP TO BOTTOM, RIGHT?
NOT NECES-SARILY THEIR WHOLE BODY.
AN ALBINO STAG BEETLE IS ONLY WHITE IN ITS EYES.
THEY'RE CALLED "WHITE EYES."
A NATURAL WHITE EYE MIYAMA STAG BEETLE IS INCREDIBLY RARE.
IT HAS GREAT RESEARCH VALUE TOO.
IF YOU SOLD IT, IT WOULD PROBABLY BE WORTH A QUARTER MILLION OR SO.
A Q-QUARTER MILLION...
I TOLD KORO SENSEI I WANTED TO SEE ONE...
...AND HE PROMISED ME HE'D SEARCH FOR IT WITH HIS ZOOM EYES!!

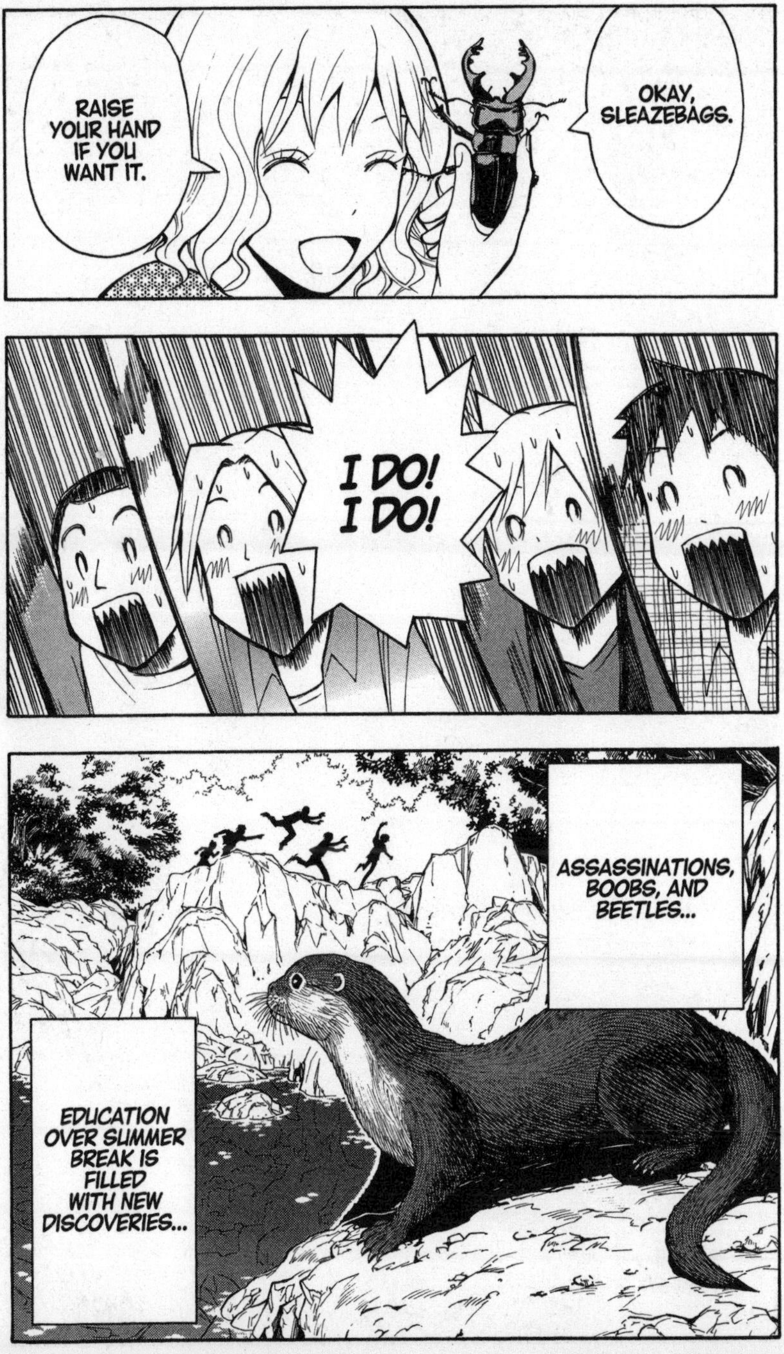
OKAY, SLEAZEBAGS.
RAISE YOUR HAND IF YOU WANT IT.
I DO! I DO!
ASSASSINATIONS, BOOBS, AND BEETLES...
EDUCATION OVER SUMMER BREAK IS FILLED WITH NEW DISCOVERIES...

Actually, there was something
even RARER in the vicinity.

Japanese River Otter
Declared extinct in 2012
Price: Priceless

CLASS 57 PLOTTING AND PLANNING TIME

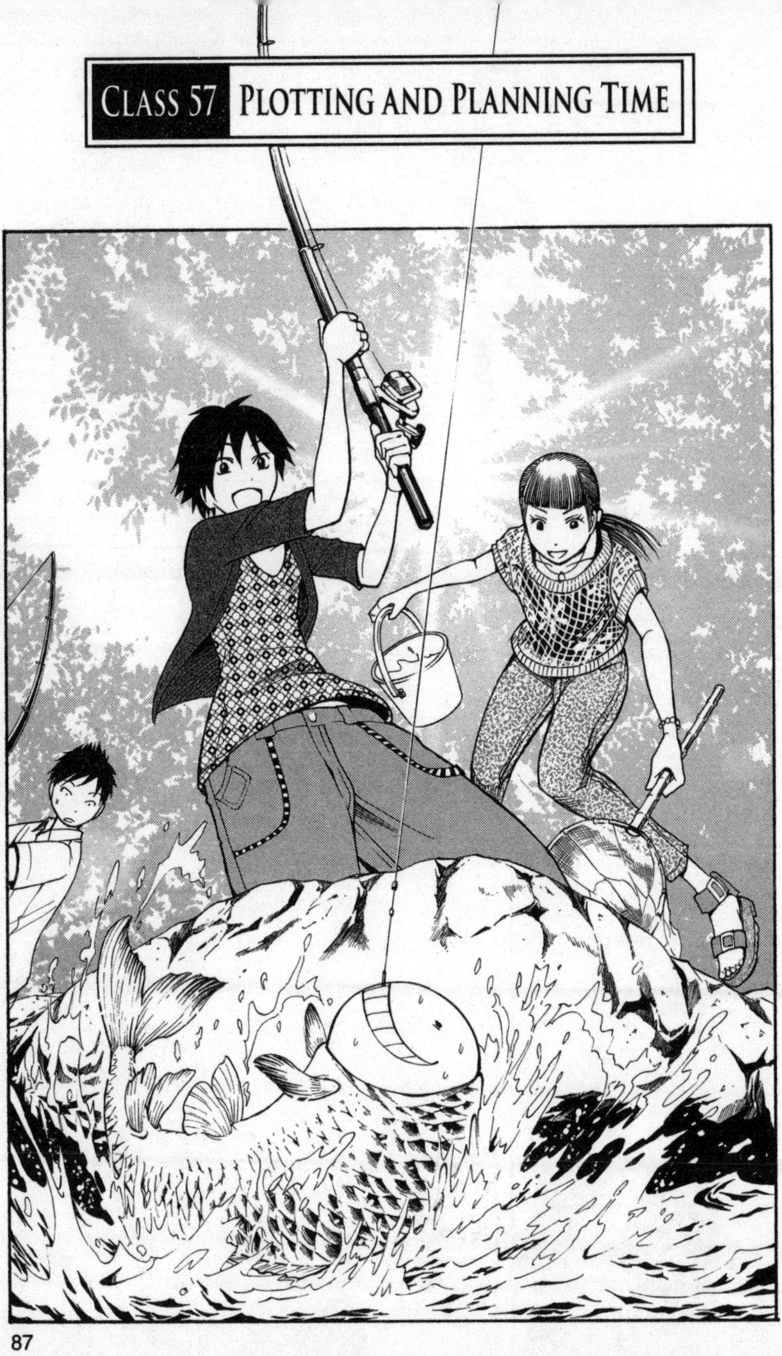

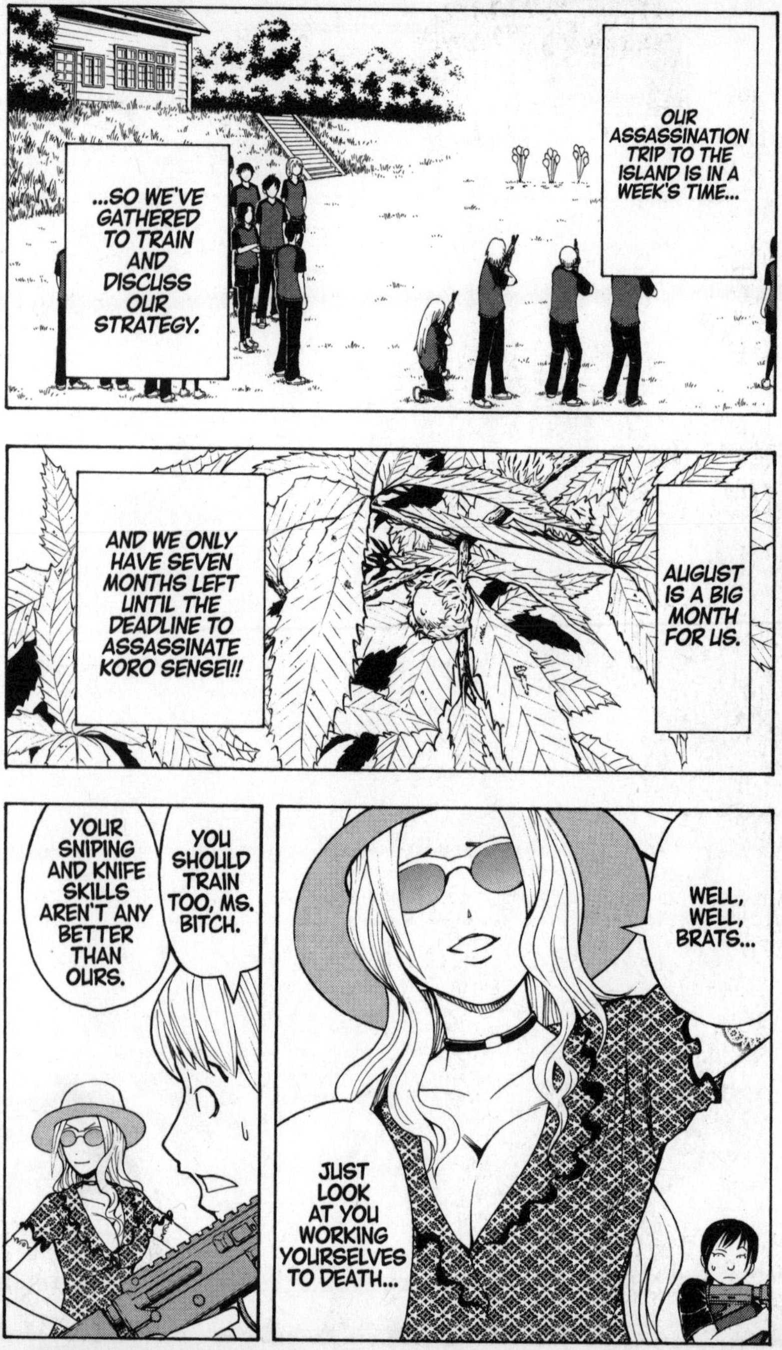
OUR ASSASSINATION TRIP TO THE ISLAND IS IN A WEEK'S TIME...
...SO WE'VE GATHERED TO TRAIN AND DISCUSS OUR STRATEGY.
AUGUST IS A BIG MONTH FOR US.
AND WE ONLY HAVE SEVEN MONTHS LEFT UNTIL THE DEADLINE TO ASSASSINATE KORO SENSEI!!
WELL, WELL, BRATS...
JUST LOOK AT YOU WORKING YOURSELVES TO DEATH...
YOU SHOULD TRAIN TOO, MS. BITCH.
YOUR SNIPING AND KNIFE SKILLS AREN'T ANY BETTER THAN OURS.

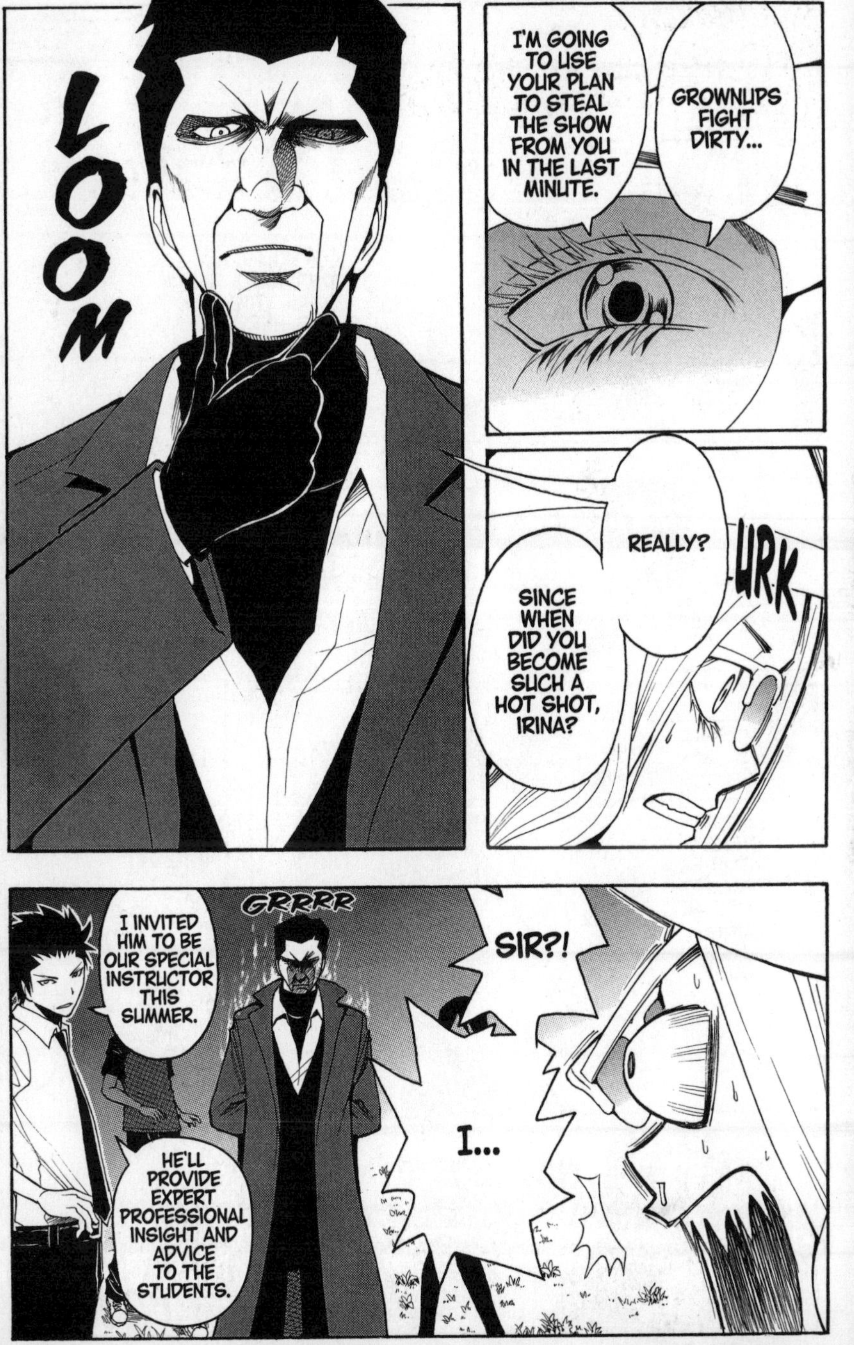
GROWNUPS FIGHT DIRTY...
I'M GOING TO USE YOUR PLAN TO STEAL THE SHOW FROM YOU IN THE LAST MINUTE.
REALLY?
URK
SINCE WHEN DID YOU BECOME SUCH A HOT SHOT, IRINA?
LOOM
SIR?!
I...
GRRRR
I INVITED HIM TO BE OUR SPECIAL INSTRUCTOR THIS SUMMER.
HE'LL PROVIDE EXPERT PROFESSIONAL INSIGHT AND ADVICE TO THE STUDENTS.

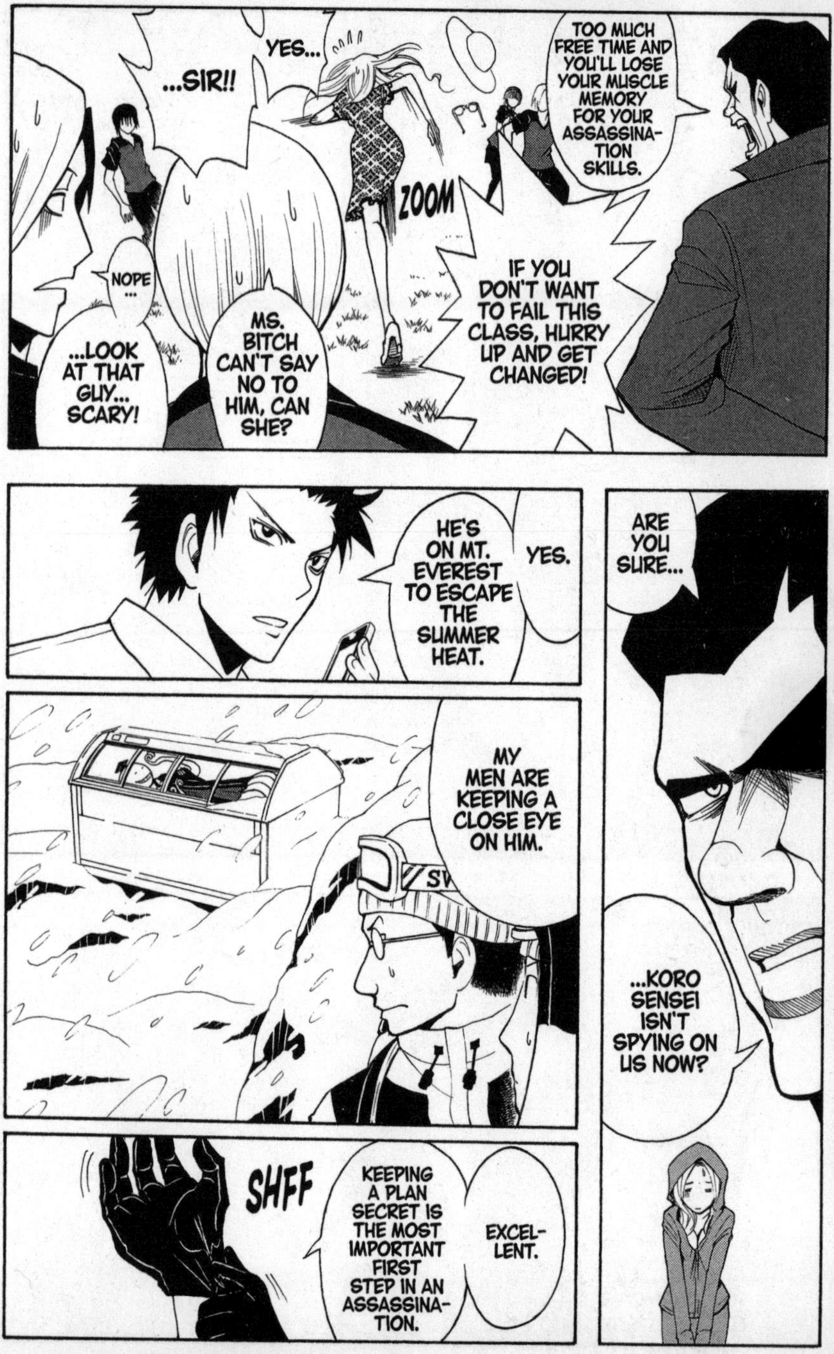
TOO MUCH FREE TIME AND YOU'LL LOSE YOUR MUSCLE MEMORY FOR YOUR ASSASSINATION SKILLS.
YES...
...SIR!!
ZOOM
IF YOU DON'T WANT TO FAIL THIS CLASS, HURRY UP AND GET CHANGED!
NOPE ...
MS. BITCH CAN'T SAY NO TO HIM, CAN SHE?
...LOOK AT THAT GUY... SCARY!
ARE YOU SURE...
...KORO SENSEI ISN'T SPYING ON US NOW?
YES.
HE'S ON MT. EVEREST TO ESCAPE THE SUMMER HEAT.
MY MEN ARE KEEPING A CLOSE EYE ON HIM.
EXCEL-LENT.
KEEPING A PLAN SECRET IS THE MOST IMPORTANT FIRST STEP IN AN ASSASSINATION.
SHFF

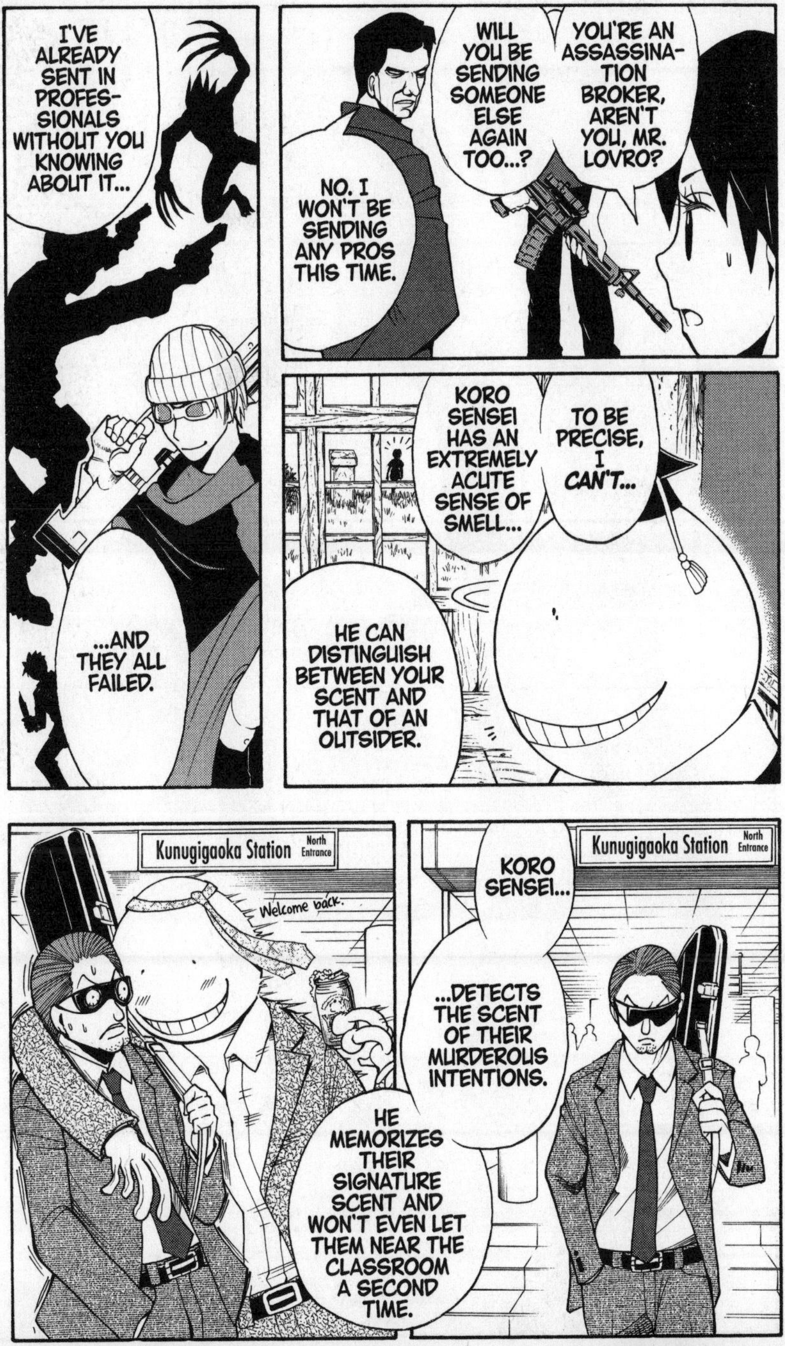
YOU'RE AN ASSASSINATION BROKER, AREN'T YOU, MR. LOVRO?
WILL YOU BE SENDING SOMEONE ELSE AGAIN TOO...?
NO. I WON'T BE SENDING ANY PROS THIS TIME.
TO BE PRECISE, I CAN'T...
KORO SENSEI HAS AN EXTREMELY ACUTE SENSE OF SMELL...
HE CAN DISTINGUISH BETWEEN YOUR SCENT AND THAT OF AN OUTSIDER.
I'VE ALREADY SENT IN PROFESSIONALS WITHOUT YOU KNOWING ABOUT IT...
...AND THEY ALL FAILED.
Kunugigaoka Station North Entrance
KORO SENSEI...
...DETECTS THE SCENT OF THEIR MURDEROUS INTENTIONS.
HE MEMORIZES THEIR SIGNATURE SCENT AND WON'T EVEN LET THEM NEAR THE CLASSROOM A SECOND TIME.
Kunugigaoka Station North Entrance
Welcome back.

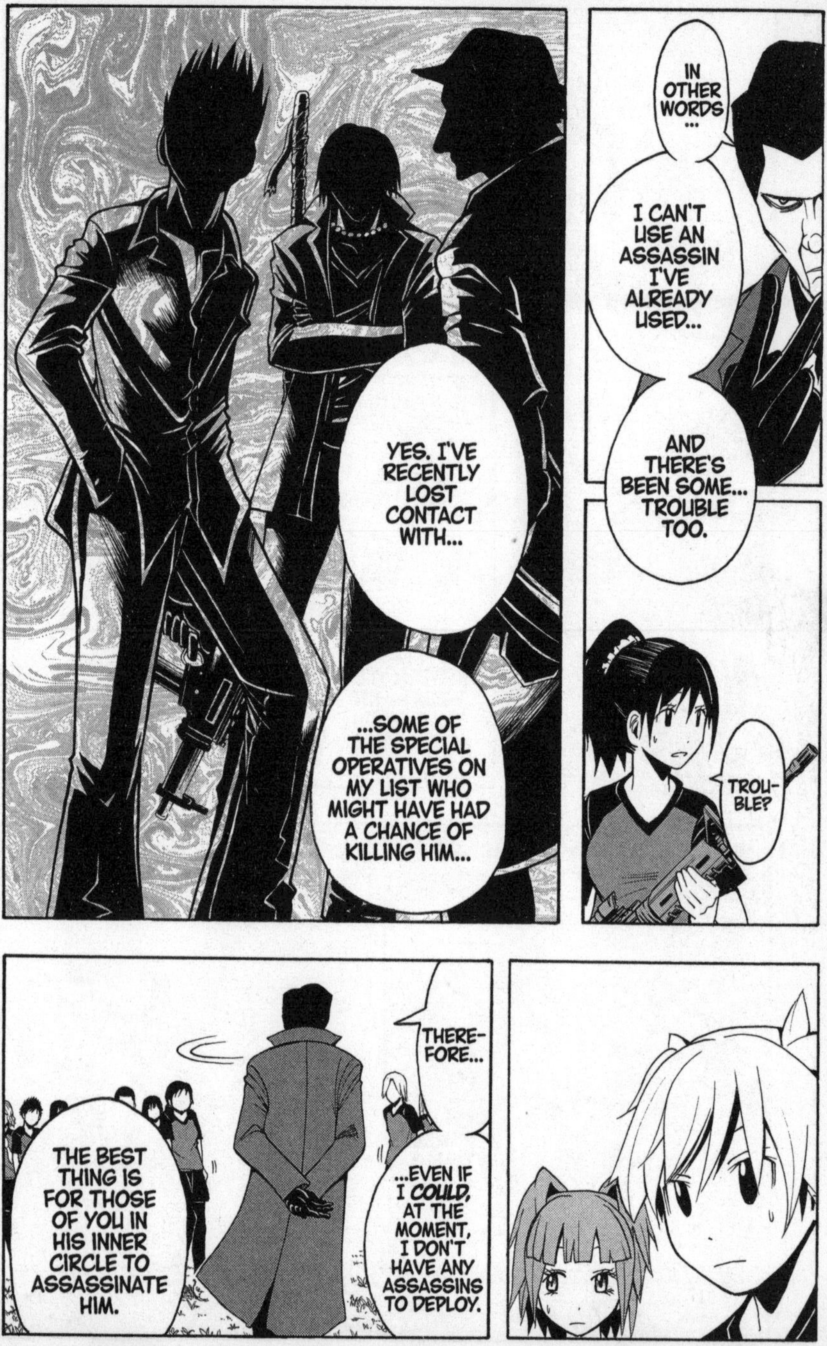
IN OTHER WORDS...
I CAN'T USE AN ASSASSIN I'VE ALREADY USED...
AND THERE'S BEEN SOME... TROUBLE TOO.
TROUBLE?
YES. I'VE RECENTLY LOST CONTACT WITH...
...SOME OF THE SPECIAL OPERATIVES ON MY LIST WHO MIGHT HAVE HAD A CHANCE OF KILLING HIM...
THEREFORE...
...EVEN IF I *COULD*, AT THE MOMENT, I DON'T HAVE ANY ASSASSINS TO DEPLOY.
THE BEST THING IS FOR THOSE OF YOU IN HIS INNER CIRCLE TO ASSASSINATE HIM.

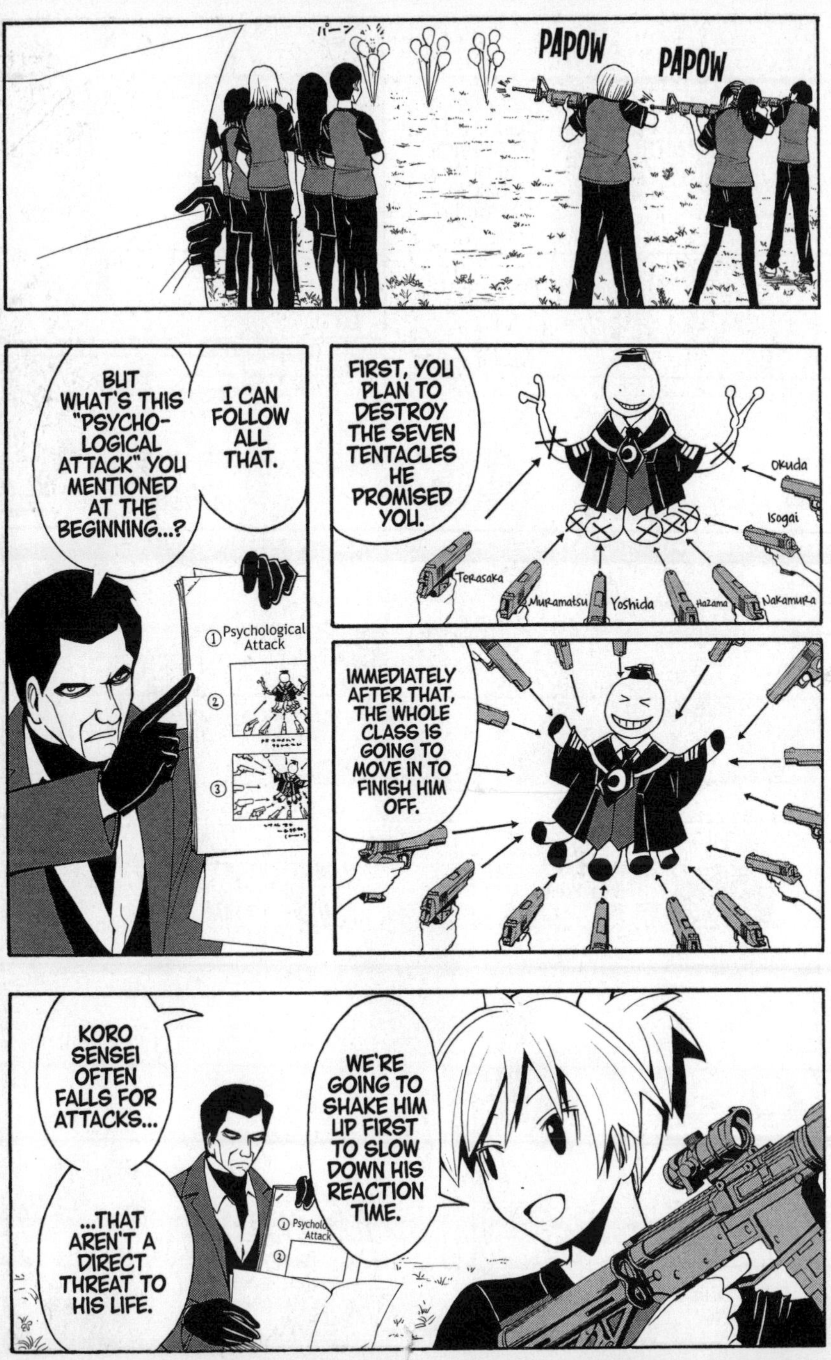

パーン
PAPOW
PAPOW
FIRST, YOU PLAN TO DESTROY THE SEVEN TENTACLES HE PROMISED YOU.
Okuda
Isogai
Terasaka
Muramatsu
Yoshida
Hazama
Nakamura
IMMEDIATELY AFTER THAT, THE WHOLE CLASS IS GOING TO MOVE IN TO FINISH HIM OFF.
I CAN FOLLOW ALL THAT.
BUT WHAT'S THIS "PSYCHOLOGICAL ATTACK" YOU MENTIONED AT THE BEGINNING...?
① Psychological Attack
②
③
WE'RE GOING TO SHAKE HIM UP FIRST TO SLOW DOWN HIS REACTION TIME.
KORO SENSEI OFTEN FALLS FOR ATTACKS...
...THAT AREN'T A DIRECT THREAT TO HIS LIFE.

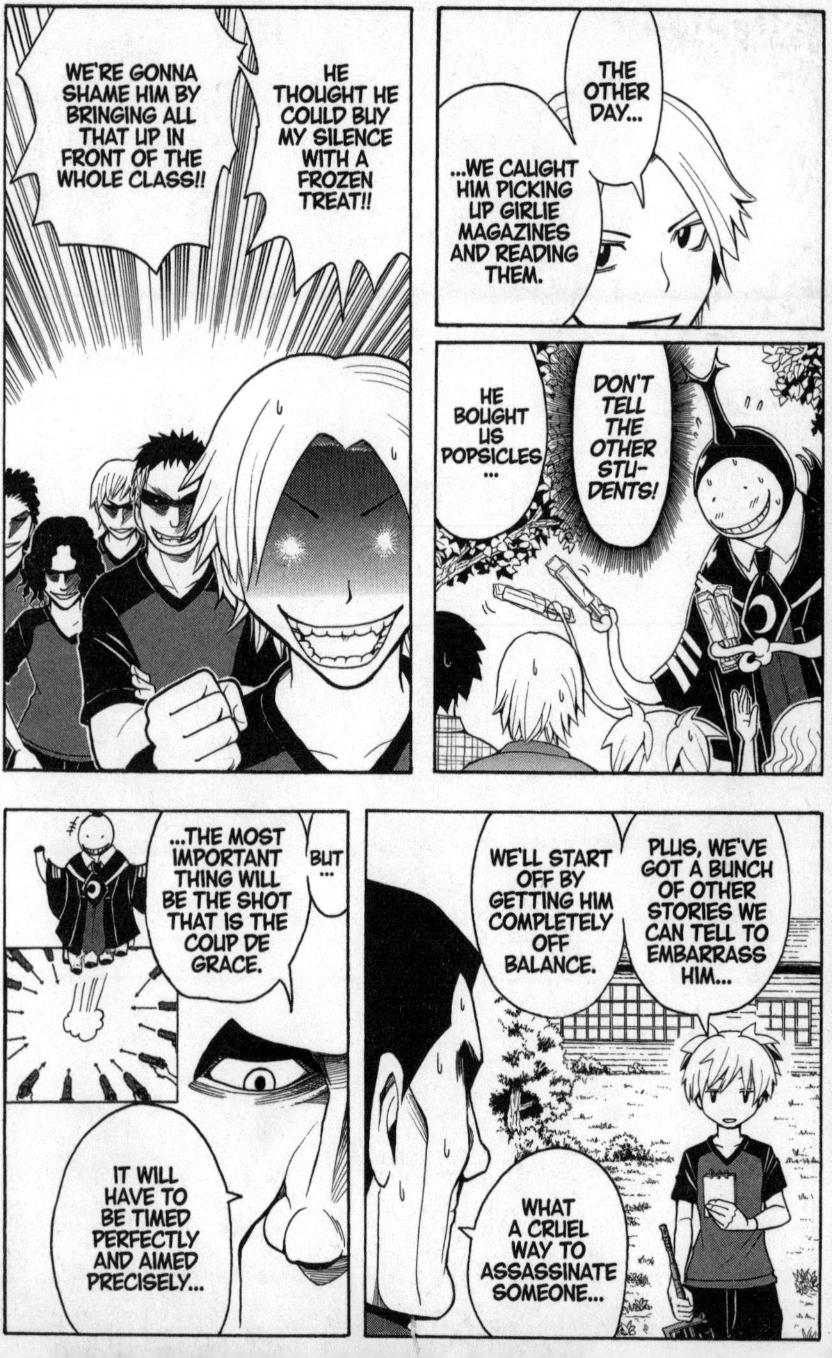
THE OTHER DAY...
...WE CAUGHT HIM PICKING UP GIRLIE MAGAZINES AND READING THEM.
DON'T TELL THE OTHER STU-DENTS!
HE BOUGHT US POPSICLES...
HE THOUGHT HE COULD BUY MY SILENCE WITH A FROZEN TREAT!!
WE'RE GONNA SHAME HIM BY BRINGING ALL THAT UP IN FRONT OF THE WHOLE CLASS!!
PLUS, WE'VE GOT A BUNCH OF OTHER STORIES WE CAN TELL TO EMBARRASS HIM...
WE'LL START OFF BY GETTING HIM COMPLETELY OFF BALANCE.
WHAT A CRUEL WAY TO ASSASSINATE SOMEONE...
BUT...
...THE MOST IMPORTANT THING WILL BE THE SHOT THAT IS THE COUP DE GRACE.
IT WILL HAVE TO BE TIMED PERFECTLY AND AIMED PRECISELY...

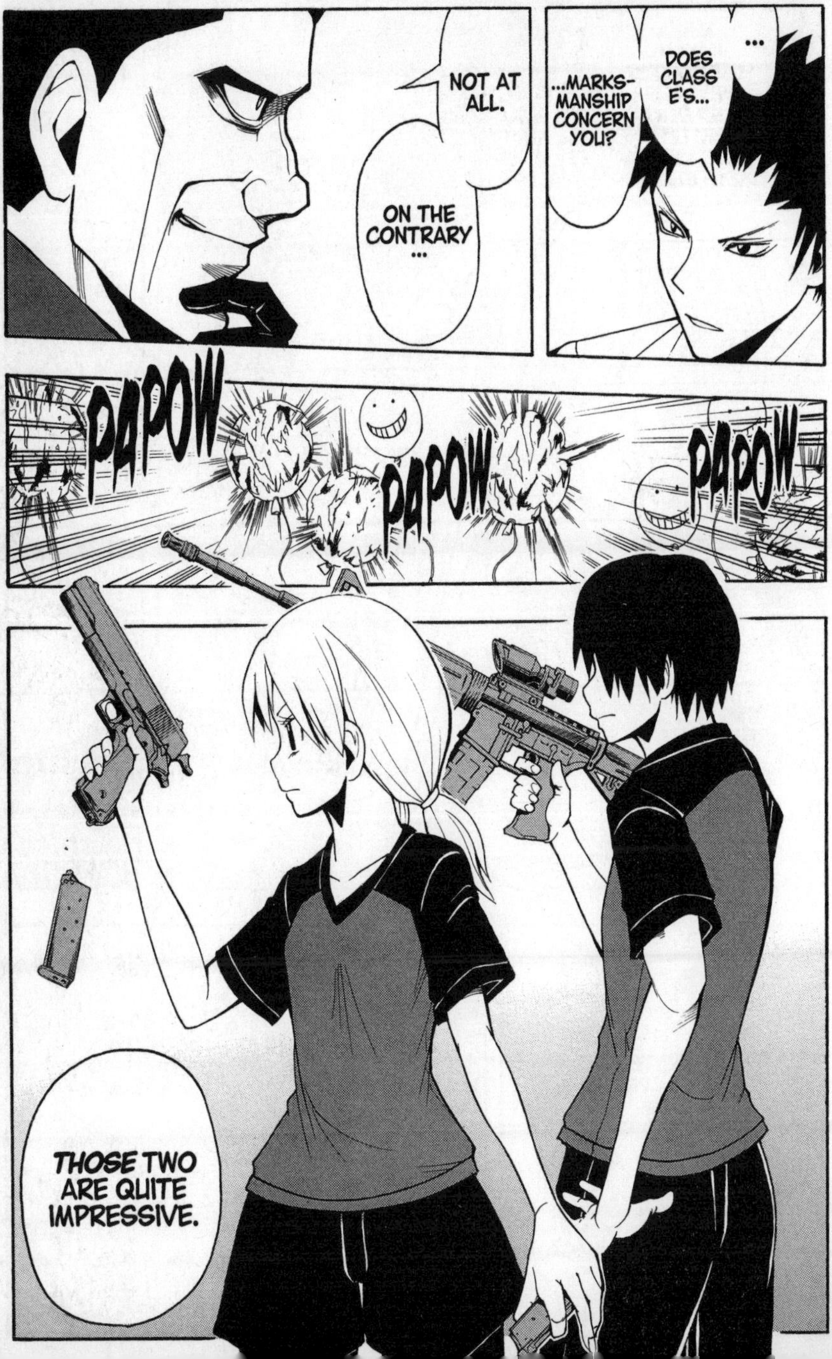
...
DOES CLASS E'S...
...MARKS-MANSHIP CONCERN YOU?
NOT AT ALL.
ON THE CONTRARY ...
PAPOW
PAPOW
PAPOW
THOSE TWO ARE QUITE IMPRESSIVE.

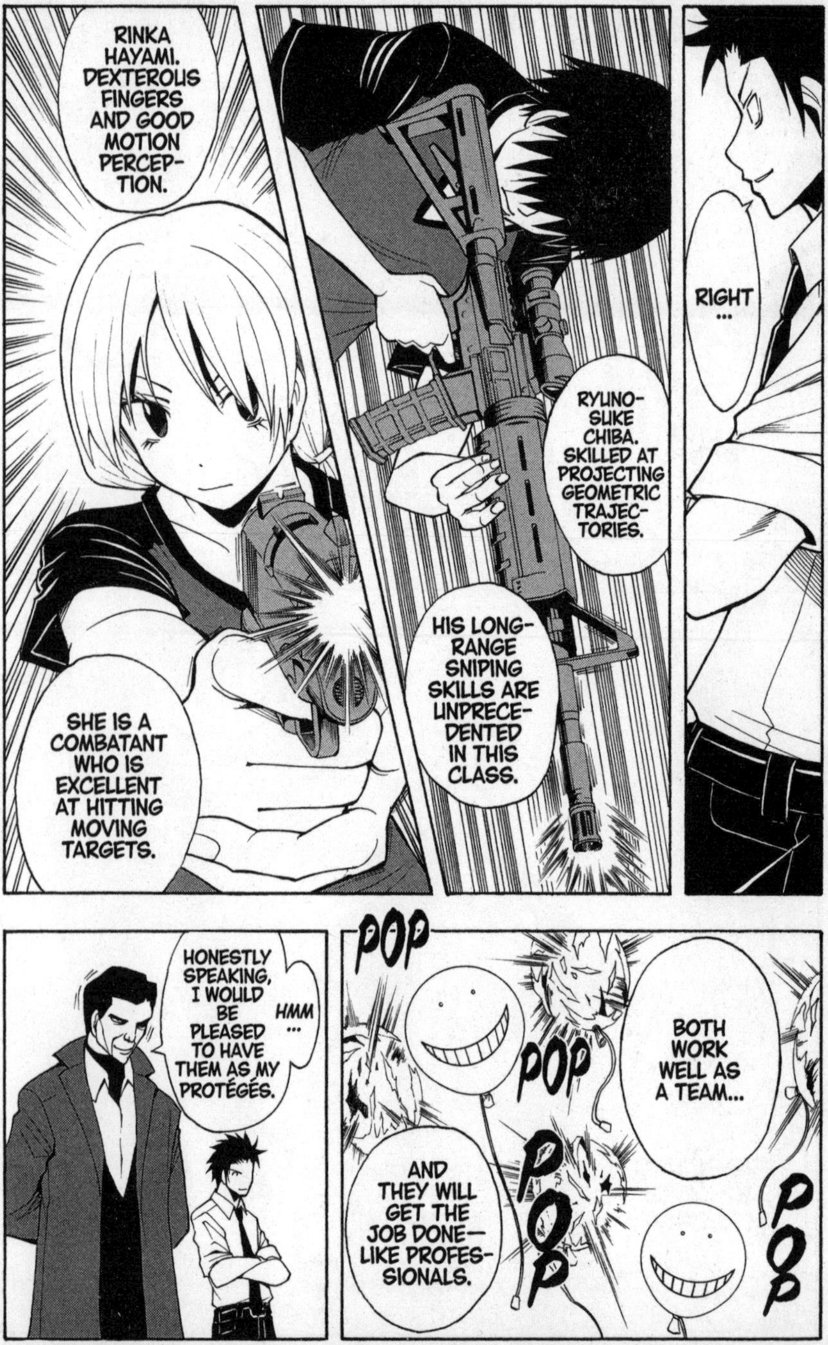
RIGHT ...
RYUNOSUKE CHIBA. SKILLED AT PROJECTING GEOMETRIC TRAJECTORIES.
HIS LONG-RANGE SNIPING SKILLS ARE UNPRECEDENTED IN THIS CLASS.
RINKA HAYAMI. DEXTEROUS FINGERS AND GOOD MOTION PERCEPTION.
SHE IS A COMBATANT WHO IS EXCELLENT AT HITTING MOVING TARGETS.
POP
BOTH WORK WELL AS A TEAM...
POP
AND THEY WILL GET THE JOB DONE—LIKE PROFESSIONALS.
POP
POP
POP
POP
HMM ...
HONESTLY SPEAKING, I WOULD BE PLEASED TO HAVE THEM AS MY PROTÉGÉS.

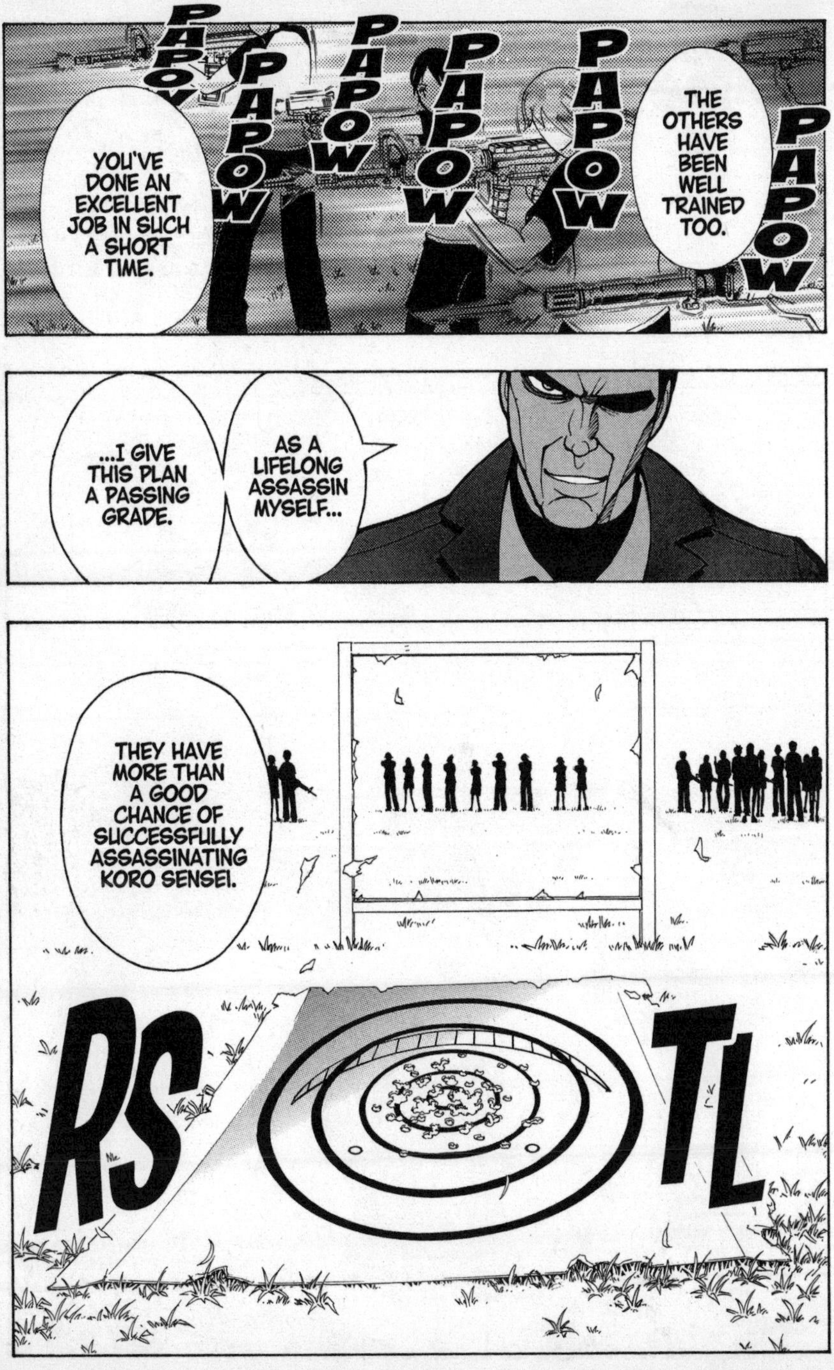
PAPOW
THE OTHERS HAVE BEEN WELL TRAINED TOO.
PAPOW
PAPOW
PAPOW
PAPOW
PAPOW
PAPOW
YOU'VE DONE AN EXCELLENT JOB IN SUCH A SHORT TIME.
AS A LIFELONG ASSASSIN MYSELF...
...I GIVE THIS PLAN A PASSING GRADE.
THEY HAVE MORE THAN A GOOD CHANCE OF SUCCESSFULLY ASSASSINATING KORO SENSEI.
RSTL

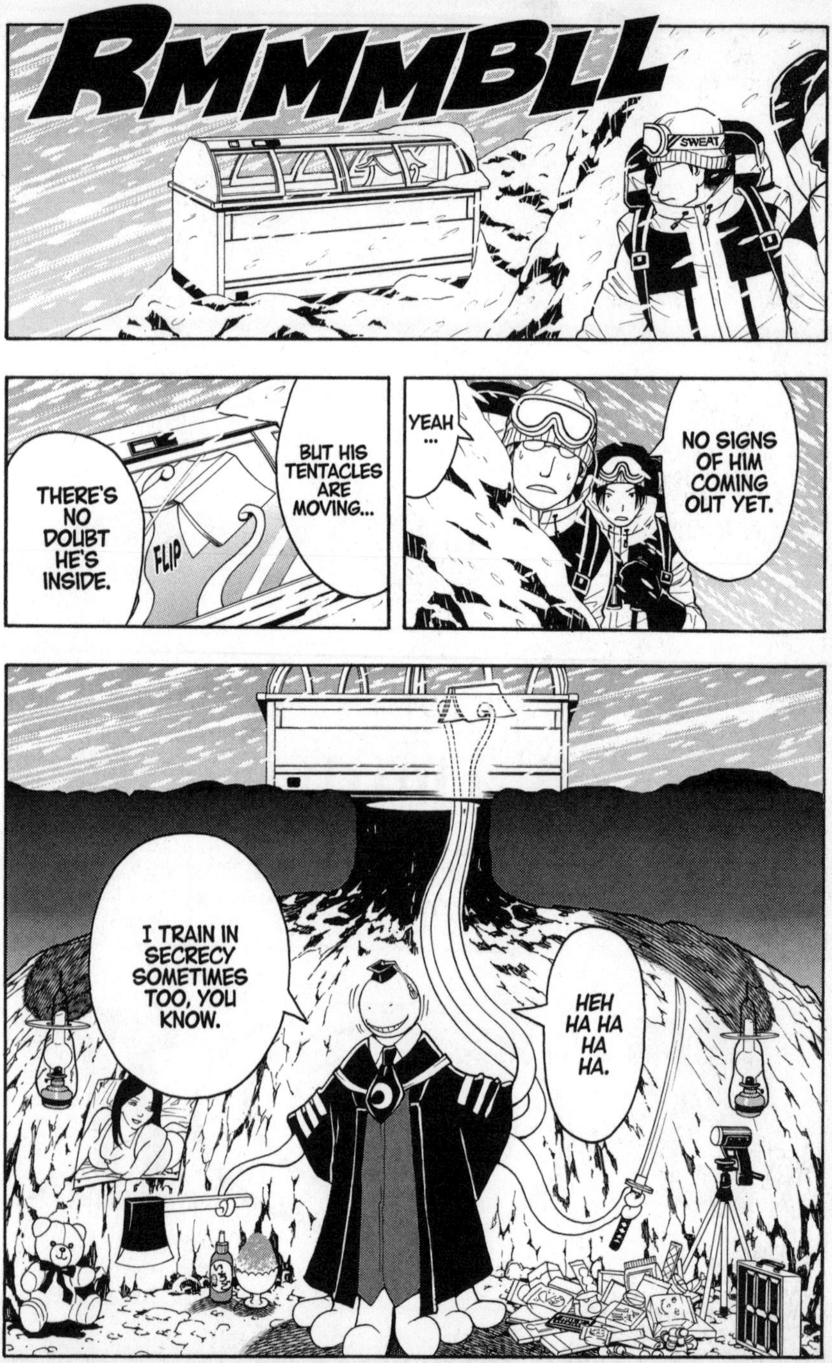
RMMMBLL
SWEAT
NO SIGNS OF HIM COMING OUT YET.
YEAH ...
BUT HIS TENTACLES ARE MOVING...
THERE'S NO DOUBT HE'S INSIDE.
FLIP
HEH HA HA HA HA.
I TRAIN IN SECRECY SOMETIMES TOO, YOU KNOW.

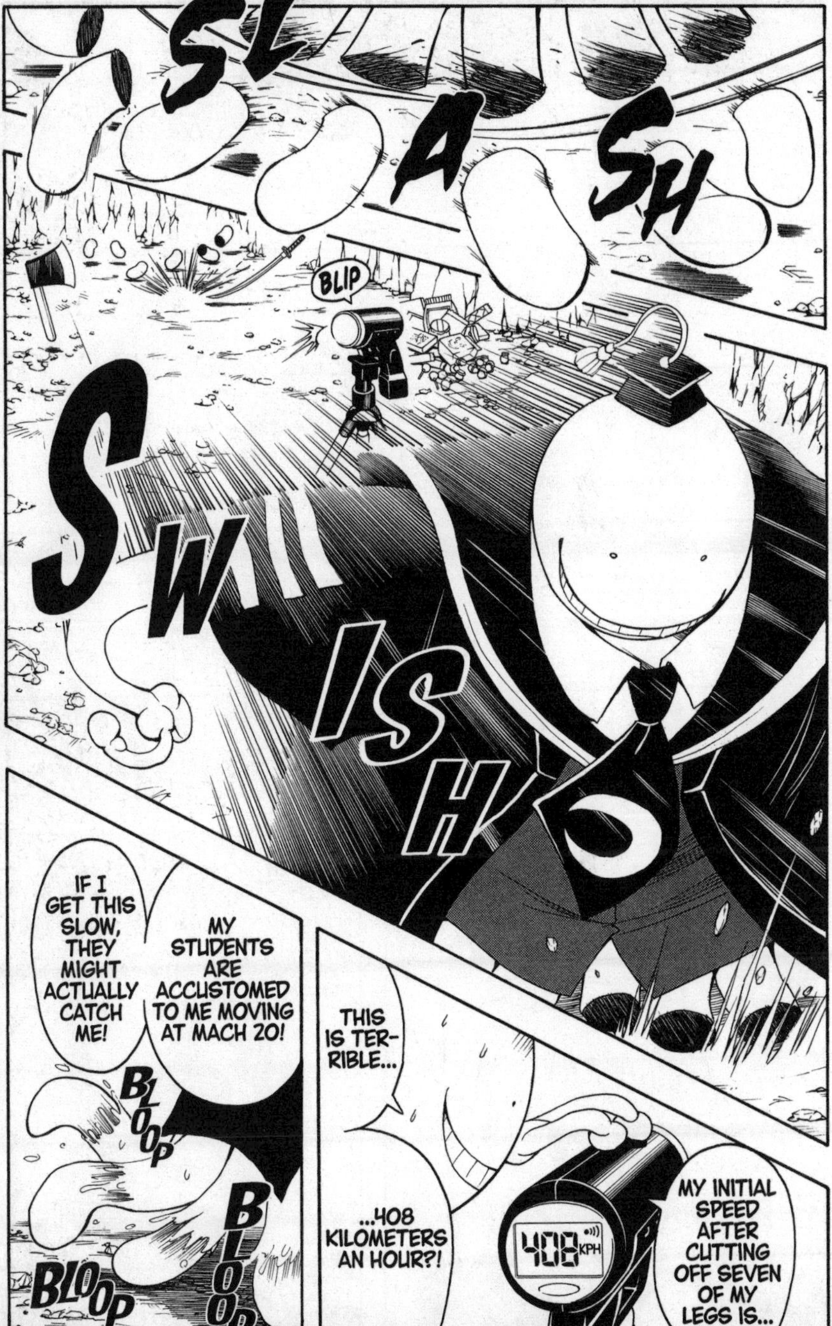
SLASH
BLIP
SWISH
MY INITIAL SPEED AFTER CUTTING OFF SEVEN OF MY LEGS IS...
...408 KILOMETERS AN HOUR?!
408 KPH
THIS IS TER-RIBLE...
MY STUDENTS ARE ACCUSTOMED TO ME MOVING AT MACH 20!
IF I GET THIS SLOW, THEY MIGHT ACTUALLY CATCH ME!
BLOOP
BLOOP
BLOOP

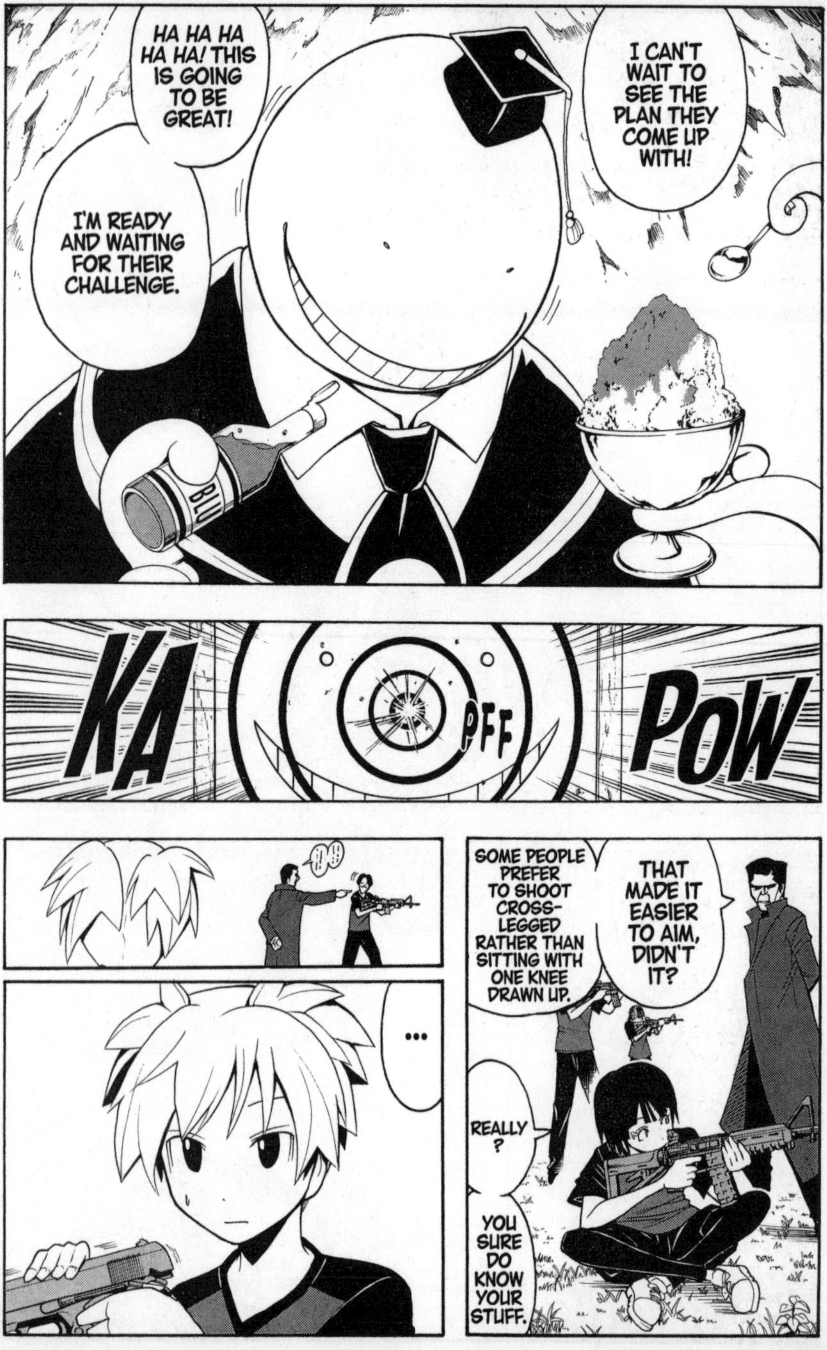
I CAN'T WAIT TO SEE THE PLAN THEY COME UP WITH!
HA HA HA HA HA! THIS IS GOING TO BE GREAT!
I'M READY AND WAITING FOR THEIR CHALLENGE.
KA
POW
PFF
THAT MADE IT EASIER TO AIM, DIDN'T IT?
SOME PEOPLE PREFER TO SHOOT CROSS-LEGGED RATHER THAN SITTING WITH ONE KNEE DRAWN UP.
REALLY?
YOU SURE DO KNOW YOUR STUFF.
...

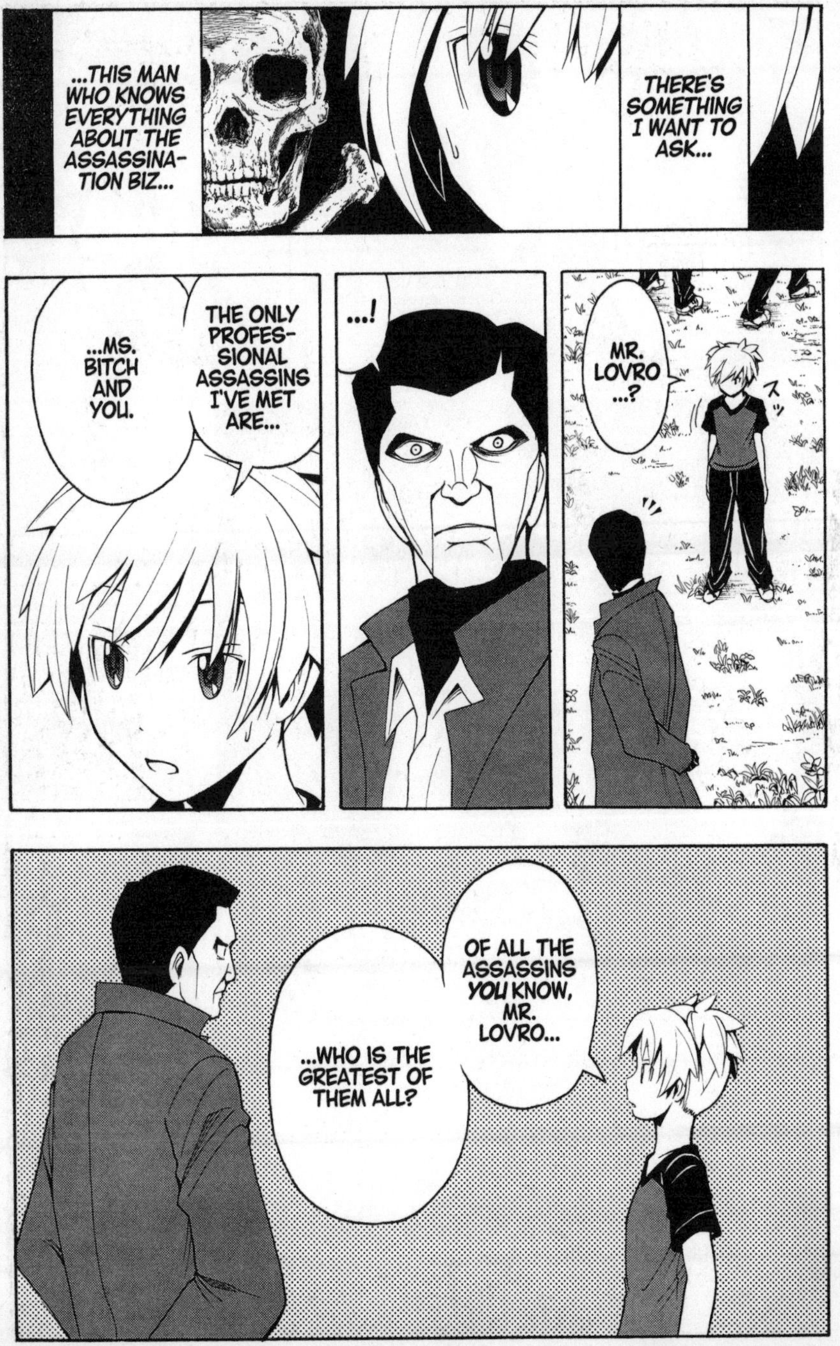
THERE'S SOMETHING I WANT TO ASK...
...THIS MAN WHO KNOWS EVERYTHING ABOUT THE ASSASSINATION BIZ...
MR. LOVRO ...?
スッ
...!
THE ONLY PROFESSIONAL ASSASSINS I'VE MET ARE...
...MS. BITCH AND YOU.
OF ALL THE ASSASSINS *YOU* KNOW, MR. LOVRO...
...WHO IS THE GREATEST OF THEM ALL?

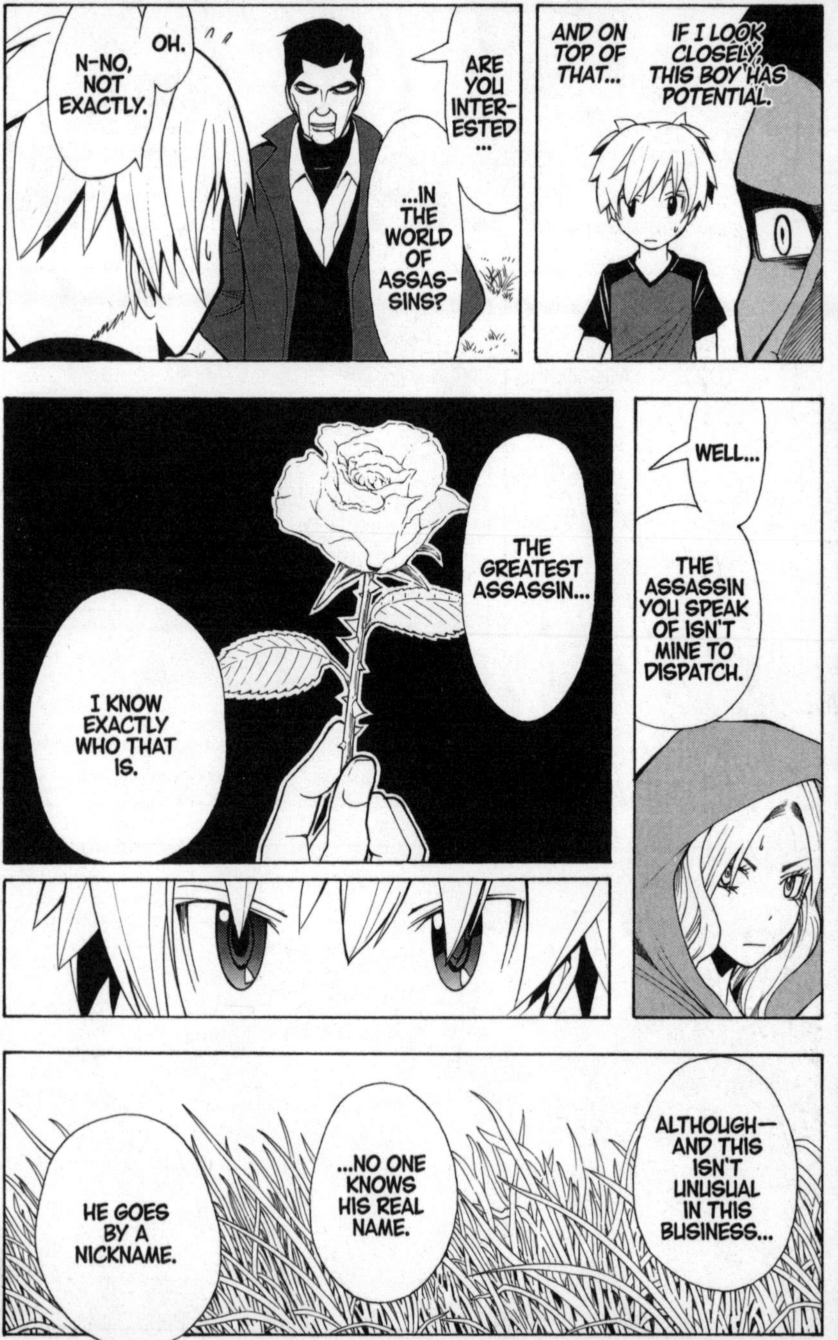
IF I LOOK CLOSELY, THIS BOY HAS POTENTIAL.
AND ON TOP OF THAT...
ARE YOU INTERESTED...
...IN THE WORLD OF ASSASSINS?
OH.
N-NO, NOT EXACTLY.
WELL...
THE ASSASSIN YOU SPEAK OF ISN'T MINE TO DISPATCH.
THE GREATEST ASSASSIN...
I KNOW EXACTLY WHO THAT IS.
ALTHOUGH—AND THIS ISN'T UNUSUAL IN THIS BUSINESS...
...NO ONE KNOWS HIS REAL NAME.
HE GOES BY A NICKNAME.

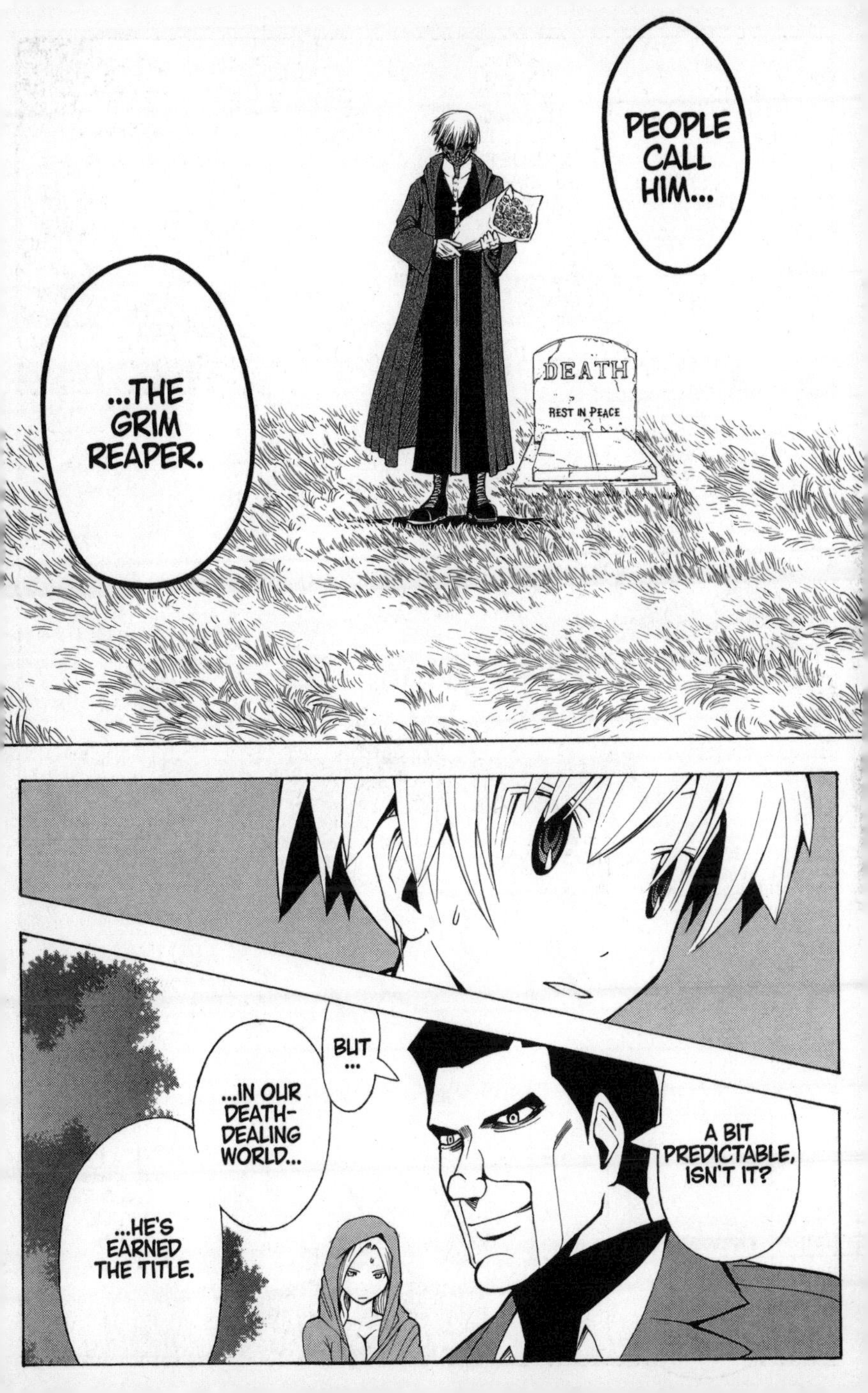
PEOPLE CALL HIM...
DEATH
REST IN PEACE
...THE GRIM REAPER.
A BIT PREDICTABLE, ISN'T IT?
BUT...
...IN OUR DEATH-DEALING WORLD...
...HE'S EARNED THE TITLE.

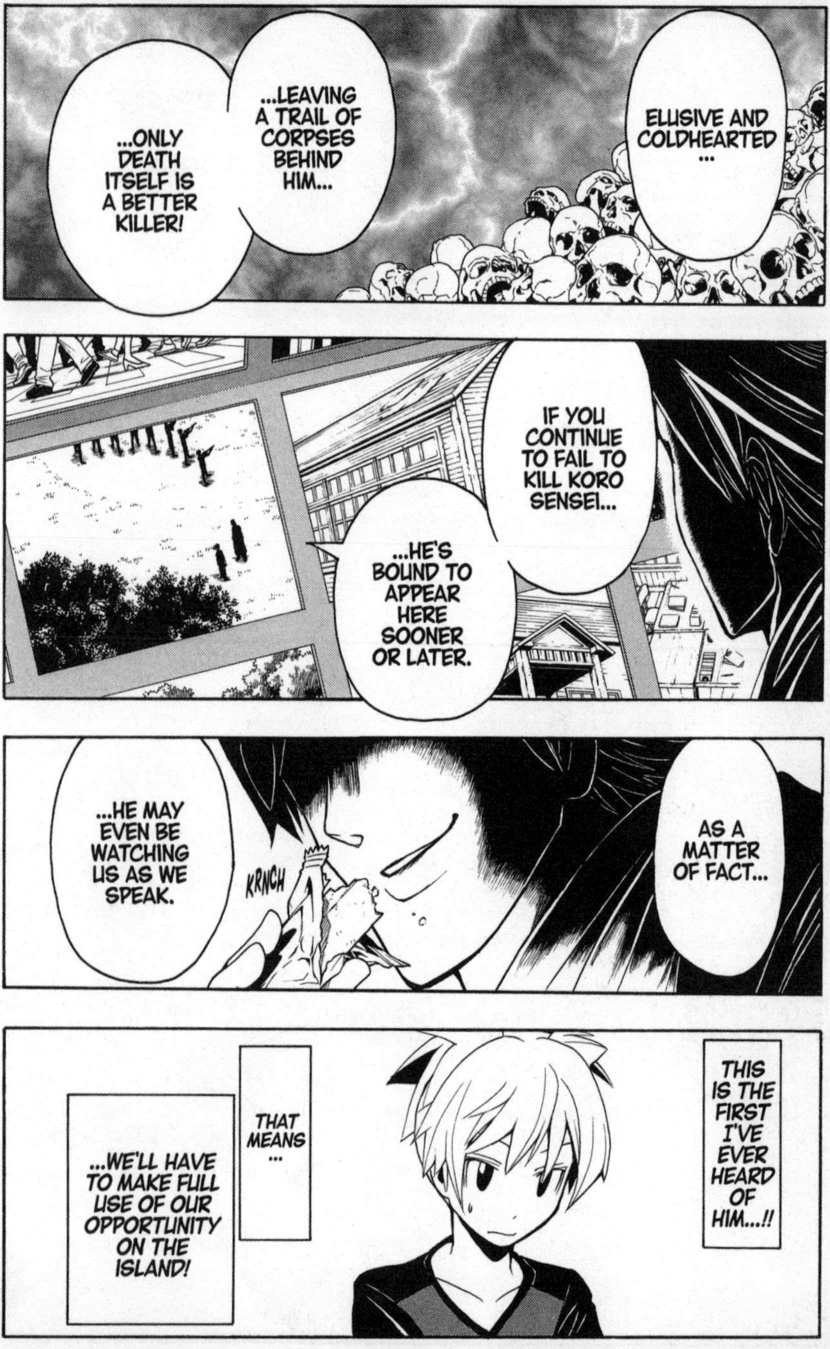
ELUSIVE AND COLDHEARTED ...
...LEAVING A TRAIL OF CORPSES BEHIND HIM...
...ONLY DEATH ITSELF IS A BETTER KILLER!
IF YOU CONTINUE TO FAIL TO KILL KORO SENSEI...
...HE'S BOUND TO APPEAR HERE SOONER OR LATER.
AS A MATTER OF FACT...
KRNCH
...HE MAY EVEN BE WATCHING US AS WE SPEAK.
THIS IS THE FIRST I'VE EVER HEARD OF HIM...!!
THAT MEANS ...
...WE'LL HAVE TO MAKE FULL USE OF OUR OPPORTUNITY ON THE ISLAND!

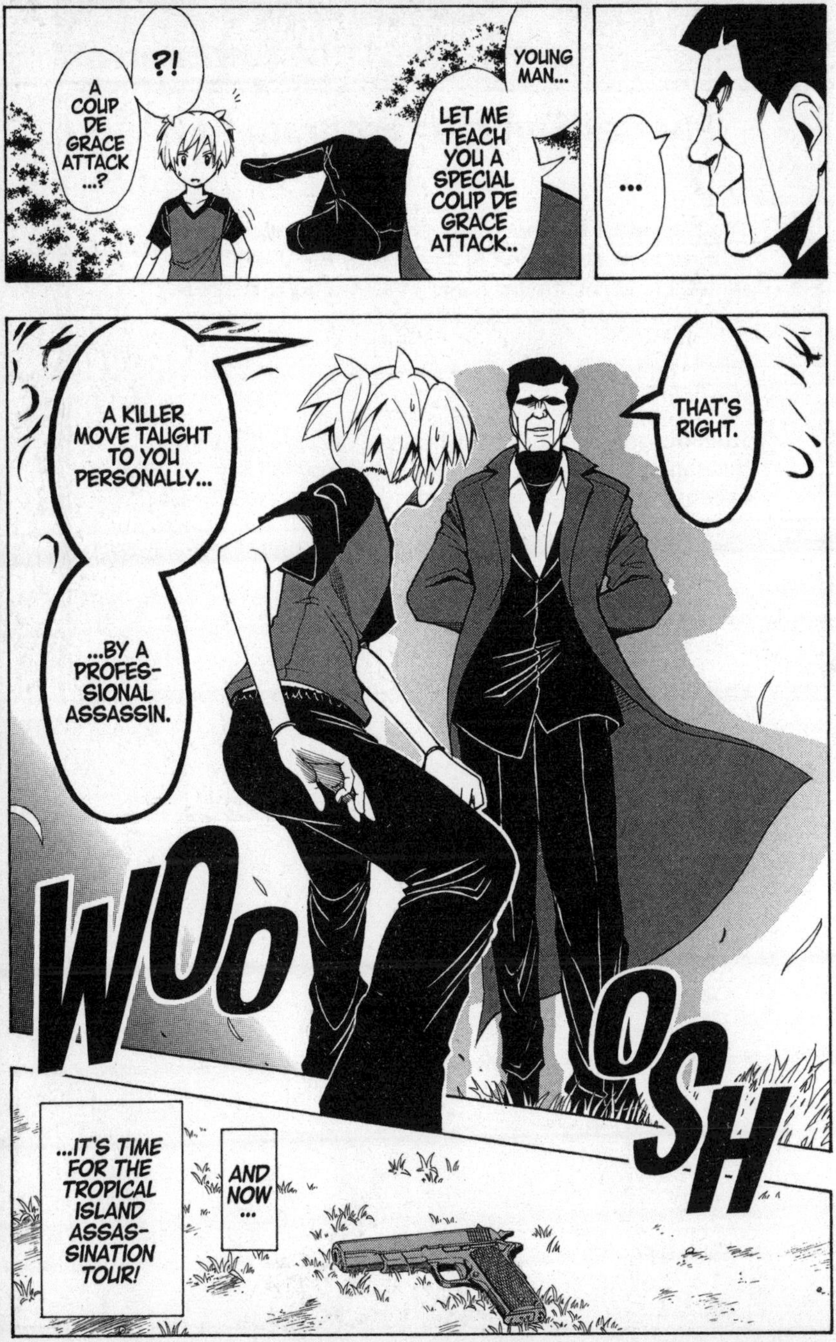
...
YOUNG MAN...
LET ME TEACH YOU A SPECIAL COUP DE GRACE ATTACK..
?!
A COUP DE GRACE ATTACK ...?
A KILLER MOVE TAUGHT TO YOU PERSONALLY...
...BY A PROFES-SIONAL ASSASSIN.
THAT'S RIGHT.
WOOOSH
AND NOW ...
...IT'S TIME FOR THE TROPICAL ISLAND ASSAS-SINATION TOUR!

Kunugigaoka Junior High Bulletin Board

Special Summer Program FAQ

- The class with the most outstanding academic achievement at the end of the first of the three semesters earns the privilege of attending the three-day, two-night trip to Okinawa to study even more.

- Students are free to learn whatever they want during this summer program. The school will pay for any expenses connected to the hotel services.

- We expect and trust you will choose wisely to make your future an even brighter one.

Kunugigaoka School Mascot Kunudon

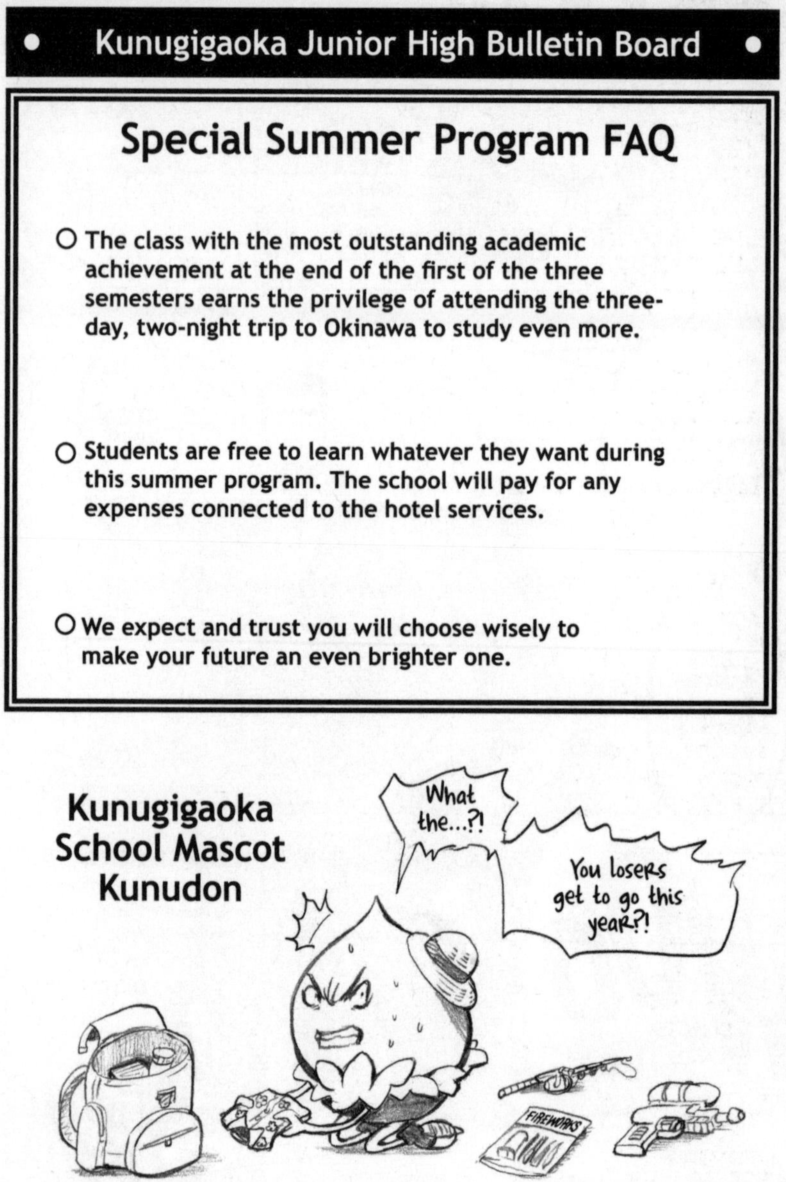
What the...?!
You losers get to go this year?!
FIREWORKS

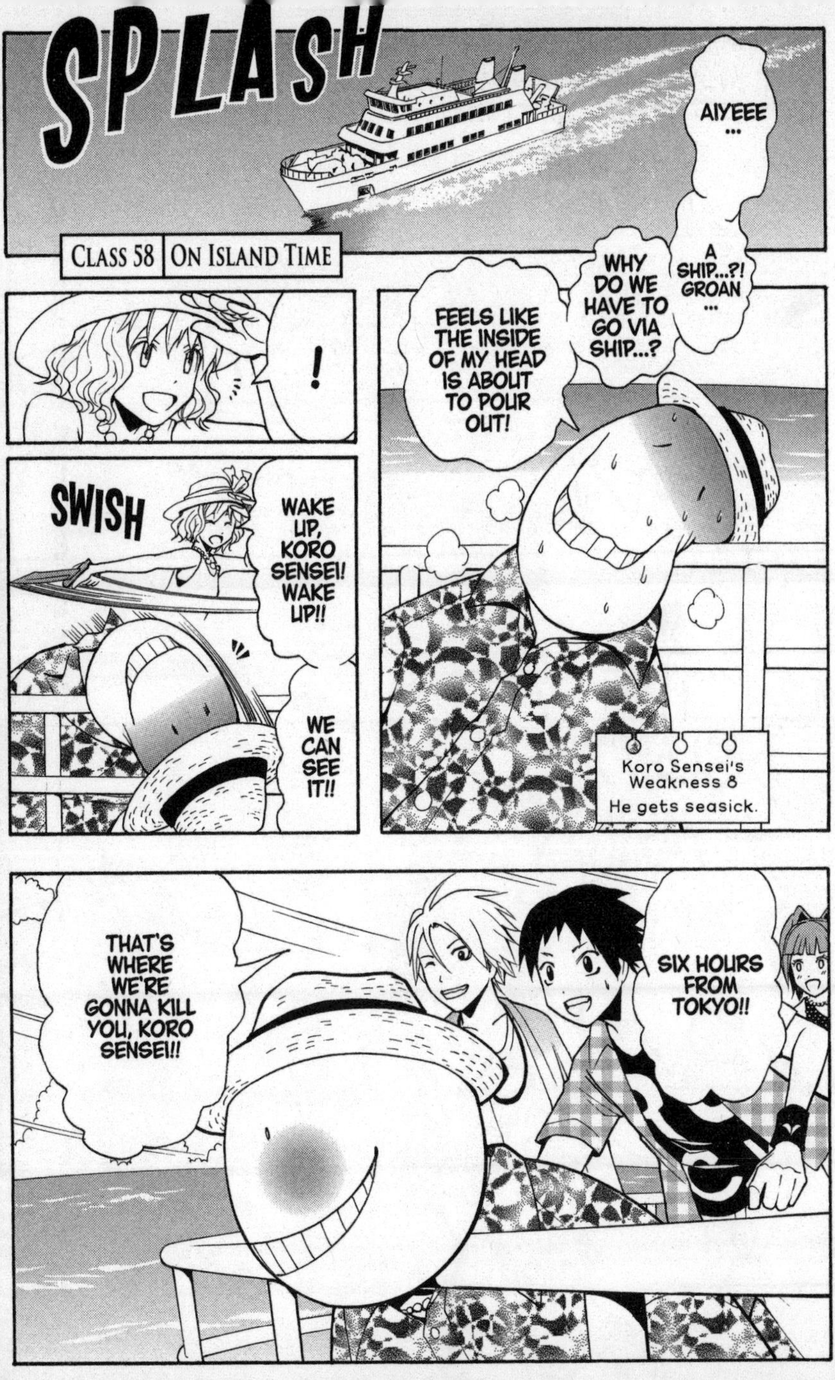
SPLASH
AIYEEE ...
Class 58 On Island Time
A SHIP...?! GROAN ...
WHY DO WE HAVE TO GO VIA SHIP...?
FEELS LIKE THE INSIDE OF MY HEAD IS ABOUT TO POUR OUT!
Koro Sensei's Weakness 8
He gets seasick.
!
SWISH
WAKE UP, KORO SENSEI! WAKE UP!!
WE CAN SEE IT!!
SIX HOURS FROM TOKYO!!
THAT'S WHERE WE'RE GONNA KILL YOU, KORO SENSEI!!

CLASS 58 ON ISLAND TIME

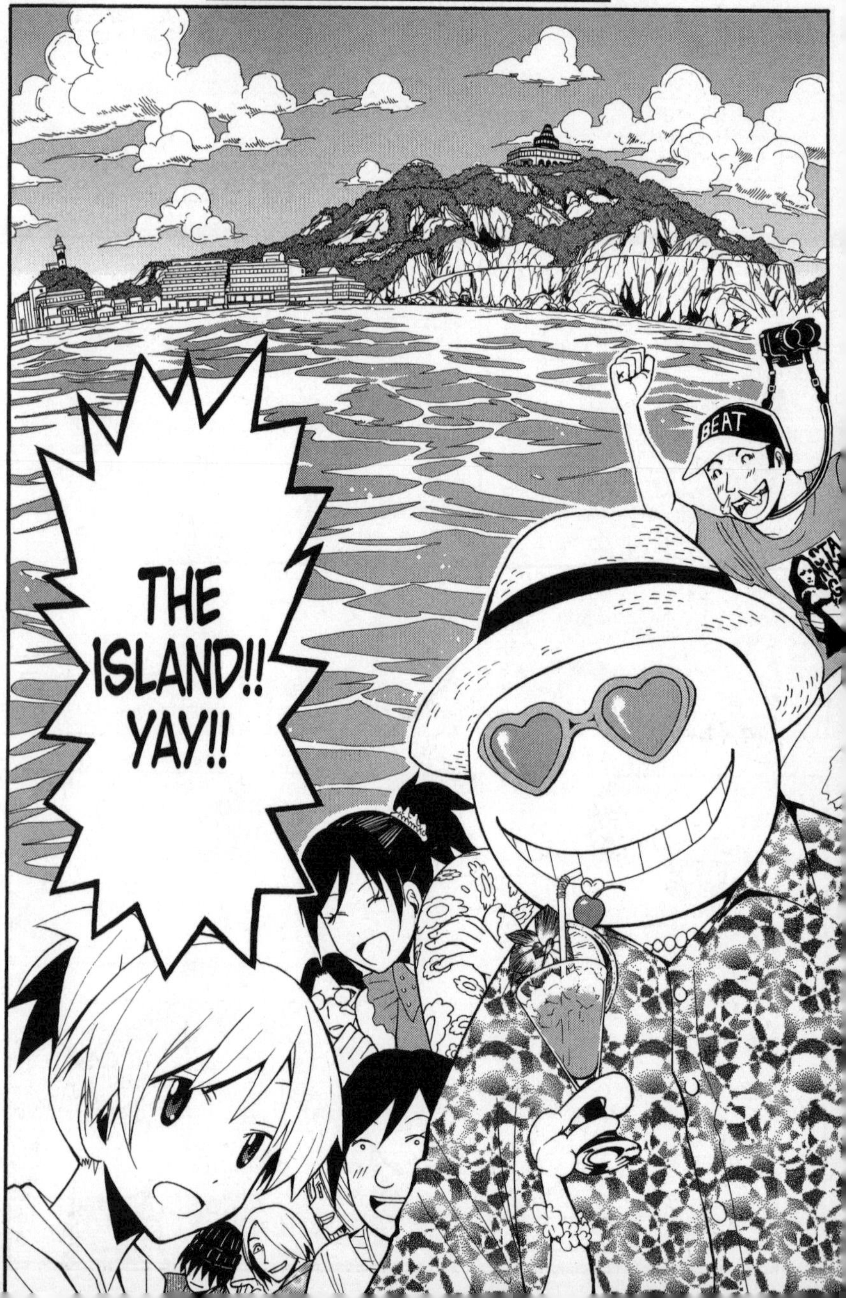
THE ISLAND!! YAY!!
BEAT

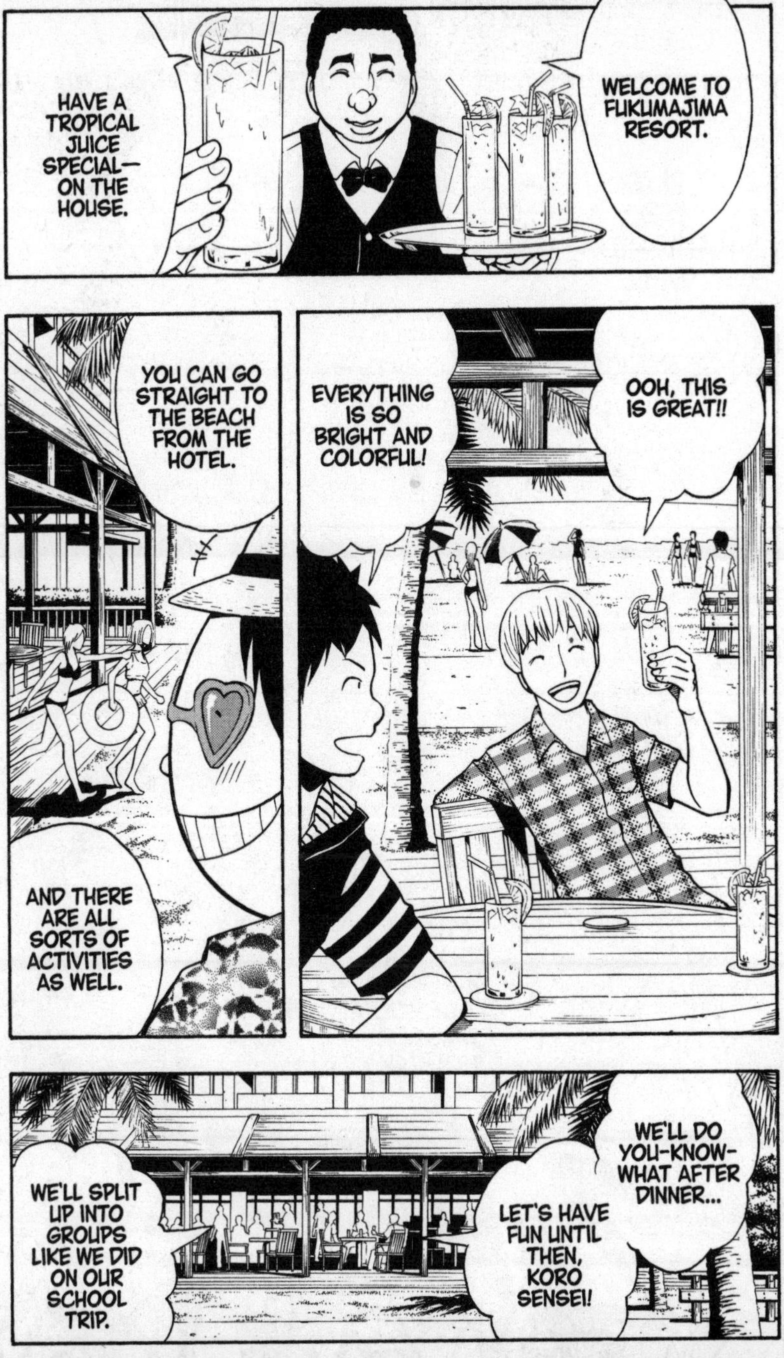
WELCOME TO FUKUMAJIMA RESORT.
HAVE A TROPICAL JUICE SPECIAL—ON THE HOUSE.
OOH, THIS IS GREAT!!
EVERYTHING IS SO BRIGHT AND COLORFUL!
YOU CAN GO STRAIGHT TO THE BEACH FROM THE HOTEL.
AND THERE ARE ALL SORTS OF ACTIVITIES AS WELL.
WE'LL DO YOU-KNOW-WHAT AFTER DINNER...
LET'S HAVE FUN UNTIL THEN, KORO SENSEI!
WE'LL SPLIT UP INTO GROUPS LIKE WE DID ON OUR SCHOOL TRIP.

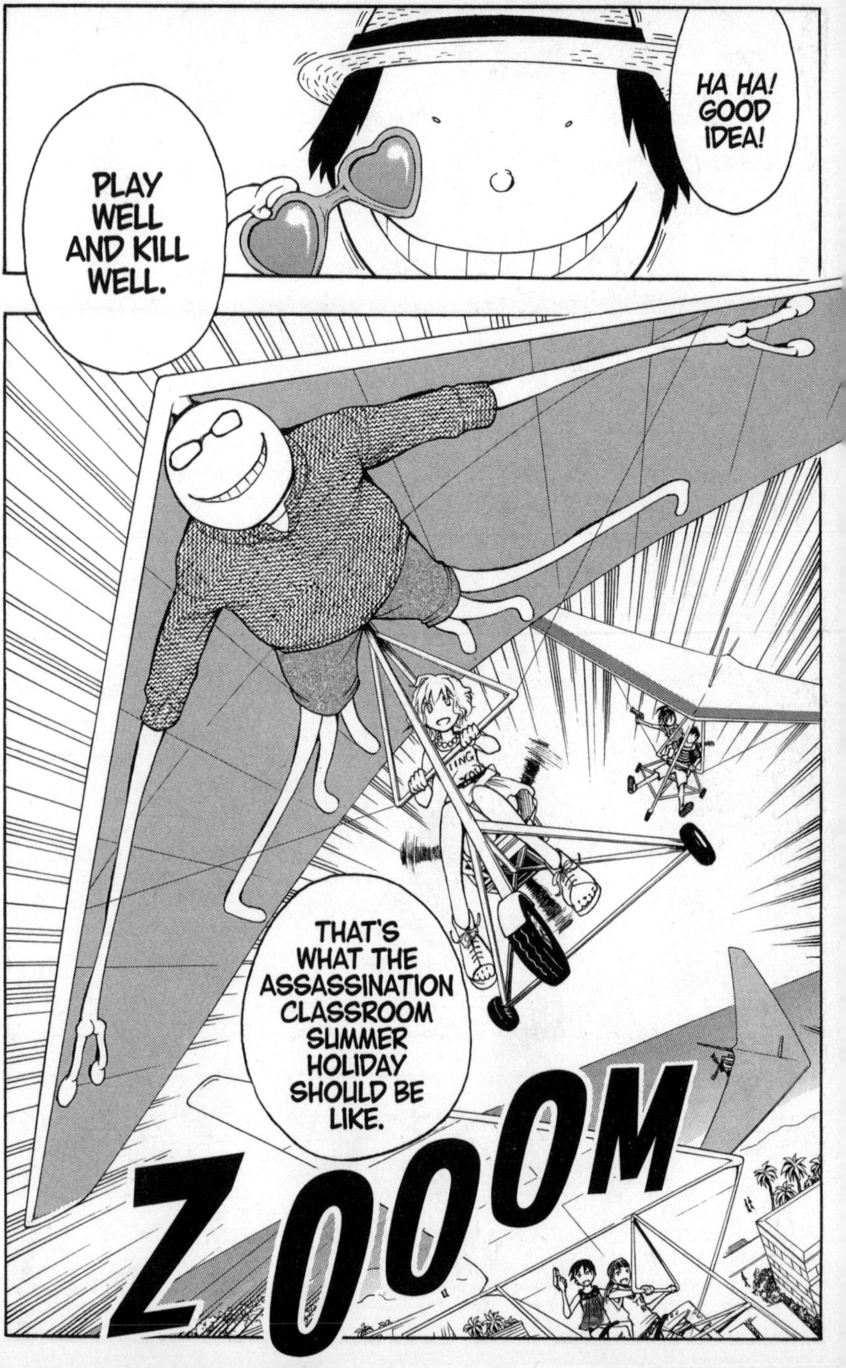
HA HA! GOOD IDEA!
PLAY WELL AND KILL WELL.
THAT'S WHAT THE ASSASSINATION CLASSROOM SUMMER HOLIDAY SHOULD BE LIKE.
ZOOOOM

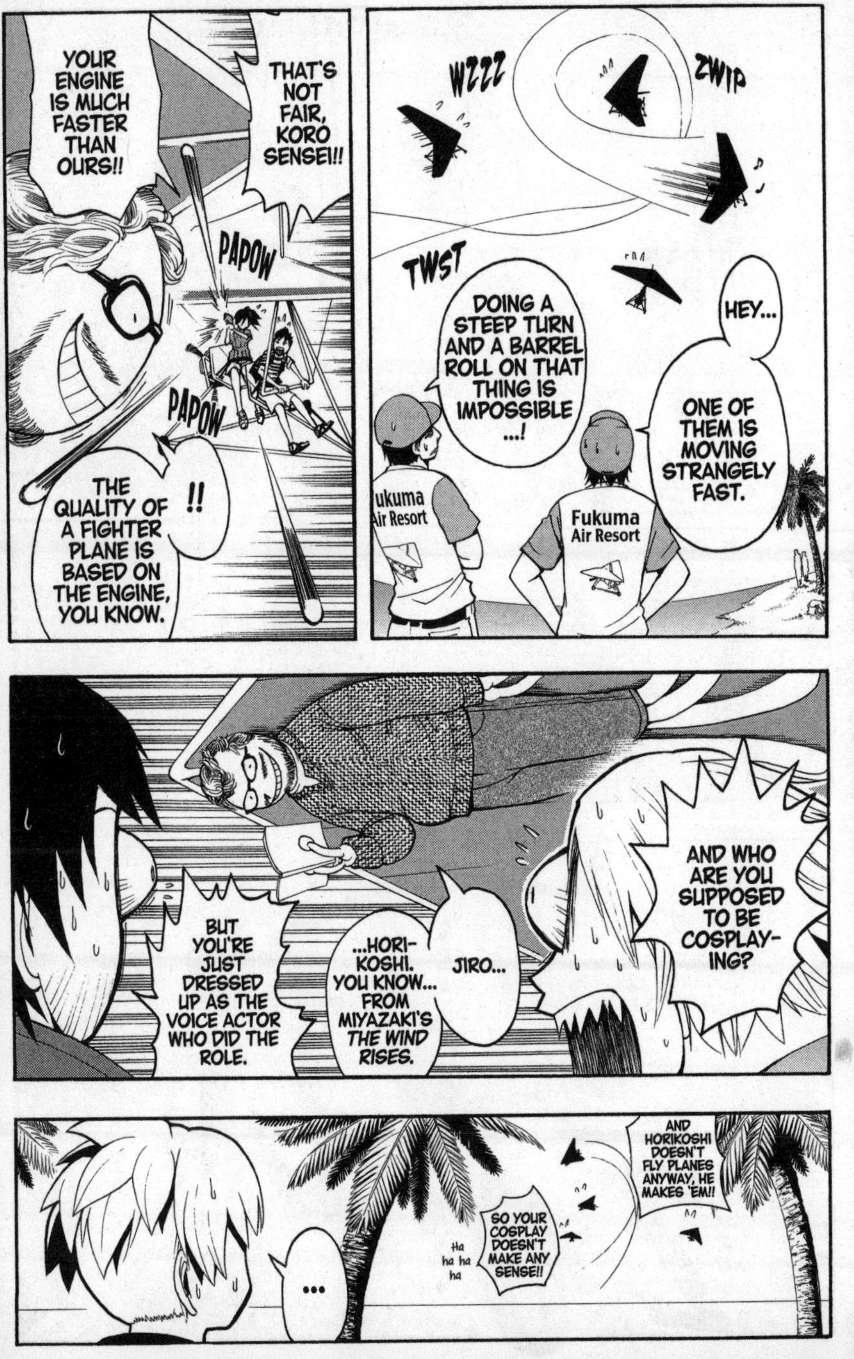
ZWIP
WZZZ
TWST
HEY...
ONE OF THEM IS MOVING STRANGELY FAST.
DOING A STEEP TURN AND A BARREL ROLL ON THAT THING IS IMPOSSIBLE ...!
Fukuma Air Resort
ukuma Air Resort
THAT'S NOT FAIR, KORO SENSEI!!
YOUR ENGINE IS MUCH FASTER THAN OURS!!
PAPOW
PAPOW
!!
THE QUALITY OF A FIGHTER PLANE IS BASED ON THE ENGINE, YOU KNOW.
AND WHO ARE YOU SUPPOSED TO BE COSPLAYING?
JIRO...
...HORI-KOSHI. YOU KNOW... FROM MIYAZAKI'S *THE WIND RISES*.
BUT YOU'RE JUST DRESSED UP AS THE VOICE ACTOR WHO DID THE ROLE.
AND HORIKOSHI DOESN'T FLY PLANES ANYWAY, HE MAKES 'EM!!
SO YOUR COSPLAY DOESN'T MAKE ANY SENSE!!
Ha ha ha ha
...

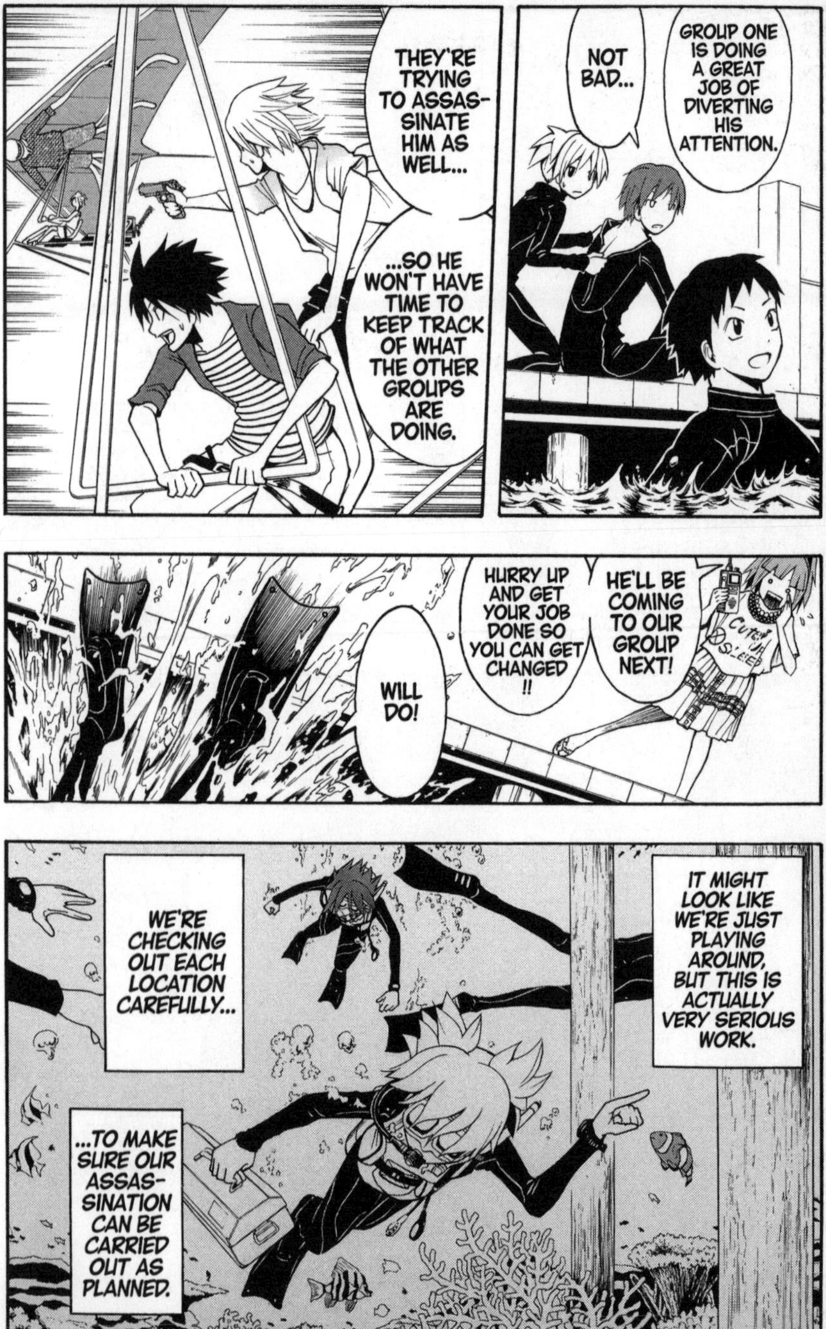
GROUP ONE IS DOING A GREAT JOB OF DIVERTING HIS ATTENTION.
NOT BAD...
THEY'RE TRYING TO ASSAS-SINATE HIM AS WELL...
...SO HE WON'T HAVE TIME TO KEEP TRACK OF WHAT THE OTHER GROUPS ARE DOING.
HE'LL BE COMING TO OUR GROUP NEXT!
HURRY UP AND GET YOUR JOB DONE SO YOU CAN GET CHANGED !!
WILL DO!
IT MIGHT LOOK LIKE WE'RE JUST PLAYING AROUND, BUT THIS IS ACTUALLY VERY SERIOUS WORK.
WE'RE CHECKING OUT EACH LOCATION CAREFULLY...
...TO MAKE SURE OUR ASSAS-SINATION CAN BE CARRIED OUT AS PLANNED.

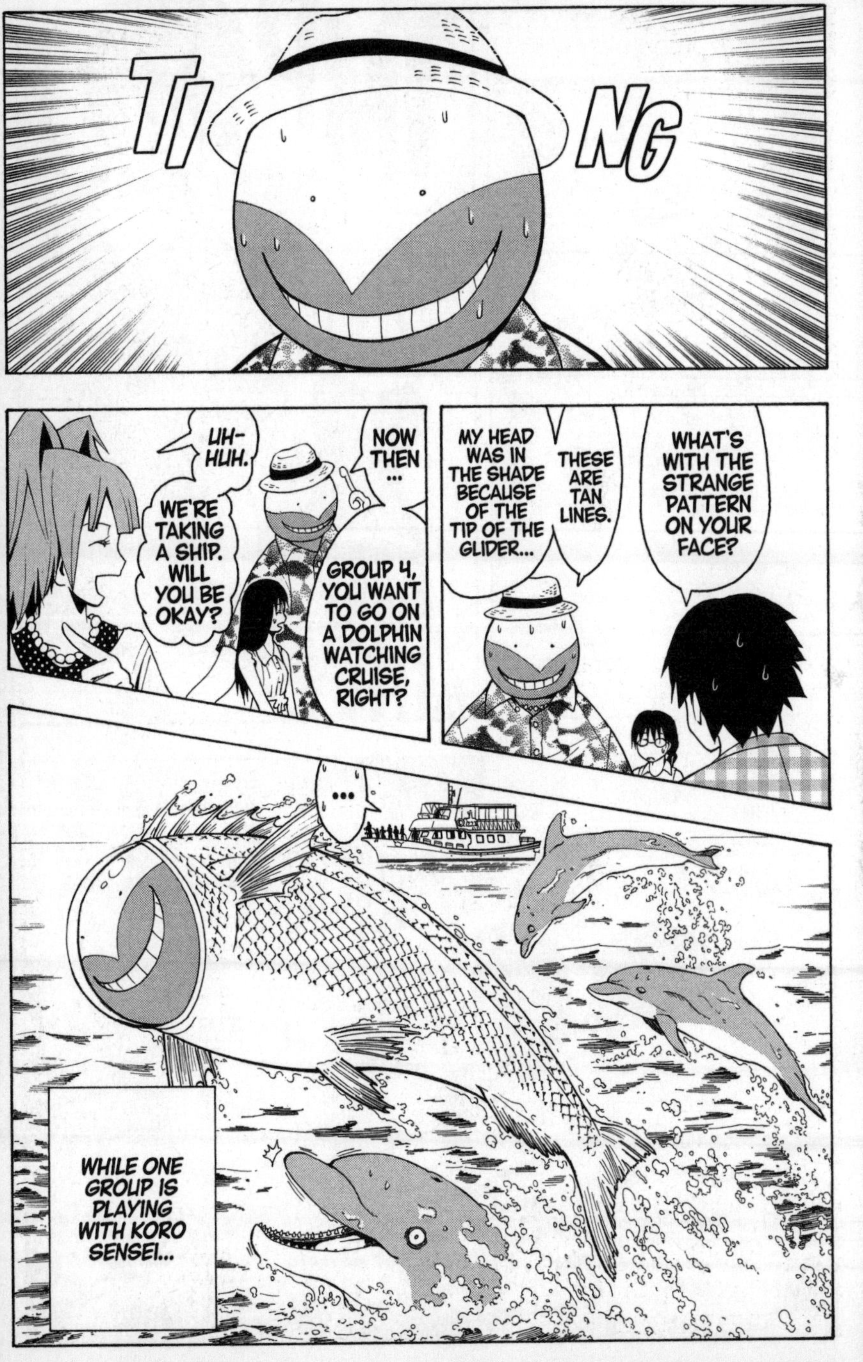
TING
WHAT'S WITH THE STRANGE PATTERN ON YOUR FACE?
THESE ARE TAN LINES.
MY HEAD WAS IN THE SHADE BECAUSE OF THE TIP OF THE GLIDER...
NOW THEN...
GROUP 4, YOU WANT TO GO ON A DOLPHIN WATCHING CRUISE, RIGHT?
UH-HUH.
WE'RE TAKING A SHIP. WILL YOU BE OKAY?
...
WHILE ONE GROUP IS PLAYING WITH KORO SENSEI...

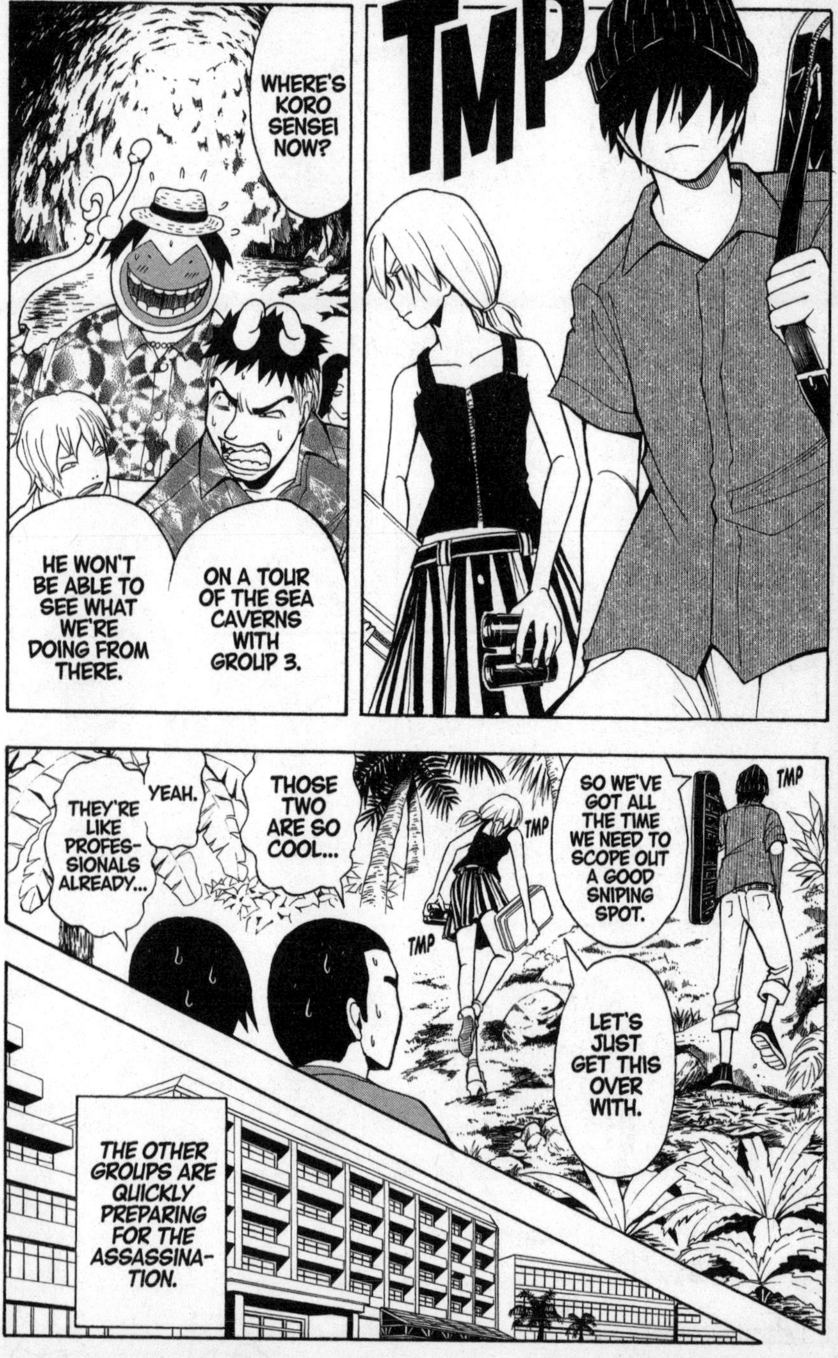
TMP
WHERE'S KORO SENSEI NOW?
ON A TOUR OF THE SEA CAVERNS WITH GROUP 3.
HE WON'T BE ABLE TO SEE WHAT WE'RE DOING FROM THERE.
TMP
SO WE'VE GOT ALL THE TIME WE NEED TO SCOPE OUT A GOOD SNIPING SPOT.
TMP
TMP
LET'S JUST GET THIS OVER WITH.
THOSE TWO ARE SO COOL...
YEAH.
THEY'RE LIKE PROFES-SIONALS ALREADY...
THE OTHER GROUPS ARE QUICKLY PREPARING FOR THE ASSASSINA-TION.

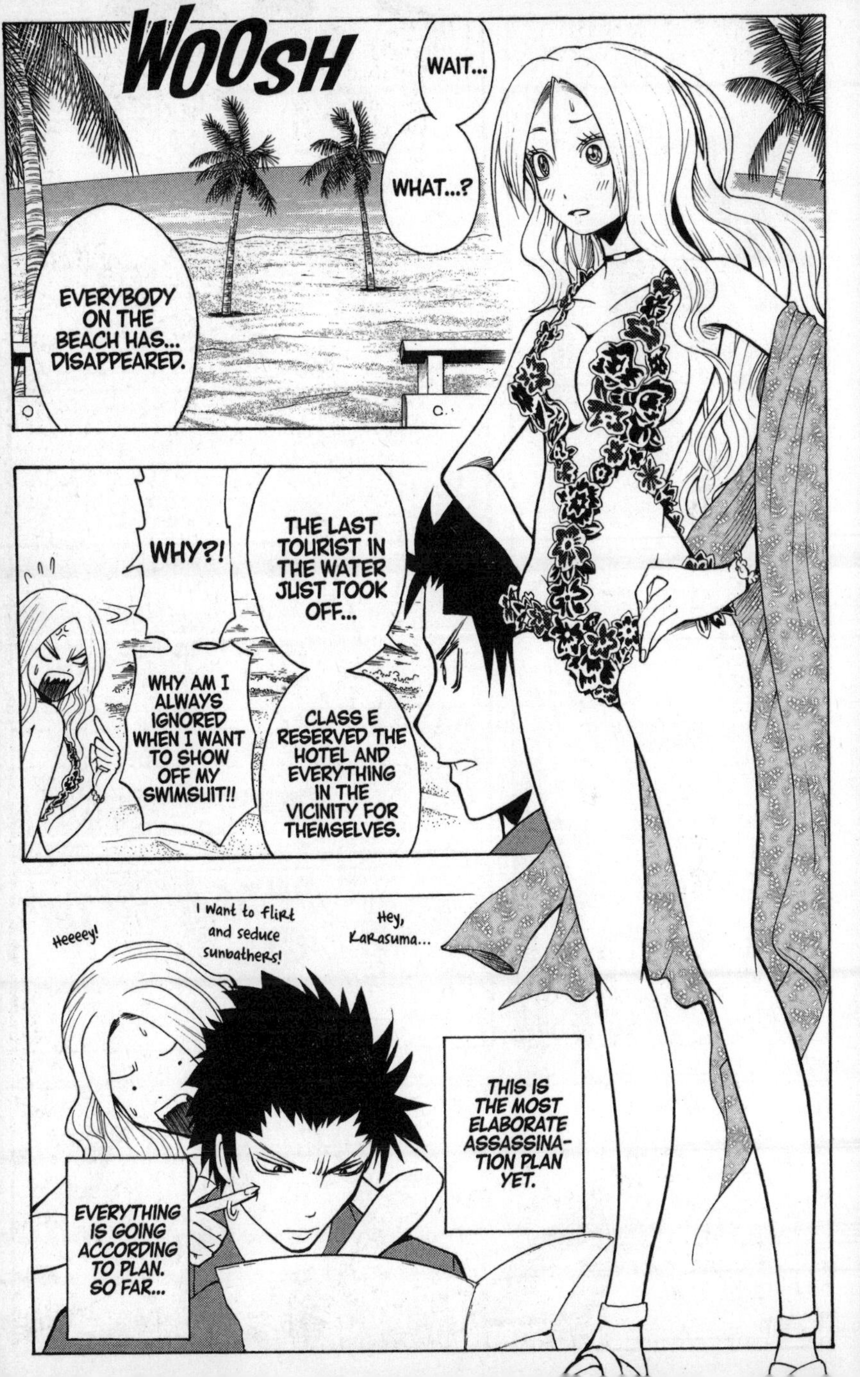
WOOSH
WAIT...
WHAT...?
EVERYBODY ON THE BEACH HAS... DISAPPEARED.
THE LAST TOURIST IN THE WATER JUST TOOK OFF...
CLASS E RESERVED THE HOTEL AND EVERYTHING IN THE VICINITY FOR THEMSELVES.
WHY?!
WHY AM I ALWAYS IGNORED WHEN I WANT TO SHOW OFF MY SWIMSUIT!!
Hey, Karasuma...
I want to flirt and seduce sunbathers!
Heeeey!
THIS IS THE MOST ELABORATE ASSASSINA-TION PLAN YET.
EVERYTHING IS GOING ACCORDING TO PLAN. SO FAR...

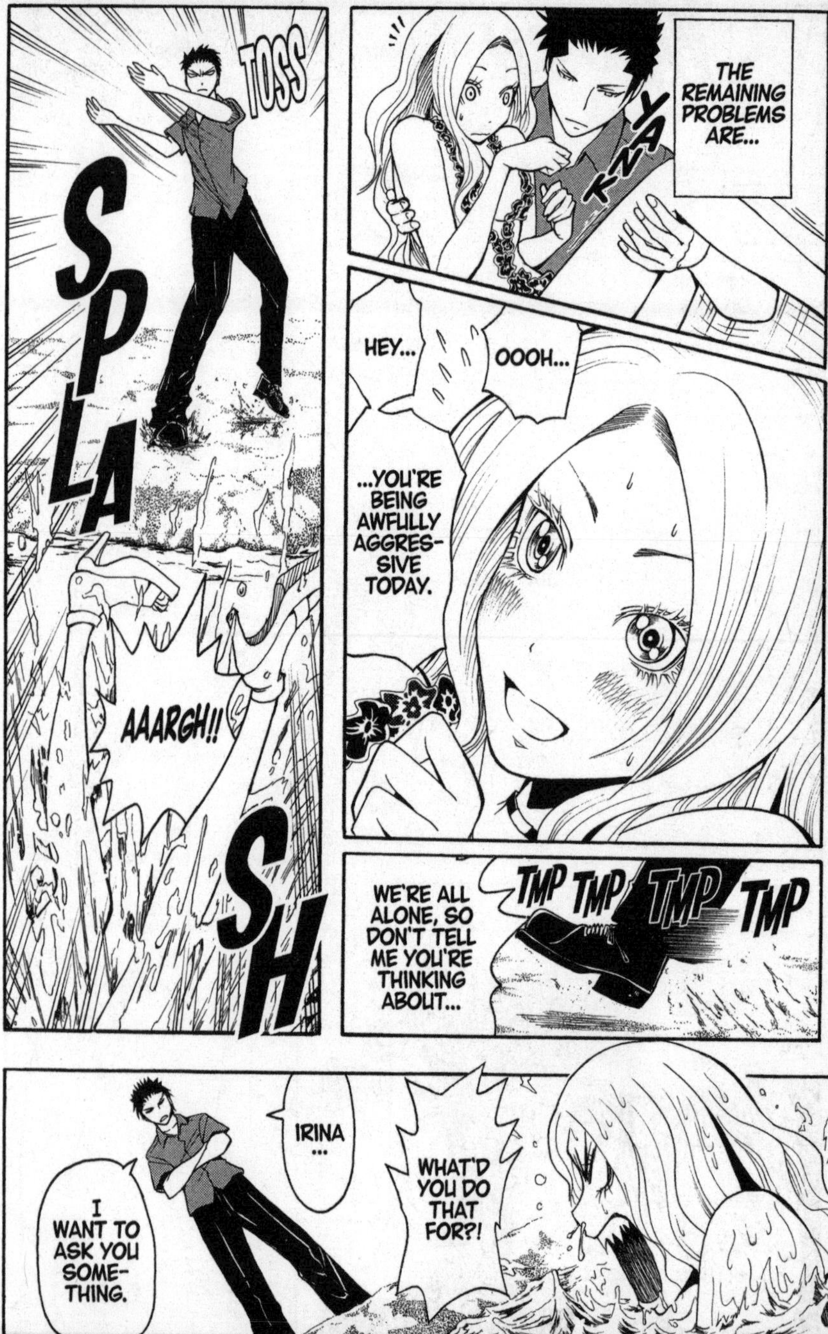
THE REMAINING PROBLEMS ARE...
YANK
OOOH...
HEY...
...YOU'RE BEING AWFULLY AGGRES-SIVE TODAY.
TMP TMP TMP TMP
WE'RE ALL ALONE, SO DON'T TELL ME YOU'RE THINKING ABOUT...
TOSS
SPLASH
AAARGH!!
WHAT'D YOU DO THAT FOR?!
IRINA...
I WANT TO ASK YOU SOME-THING.

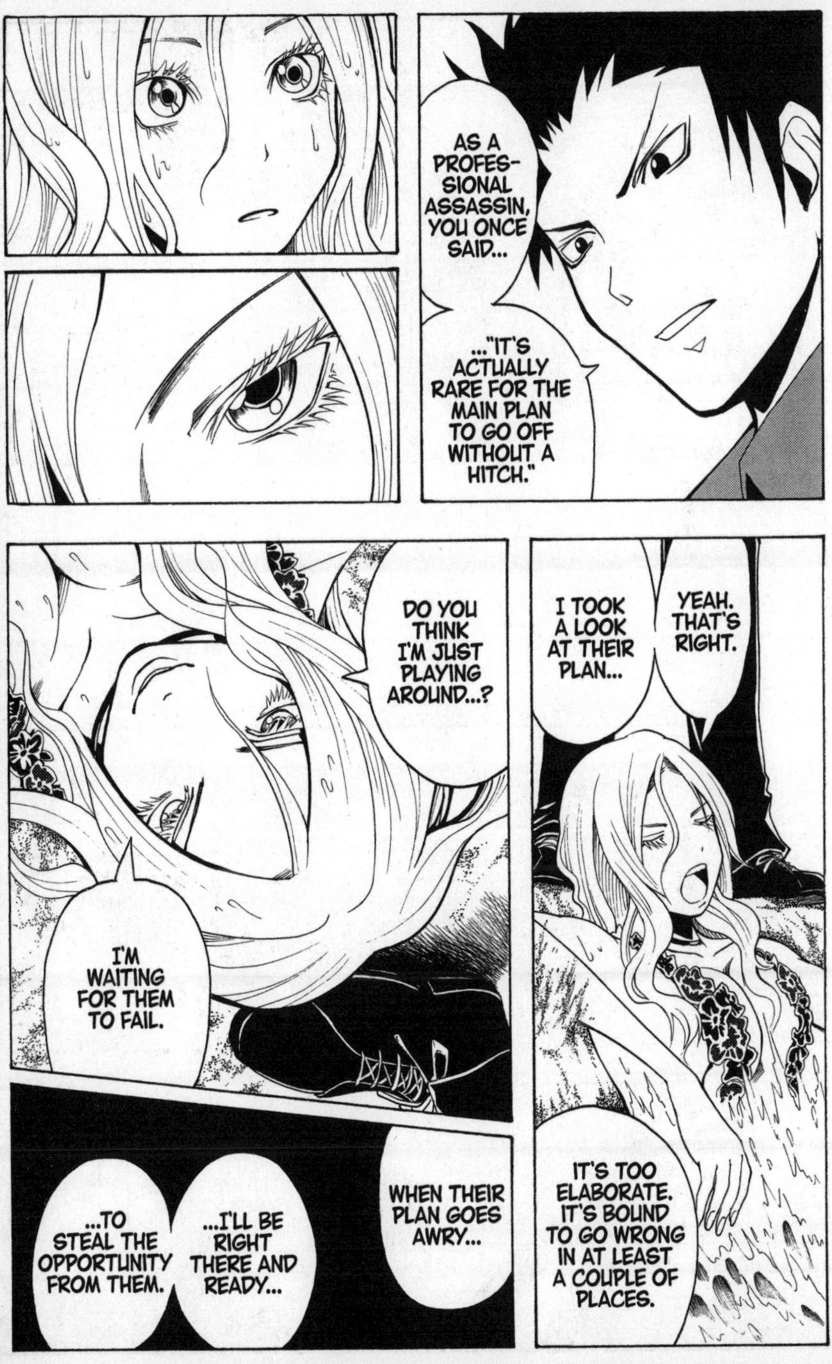
AS A PROFESSIONAL ASSASSIN, YOU ONCE SAID...
..."IT'S ACTUALLY RARE FOR THE MAIN PLAN TO GO OFF WITHOUT A HITCH."
YEAH. THAT'S RIGHT.
I TOOK A LOOK AT THEIR PLAN...
IT'S TOO ELABORATE. IT'S BOUND TO GO WRONG IN AT LEAST A COUPLE OF PLACES.
DO YOU THINK I'M JUST PLAYING AROUND...?
I'M WAITING FOR THEM TO FAIL.
WHEN THEIR PLAN GOES AWRY...
...I'LL BE RIGHT THERE AND READY...
...TO STEAL THE OPPORTUNITY FROM THEM.

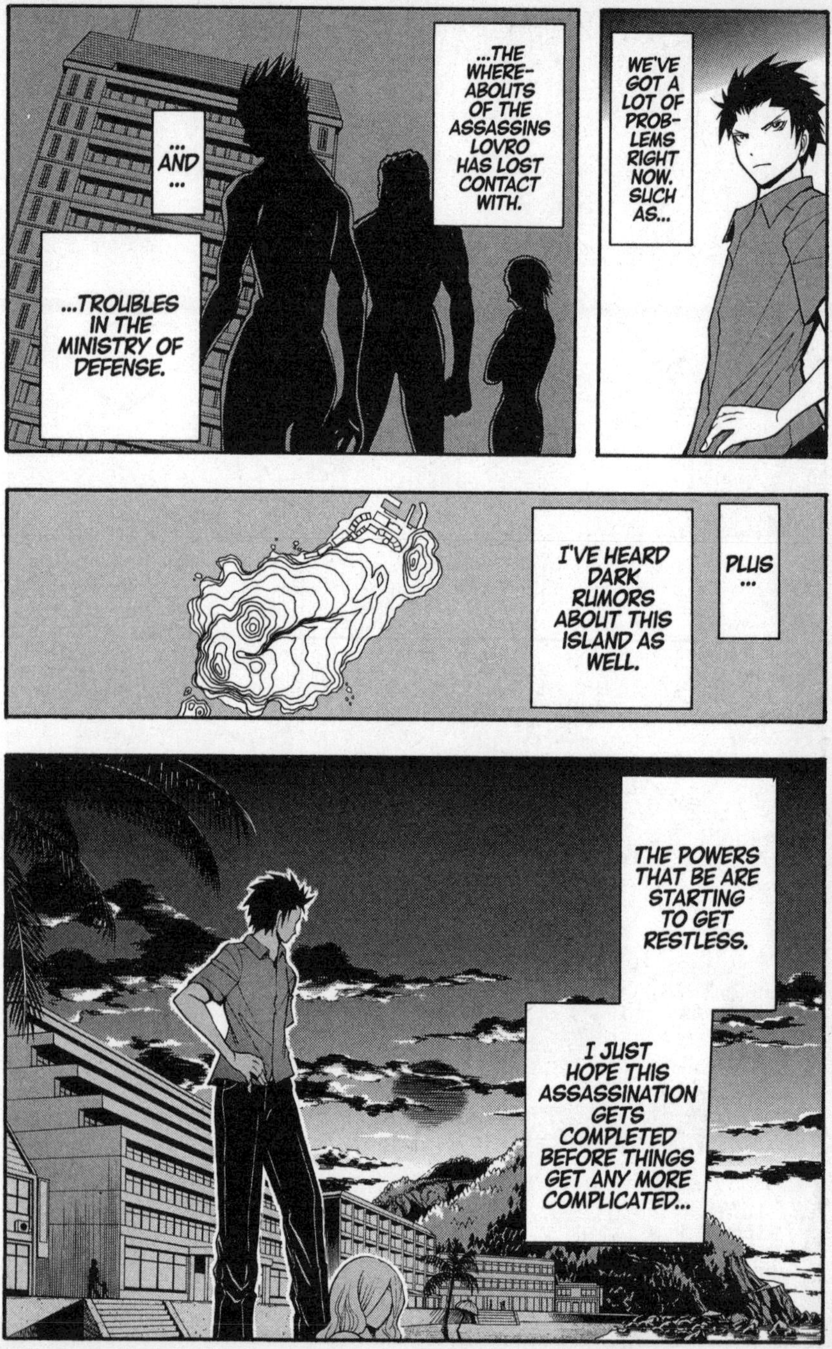
WE'VE GOT A LOT OF PROBLEMS RIGHT NOW. SUCH AS...
...THE WHEREABOUTS OF THE ASSASSINS LOVRO HAS LOST CONTACT WITH.
... AND ...
...TROUBLES IN THE MINISTRY OF DEFENSE.
PLUS ...
I'VE HEARD DARK RUMORS ABOUT THIS ISLAND AS WELL.
THE POWERS THAT BE ARE STARTING TO GET RESTLESS.
I JUST HOPE THIS ASSASSINATION GETS COMPLETED BEFORE THINGS GET ANY MORE COMPLICATED...

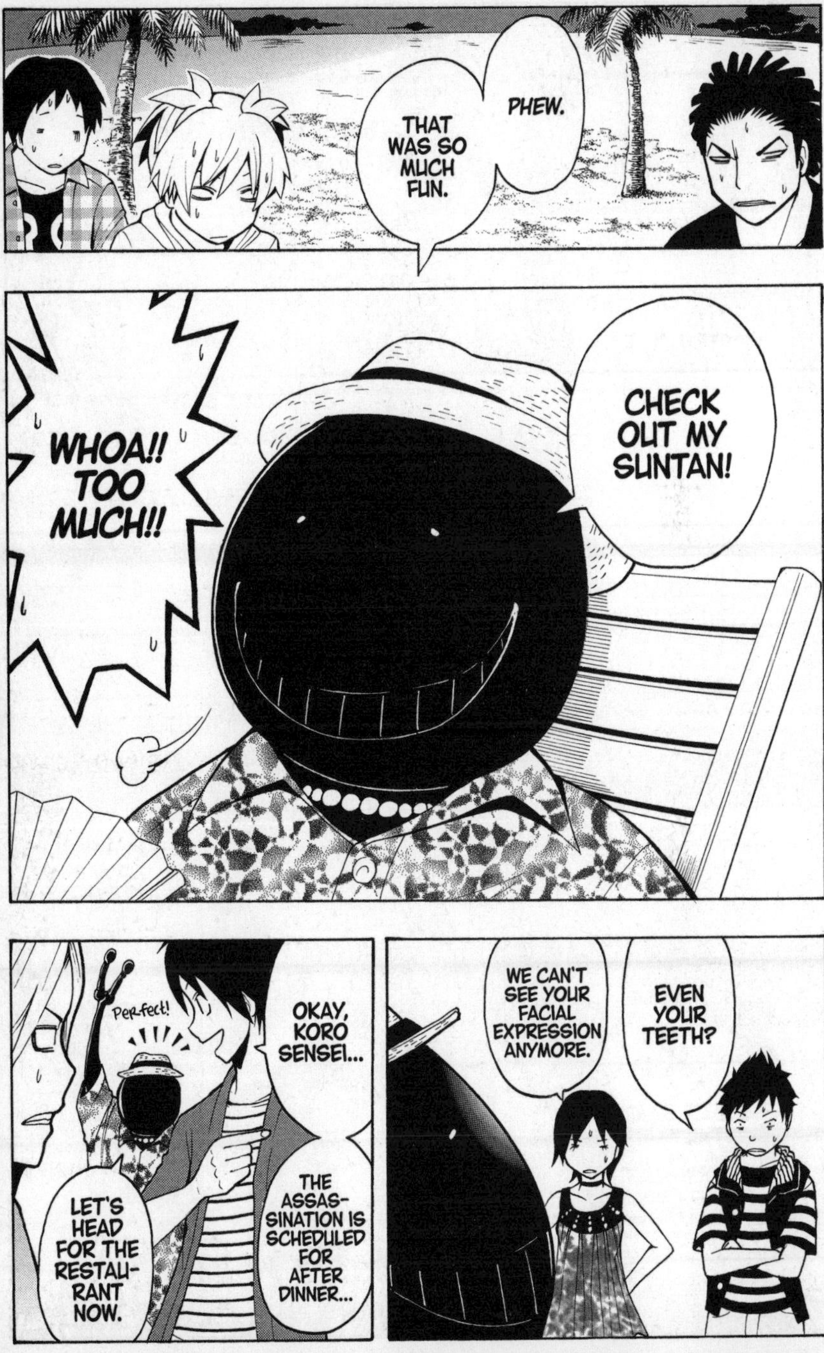
PHEW.
THAT WAS SO MUCH FUN.
CHECK OUT MY SUNTAN!
WHOA!! TOO MUCH!!
EVEN YOUR TEETH?
WE CAN'T SEE YOUR FACIAL EXPRESSION ANYMORE.
OKAY, KORO SENSEI...
Perfect!
THE ASSAS-SINATION IS SCHEDULED FOR AFTER DINNER...
LET'S HEAD FOR THE RESTAU-RANT NOW.

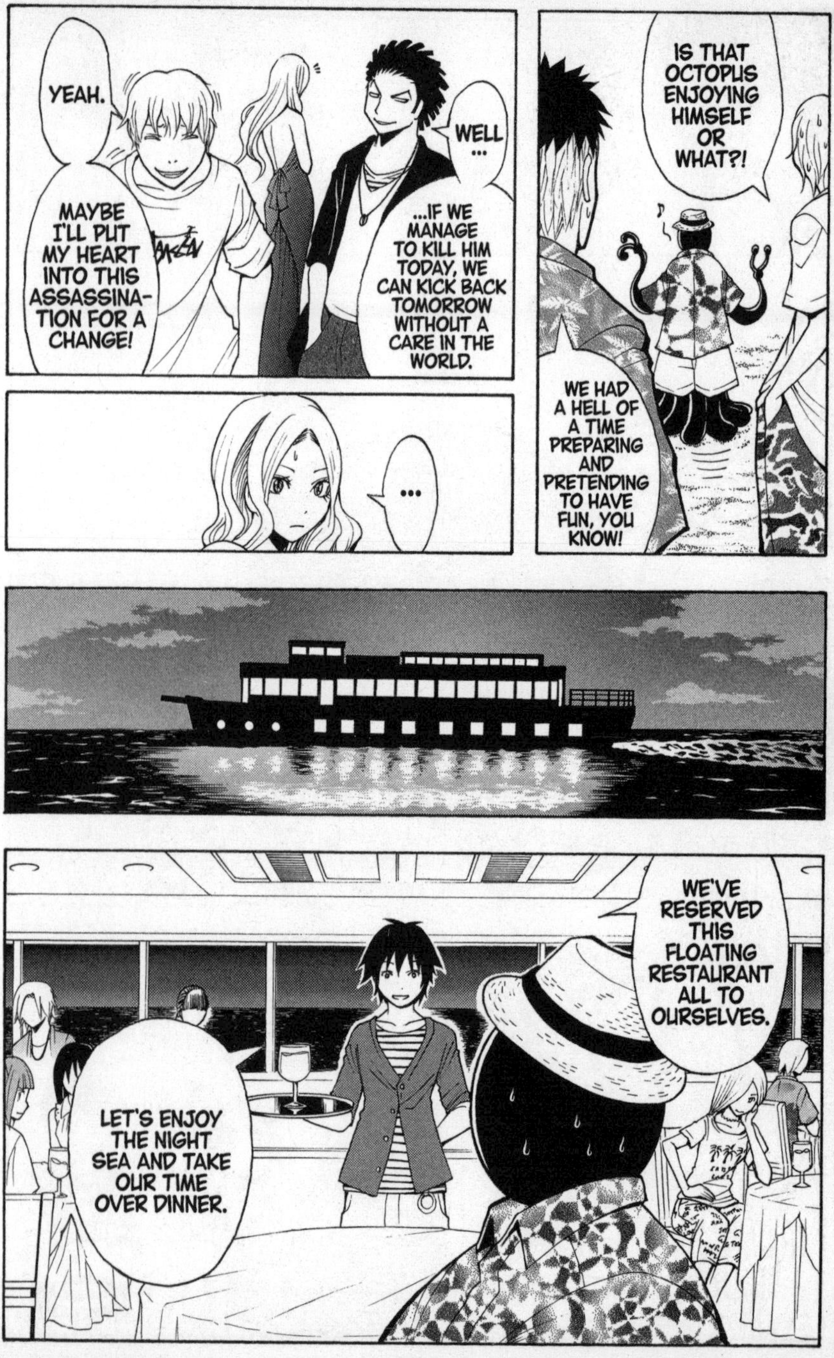
IS THAT OCTOPUS ENJOYING HIMSELF OR WHAT?!
WE HAD A HELL OF A TIME PREPARING AND PRETENDING TO HAVE FUN, YOU KNOW!
WELL ...
...IF WE MANAGE TO KILL HIM TODAY, WE CAN KICK BACK TOMORROW WITHOUT A CARE IN THE WORLD.
YEAH.
MAYBE I'LL PUT MY HEART INTO THIS ASSASSINATION FOR A CHANGE!
...
WE'VE RESERVED THIS FLOATING RESTAURANT ALL TO OURSELVES.
LET'S ENJOY THE NIGHT SEA AND TAKE OUR TIME OVER DINNER.

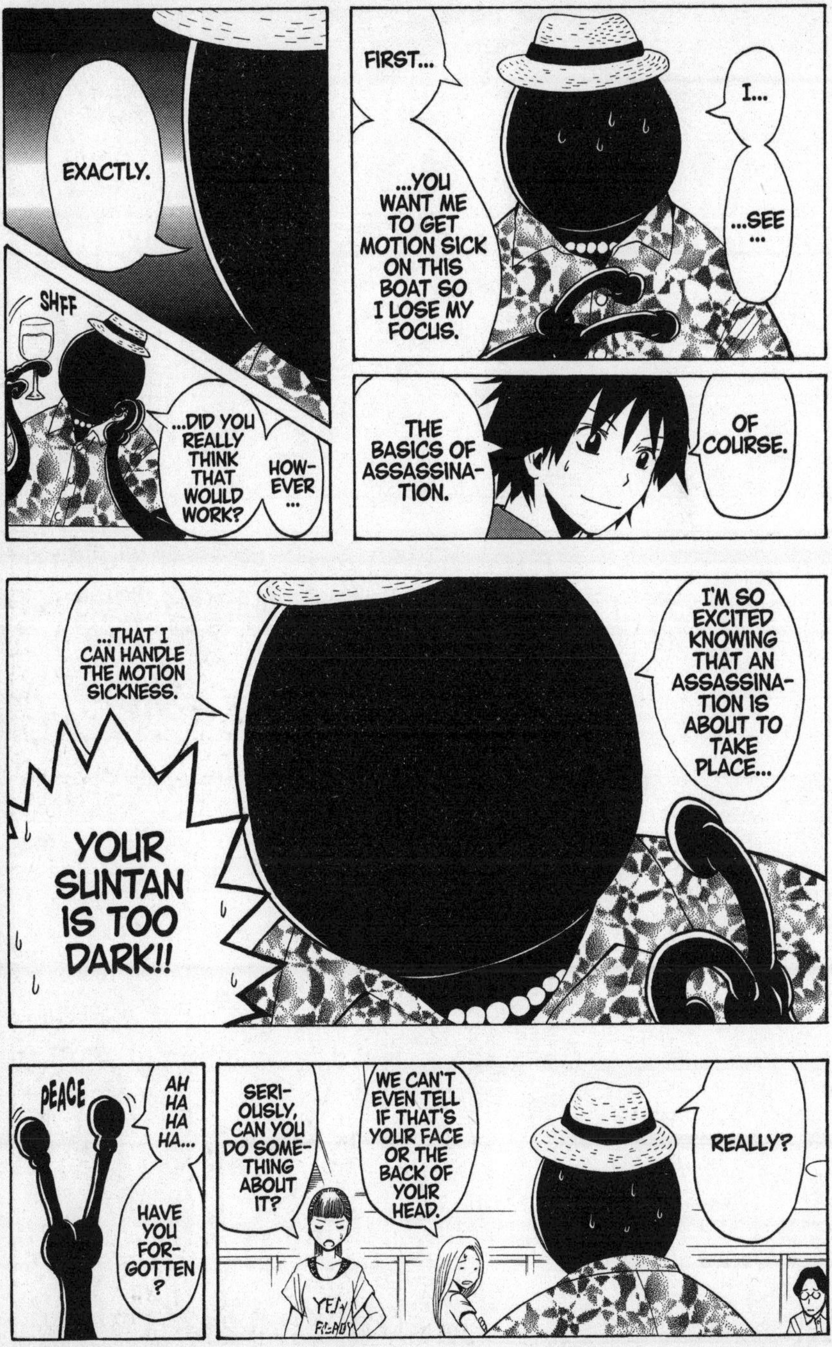
I...
...SEE...
FIRST...
...YOU WANT ME TO GET MOTION SICK ON THIS BOAT SO I LOSE MY FOCUS.
OF COURSE.
THE BASICS OF ASSASSINA-TION.
EXACTLY.
SHFF
HOW-EVER...
...DID YOU REALLY THINK THAT WOULD WORK?
I'M SO EXCITED KNOWING THAT AN ASSASSINA-TION IS ABOUT TO TAKE PLACE...
...THAT I CAN HANDLE THE MOTION SICKNESS.
YOUR SUNTAN IS TOO DARK!!
REALLY?
WE CAN'T EVEN TELL IF THAT'S YOUR FACE OR THE BACK OF YOUR HEAD.
SERI-OUSLY, CAN YOU DO SOME-THING ABOUT IT?
AH HA HA HA...
HAVE YOU FOR-GOTTEN?
PEACE

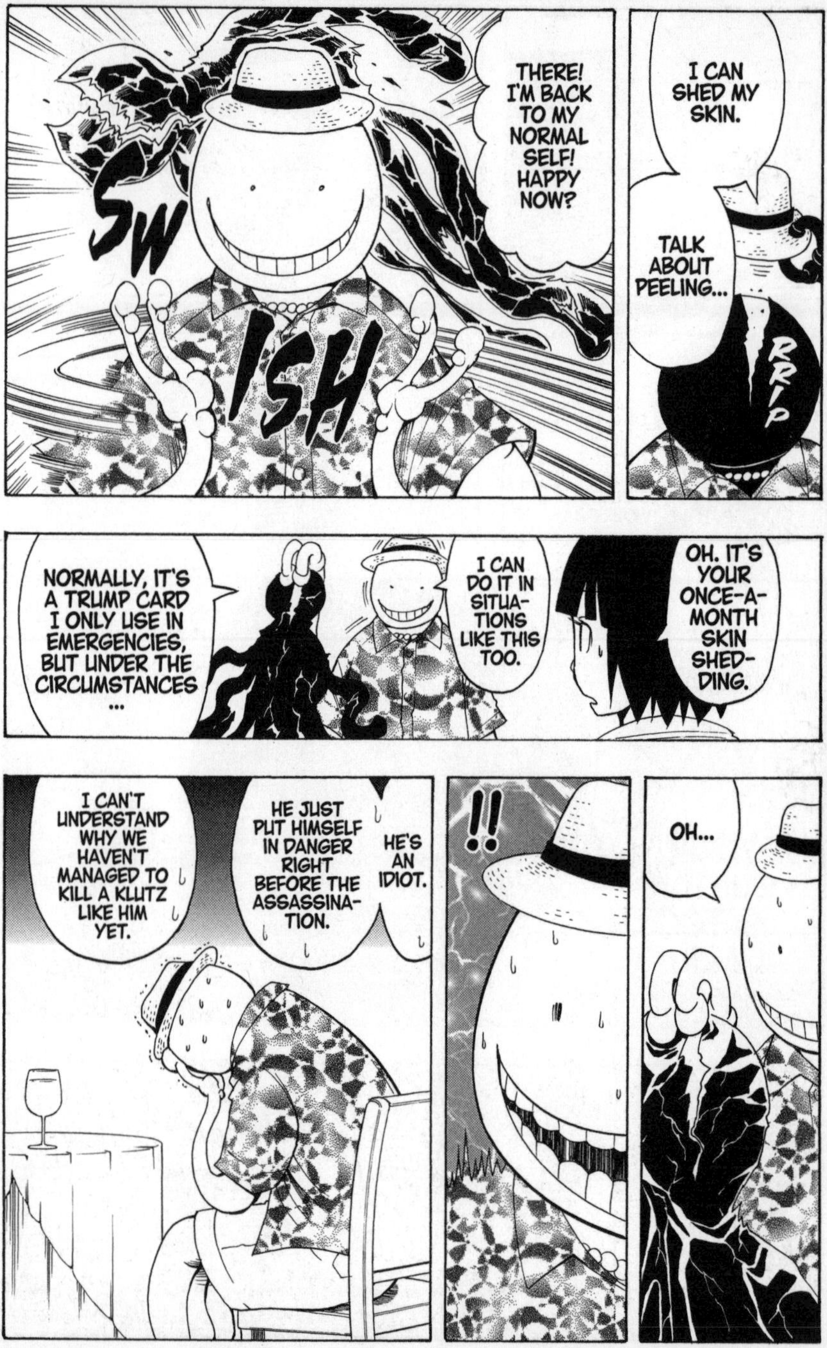
I CAN SHED MY SKIN.
TALK ABOUT PEELING...
RRIP
SWISH
THERE! I'M BACK TO MY NORMAL SELF! HAPPY NOW?
OH. IT'S YOUR ONCE-A-MONTH SKIN SHED-DING.
I CAN DO IT IN SITUA-TIONS LIKE THIS TOO.
NORMALLY, IT'S A TRUMP CARD I ONLY USE IN EMERGENCIES, BUT UNDER THE CIRCUMSTANCES ...
OH...
!!
HE'S AN IDIOT.
HE JUST PUT HIMSELF IN DANGER RIGHT BEFORE THE ASSASSINA-TION.
I CAN'T UNDERSTAND WHY WE HAVEN'T MANAGED TO KILL A KLUTZ LIKE HIM YET.

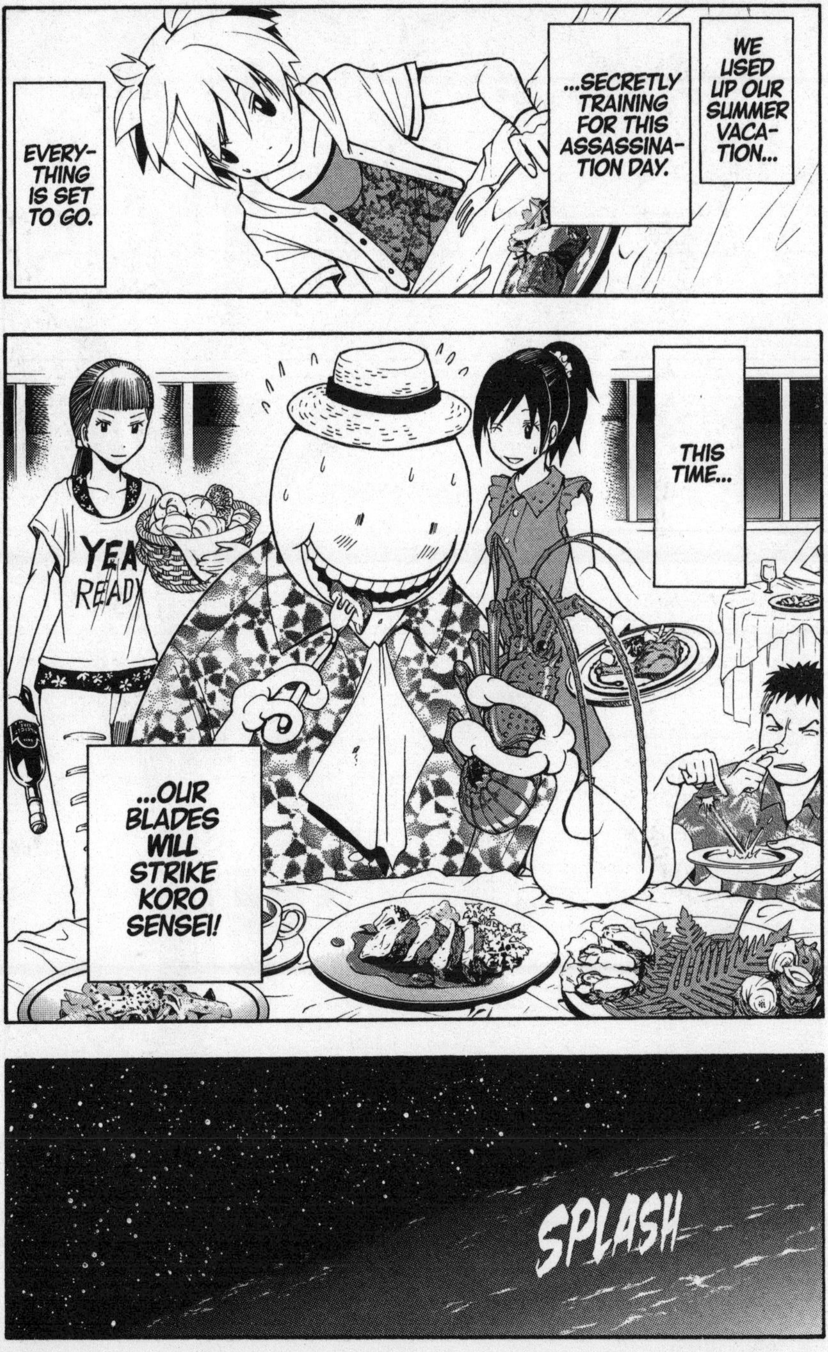
WE USED UP OUR SUMMER VACATION...
...SECRETLY TRAINING FOR THIS ASSASSINATION DAY.
EVERYTHING IS SET TO GO.
THIS TIME...
YEA READY
...OUR BLADES WILL STRIKE KORO SENSEI!
SPLASH

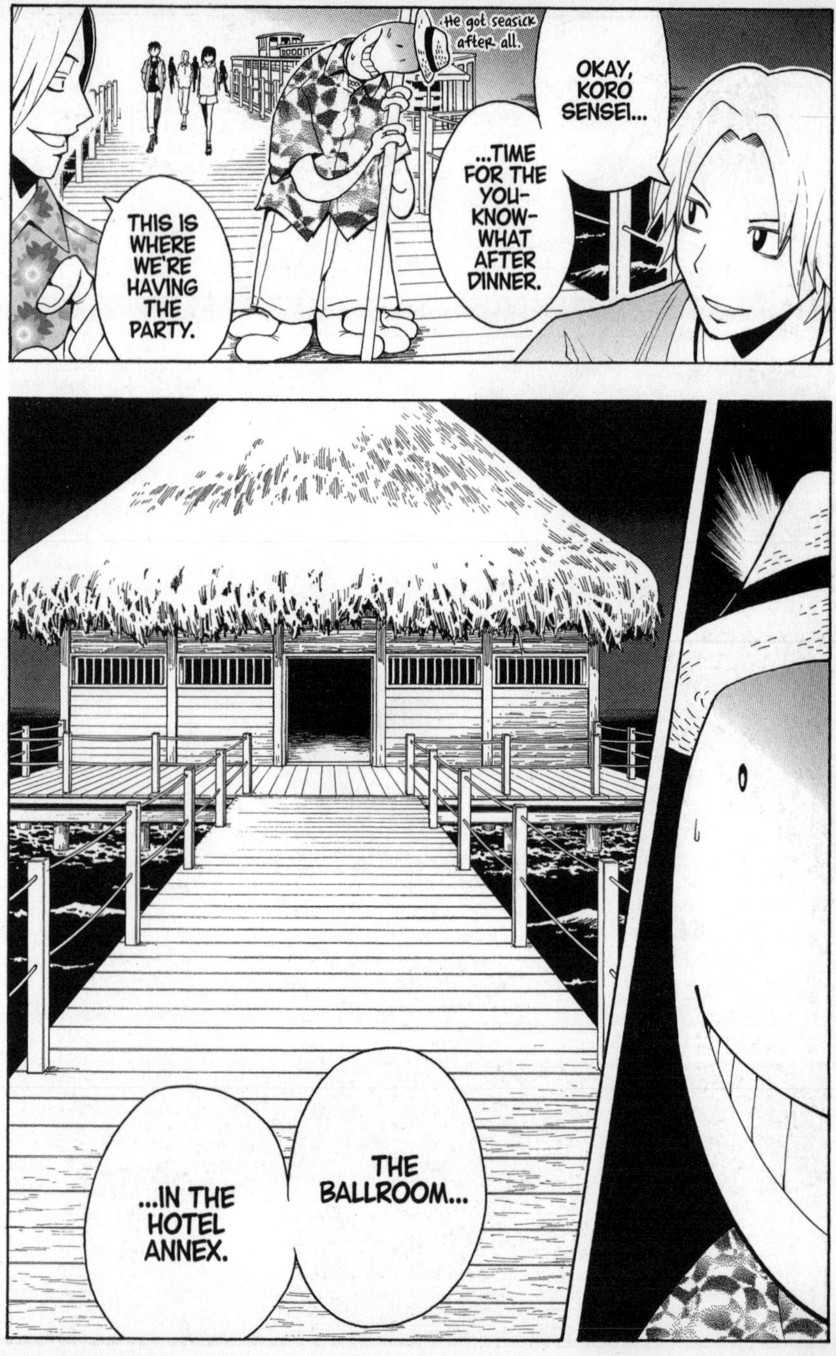
OKAY, KORO SENSEI...
...TIME FOR THE YOU-KNOW-WHAT AFTER DINNER.
He got seasick after all.
THIS IS WHERE WE'RE HAVING THE PARTY.
THE BALLROOM...
...IN THE HOTEL ANNEX.

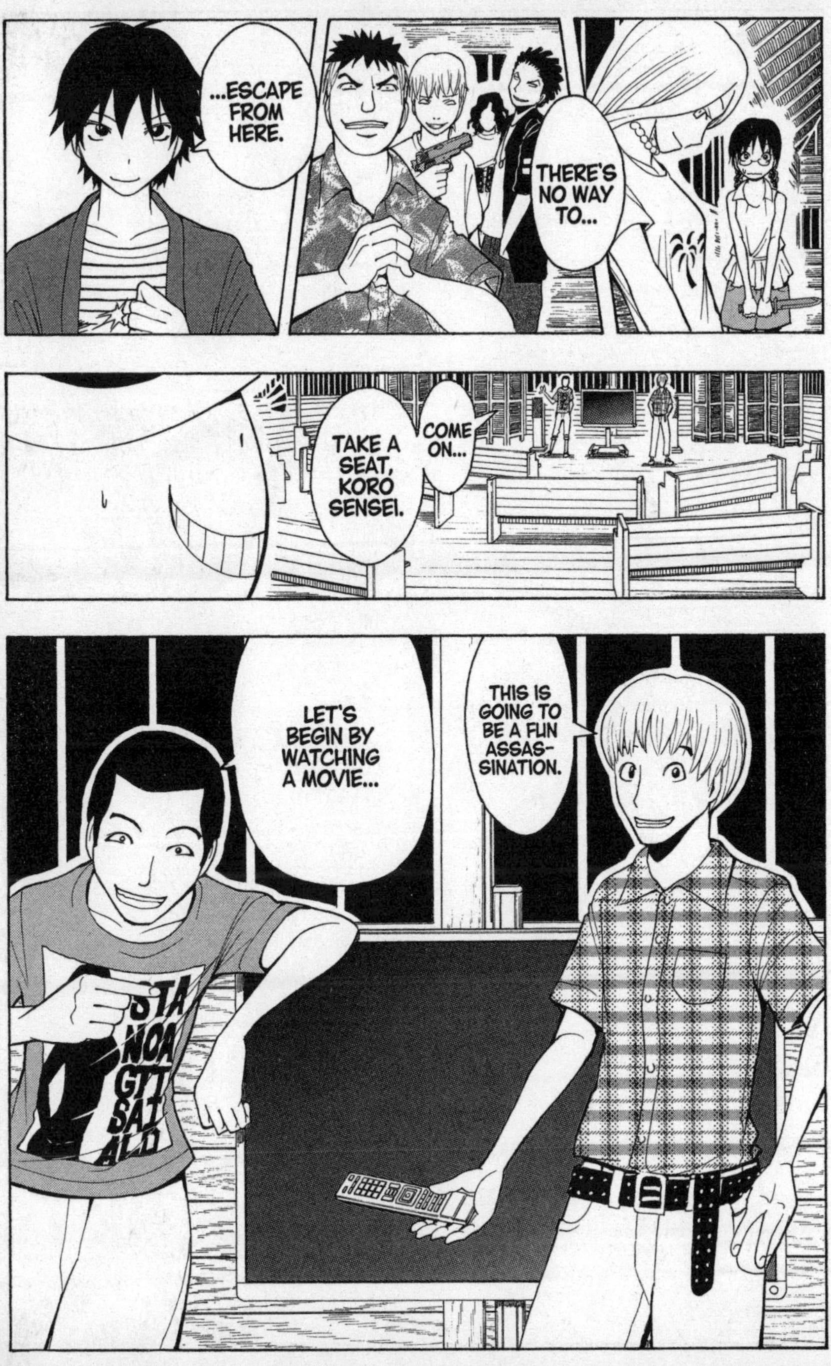
THERE'S NO WAY TO...
...ESCAPE FROM HERE.
COME ON...
TAKE A SEAT, KORO SENSEI.
THIS IS GOING TO BE A FUN ASSAS-SINATION.
LET'S BEGIN BY WATCHING A MOVIE...

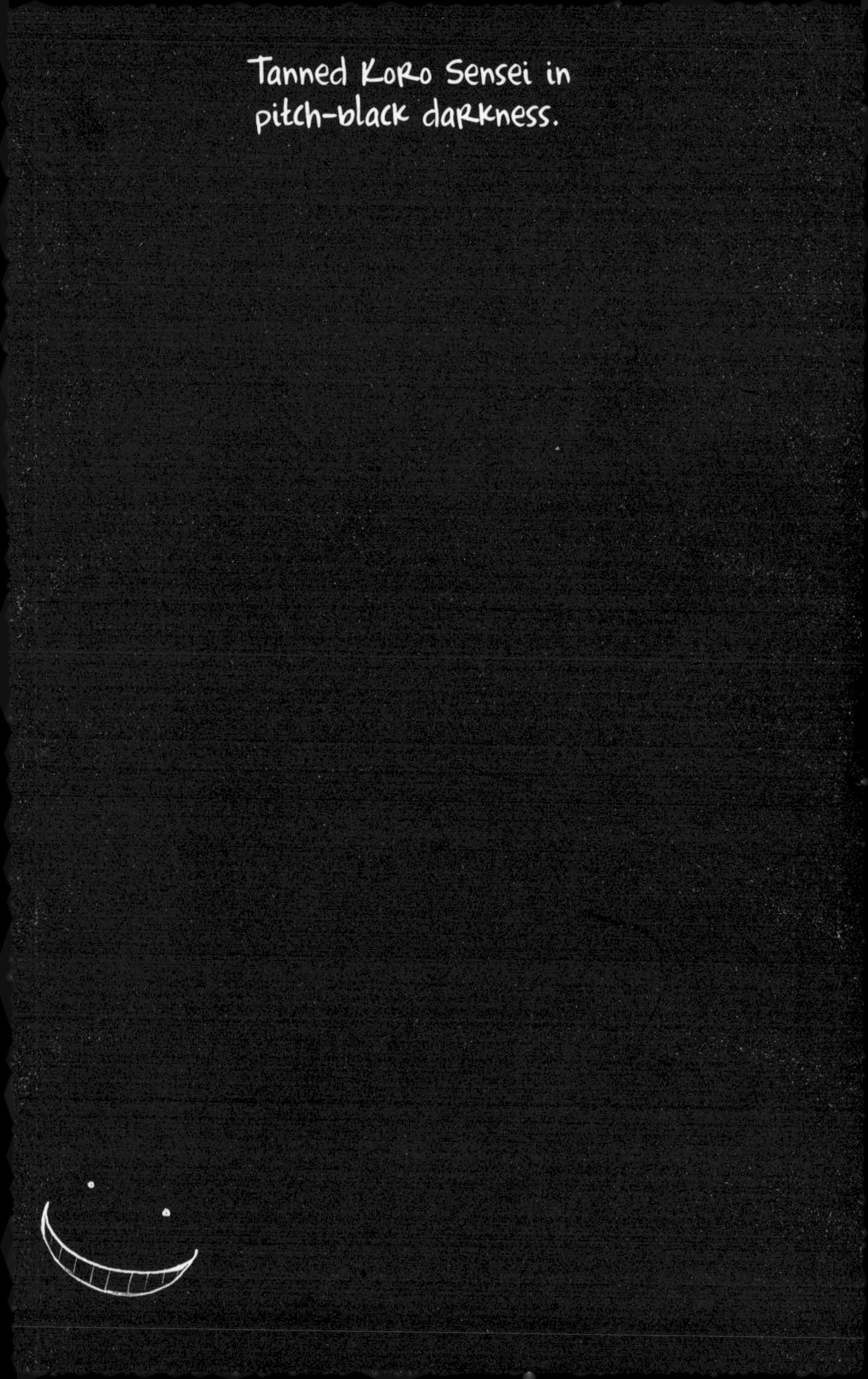
Tanned Koro Sensei in
pitch-black darkness.

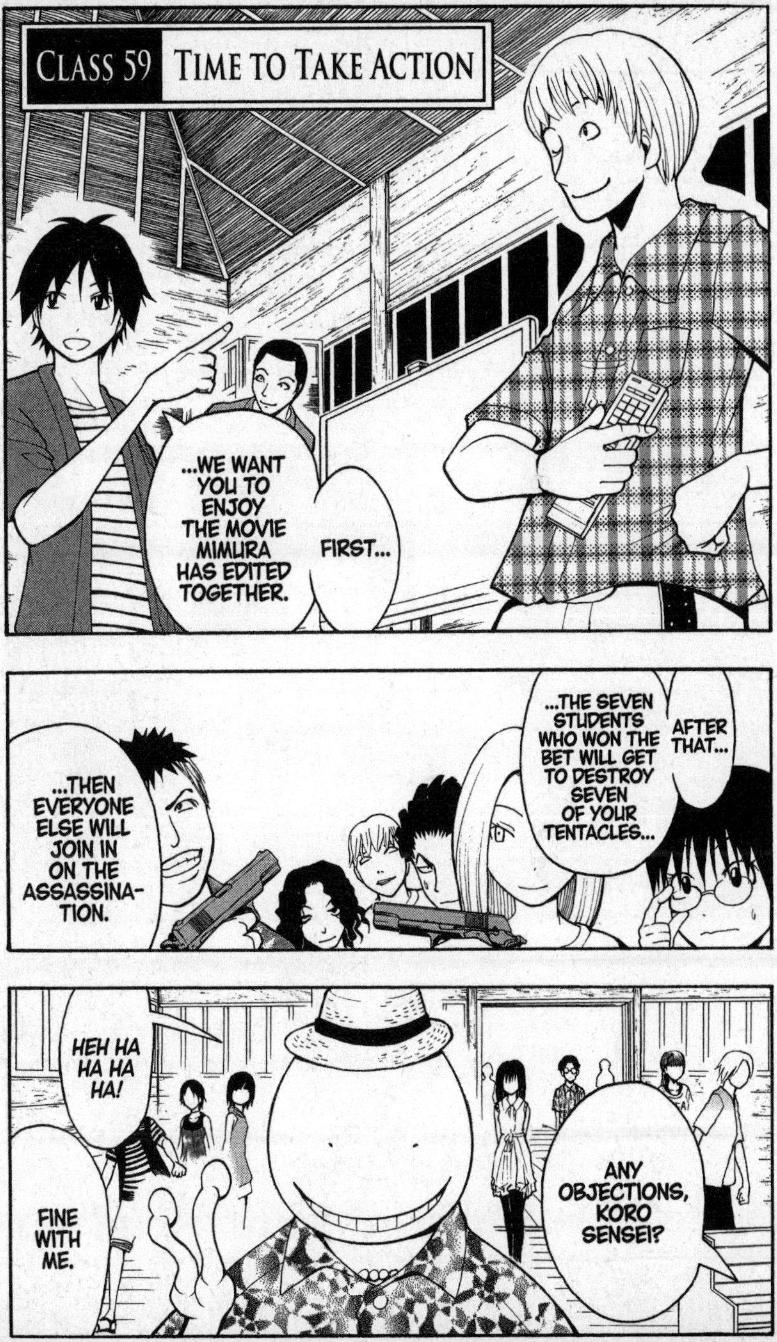
CLASS 59 TIME TO TAKE ACTION
FIRST...
...WE WANT YOU TO ENJOY THE MOVIE MIMURA HAS EDITED TOGETHER.
AFTER THAT...
...THE SEVEN STUDENTS WHO WON THE BET WILL GET TO DESTROY SEVEN OF YOUR TENTACLES...
...THEN EVERYONE ELSE WILL JOIN IN ON THE ASSASSINA-TION.
ANY OBJECTIONS, KORO SENSEI?
HEH HA HA HA HA!
FINE WITH ME.

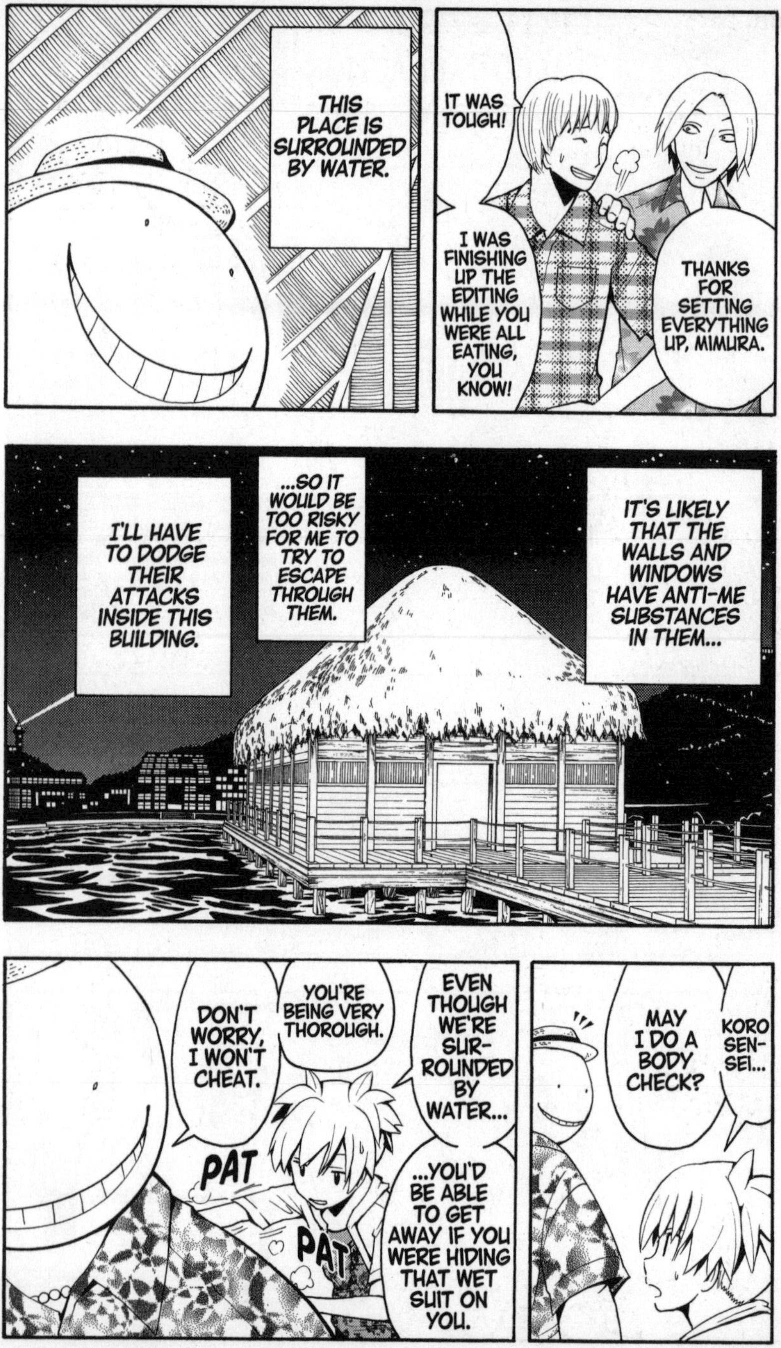
THANKS FOR SETTING EVERYTHING UP, MIMURA.
IT WAS TOUGH!
I WAS FINISHING UP THE EDITING WHILE YOU WERE ALL EATING, YOU KNOW!
THIS PLACE IS SURROUNDED BY WATER.
IT'S LIKELY THAT THE WALLS AND WINDOWS HAVE ANTI-ME SUBSTANCES IN THEM...
...SO IT WOULD BE TOO RISKY FOR ME TO TRY TO ESCAPE THROUGH THEM.
I'LL HAVE TO DODGE THEIR ATTACKS INSIDE THIS BUILDING.
KORO SEN-SEI...
MAY I DO A BODY CHECK?
EVEN THOUGH WE'RE SUR-ROUNDED BY WATER...
...YOU'D BE ABLE TO GET AWAY IF YOU WERE HIDING THAT WET SUIT ON YOU.
YOU'RE BEING VERY THOROUGH.
DON'T WORRY, I WON'T CHEAT.
PAT
PAT

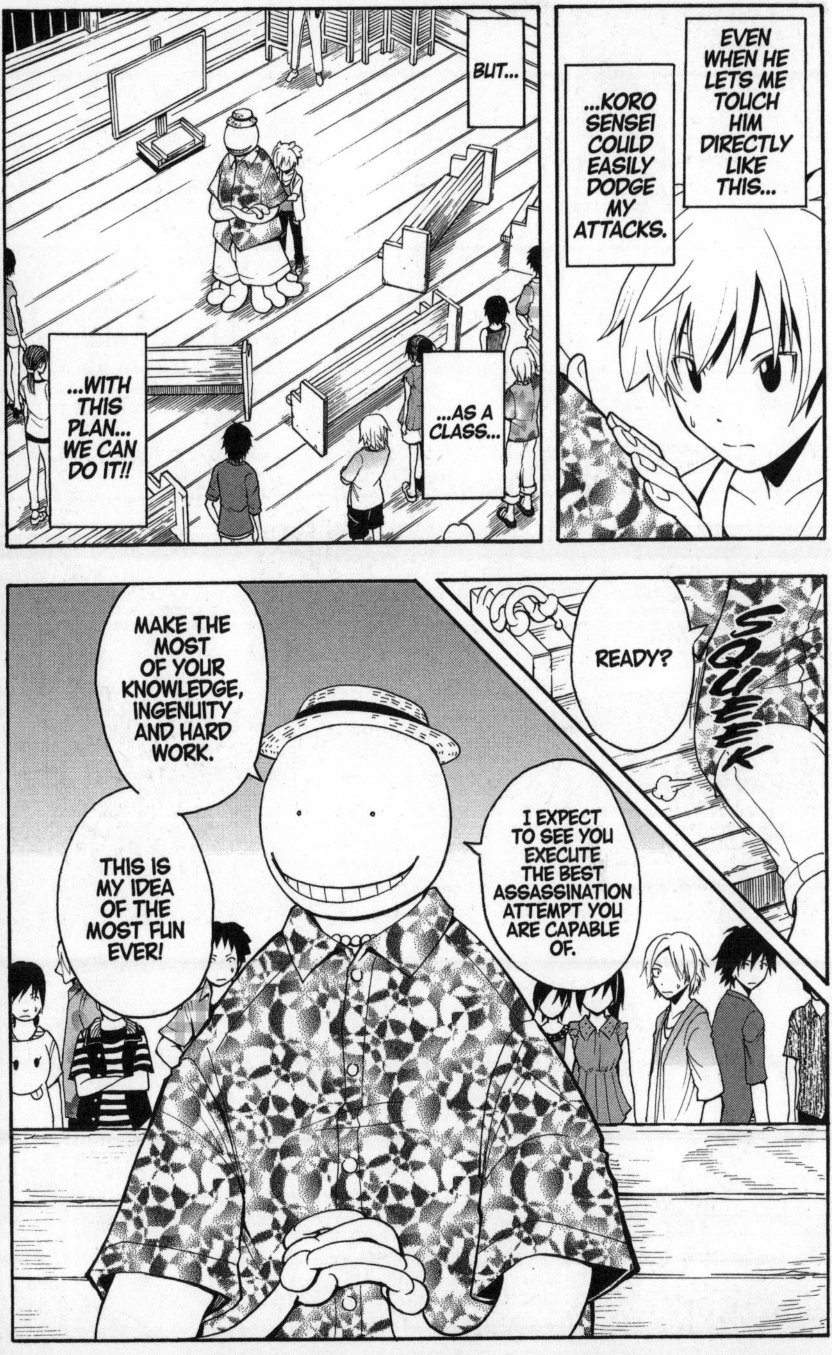
EVEN WHEN HE LETS ME TOUCH HIM DIRECTLY LIKE THIS...
...KORO SENSEI COULD EASILY DODGE MY ATTACKS.
BUT...
...AS A CLASS...
...WITH THIS PLAN... WE CAN DO IT!!
READY?
SQUEEEK
MAKE THE MOST OF YOUR KNOWLEDGE, INGENUITY AND HARD WORK.
I EXPECT TO SEE YOU EXECUTE THE BEST ASSASSINATION ATTEMPT YOU ARE CAPABLE OF.
THIS IS MY IDEA OF THE MOST FUN EVER!

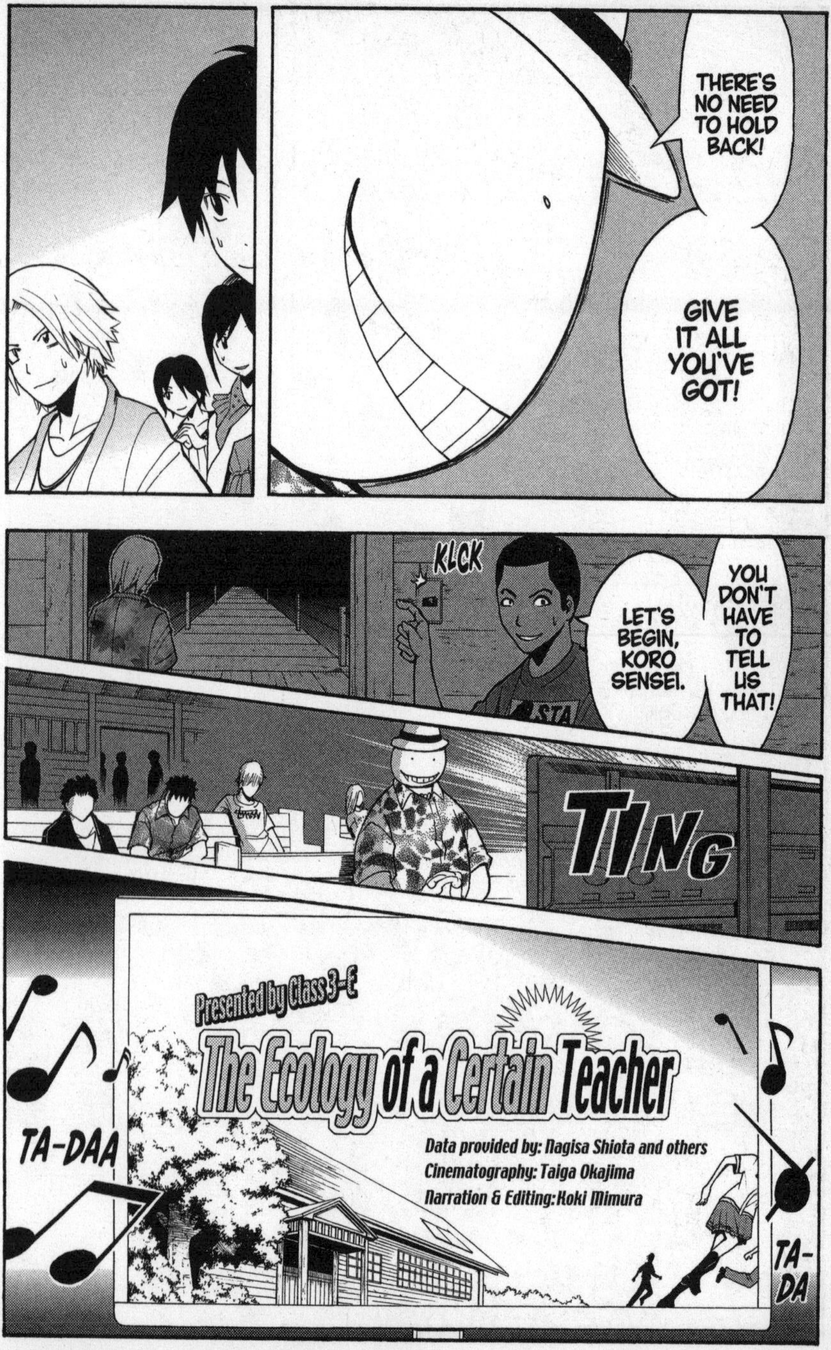
THERE'S NO NEED TO HOLD BACK!
GIVE IT ALL YOU'VE GOT!
YOU DON'T HAVE TO TELL US THAT!
LET'S BEGIN, KORO SENSEI.
KLCK
TING
Presented by Class 3-E
The Ecology of a Certain Teacher
Data provided by: Nagisa Shiota and others
Cinematography: Taiga Okajima
Narration & Editing: Koki Mimura
TA-DA
TA-DAA

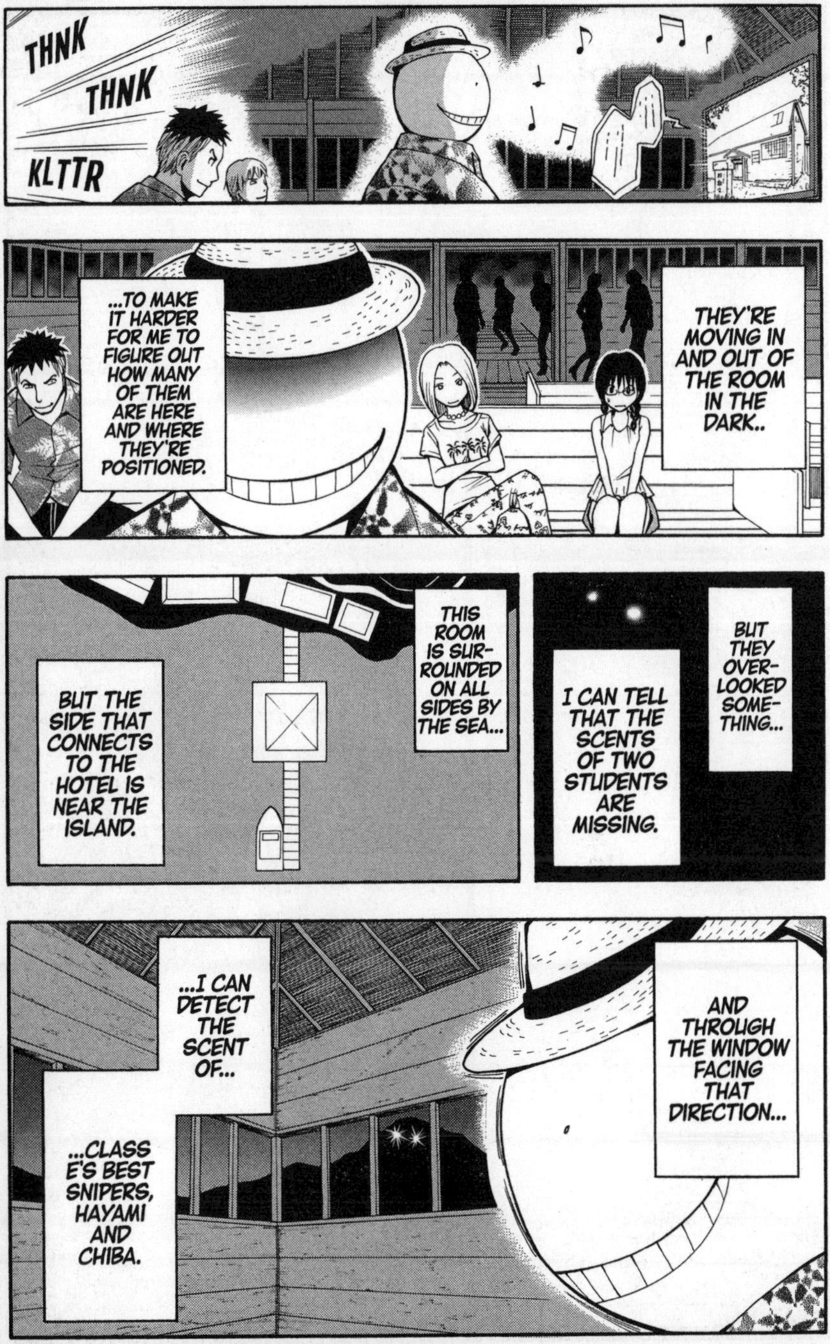
THNK
THNK
KLTTR
THEY'RE MOVING IN AND OUT OF THE ROOM IN THE DARK..
...TO MAKE IT HARDER FOR ME TO FIGURE OUT HOW MANY OF THEM ARE HERE AND WHERE THEY'RE POSITIONED.
BUT THEY OVERLOOKED SOMETHING...
I CAN TELL THAT THE SCENTS OF TWO STUDENTS ARE MISSING.
THIS ROOM IS SURROUNDED ON ALL SIDES BY THE SEA...
BUT THE SIDE THAT CONNECTS TO THE HOTEL IS NEAR THE ISLAND.
AND THROUGH THE WINDOW FACING THAT DIRECTION...
...I CAN DETECT THE SCENT OF...
...CLASS E'S BEST SNIPERS, HAYAMI AND CHIBA.

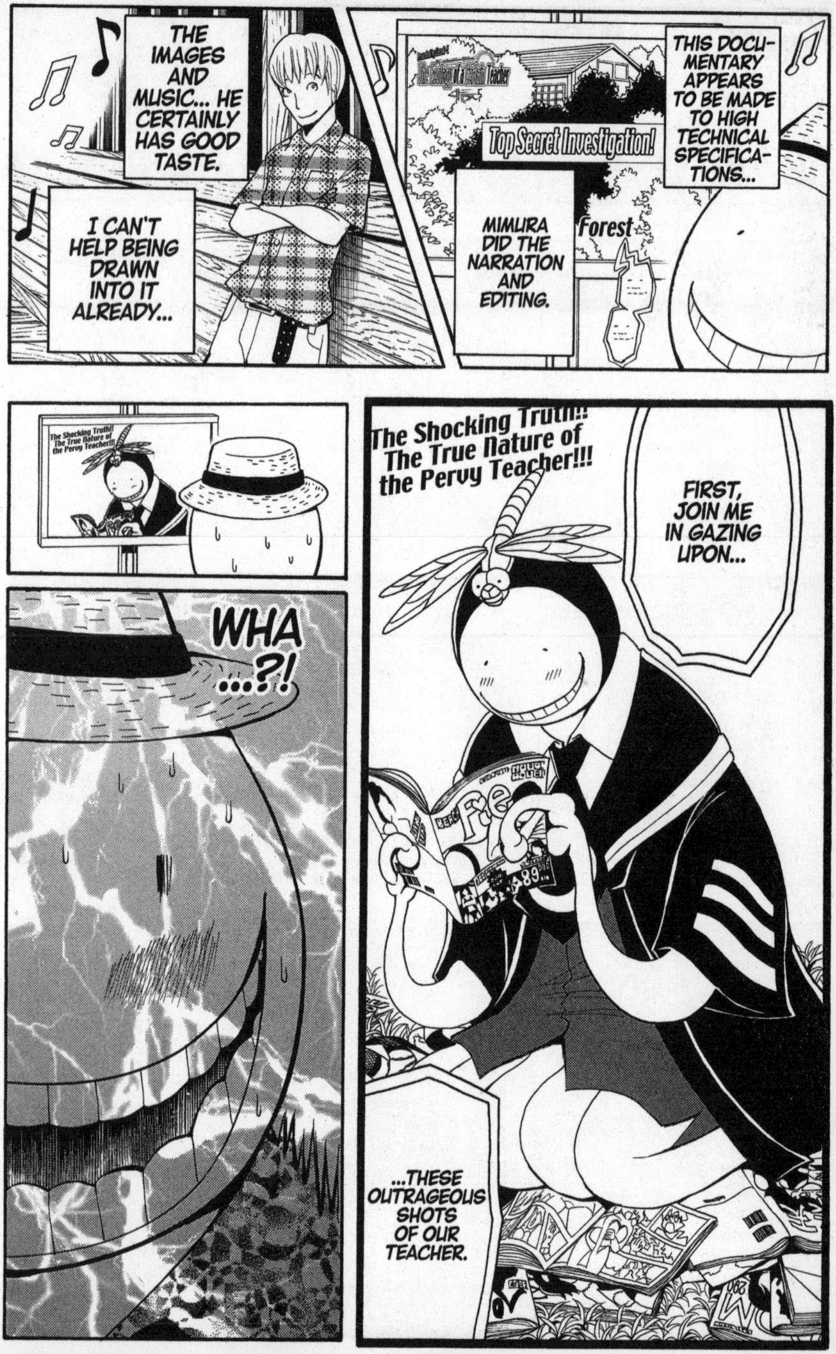

THIS DOCUMENTARY APPEARS TO BE MADE TO HIGH TECHNICAL SPECIFICATIONS...
The Ecology of a Certain Teacher
Top Secret Investigation!
Forest
MIMURA DID THE NARRATION AND EDITING.
THE IMAGES AND MUSIC... HE CERTAINLY HAS GOOD TASTE.
I CAN'T HELP BEING DRAWN INTO IT ALREADY...
The Shocking Truth!! The True Nature of the Pervy Teacher!!!
FIRST, JOIN ME IN GAZING UPON...
...THESE OUTRAGEOUS SHOTS OF OUR TEACHER.
The Shocking Truth!! The True Nature of the Pervy Teacher!!!
WHA ...?!

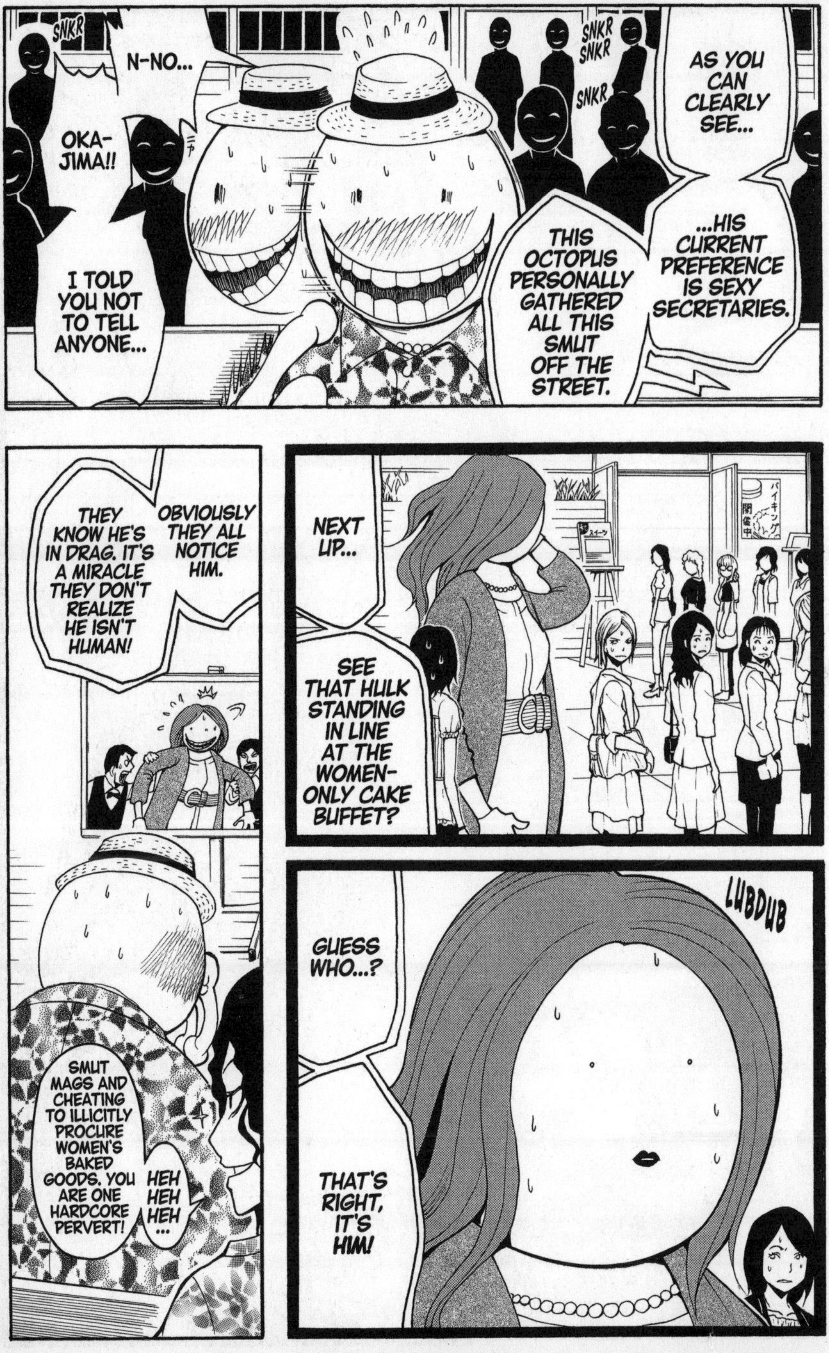
AS YOU CAN CLEARLY SEE...
...HIS CURRENT PREFERENCE IS SEXY SECRETARIES.
THIS OCTOPUS PERSONALLY GATHERED ALL THIS SMUT OFF THE STREET.
SNKR SNKR
SNKR
N-NO...
SNKR
OKA-JIMA!!
I TOLD YOU NOT TO TELL ANYONE...
LUBDUB
NEXT UP...
SEE THAT HULK STANDING IN LINE AT THE WOMEN-ONLY CAKE BUFFET?
GUESS WHO...?
THAT'S RIGHT, IT'S HIM!
OBVIOUSLY THEY ALL NOTICE HIM.
THEY KNOW HE'S IN DRAG. IT'S A MIRACLE THEY DON'T REALIZE HE ISN'T HUMAN!
HEH HEH HEH...
SMUT MAGS AND CHEATING TO ILLICITLY PROCURE WOMEN'S BAKED GOODS. YOU ARE ONE HARDCORE PERVERT!

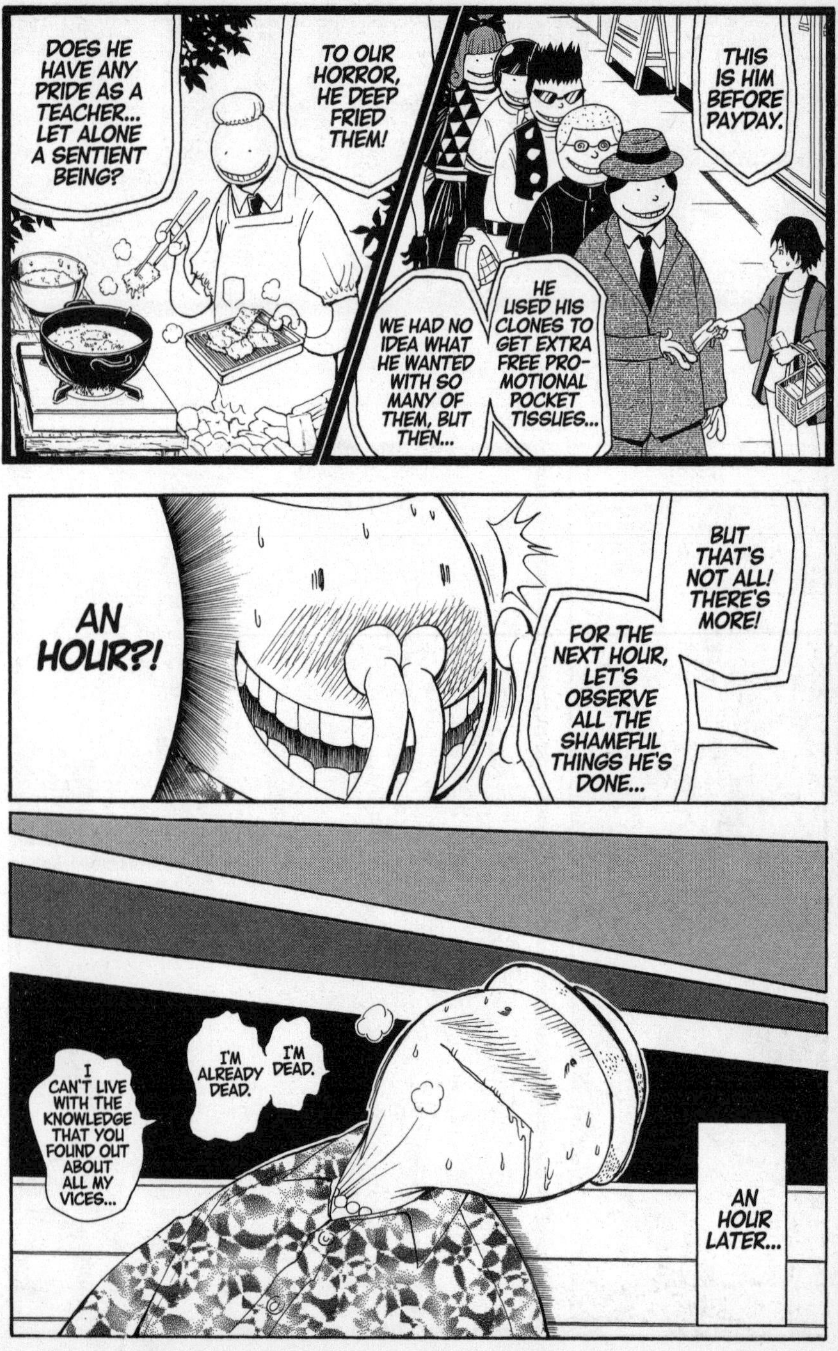
THIS IS HIM BEFORE PAYDAY.
HE USED HIS CLONES TO GET EXTRA FREE PROMOTIONAL POCKET TISSUES...
WE HAD NO IDEA WHAT HE WANTED WITH SO MANY OF THEM, BUT THEN...
TO OUR HORROR, HE DEEP FRIED THEM!
DOES HE HAVE ANY PRIDE AS A TEACHER... LET ALONE A SENTIENT BEING?
BUT THAT'S NOT ALL! THERE'S MORE!
FOR THE NEXT HOUR, LET'S OBSERVE ALL THE SHAMEFUL THINGS HE'S DONE...
AN HOUR?!
AN HOUR LATER...
I'M DEAD.
I'M ALREADY DEAD.
I CAN'T LIVE WITH THE KNOWLEDGE THAT YOU FOUND OUT ABOUT ALL MY VICES...

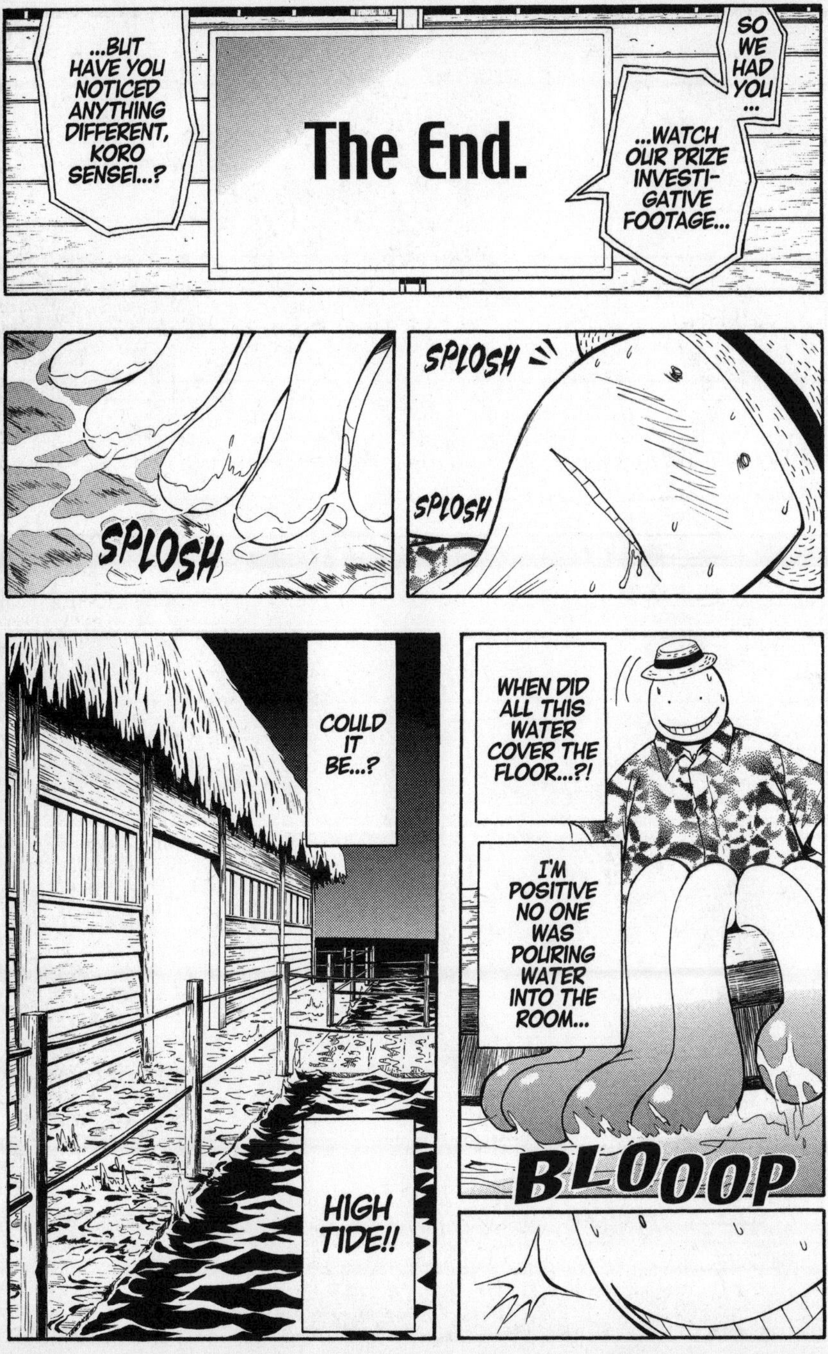
SO WE HAD YOU...
...WATCH OUR PRIZE INVESTIGATIVE FOOTAGE...
The End.
...BUT HAVE YOU NOTICED ANYTHING DIFFERENT, KORO SENSEI...?
SPLOSH
SPLOSH
SPLOSH
WHEN DID ALL THIS WATER COVER THE FLOOR...?!
I'M POSITIVE NO ONE WAS POURING WATER INTO THE ROOM...
BLOOOP
COULD IT BE...?
HIGH TIDE!!

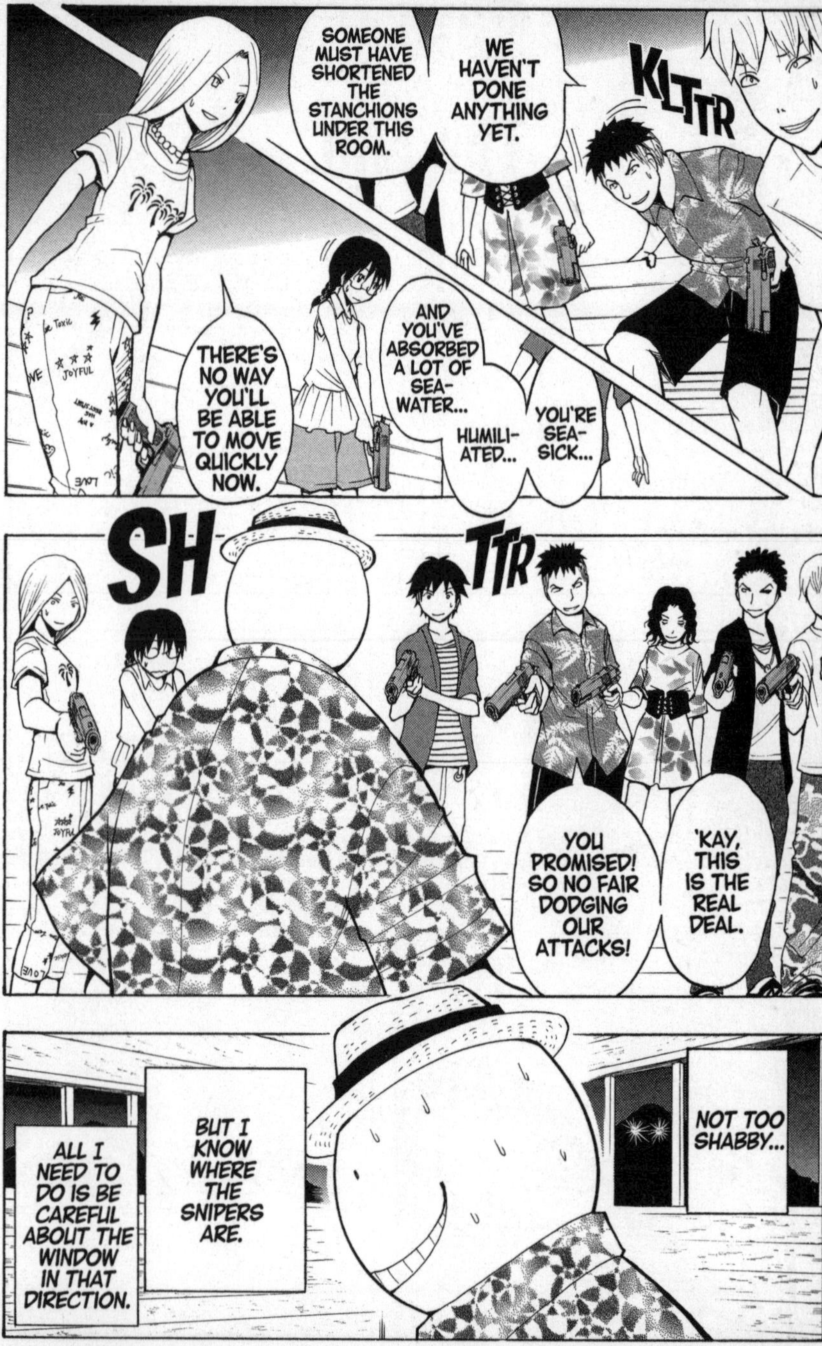
KLTTR
WE HAVEN'T DONE ANYTHING YET.
SOMEONE MUST HAVE SHORTENED THE STANCHIONS UNDER THIS ROOM.
YOU'RE SEA-SICK...
HUMILI-ATED...
AND YOU'VE ABSORBED A LOT OF SEA-WATER...
THERE'S NO WAY YOU'LL BE ABLE TO MOVE QUICKLY NOW.
SH TTR
'KAY, THIS IS THE REAL DEAL.
YOU PROMISED! SO NO FAIR DODGING OUR ATTACKS!
NOT TOO SHABBY...
BUT I KNOW WHERE THE SNIPERS ARE.
ALL I NEED TO DO IS BE CAREFUL ABOUT THE WINDOW IN THAT DIRECTION.

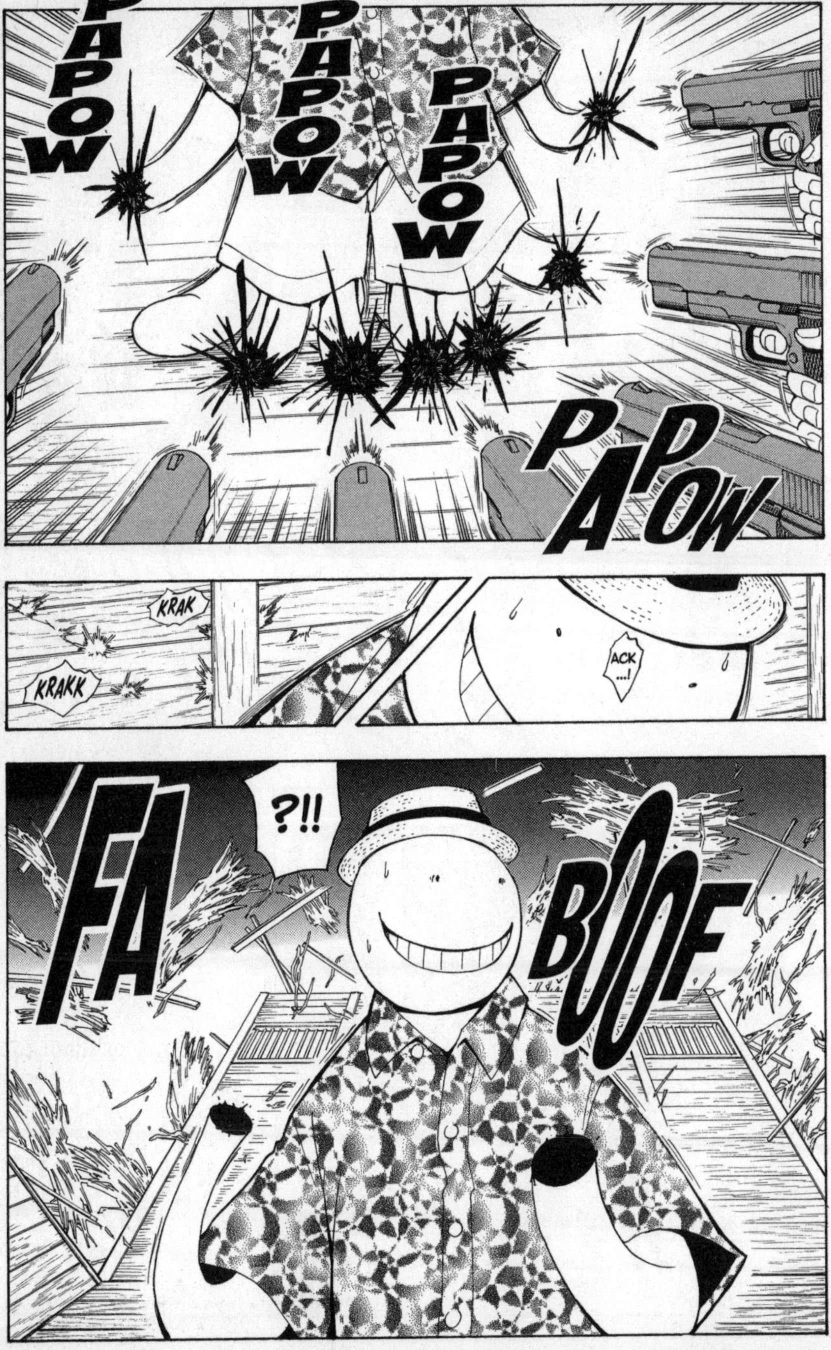
PAPOW
PAPOW
PAPOW
PAPOW
ACK ...!
KRAK
KRAKK
?!!
FA BOOF

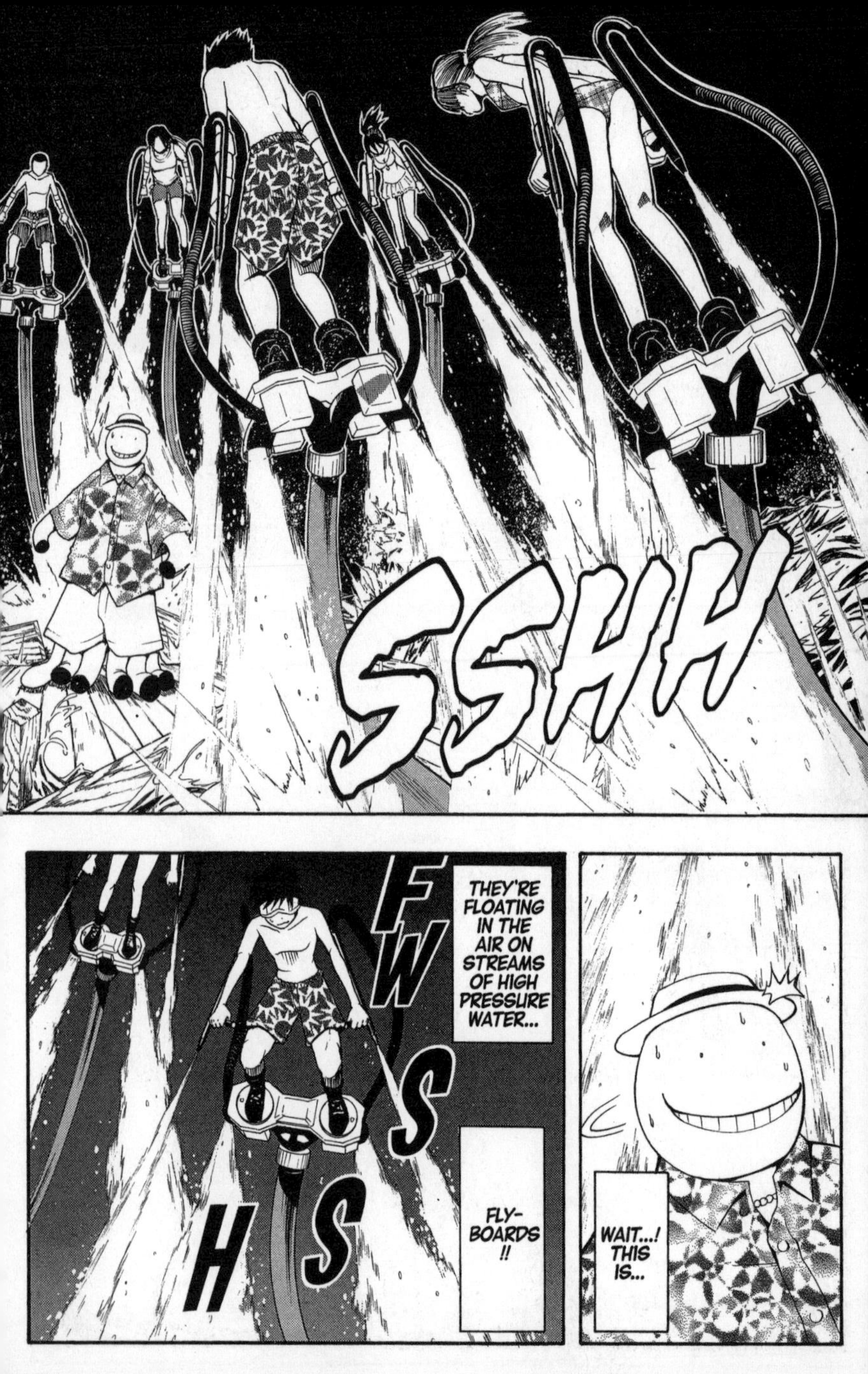
SSHH
WAIT...! THIS IS...
FWSS
THEY'RE FLOATING IN THE AIR ON STREAMS OF HIGH PRESSURE WATER...
FLY-BOARDS !!
HS

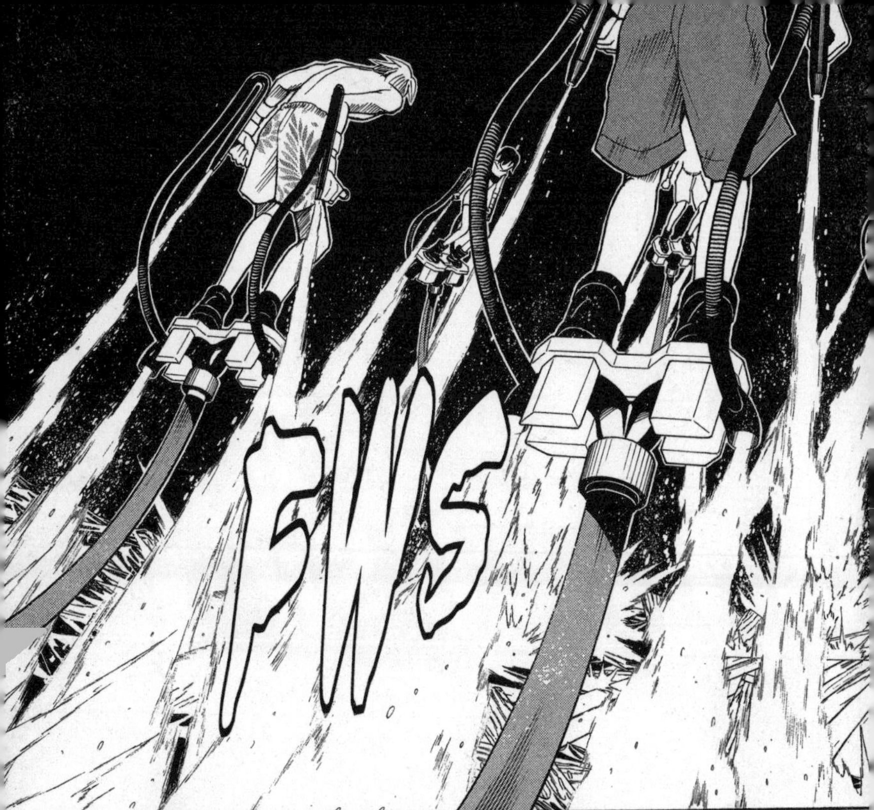
FWSH
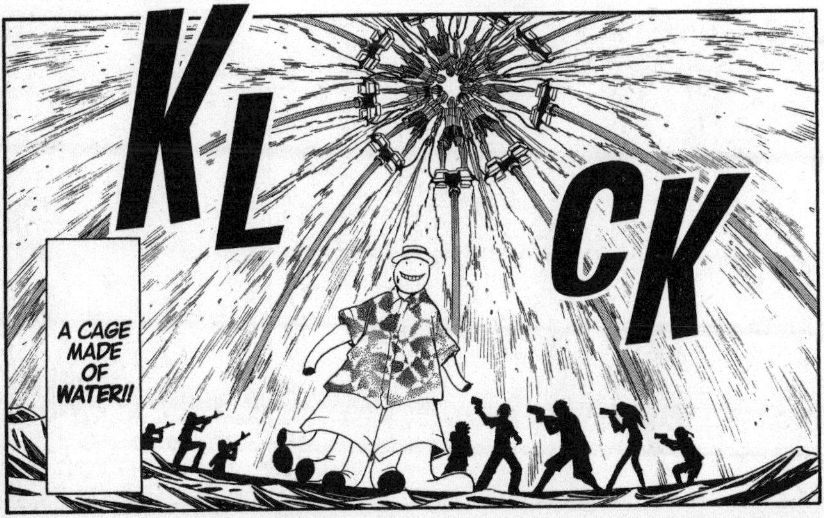
KLICK
A CAGE MADE OF WATER!!

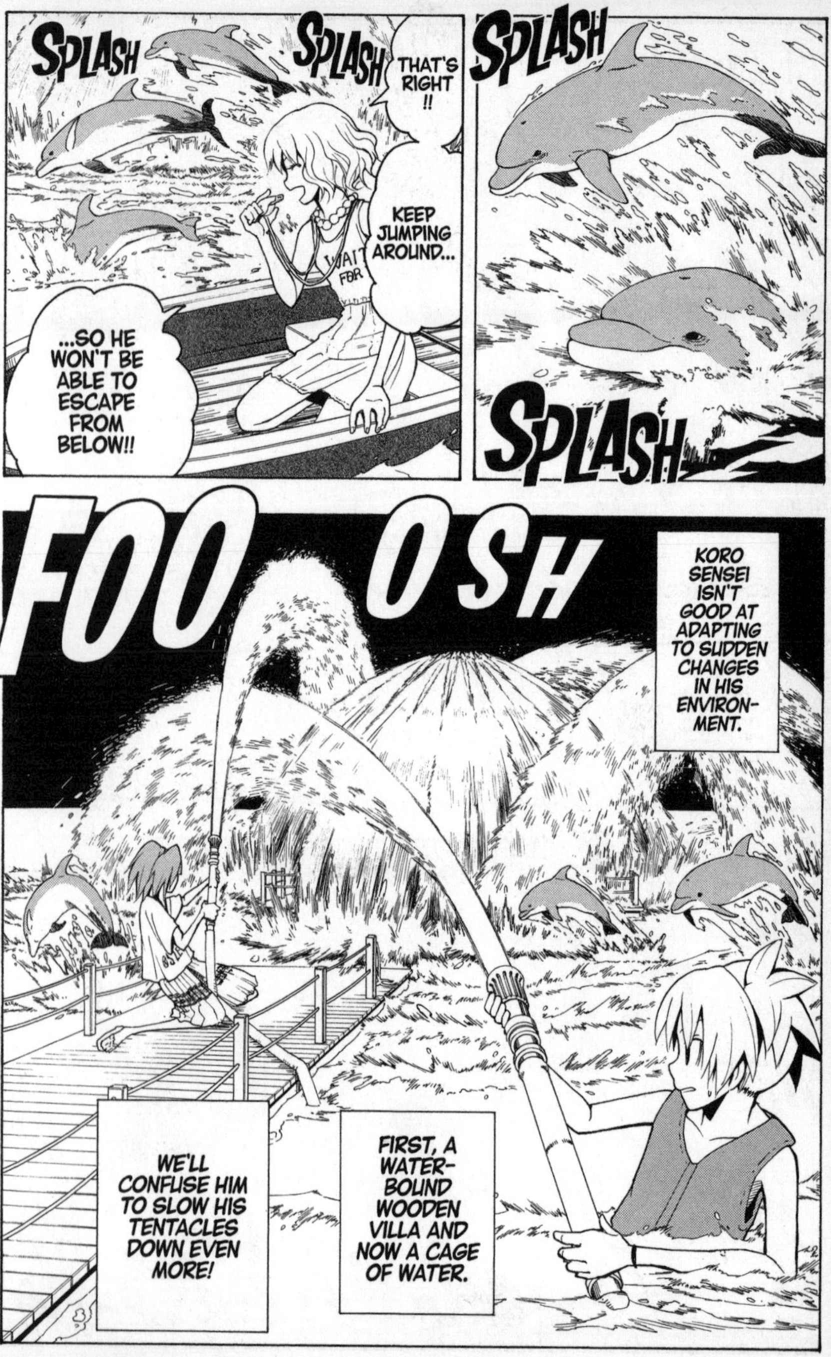
SPLASH
SPLASH
THAT'S RIGHT !!
SPLASH
SPLASH
KEEP JUMPING AROUND...
...SO HE WON'T BE ABLE TO ESCAPE FROM BELOW!!
KORO SENSEI ISN'T GOOD AT ADAPTING TO SUDDEN CHANGES IN HIS ENVIRON-MENT.
FOOOSH
FIRST, A WATER-BOUND WOODEN VILLA AND NOW A CAGE OF WATER.
WE'LL CONFUSE HIM TO SLOW HIS TENTACLES DOWN EVEN MORE!

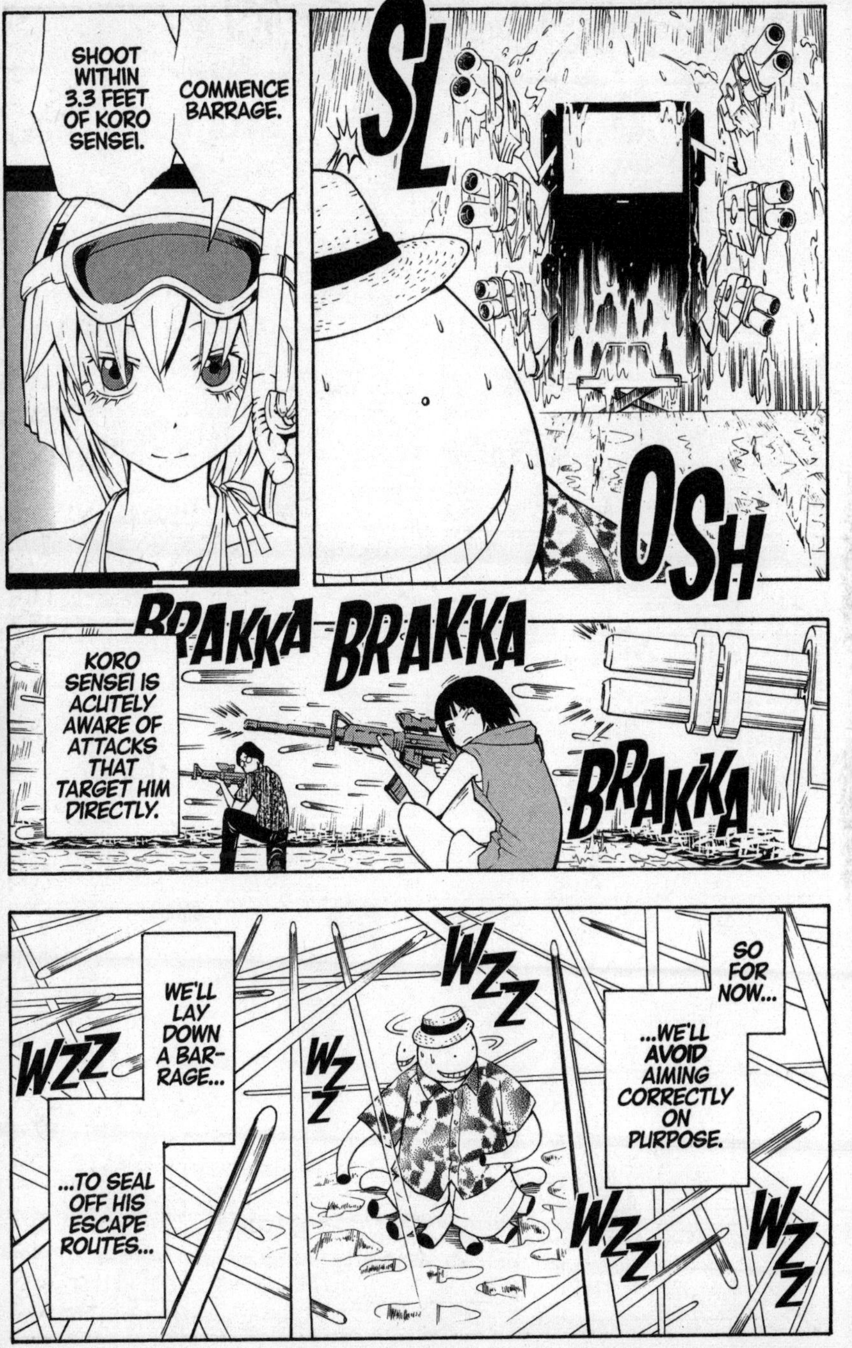
SLOSH
COMMENCE BARRAGE.
SHOOT WITHIN 3.3 FEET OF KORO SENSEI.
BRAKKA BRAKKA
BRAKKA
KORO SENSEI IS ACUTELY AWARE OF ATTACKS THAT TARGET HIM DIRECTLY.
SO FOR NOW...
...WE'LL AVOID AIMING CORRECTLY ON PURPOSE.
WZZ
WZZ
WE'LL LAY DOWN A BAR-RAGE...
WZZ
...TO SEAL OFF HIS ESCAPE ROUTES...
WZZ
WZZ

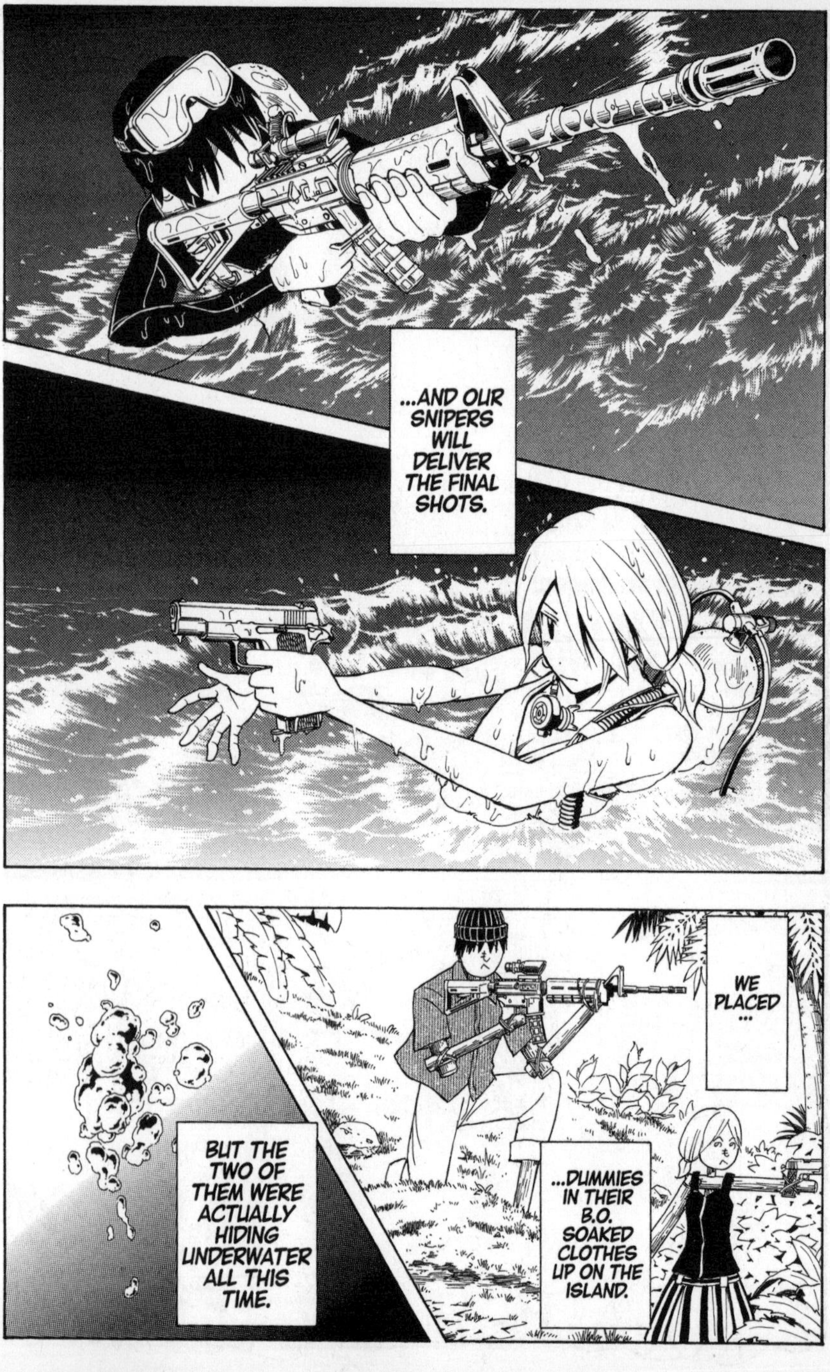
...AND OUR SNIPERS WILL DELIVER THE FINAL SHOTS.
WE PLACED...
...DUMMIES IN THEIR B.O. SOAKED CLOTHES UP ON THE ISLAND.
BUT THE TWO OF THEM WERE ACTUALLY HIDING UNDERWATER ALL THIS TIME.

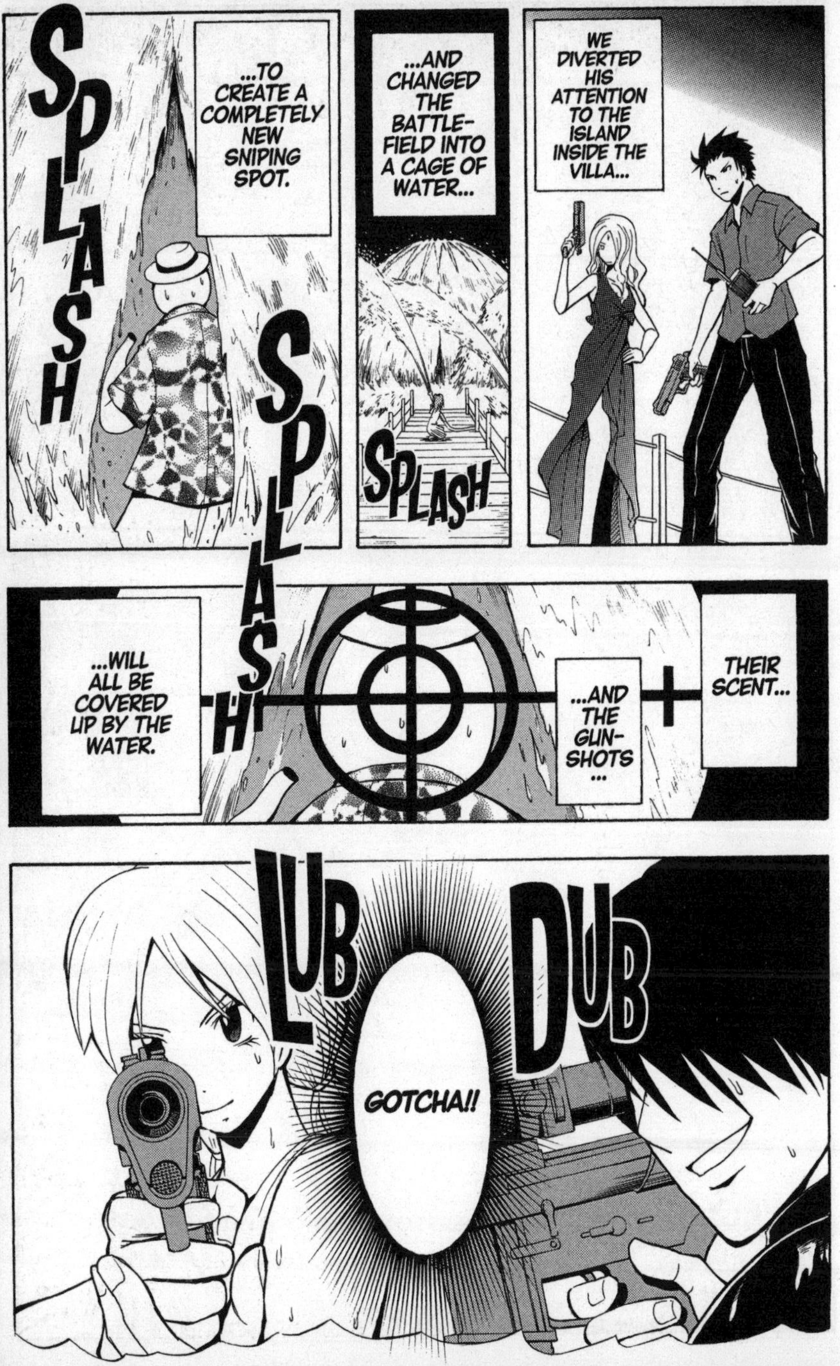
WE DIVERTED HIS ATTENTION TO THE ISLAND INSIDE THE VILLA...
...AND CHANGED THE BATTLE-FIELD INTO A CAGE OF WATER...
SPLASH
...TO CREATE A COMPLETELY NEW SNIPING SPOT.
SPLASH
SPLASH
THEIR SCENT...
...AND THE GUN-SHOTS...
...WILL ALL BE COVERED UP BY THE WATER.
LUB
DUB
GOTCHA!!

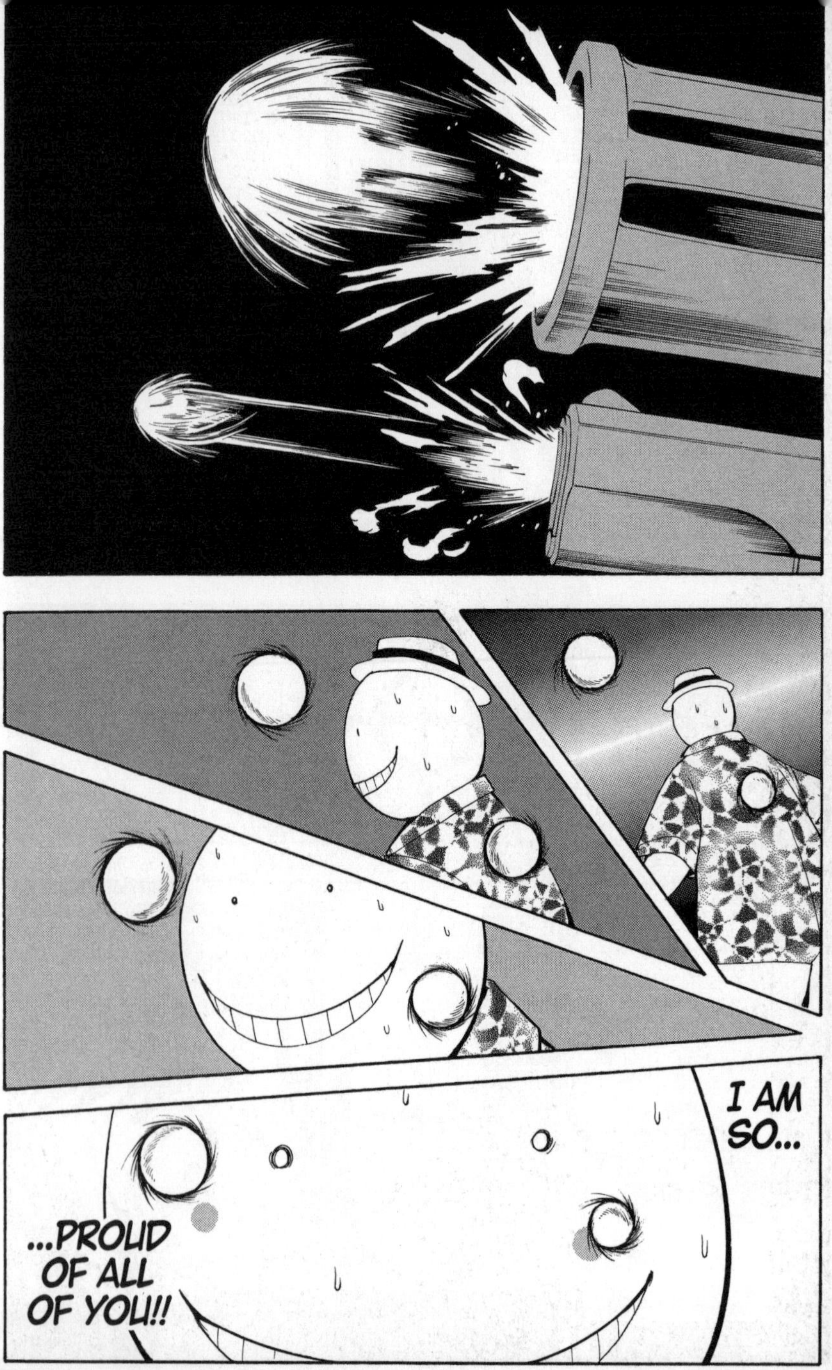
I AM SO...
...PROUD OF ALL OF YOU!!

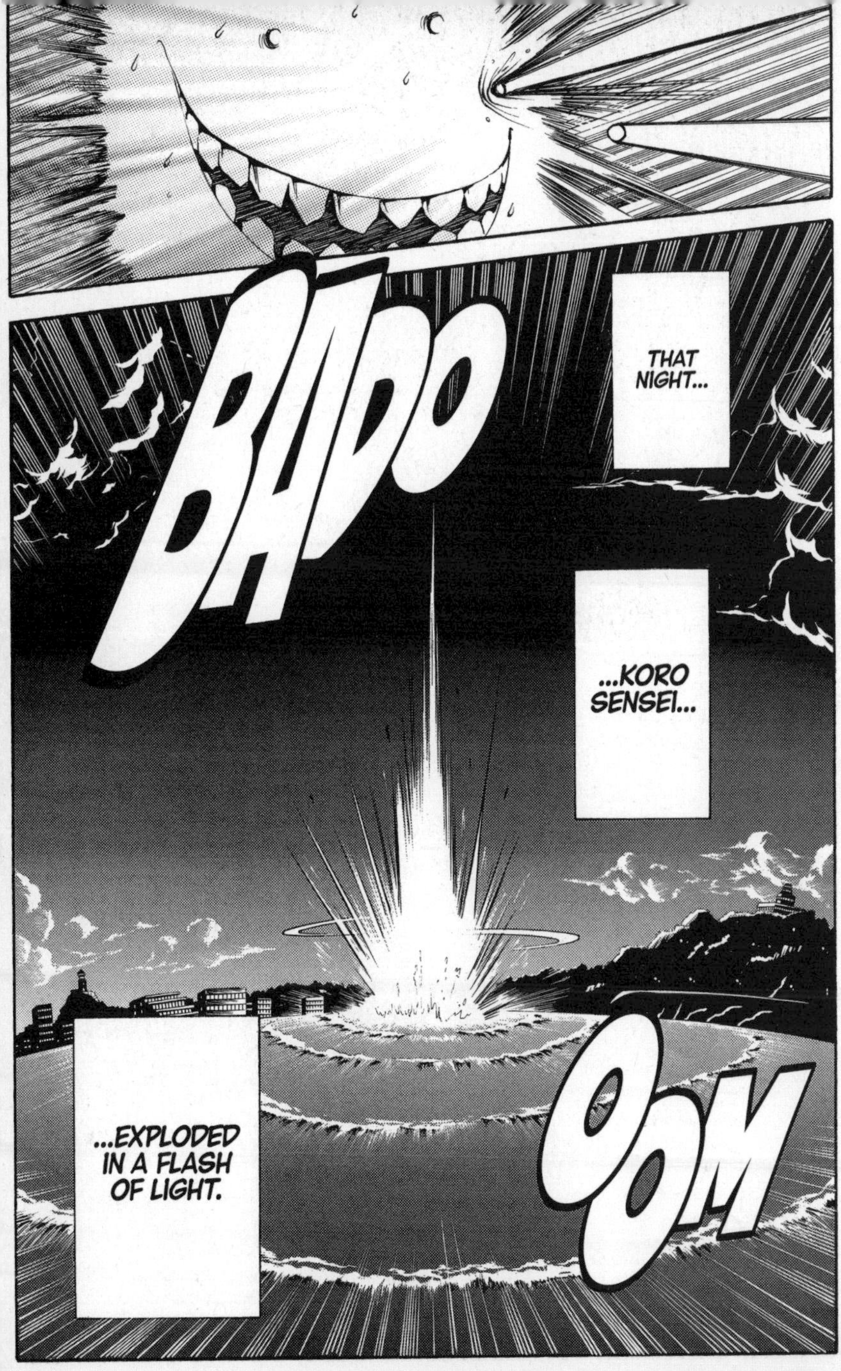
THAT NIGHT...
...KORO SENSEI...
BADO
OOM
...EXPLODED IN A FLASH OF LIGHT.

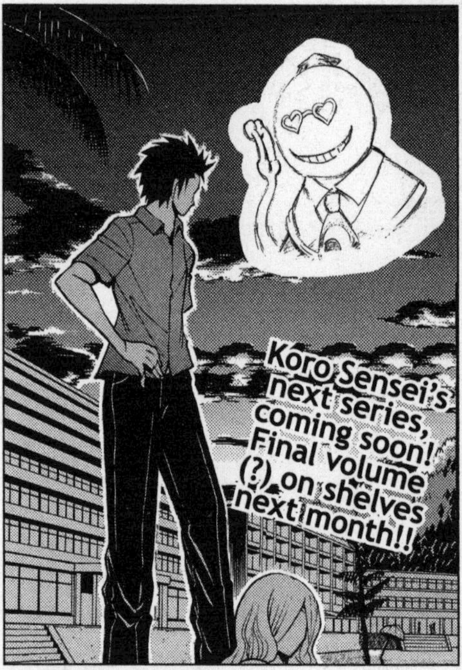
Koro Sensei's next series, coming soon! Final volume (?) on shelves next month!!

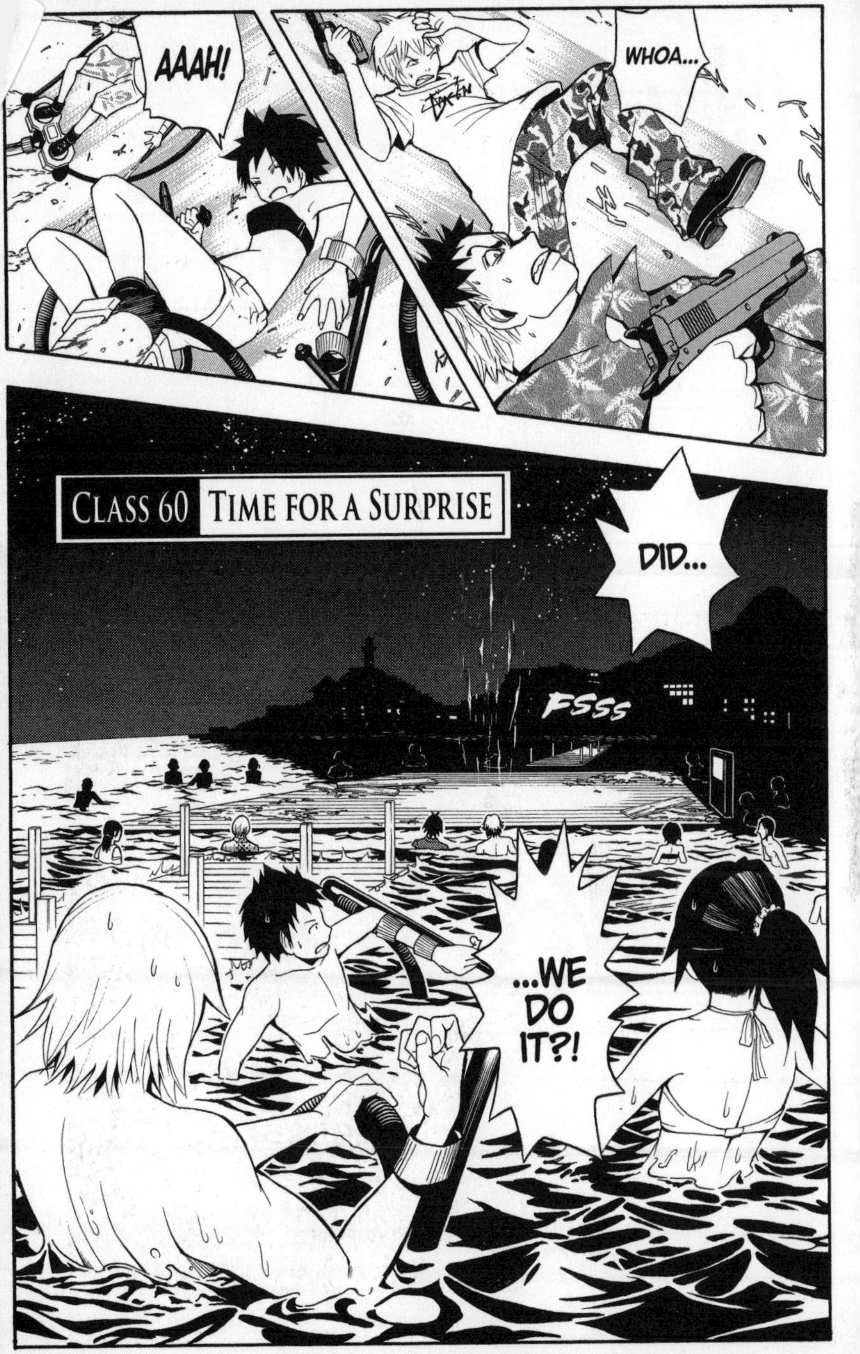
WHOA...
AAAH!
CLASS 60 TIME FOR A SURPRISE
DID...
FSSS
...WE DO IT?!

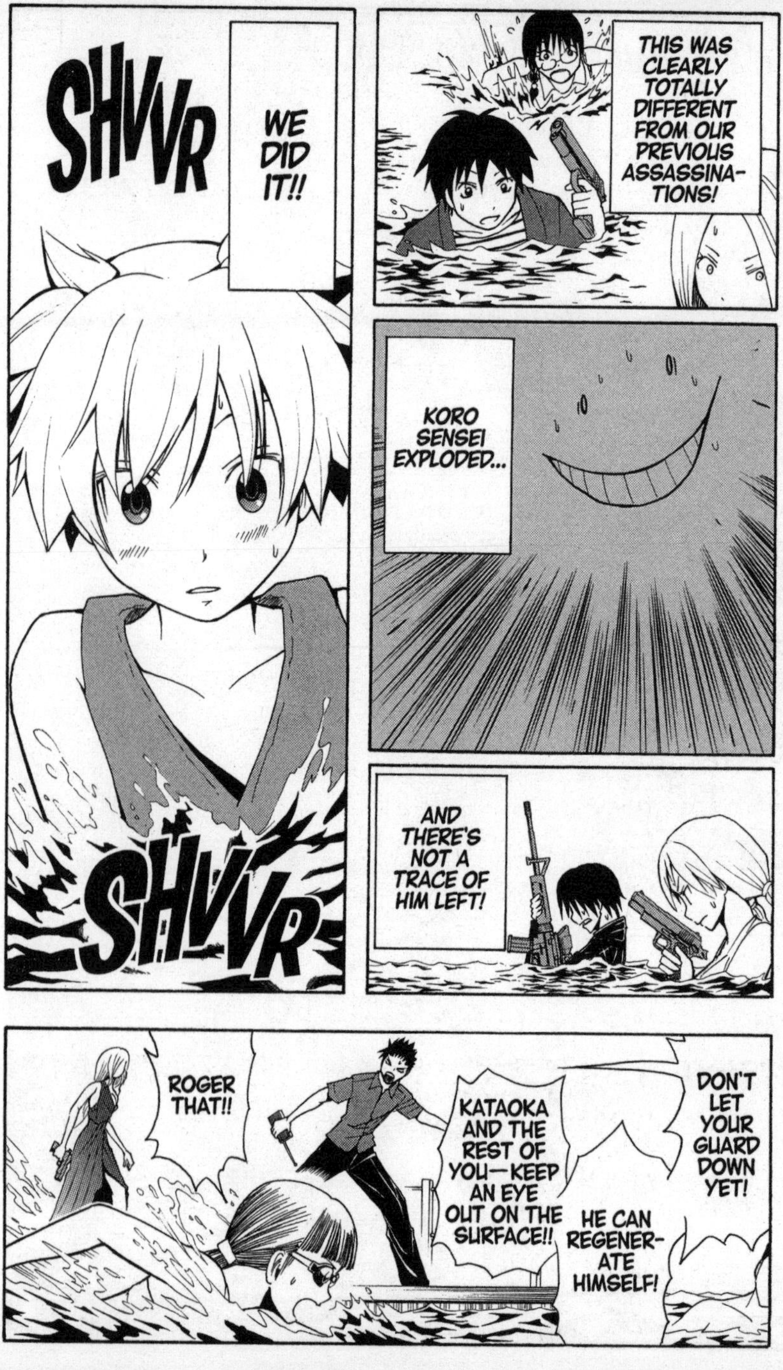
THIS WAS CLEARLY TOTALLY DIFFERENT FROM OUR PREVIOUS ASSASSINA-TIONS!
KORO SENSEI EXPLODED...
AND THERE'S NOT A TRACE OF HIM LEFT!
WE DID IT!!
SHVVR
SHVVR
DON'T LET YOUR GUARD DOWN YET!
HE CAN REGENER-ATE HIMSELF!
KATAOKA AND THE REST OF YOU—KEEP AN EYE OUT ON THE SURFACE!!
ROGER THAT!!

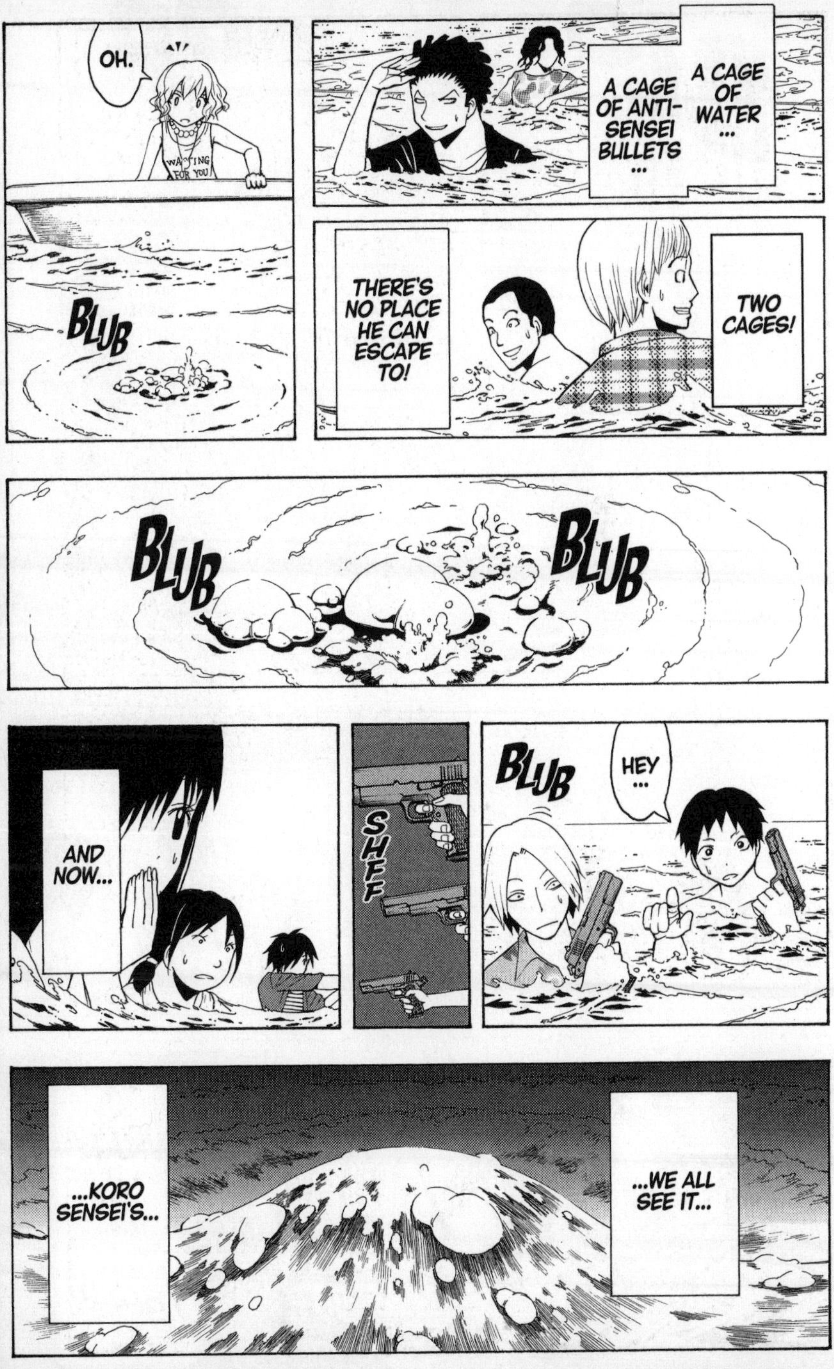
A CAGE OF WATER...
A CAGE OF ANTI-SENSEI BULLETS...
OH.
TWO CAGES!
THERE'S NO PLACE HE CAN ESCAPE TO!
BLUB
BLUB
BLUB
HEY...
BLUB
SHFF
AND NOW...
...WE ALL SEE IT...
...KORO SENSEI'S...

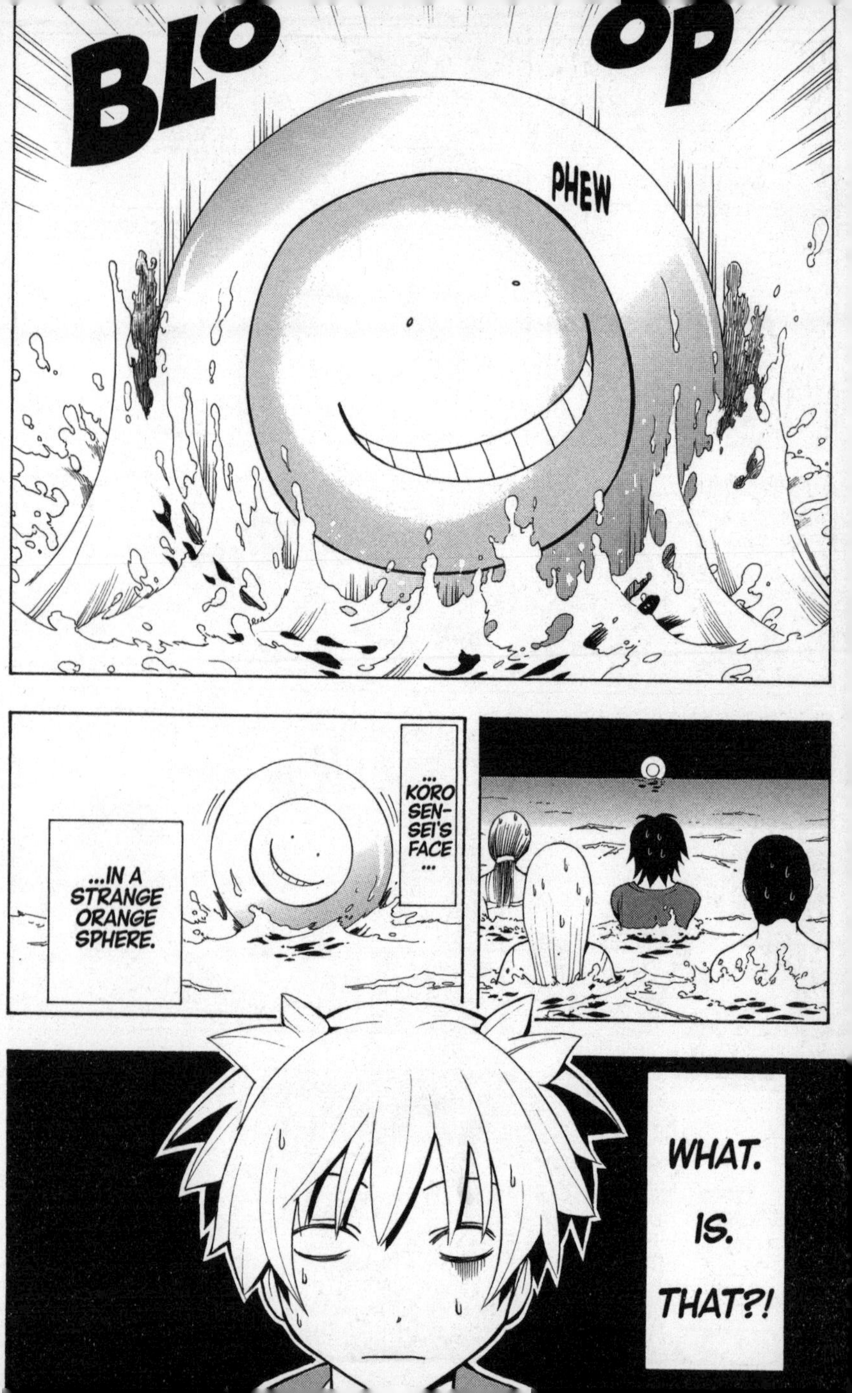
BLOOP
PHEW
...KŌRO SEN-SEI'S FACE...
...IN A STRANGE ORANGE SPHERE.
WHAT. IS. THAT?!

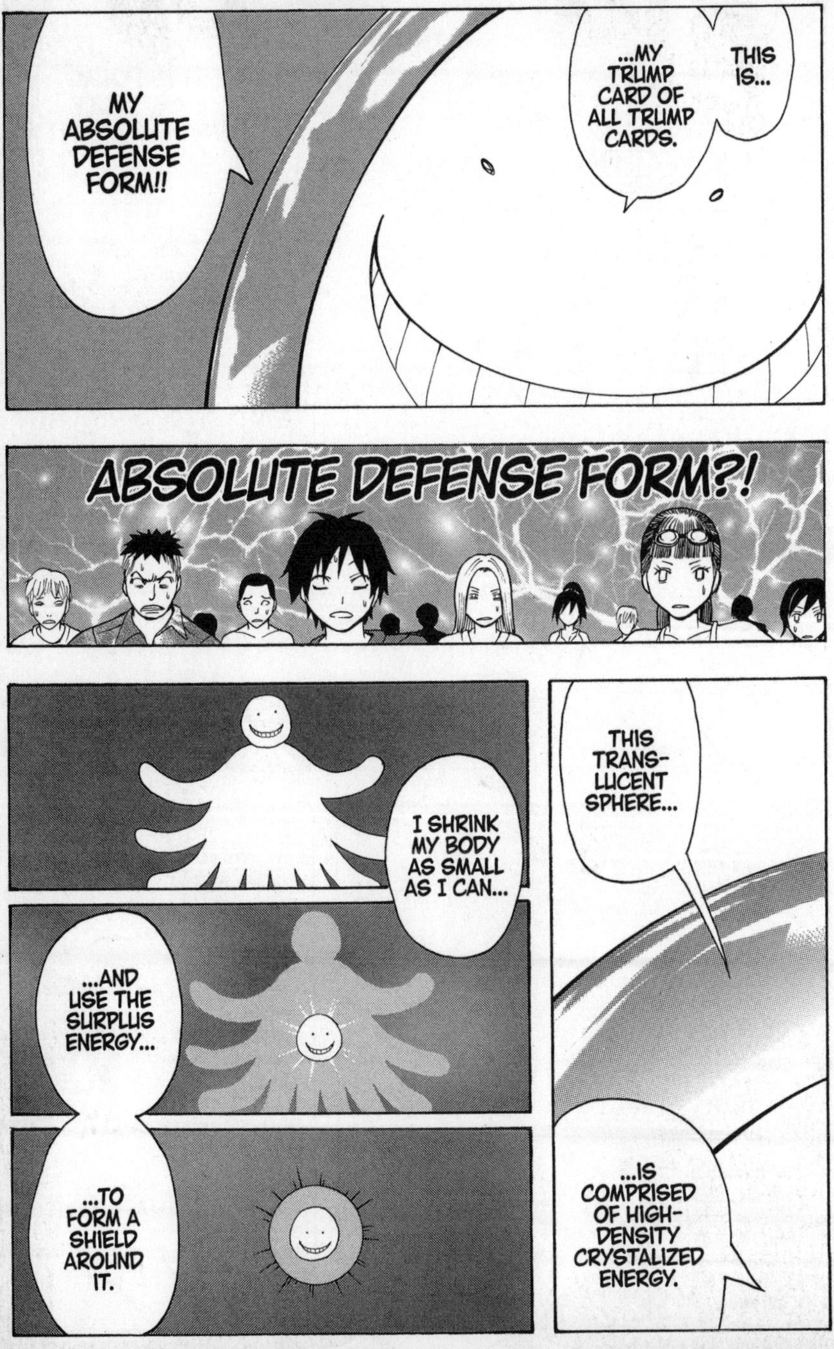
THIS IS...
...MY TRUMP CARD OF ALL TRUMP CARDS.
MY ABSOLUTE DEFENSE FORM!!
ABSOLUTE DEFENSE FORM?!
THIS TRANS-LUCENT SPHERE...
...IS COMPRISED OF HIGH-DENSITY CRYSTALIZED ENERGY.
I SHRINK MY BODY AS SMALL AS I CAN...
...AND USE THE SURPLUS ENERGY...
...TO FORM A SHIELD AROUND IT.

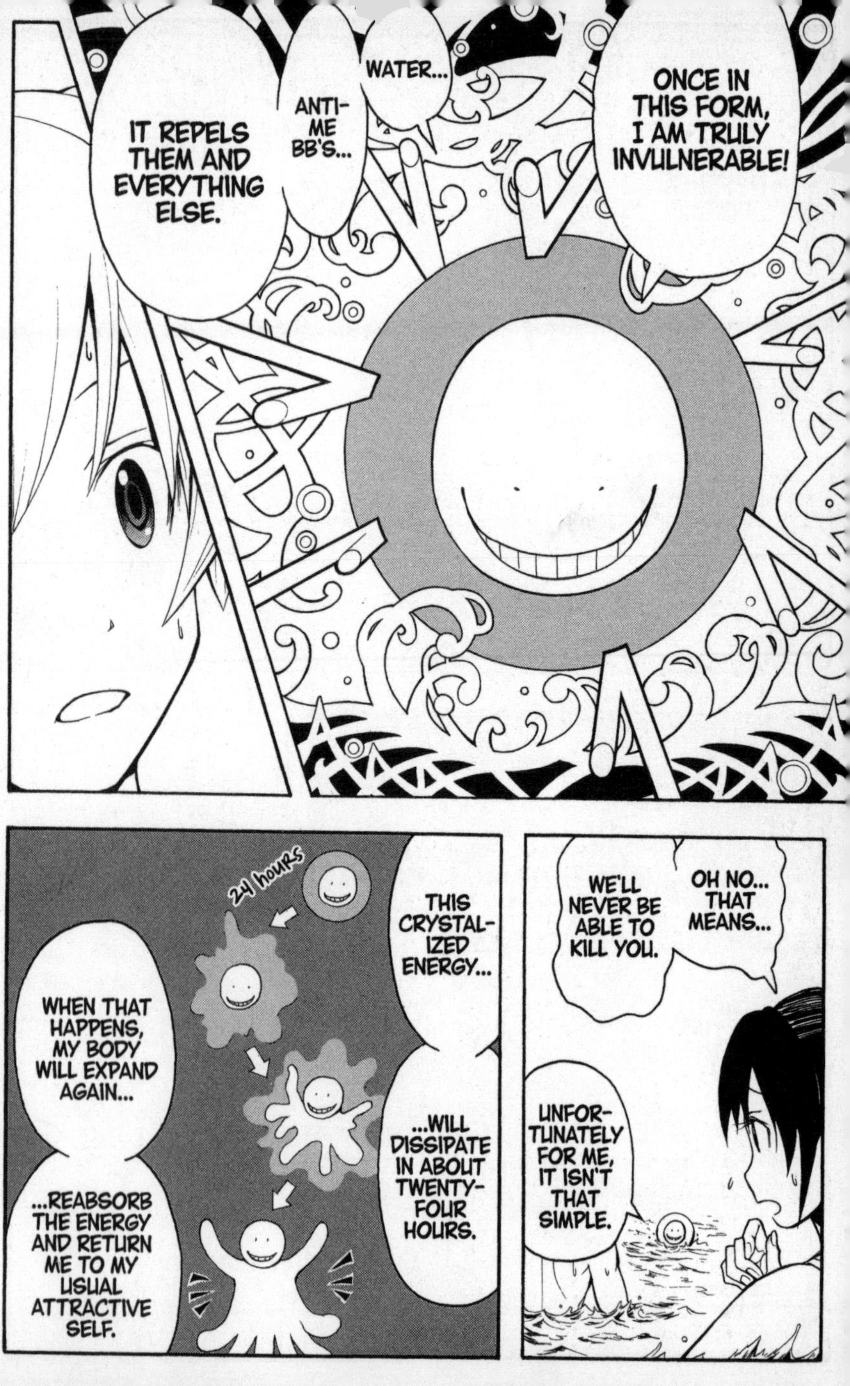
ONCE IN THIS FORM, I AM TRULY INVULNERABLE!
WATER...
ANTI-ME BB'S...
IT REPELS THEM AND EVERYTHING ELSE.
OH NO... THAT MEANS...
WE'LL NEVER BE ABLE TO KILL YOU.
UNFORTUNATELY FOR ME, IT ISN'T THAT SIMPLE.
THIS CRYSTALIZED ENERGY...
...WILL DISSIPATE IN ABOUT TWENTY-FOUR HOURS.
24 hours
WHEN THAT HAPPENS, MY BODY WILL EXPAND AGAIN...
...REABSORB THE ENERGY AND RETURN ME TO MY USUAL ATTRACTIVE SELF.

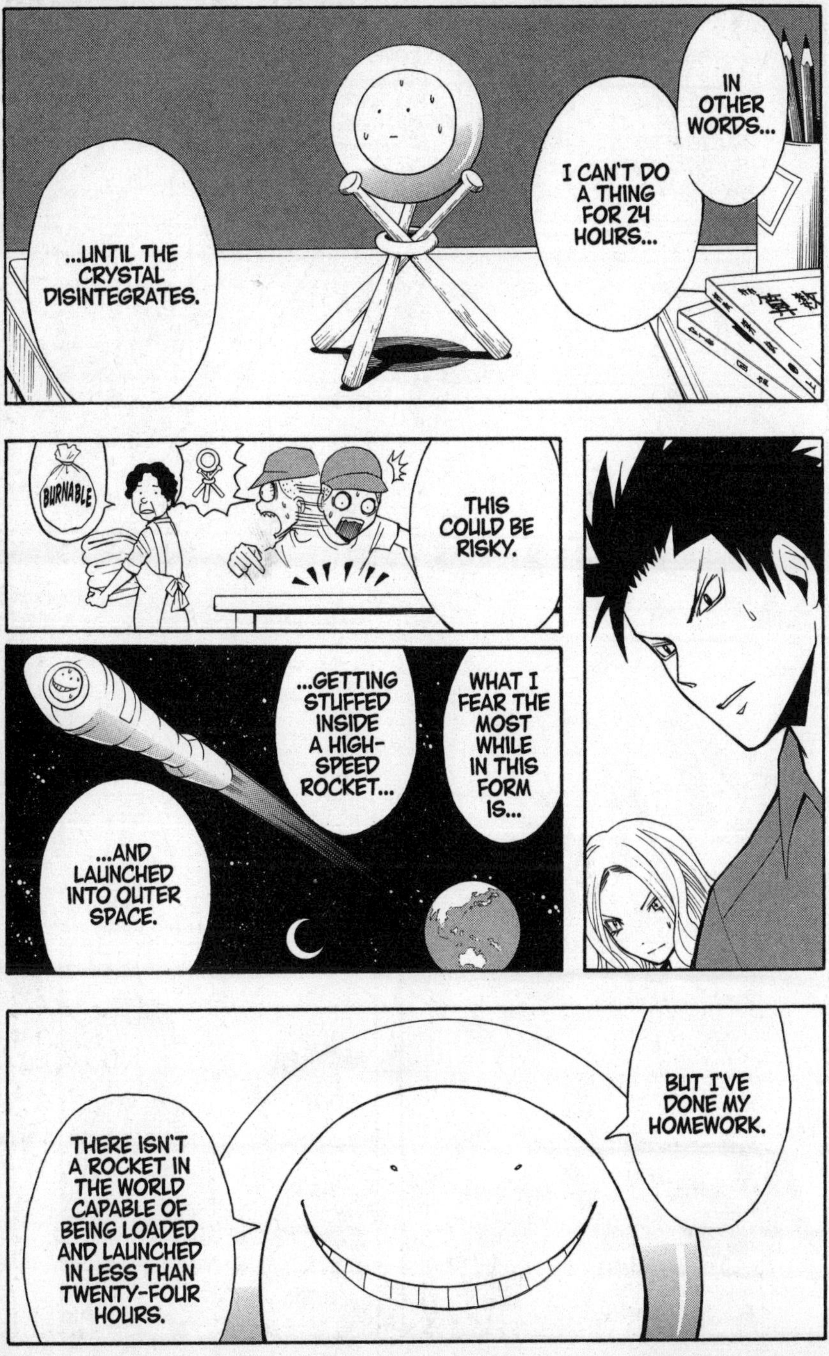
IN OTHER WORDS...
I CAN'T DO A THING FOR 24 HOURS...
...UNTIL THE CRYSTAL DISINTEGRATES.
THIS COULD BE RISKY.
BURNABLE
WHAT I FEAR THE MOST WHILE IN THIS FORM IS...
...GETTING STUFFED INSIDE A HIGH-SPEED ROCKET...
...AND LAUNCHED INTO OUTER SPACE.
BUT I'VE DONE MY HOMEWORK.
THERE ISN'T A ROCKET IN THE WORLD CAPABLE OF BEING LOADED AND LAUNCHED IN LESS THAN TWENTY-FOUR HOURS.

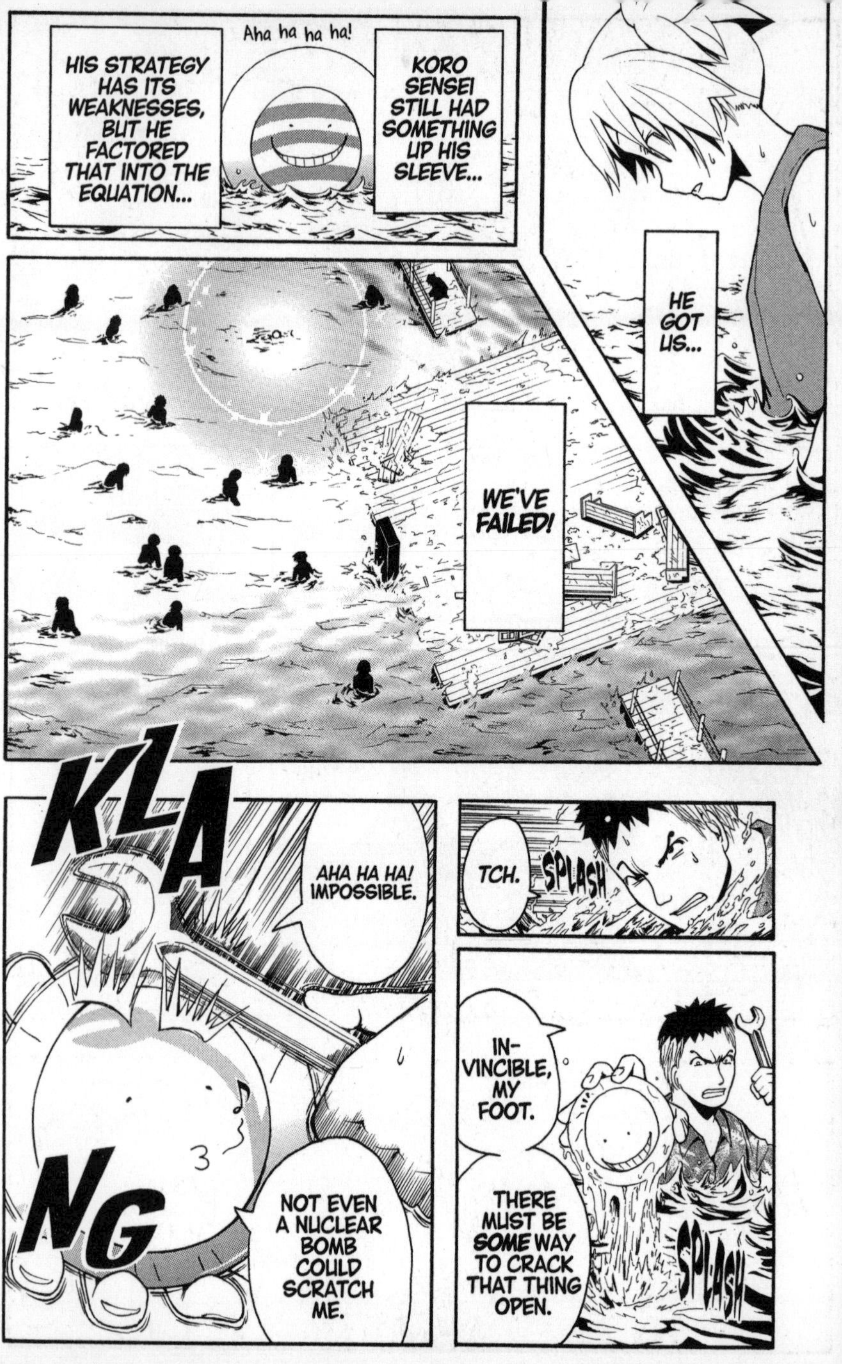
HE GOT US...
KORO SENSEI STILL HAD SOMETHING UP HIS SLEEVE...
Aha ha ha ha!
HIS STRATEGY HAS ITS WEAKNESSES, BUT HE FACTORED THAT INTO THE EQUATION...
WE'VE FAILED!
TCH.
SPLASH
IN-VINCIBLE, MY FOOT.
THERE MUST BE SOME WAY TO CRACK THAT THING OPEN.
SPLASH
KLANG
AHA HA HA! IMPOSSIBLE.
NOT EVEN A NUCLEAR BOMB COULD SCRATCH ME.

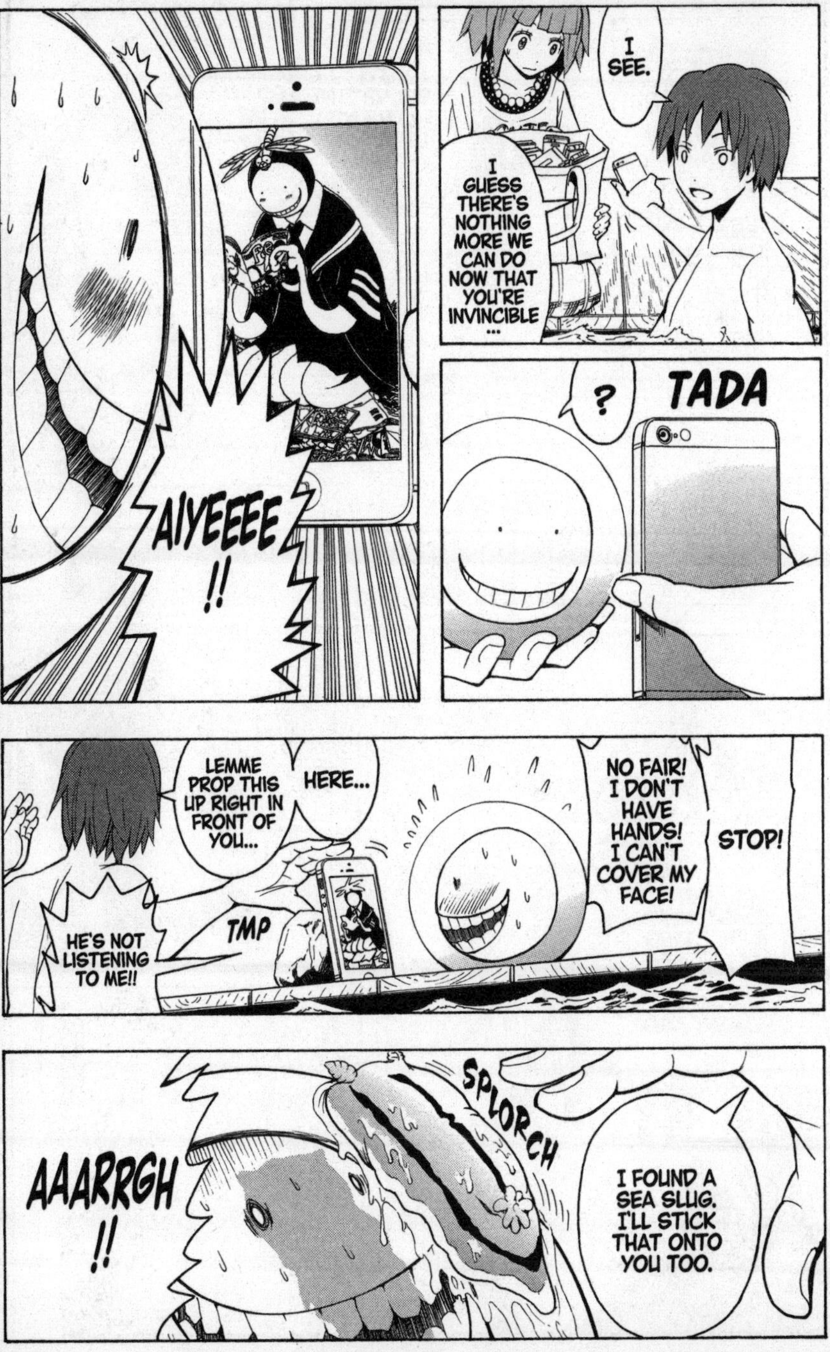
I SEE.
I GUESS THERE'S NOTHING MORE WE CAN DO NOW THAT YOU'RE INVINCIBLE...
TADA
?
AIYEEEE!!
STOP!
NO FAIR! I DON'T HAVE HANDS! I CAN'T COVER MY FACE!
HERE...
LEMME PROP THIS UP RIGHT IN FRONT OF YOU...
TMP
HE'S NOT LISTENING TO ME!!
I FOUND A SEA SLUG. I'LL STICK THAT ONTO YOU TOO.
SPLORCH
AAARRGH!!

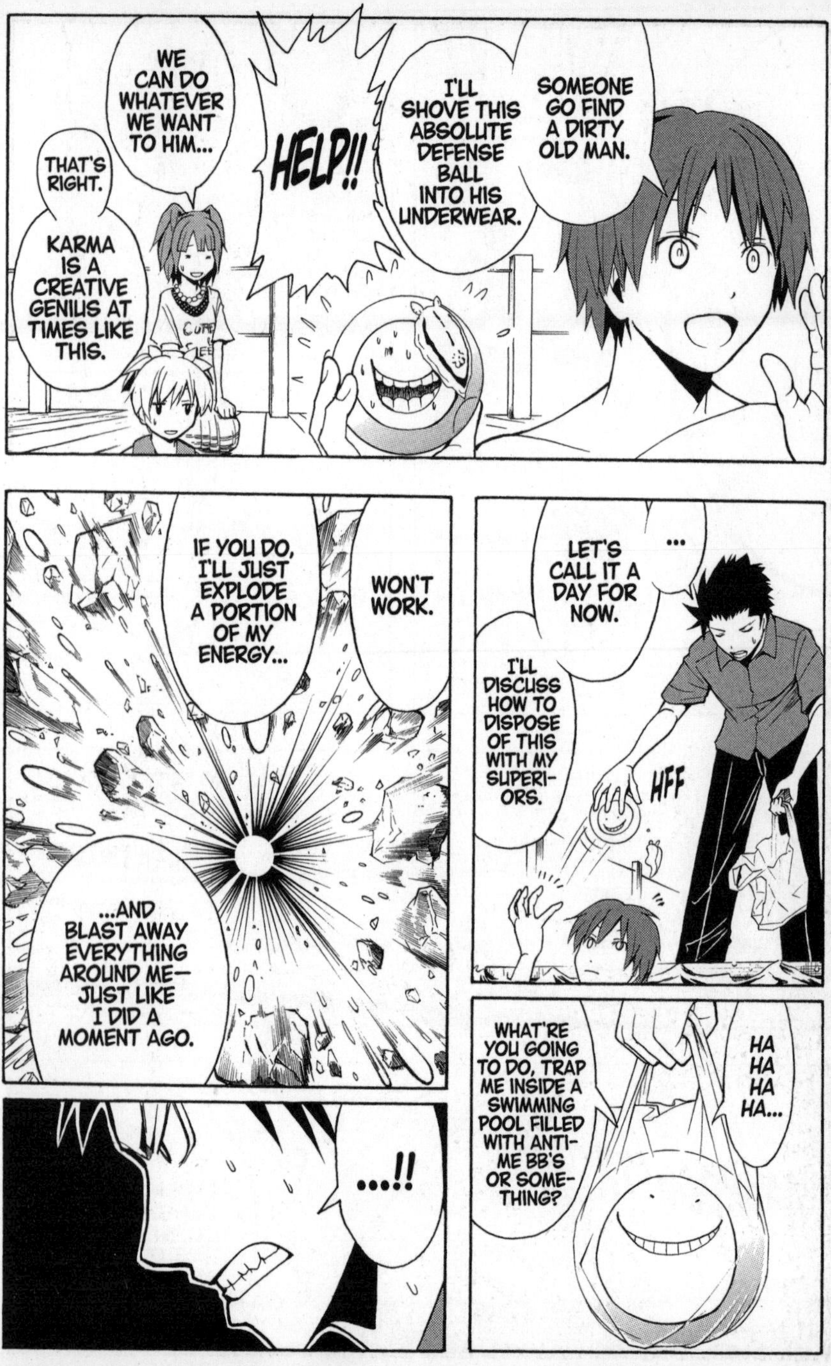
SOMEONE GO FIND A DIRTY OLD MAN.
I'LL SHOVE THIS ABSOLUTE DEFENSE BALL INTO HIS UNDERWEAR.
HELP!!
WE CAN DO WHATEVER WE WANT TO HIM...
THAT'S RIGHT.
KARMA IS A CREATIVE GENIUS AT TIMES LIKE THIS.
...
LET'S CALL IT A DAY FOR NOW.
I'LL DISCUSS HOW TO DISPOSE OF THIS WITH MY SUPERIORS.
HFF
HA HA HA HA...
WHAT'RE YOU GOING TO DO, TRAP ME INSIDE A SWIMMING POOL FILLED WITH ANTI-ME BB'S OR SOMETHING?
WON'T WORK.
IF YOU DO, I'LL JUST EXPLODE A PORTION OF MY ENERGY...
...AND BLAST AWAY EVERYTHING AROUND ME—JUST LIKE I DID A MOMENT AGO.
...!!

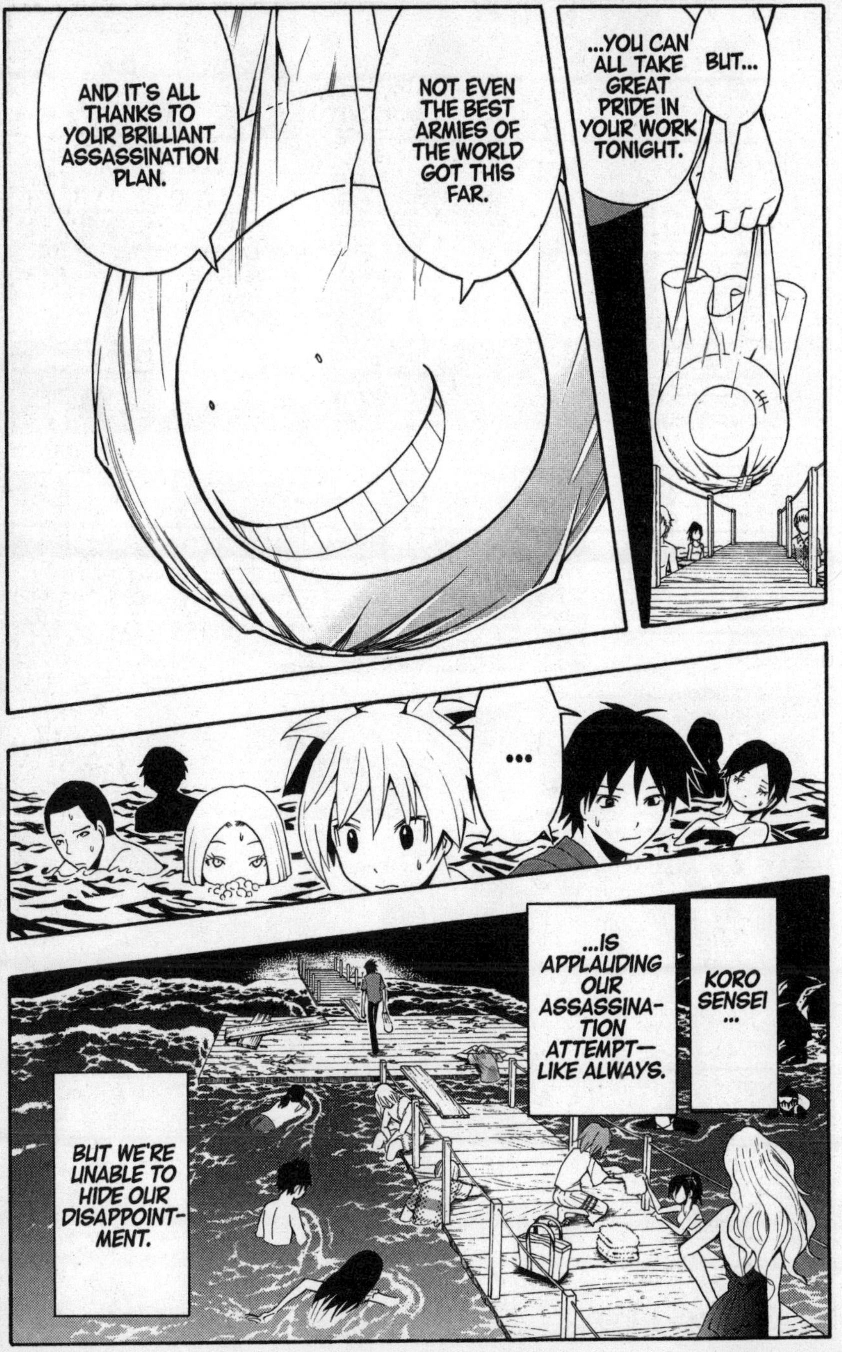
BUT...
...YOU CAN ALL TAKE GREAT PRIDE IN YOUR WORK TONIGHT.
NOT EVEN THE BEST ARMIES OF THE WORLD GOT THIS FAR.
AND IT'S ALL THANKS TO YOUR BRILLIANT ASSASSINATION PLAN.
...
KORO SENSEI ...
...IS APPLAUDING OUR ASSASSINATION ATTEMPT—LIKE ALWAYS.
BUT WE'RE UNABLE TO HIDE OUR DISAPPOINTMENT.

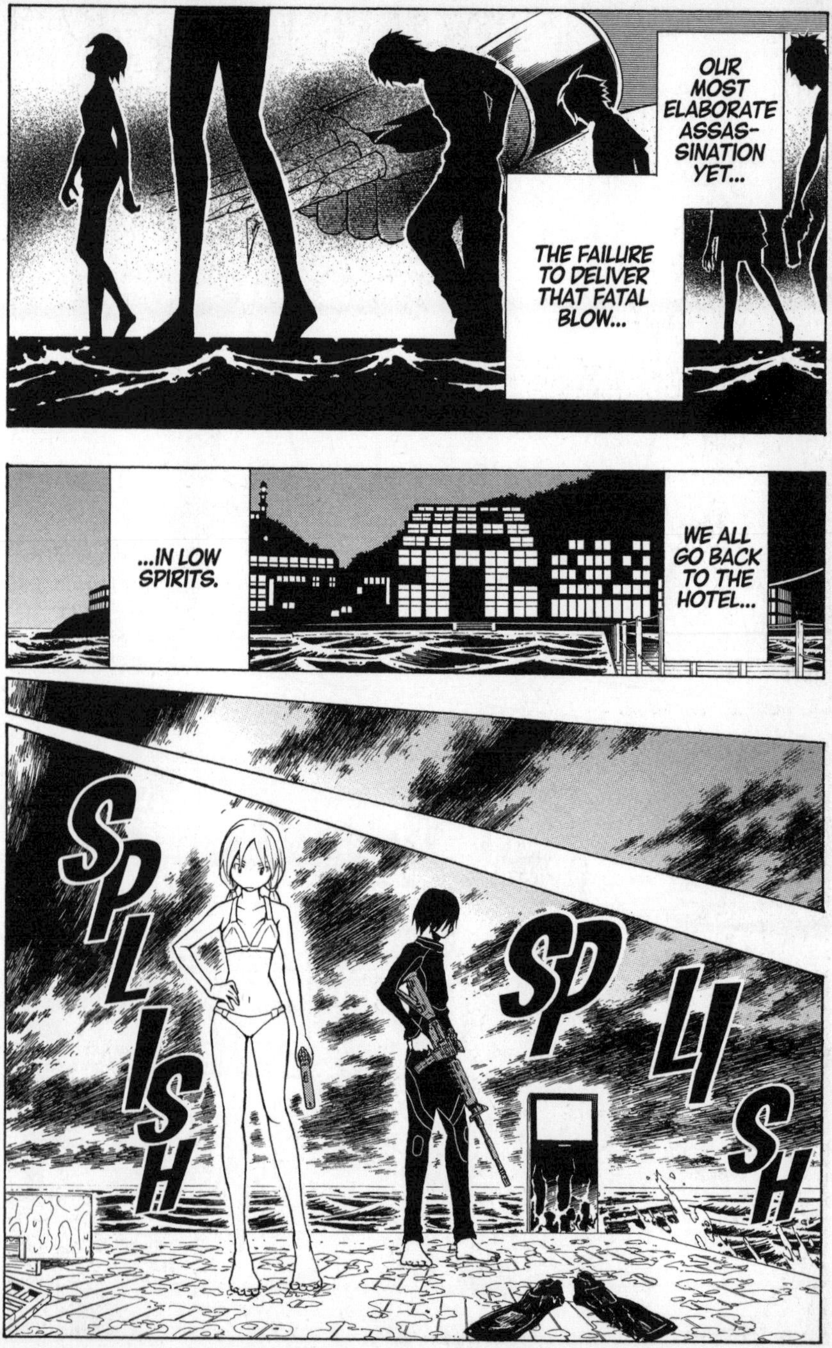
OUR MOST ELABORATE ASSAS-SINATION YET...
THE FAILURE TO DELIVER THAT FATAL BLOW...
WE ALL GO BACK TO THE HOTEL...
...IN LOW SPIRITS.
SPLISH
SPLISH

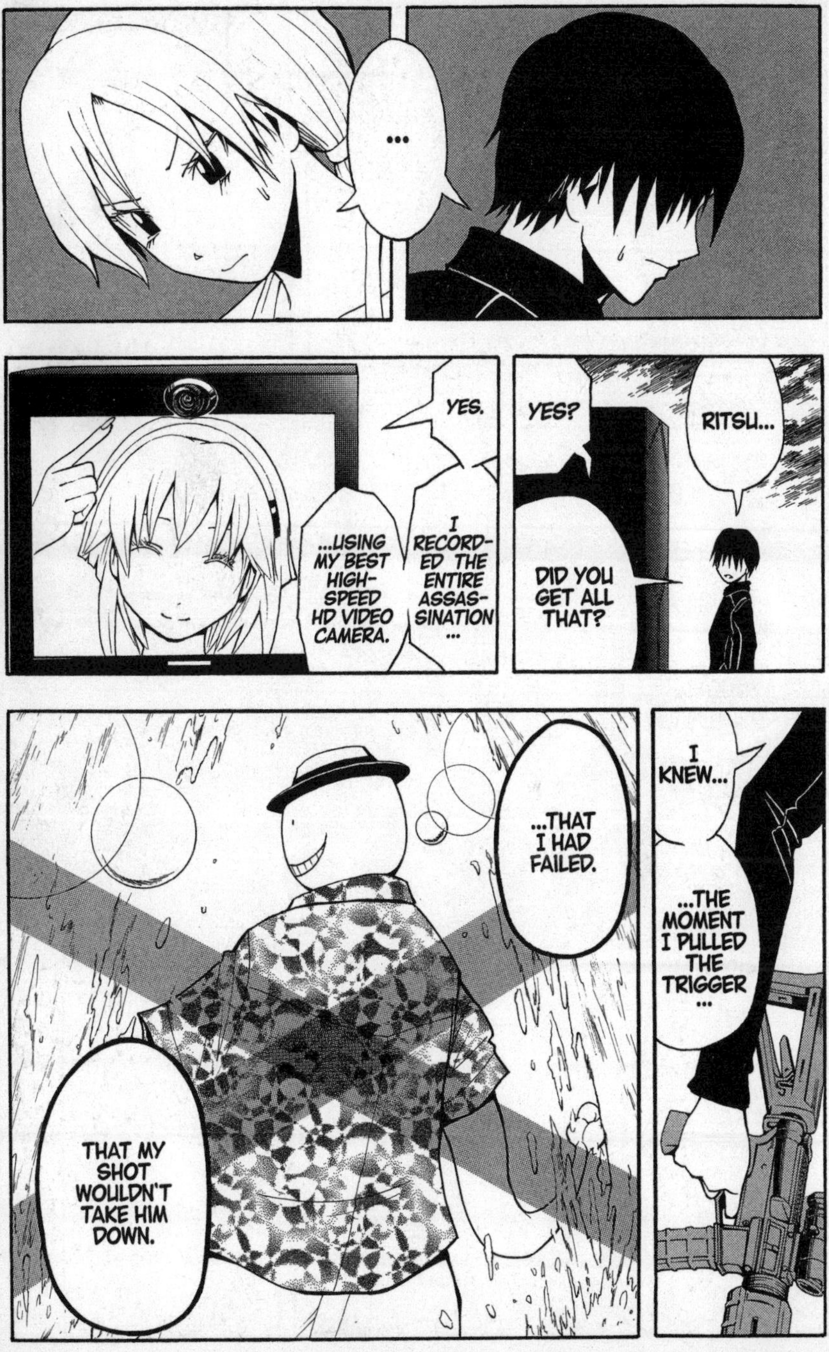
...
RITSU...
YES?
DID YOU GET ALL THAT?
YES.
I RECORDED THE ENTIRE ASSASSINATION...
...USING MY BEST HIGH-SPEED HD VIDEO CAMERA.
I KNEW...
...THE MOMENT I PULLED THE TRIGGER...
...THAT I HAD FAILED.
THAT MY SHOT WOULDN'T TAKE HIM DOWN.

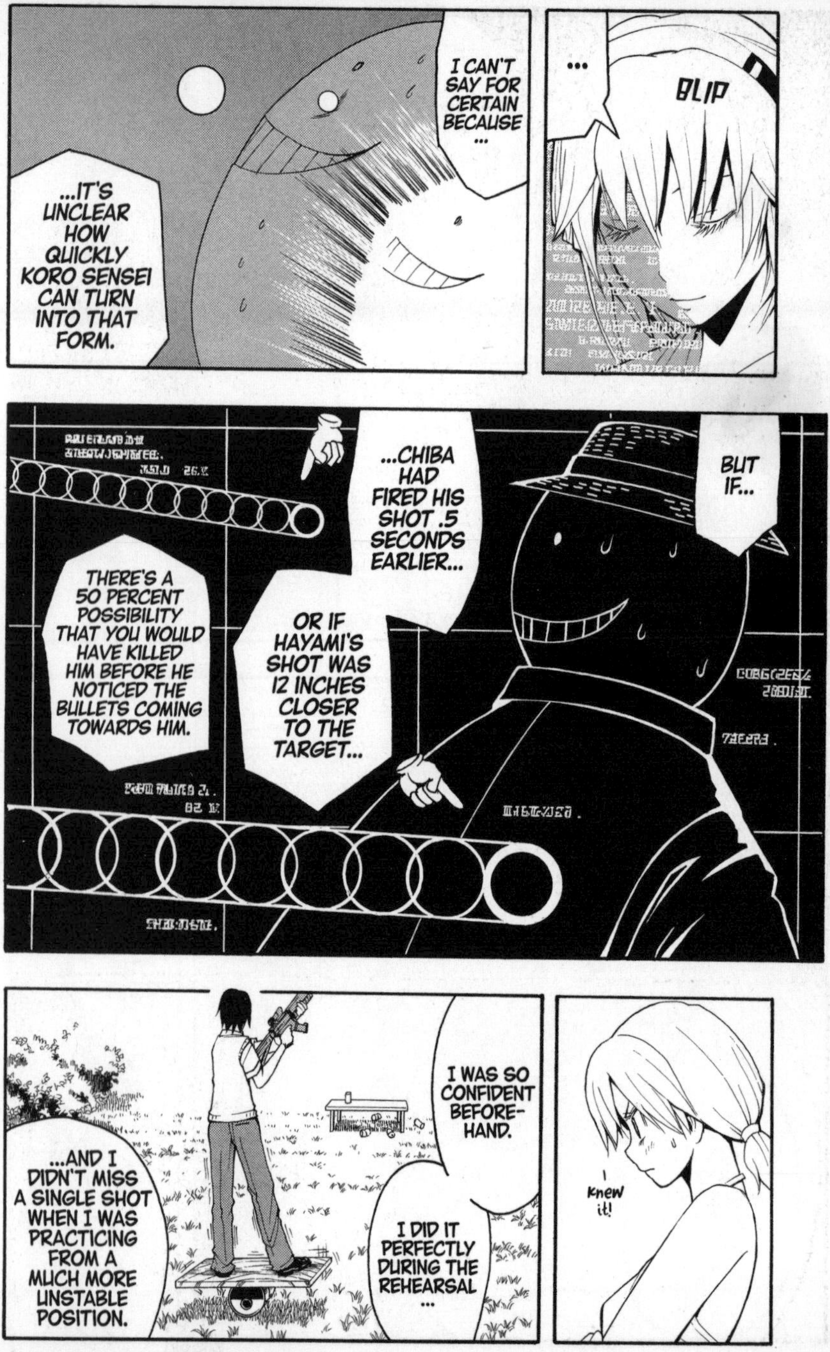
...
BLIP
I CAN'T SAY FOR CERTAIN BECAUSE ...
...IT'S UNCLEAR HOW QUICKLY KORO SENSEI CAN TURN INTO THAT FORM.
BUT IF...
...CHIBA HAD FIRED HIS SHOT .5 SECONDS EARLIER...
OR IF HAYAMI'S SHOT WAS 12 INCHES CLOSER TO THE TARGET...
THERE'S A 50 PERCENT POSSIBILITY THAT YOU WOULD HAVE KILLED HIM BEFORE HE NOTICED THE BULLETS COMING TOWARDS HIM.
I knew it!
I WAS SO CONFIDENT BEFORE-HAND.
I DID IT PERFECTLY DURING THE REHEARSAL ...
...AND I DIDN'T MISS A SINGLE SHOT WHEN I WAS PRACTICING FROM A MUCH MORE UNSTABLE POSITION.

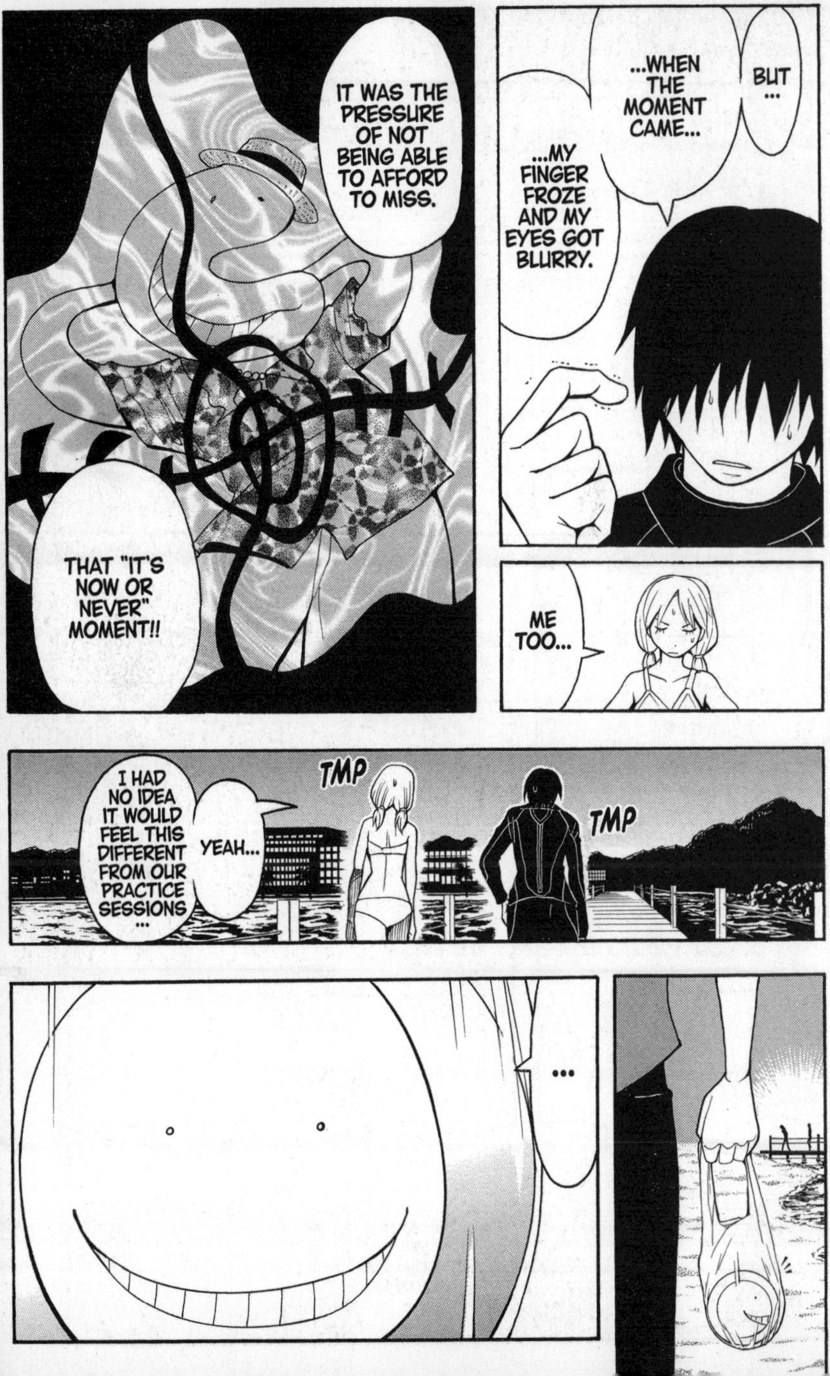
BUT ...
...WHEN THE MOMENT CAME...
...MY FINGER FROZE AND MY EYES GOT BLURRY.
IT WAS THE PRESSURE OF NOT BEING ABLE TO AFFORD TO MISS.
THAT "IT'S NOW OR NEVER" MOMENT!!
ME TOO...
TMP
TMP
YEAH...
I HAD NO IDEA IT WOULD FEEL THIS DIFFERENT FROM OUR PRACTICE SESSIONS ...
...

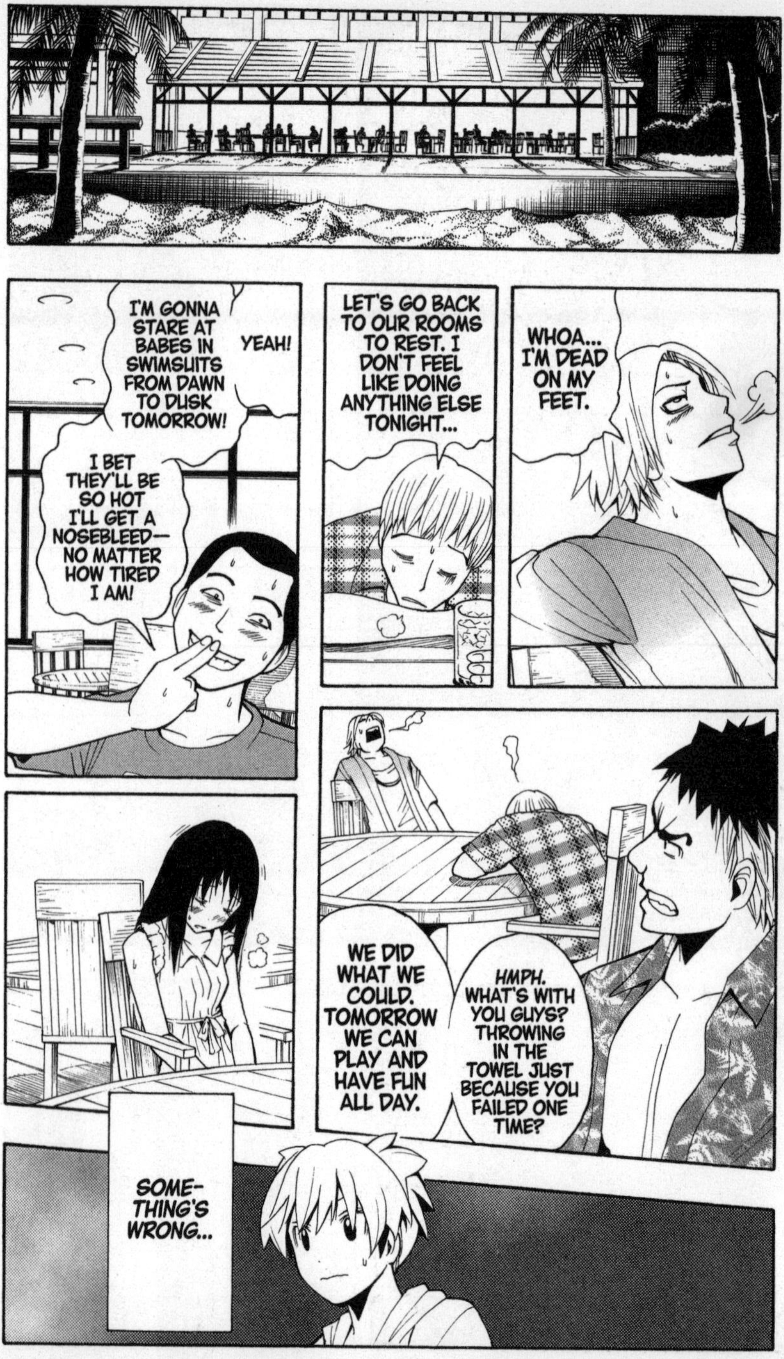
WHOA... I'M DEAD ON MY FEET.
LET'S GO BACK TO OUR ROOMS TO REST. I DON'T FEEL LIKE DOING ANYTHING ELSE TONIGHT...
I'M GONNA STARE AT BABES IN SWIMSUITS FROM DAWN TO DUSK TOMORROW!
YEAH!
I BET THEY'LL BE SO HOT I'LL GET A NOSEBLEED— NO MATTER HOW TIRED I AM!
HMPH. WHAT'S WITH YOU GUYS? THROWING IN THE TOWEL JUST BECAUSE YOU FAILED ONE TIME?
WE DID WHAT WE COULD. TOMORROW WE CAN PLAY AND HAVE FUN ALL DAY.
SOME-THING'S WRONG...

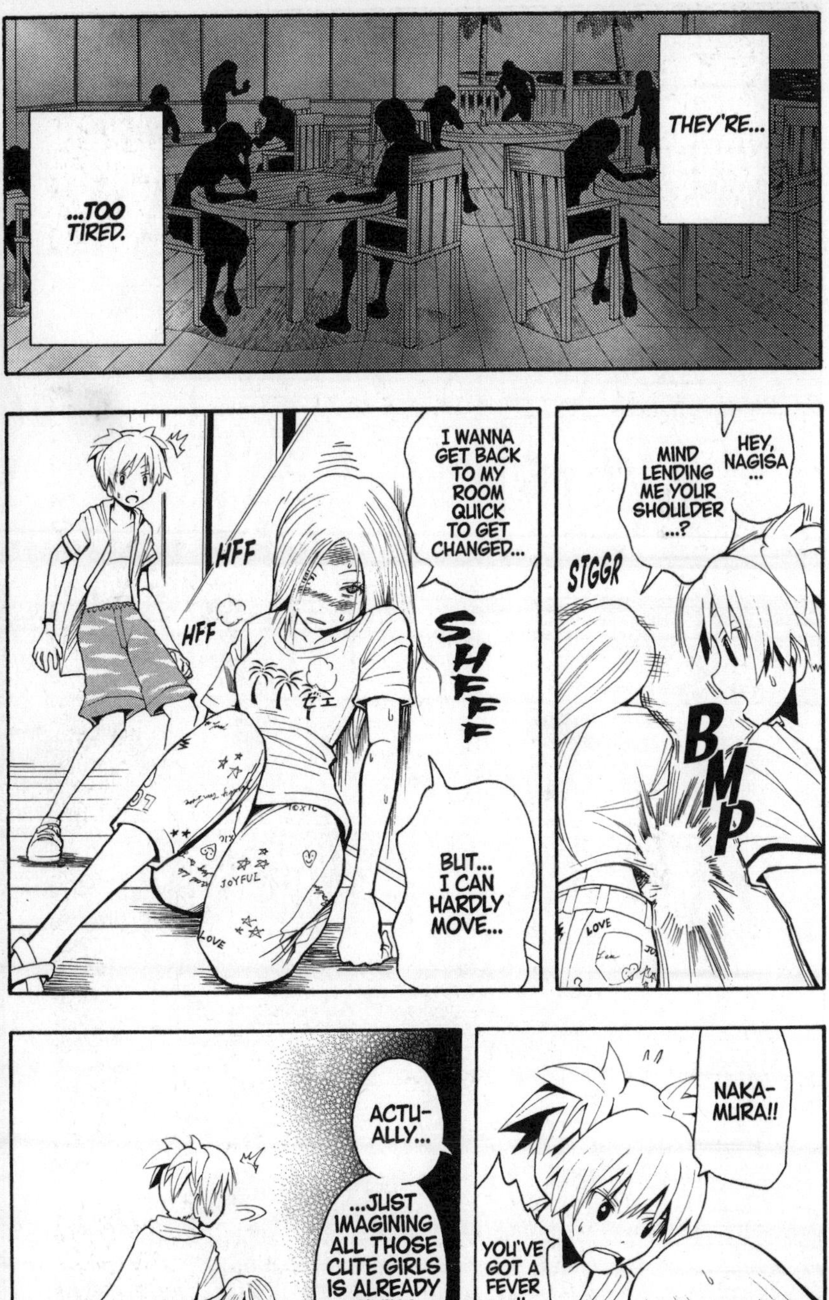
THEY'RE...
...TOO TIRED.
HEY, NAGISA...
MIND LENDING ME YOUR SHOULDER...?
STGGR
BMP
I WANNA GET BACK TO MY ROOM QUICK TO GET CHANGED...
SHFFF
HFF
HFF
BUT... I CAN HARDLY MOVE...
NAKA-MURA!!
YOU'VE GOT A FEVER...!!
ACTU-ALLY...
...JUST IMAGINING ALL THOSE CUTE GIRLS IS ALREADY GIVING ME A...

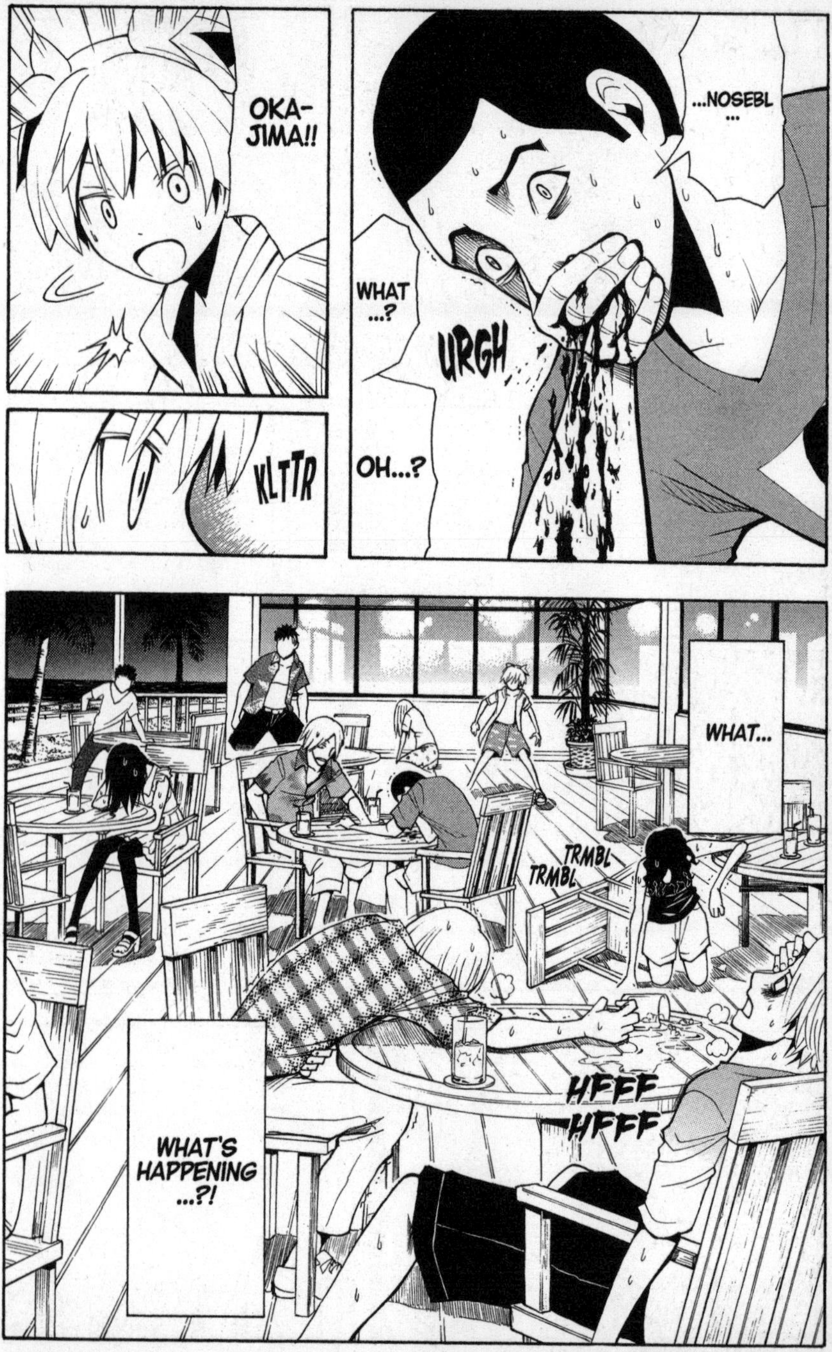
...NOSEBL ...
WHAT ...?
URGH
OH...?
OKA-JIMA!!
KLTTR
WHAT...
TRMBL TRMBL
HFFF HFFF
WHAT'S HAPPENING ...?!

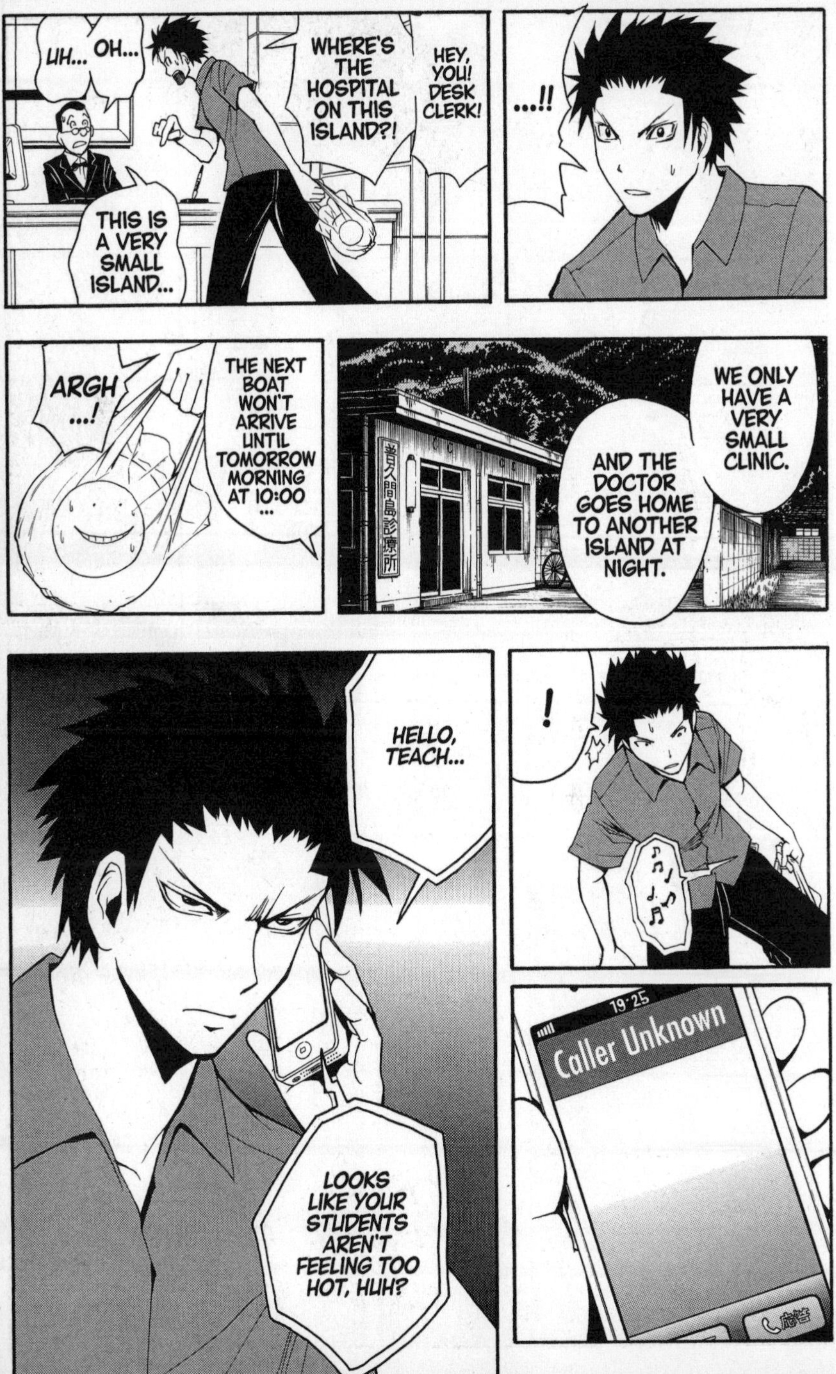
...!!
HEY, YOU! DESK CLERK!
WHERE'S THE HOSPITAL ON THIS ISLAND?!
UH... OH...
THIS IS A VERY SMALL ISLAND...
WE ONLY HAVE A VERY SMALL CLINIC.
AND THE DOCTOR GOES HOME TO ANOTHER ISLAND AT NIGHT.
普久間島診療所
THE NEXT BOAT WON'T ARRIVE UNTIL TOMORROW MORNING AT 10:00 ...
ARGH ...!
!
19:25
Caller Unknown
応答
HELLO, TEACH...
LOOKS LIKE YOUR STUDENTS AREN'T FEELING TOO HOT, HUH?

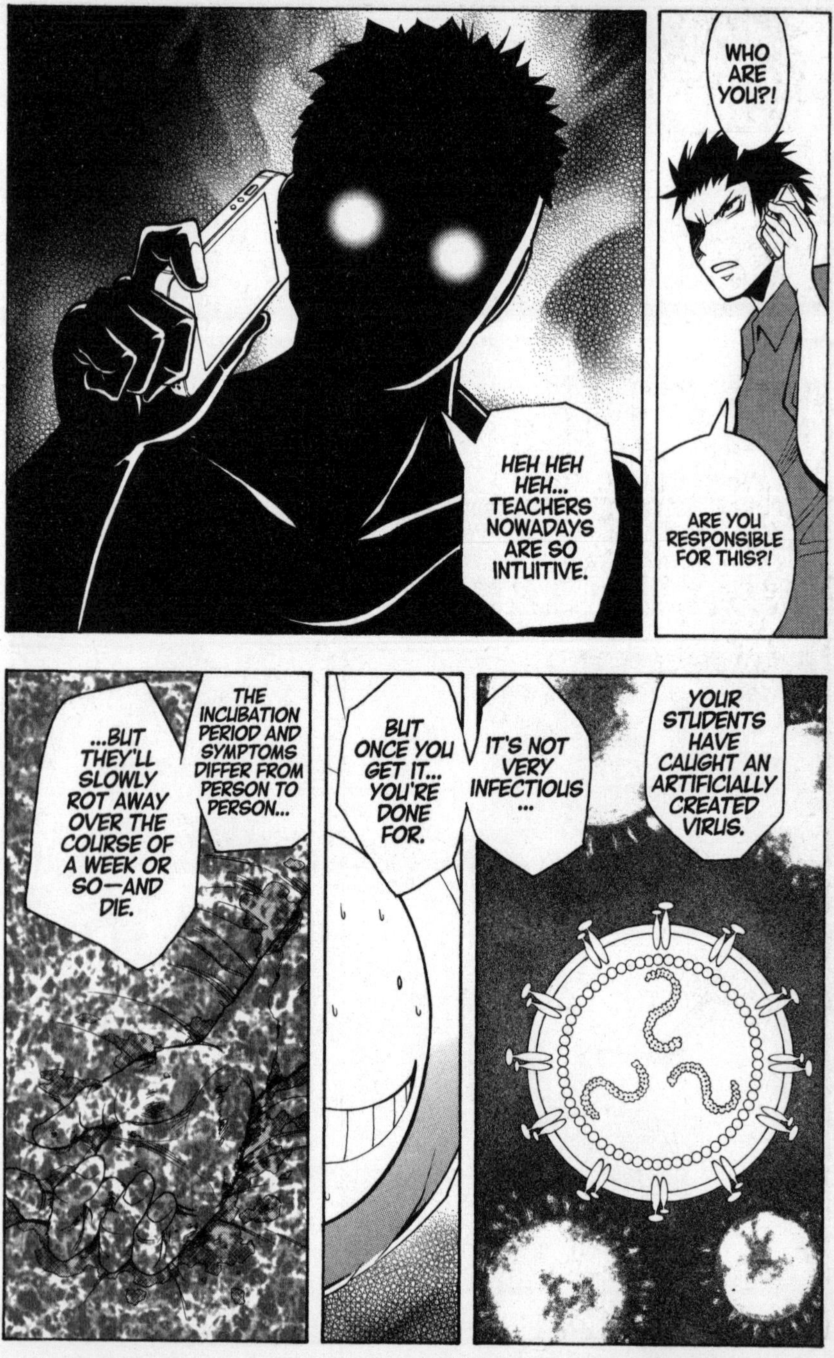
WHO ARE YOU?!
ARE YOU RESPONSIBLE FOR THIS?!
HEH HEH HEH... TEACHERS NOWADAYS ARE SO INTUITIVE.
YOUR STUDENTS HAVE CAUGHT AN ARTIFICIALLY CREATED VIRUS.
IT'S NOT VERY INFECTIOUS ...
BUT ONCE YOU GET IT... YOU'RE DONE FOR.
THE INCUBATION PERIOD AND SYMPTOMS DIFFER FROM PERSON TO PERSON...
...BUT THEY'LL SLOWLY ROT AWAY OVER THE COURSE OF A WEEK OR SO—AND DIE.

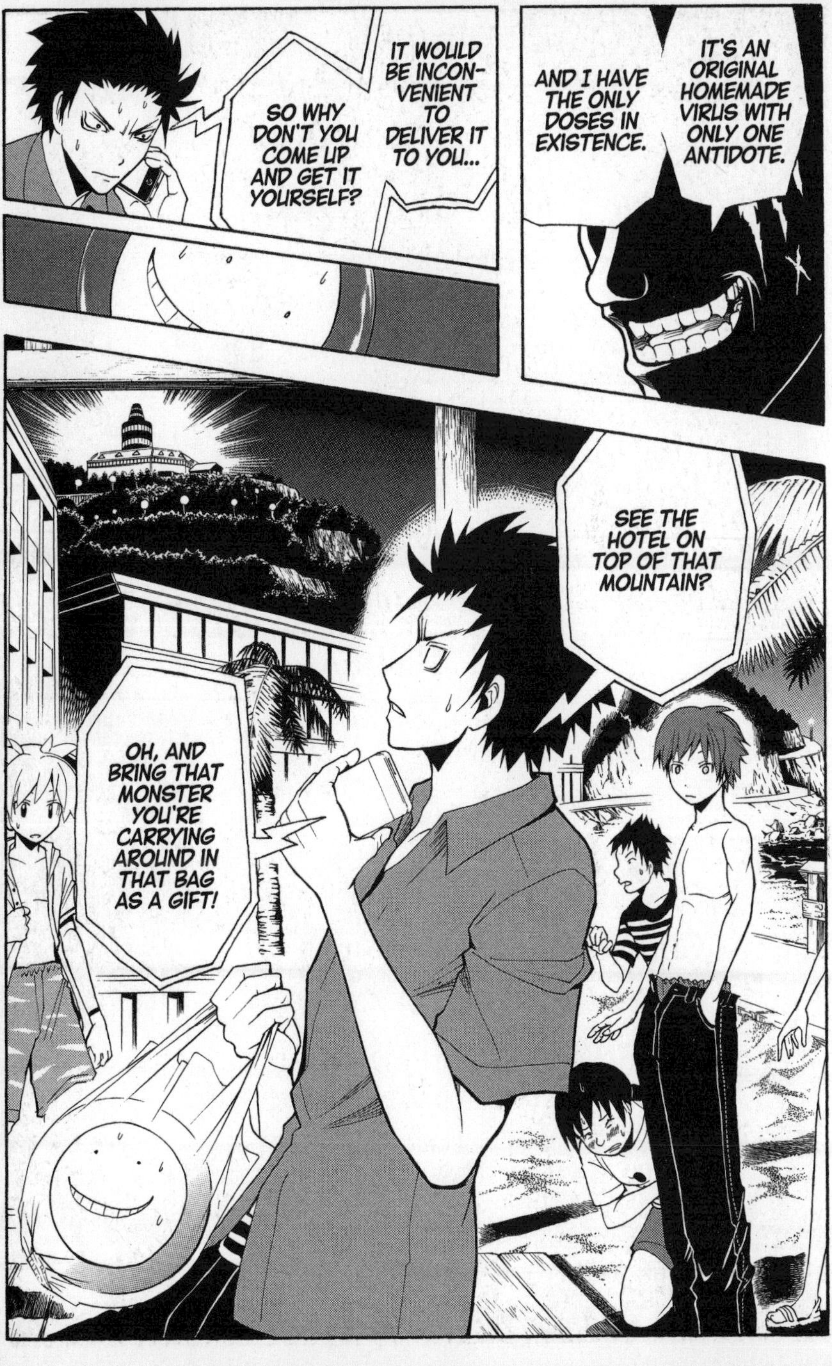
IT'S AN ORIGINAL HOMEMADE VIRUS WITH ONLY ONE ANTIDOTE.
AND I HAVE THE ONLY DOSES IN EXISTENCE.
IT WOULD BE INCON-VENIENT TO DELIVER IT TO YOU...
SO WHY DON'T YOU COME UP AND GET IT YOURSELF?
SEE THE HOTEL ON TOP OF THAT MOUNTAIN?
OH, AND BRING THAT MONSTER YOU'RE CARRYING AROUND IN THAT BAG AS A GIFT!

E-23 KOKI MIMURA

- 😊 BIRTHDAY: FEBRUARY 1

- 😊 HEIGHT: 5' 5"

- 😊 WEIGHT: 117 LBS.

- 😊 FAVORITE SUBJECT: CIVICS

- 😊 LEAST FAVORITE SUBJECT: BIOLOGY

- 😊 HOBBY/SKILL: WATCHING DVDS, AIR GUITAR

- 😊 FUTURE GOAL: TV SHOW PRODUCER

- 😊 HOW HE WAS INVITED BY SUGAYA: HEY, LET'S MAKE A MOVIE TOGETHER!

- 😊 HOW HE WAS INVITED BY OKAJIMA: YO... LET'S MAKE A MOVIE TOGETHER...

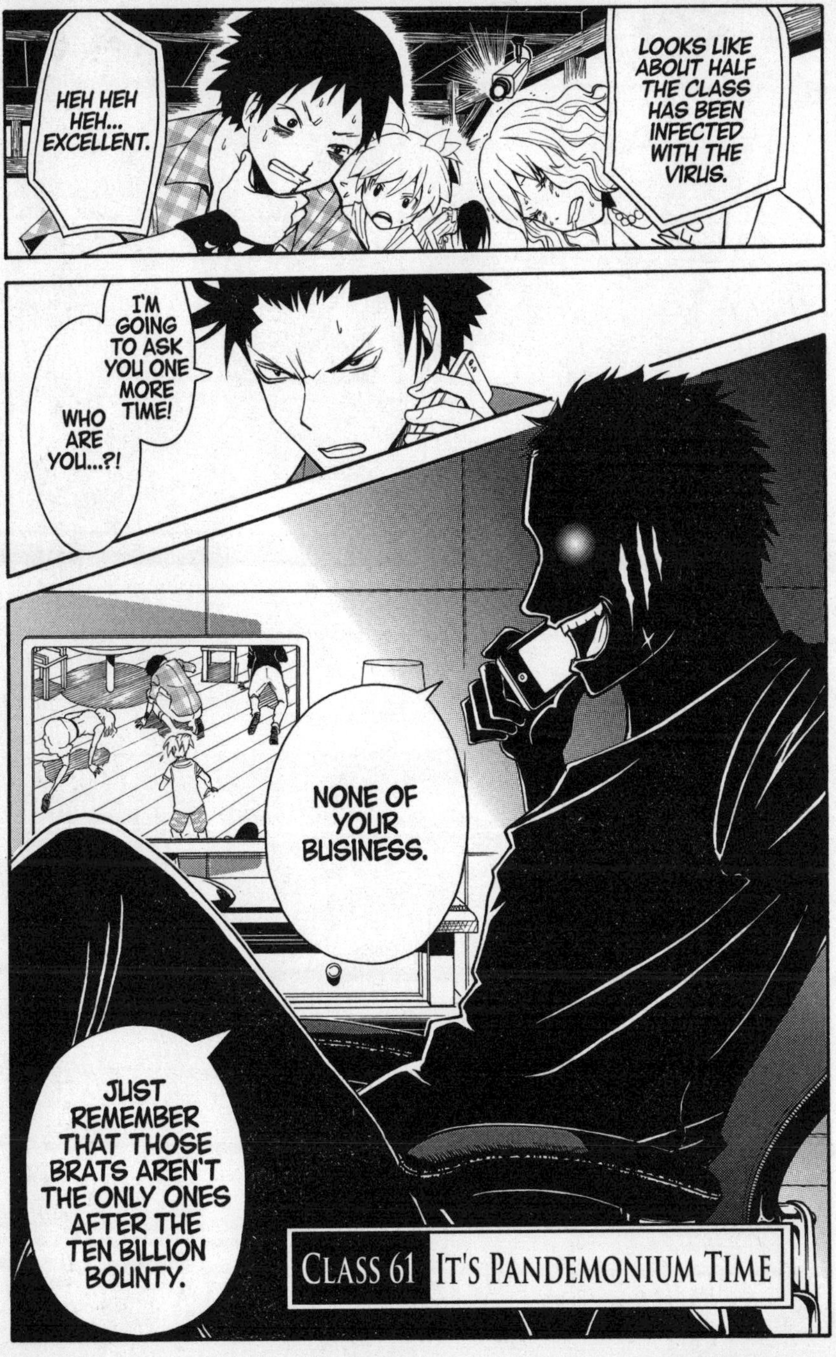
LOOKS LIKE ABOUT HALF THE CLASS HAS BEEN INFECTED WITH THE VIRUS.
HEH HEH HEH... EXCELLENT.
I'M GOING TO ASK YOU ONE MORE TIME!
WHO ARE YOU...?!
NONE OF YOUR BUSINESS.
JUST REMEMBER THAT THOSE BRATS AREN'T THE ONLY ONES AFTER THE TEN BILLION BOUNTY.
CLASS 61 IT'S PANDEMONIUM TIME

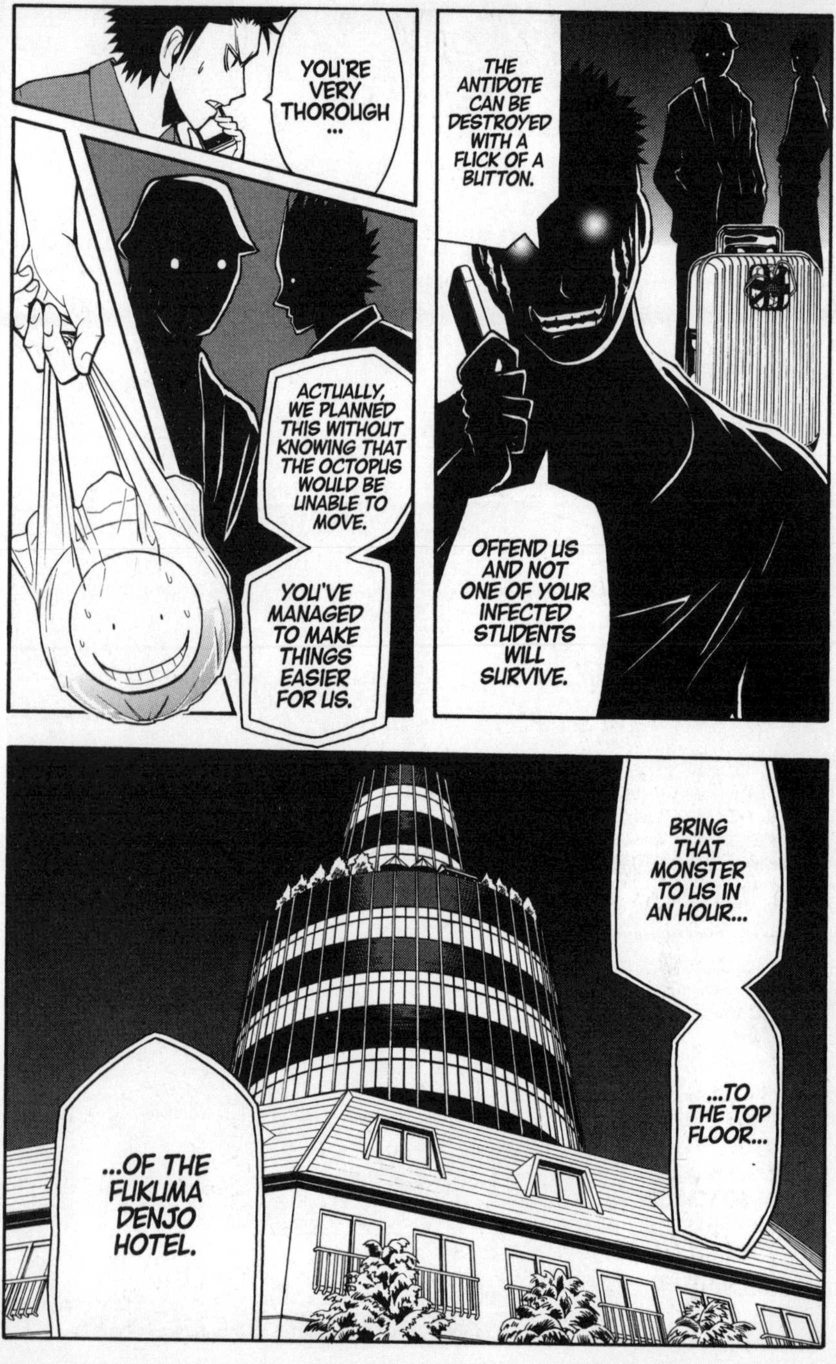
THE ANTIDOTE CAN BE DESTROYED WITH A FLICK OF A BUTTON.
OFFEND US AND NOT ONE OF YOUR INFECTED STUDENTS WILL SURVIVE.
YOU'RE VERY THOROUGH ...
ACTUALLY, WE PLANNED THIS WITHOUT KNOWING THAT THE OCTOPUS WOULD BE UNABLE TO MOVE.
YOU'VE MANAGED TO MAKE THINGS EASIER FOR US.
BRING THAT MONSTER TO US IN AN HOUR...
...TO THE TOP FLOOR...
...OF THE FUKUMA DENJO HOTEL.

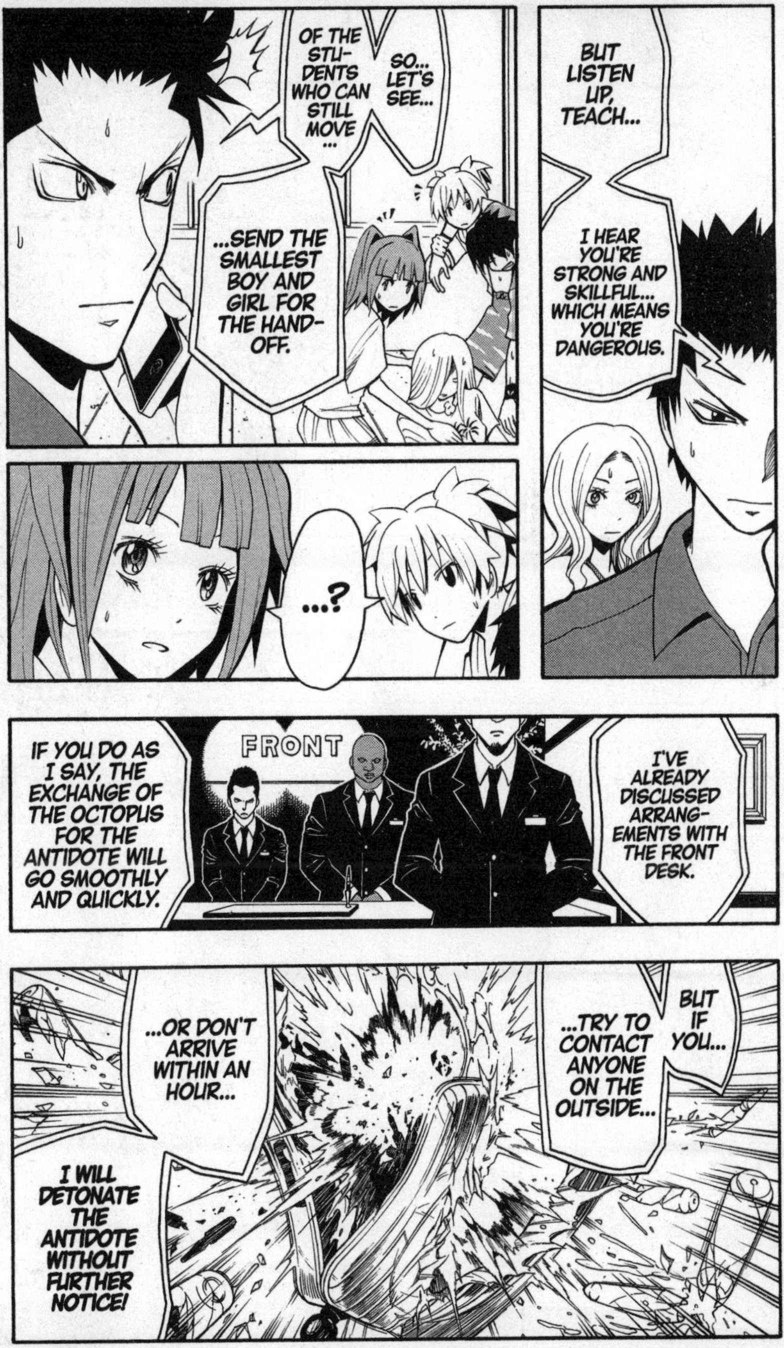
BUT LISTEN UP, TEACH...
I HEAR YOU'RE STRONG AND SKILLFUL... WHICH MEANS YOU'RE DANGEROUS.
SO... LET'S SEE...
OF THE STUDENTS WHO CAN STILL MOVE...
...SEND THE SMALLEST BOY AND GIRL FOR THE HAND-OFF.
...?
I'VE ALREADY DISCUSSED ARRANGEMENTS WITH THE FRONT DESK.
FRONT
IF YOU DO AS I SAY, THE EXCHANGE OF THE OCTOPUS FOR THE ANTIDOTE WILL GO SMOOTHLY AND QUICKLY.
BUT IF YOU...
...TRY TO CONTACT ANYONE ON THE OUTSIDE...
...OR DON'T ARRIVE WITHIN AN HOUR...
I WILL DETONATE THE ANTIDOTE WITHOUT FURTHER NOTICE!

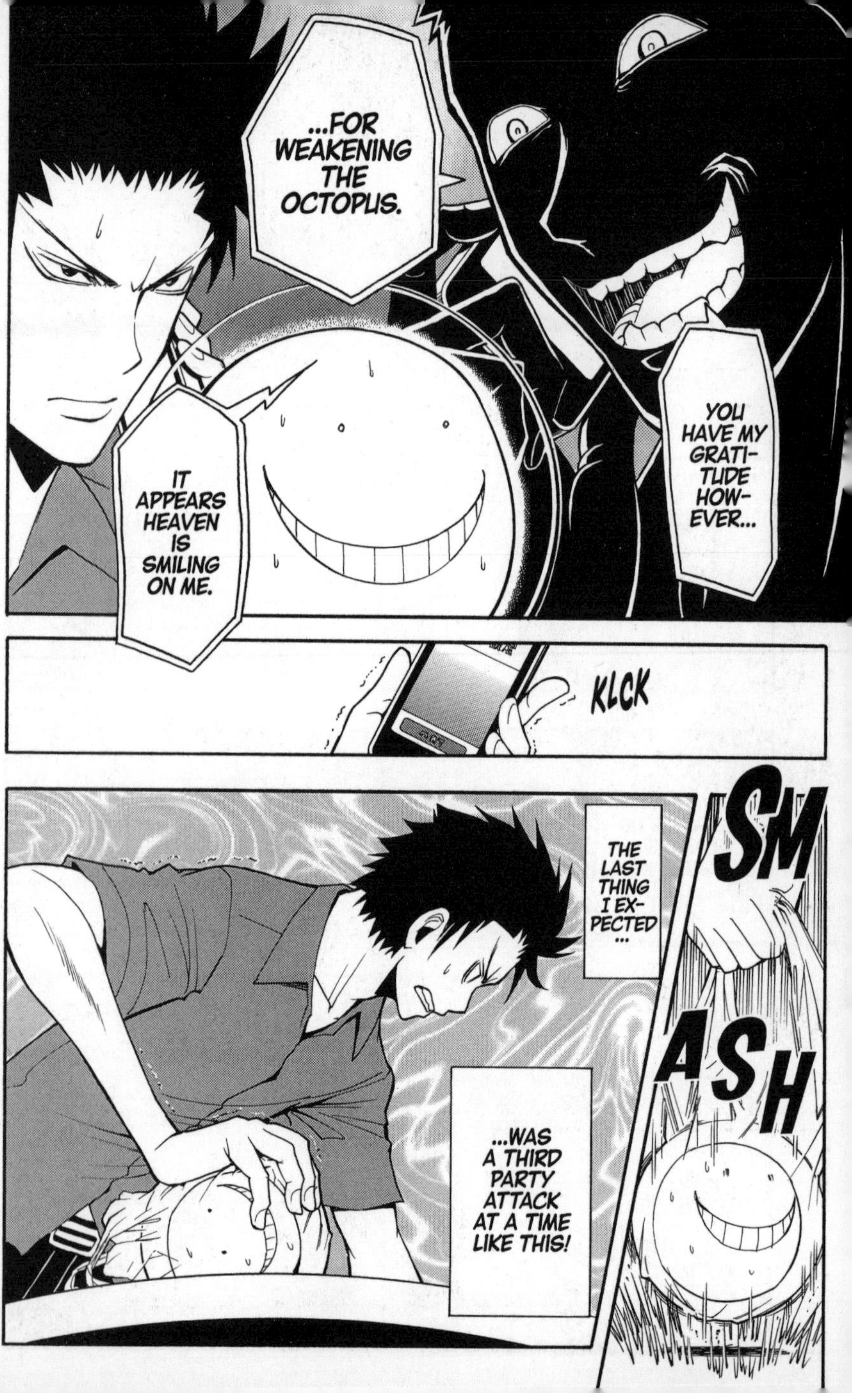
YOU HAVE MY GRATI-TUDE HOW-EVER...
...FOR WEAKENING THE OCTOPUS.
IT APPEARS HEAVEN IS SMILING ON ME.
KLCK
SMASH
THE LAST THING I EX-PECTED...
...WAS A THIRD PARTY ATTACK AT A TIME LIKE THIS!

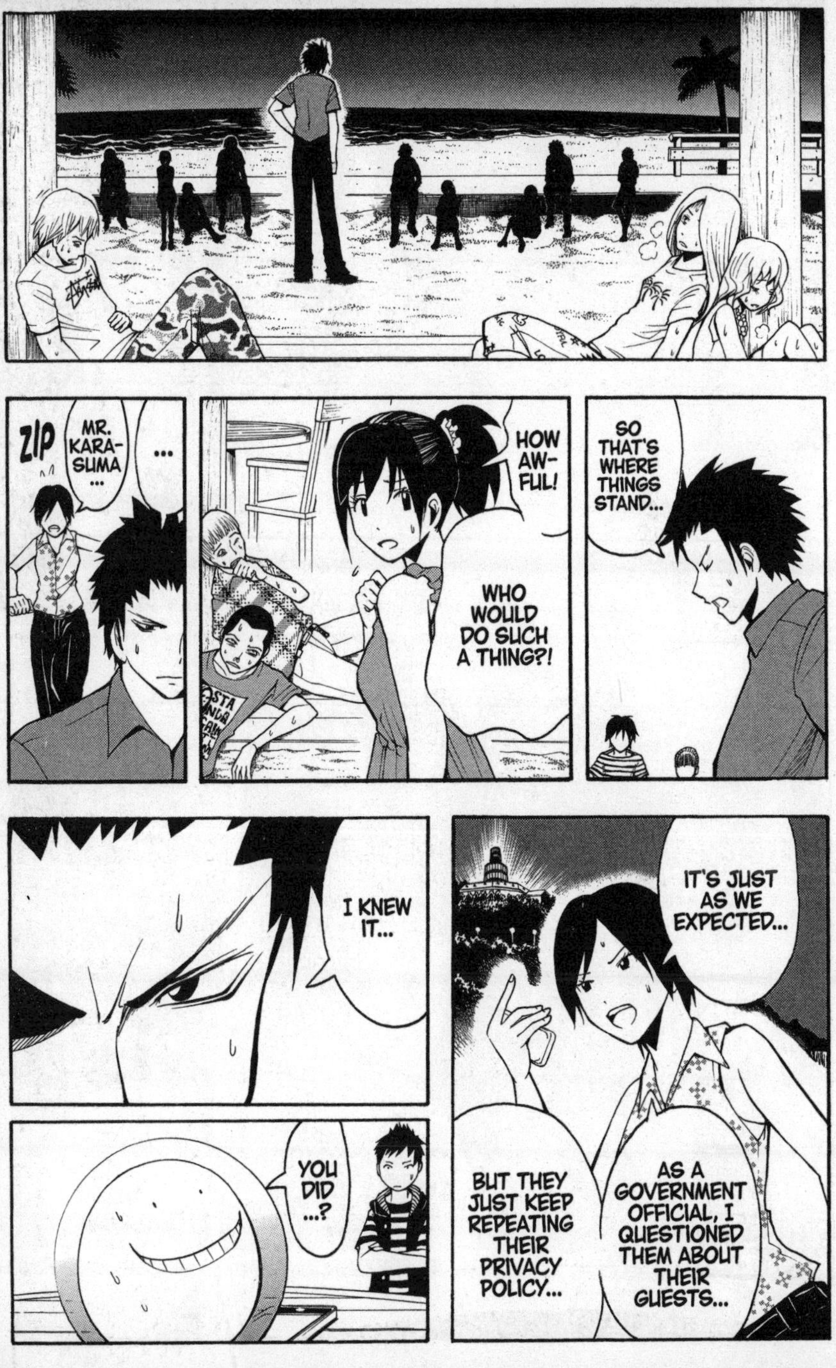
SO THAT'S WHERE THINGS STAND...
HOW AWFUL!
WHO WOULD DO SUCH A THING?!
...
MR. KARASUMA ...
ZIP
IT'S JUST AS WE EXPECTED...
AS A GOVERNMENT OFFICIAL, I QUESTIONED THEM ABOUT THEIR GUESTS...
BUT THEY JUST KEEP REPEATING THEIR PRIVACY POLICY...
I KNEW IT...
YOU DID ...?

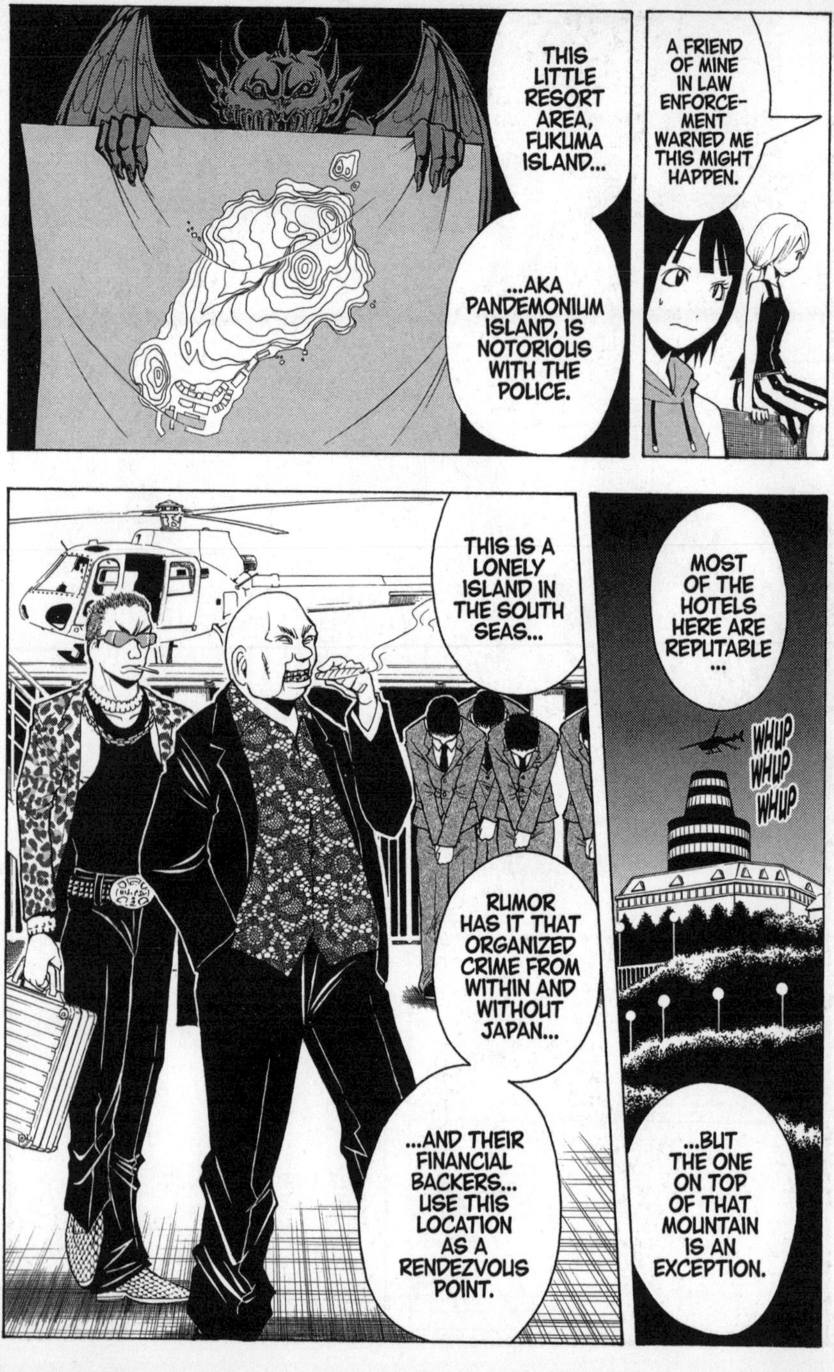
A FRIEND OF MINE IN LAW ENFORCEMENT WARNED ME THIS MIGHT HAPPEN.
THIS LITTLE RESORT AREA, FUKUMA ISLAND...
...AKA PANDEMONIUM ISLAND, IS NOTORIOUS WITH THE POLICE.
MOST OF THE HOTELS HERE ARE REPUTABLE...
WHUP WHUP WHUP
...BUT THE ONE ON TOP OF THAT MOUNTAIN IS AN EXCEPTION.
THIS IS A LONELY ISLAND IN THE SOUTH SEAS...
RUMOR HAS IT THAT ORGANIZED CRIME FROM WITHIN AND WITHOUT JAPAN...
...AND THEIR FINANCIAL BACKERS... USE THIS LOCATION AS A RENDEZVOUS POINT.

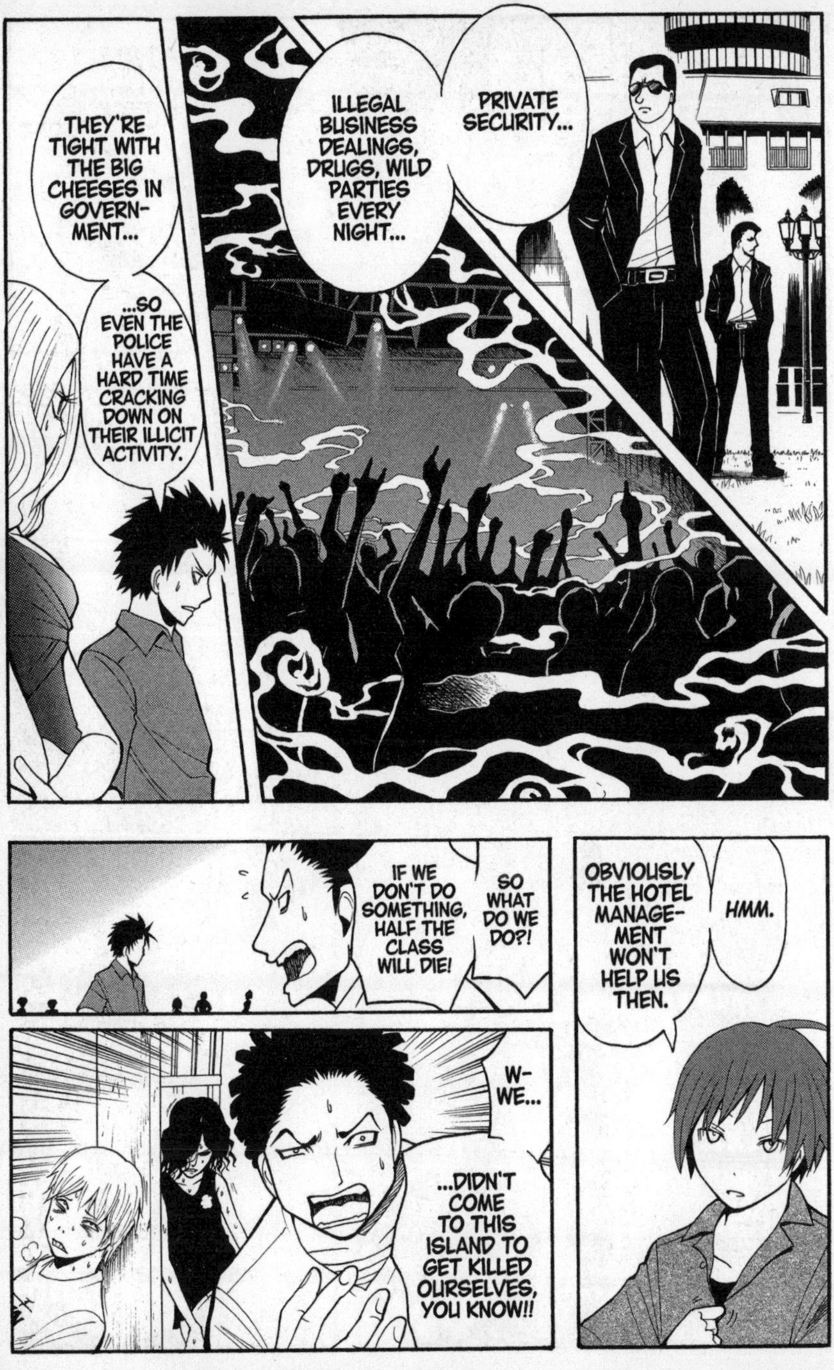
PRIVATE SECURITY...
ILLEGAL BUSINESS DEALINGS, DRUGS, WILD PARTIES EVERY NIGHT...
THEY'RE TIGHT WITH THE BIG CHEESES IN GOVERN-MENT...
...SO EVEN THE POLICE HAVE A HARD TIME CRACKING DOWN ON THEIR ILLICIT ACTIVITY.
HMM.
OBVIOUSLY THE HOTEL MANAGE-MENT WON'T HELP US THEN.
SO WHAT DO WE DO?!
IF WE DON'T DO SOMETHING, HALF THE CLASS WILL DIE!
W-WE...
...DIDN'T COME TO THIS ISLAND TO GET KILLED OURSELVES, YOU KNOW!!

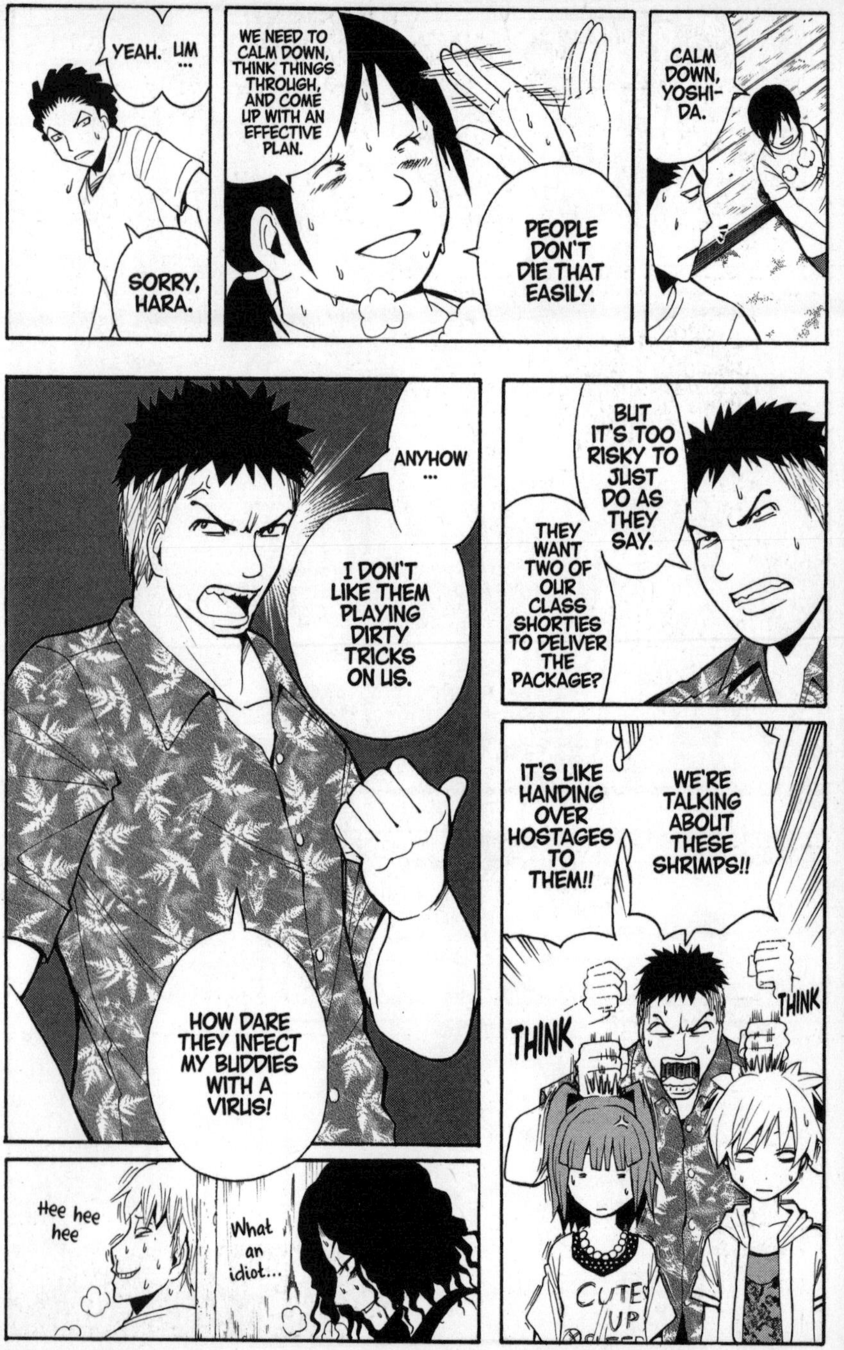
CALM DOWN, YOSHIDA.
WE NEED TO CALM DOWN, THINK THINGS THROUGH, AND COME UP WITH AN EFFECTIVE PLAN.
PEOPLE DON'T DIE THAT EASILY.
YEAH. UM ...
SORRY, HARA.
BUT IT'S TOO RISKY TO JUST DO AS THEY SAY.
THEY WANT TWO OF OUR CLASS SHORTIES TO DELIVER THE PACKAGE?
WE'RE TALKING ABOUT THESE SHRIMPS!!
IT'S LIKE HANDING OVER HOSTAGES TO THEM!!
THINK
THINK
ANYHOW ...
I DON'T LIKE THEM PLAYING DIRTY TRICKS ON US.
HOW DARE THEY INFECT MY BUDDIES WITH A VIRUS!
What an idiot...
Hee hee hee
CUTE UP

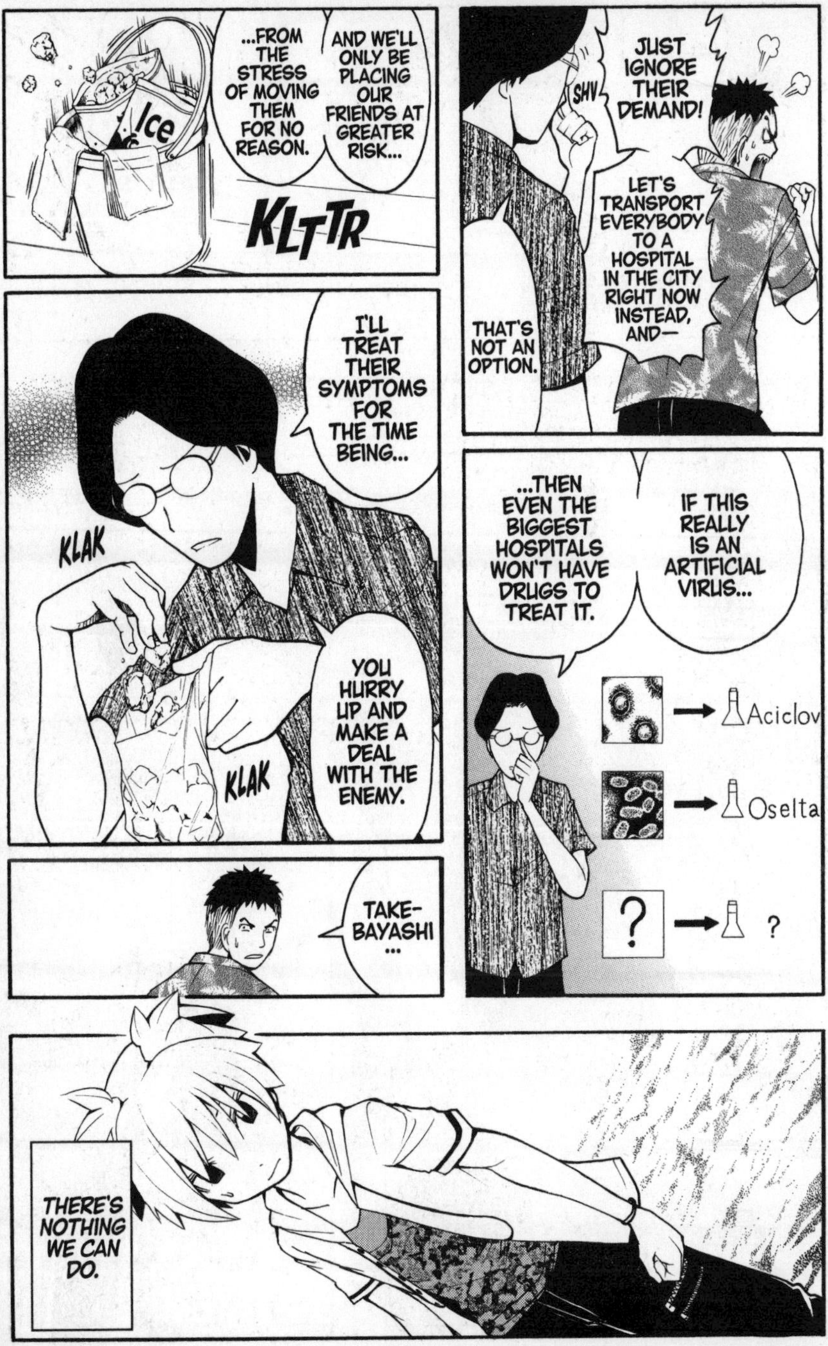
JUST IGNORE THEIR DEMAND!
SHV
LET'S TRANSPORT EVERYBODY TO A HOSPITAL IN THE CITY RIGHT NOW INSTEAD, AND—
THAT'S NOT AN OPTION.
AND WE'LL ONLY BE PLACING OUR FRIENDS AT GREATER RISK...
...FROM THE STRESS OF MOVING THEM FOR NO REASON.
Ice
KLTTR
IF THIS REALLY IS AN ARTIFICIAL VIRUS...
...THEN EVEN THE BIGGEST HOSPITALS WON'T HAVE DRUGS TO TREAT IT.
Aciclov
Oselta
?
?
I'LL TREAT THEIR SYMPTOMS FOR THE TIME BEING...
KLAK
YOU HURRY UP AND MAKE A DEAL WITH THE ENEMY.
KLAK
TAKE-BAYASHI...
THERE'S NOTHING WE CAN DO.

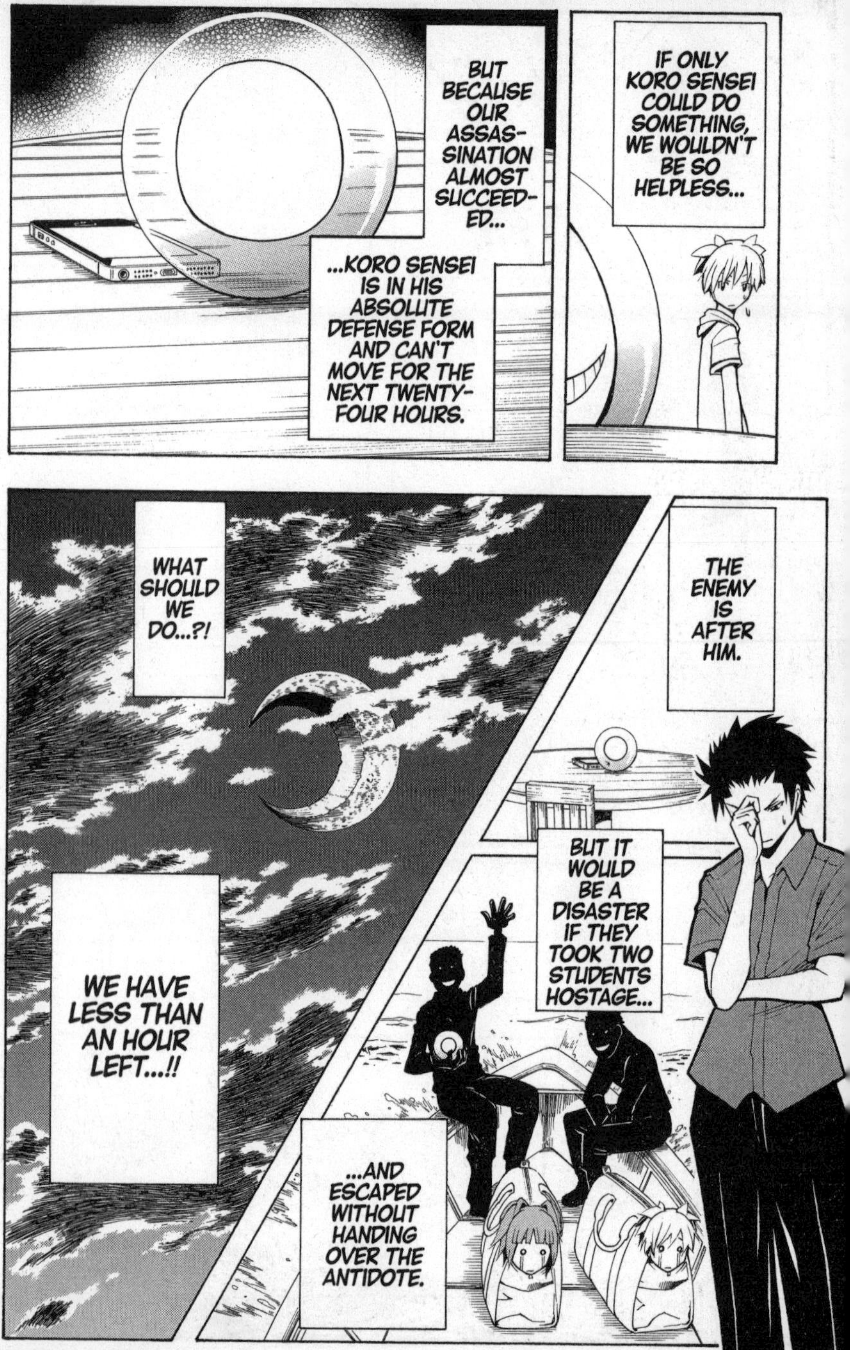
IF ONLY KORO SENSEI COULD DO SOMETHING, WE WOULDN'T BE SO HELPLESS...
BUT BECAUSE OUR ASSASSINATION ALMOST SUCCEEDED...
...KORO SENSEI IS IN HIS ABSOLUTE DEFENSE FORM AND CAN'T MOVE FOR THE NEXT TWENTY-FOUR HOURS.
THE ENEMY IS AFTER HIM.
BUT IT WOULD BE A DISASTER IF THEY TOOK TWO STUDENTS HOSTAGE...
...AND ESCAPED WITHOUT HANDING OVER THE ANTIDOTE.
WHAT SHOULD WE DO...?!
WE HAVE LESS THAN AN HOUR LEFT...!!

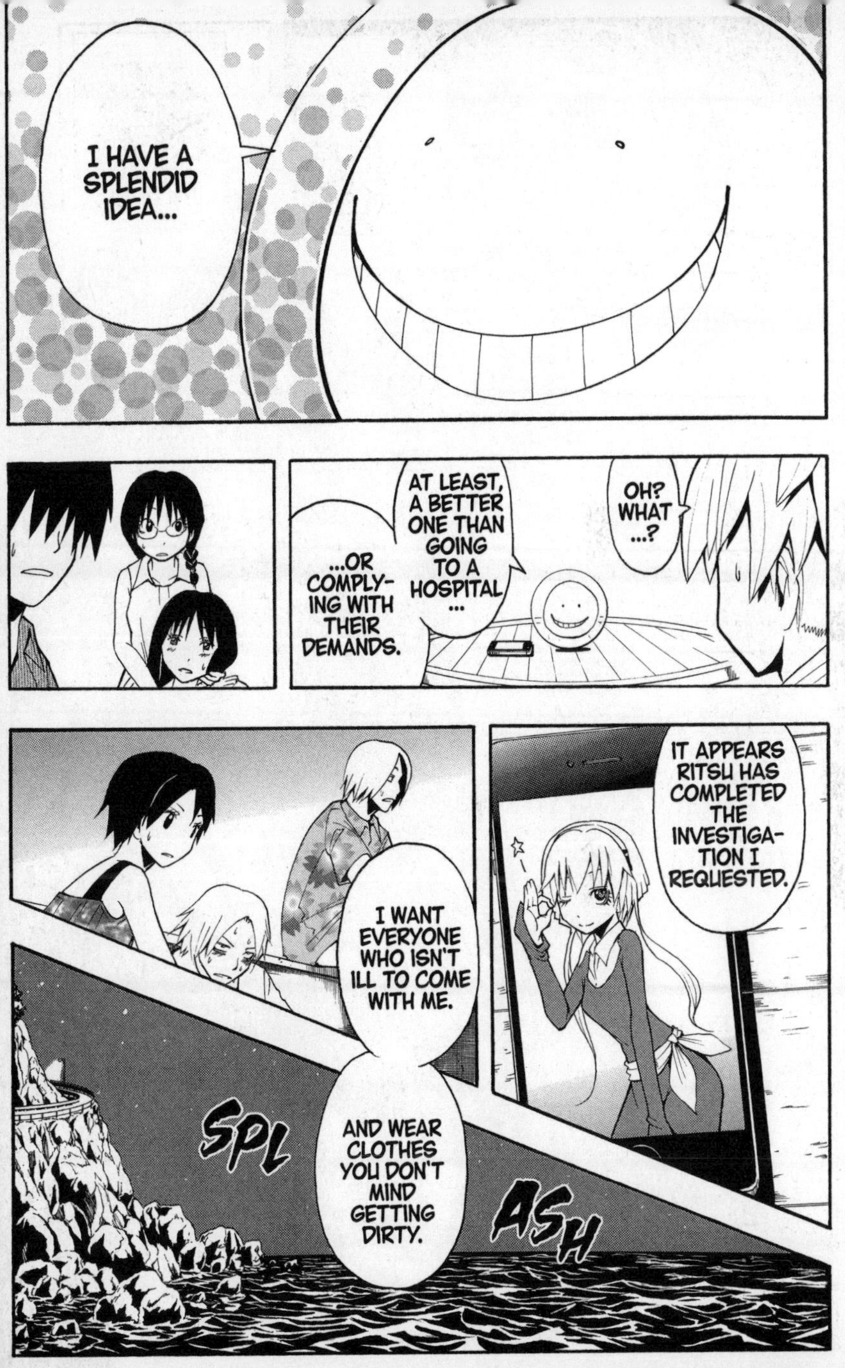
I HAVE A SPLENDID IDEA...
OH? WHAT ...?
AT LEAST, A BETTER ONE THAN GOING TO A HOSPITAL ...
...OR COMPLY-ING WITH THEIR DEMANDS.
IT APPEARS RITSU HAS COMPLETED THE INVESTIGA-TION I REQUESTED.
I WANT EVERYONE WHO ISN'T ILL TO COME WITH ME.
AND WEAR CLOTHES YOU DON'T MIND GETTING DIRTY.
SPLASH

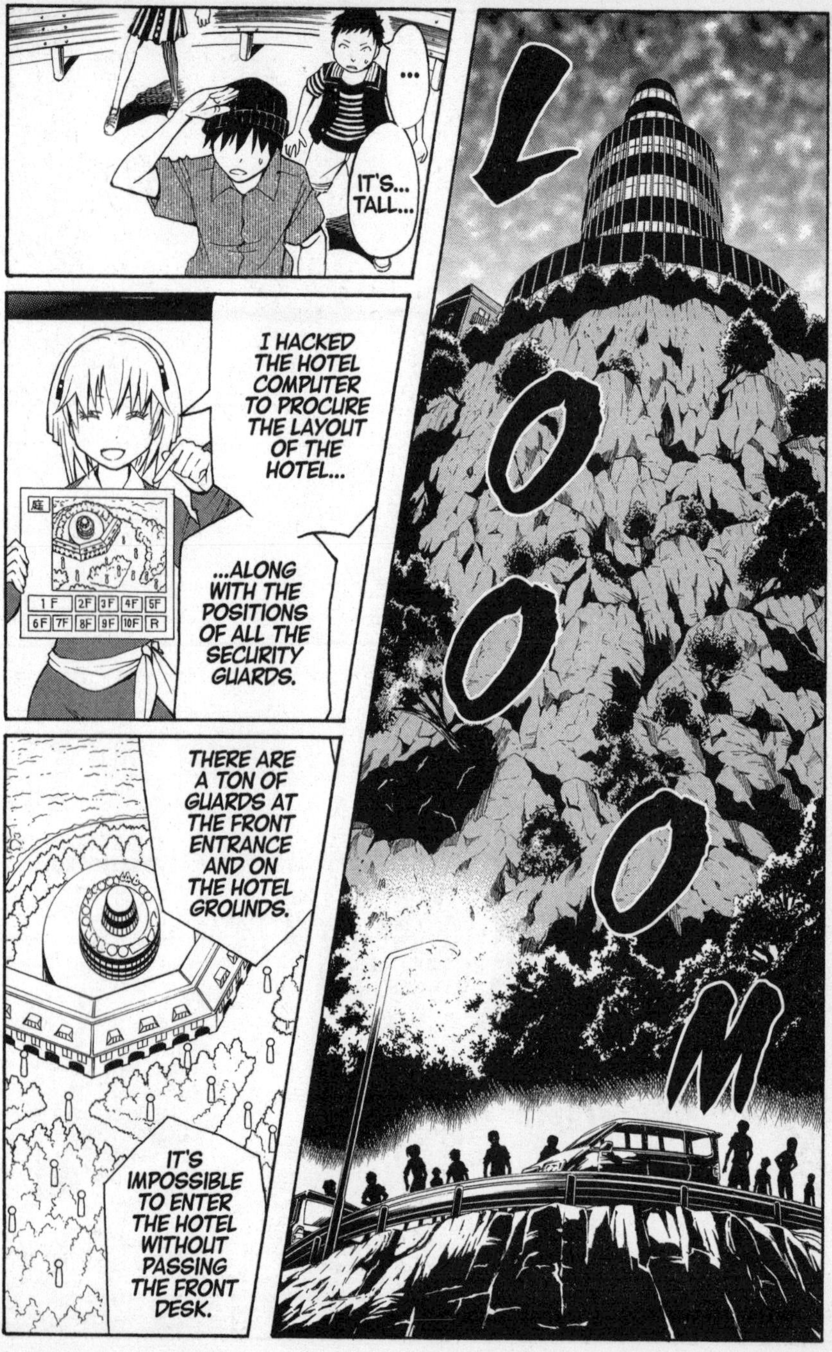
LOOOOM
...
IT'S... TALL...
I HACKED THE HOTEL COMPUTER TO PROCURE THE LAYOUT OF THE HOTEL...
庭
1F 2F 3F 4F 5F
6F 7F 8F 9F 10F R
...ALONG WITH THE POSITIONS OF ALL THE SECURITY GUARDS.
THERE ARE A TON OF GUARDS AT THE FRONT ENTRANCE AND ON THE HOTEL GROUNDS.
IT'S IMPOSSIBLE TO ENTER THE HOTEL WITHOUT PASSING THE FRONT DESK.

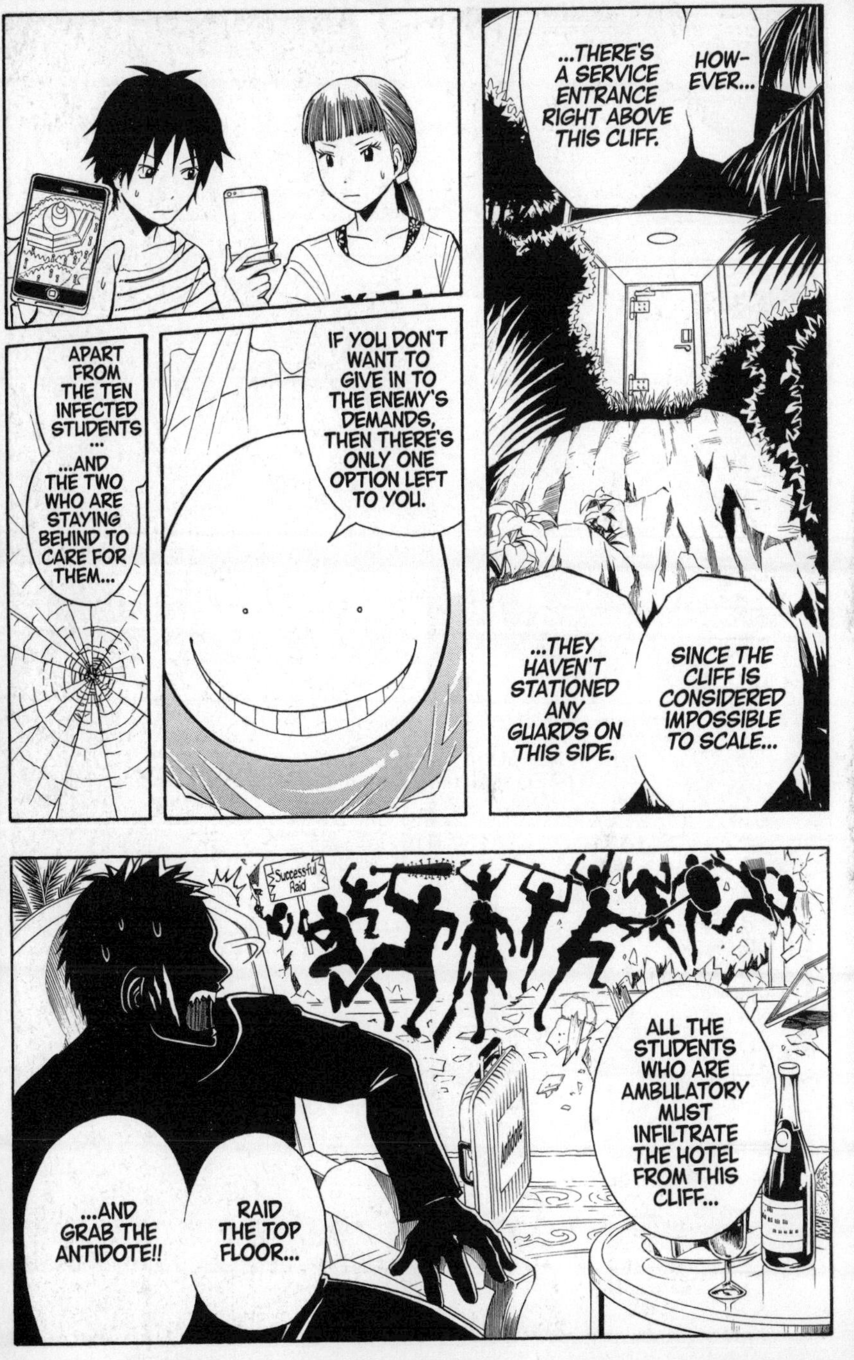
HOW-EVER...
...THERE'S A SERVICE ENTRANCE RIGHT ABOVE THIS CLIFF.
SINCE THE CLIFF IS CONSIDERED IMPOSSIBLE TO SCALE...
...THEY HAVEN'T STATIONED ANY GUARDS ON THIS SIDE.
IF YOU DON'T WANT TO GIVE IN TO THE ENEMY'S DEMANDS, THEN THERE'S ONLY ONE OPTION LEFT TO YOU.
APART FROM THE TEN INFECTED STUDENTS...
...AND THE TWO WHO ARE STAYING BEHIND TO CARE FOR THEM...
ALL THE STUDENTS WHO ARE AMBULATORY MUST INFILTRATE THE HOTEL FROM THIS CLIFF...
Successful Raid
Antidote
RAID THE TOP FLOOR...
...AND GRAB THE ANTIDOTE!!

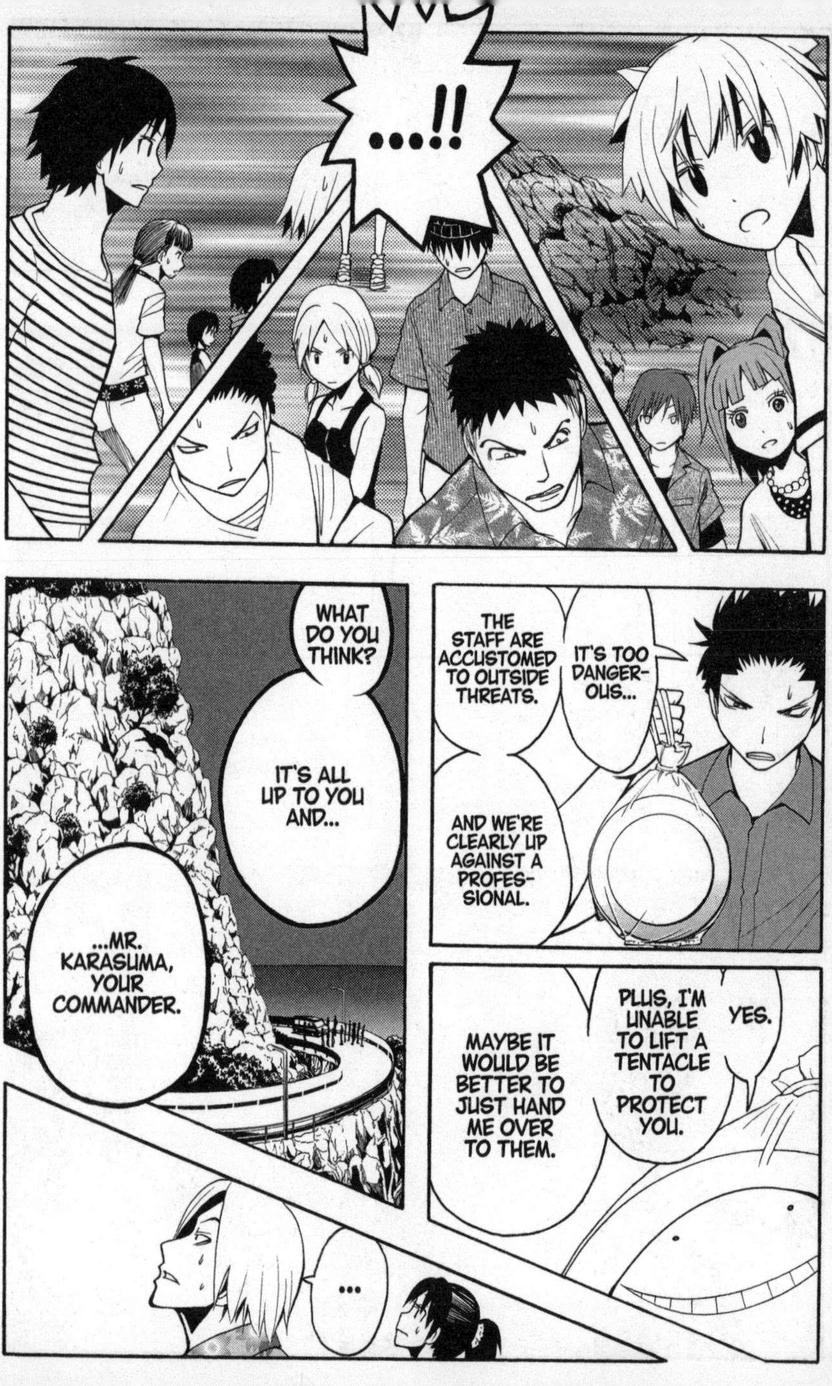
...!!
IT'S TOO DANGER-OUS...
THE STAFF ARE ACCUSTOMED TO OUTSIDE THREATS.
AND WE'RE CLEARLY UP AGAINST A PROFES-SIONAL.
YES.
PLUS, I'M UNABLE TO LIFT A TENTACLE TO PROTECT YOU.
MAYBE IT WOULD BE BETTER TO JUST HAND ME OVER TO THEM.
WHAT DO YOU THINK?
IT'S ALL UP TO YOU AND...
...MR. KARASUMA, YOUR COMMANDER.
...

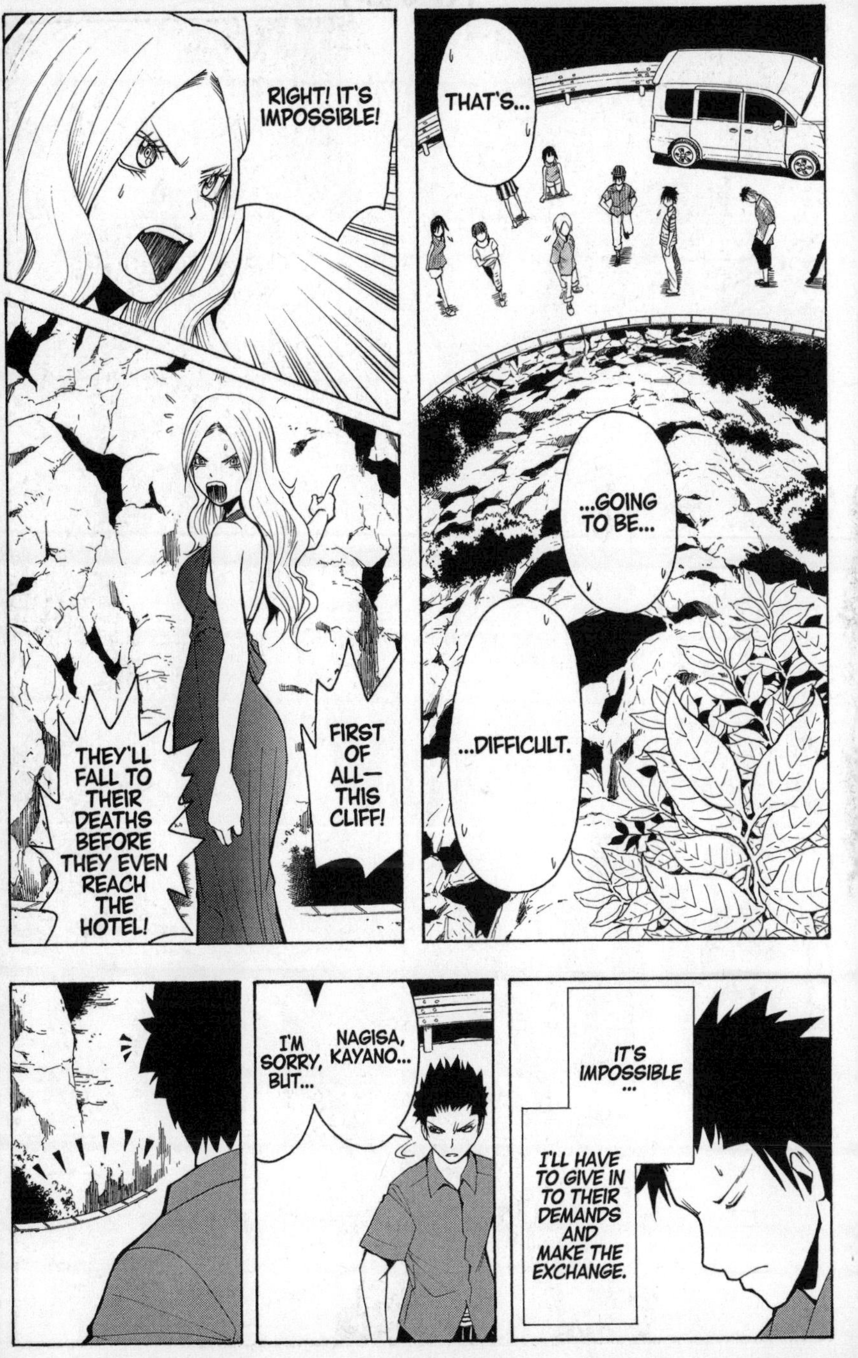
THAT'S...
...GOING TO BE...
...DIFFICULT.
RIGHT! IT'S IMPOSSIBLE!
FIRST OF ALL— THIS CLIFF!
THEY'LL FALL TO THEIR DEATHS BEFORE THEY EVEN REACH THE HOTEL!
IT'S IMPOSSIBLE...
I'LL HAVE TO GIVE IN TO THEIR DEMANDS AND MAKE THE EXCHANGE.
NAGISA, KAYANO... I'M SORRY, BUT...

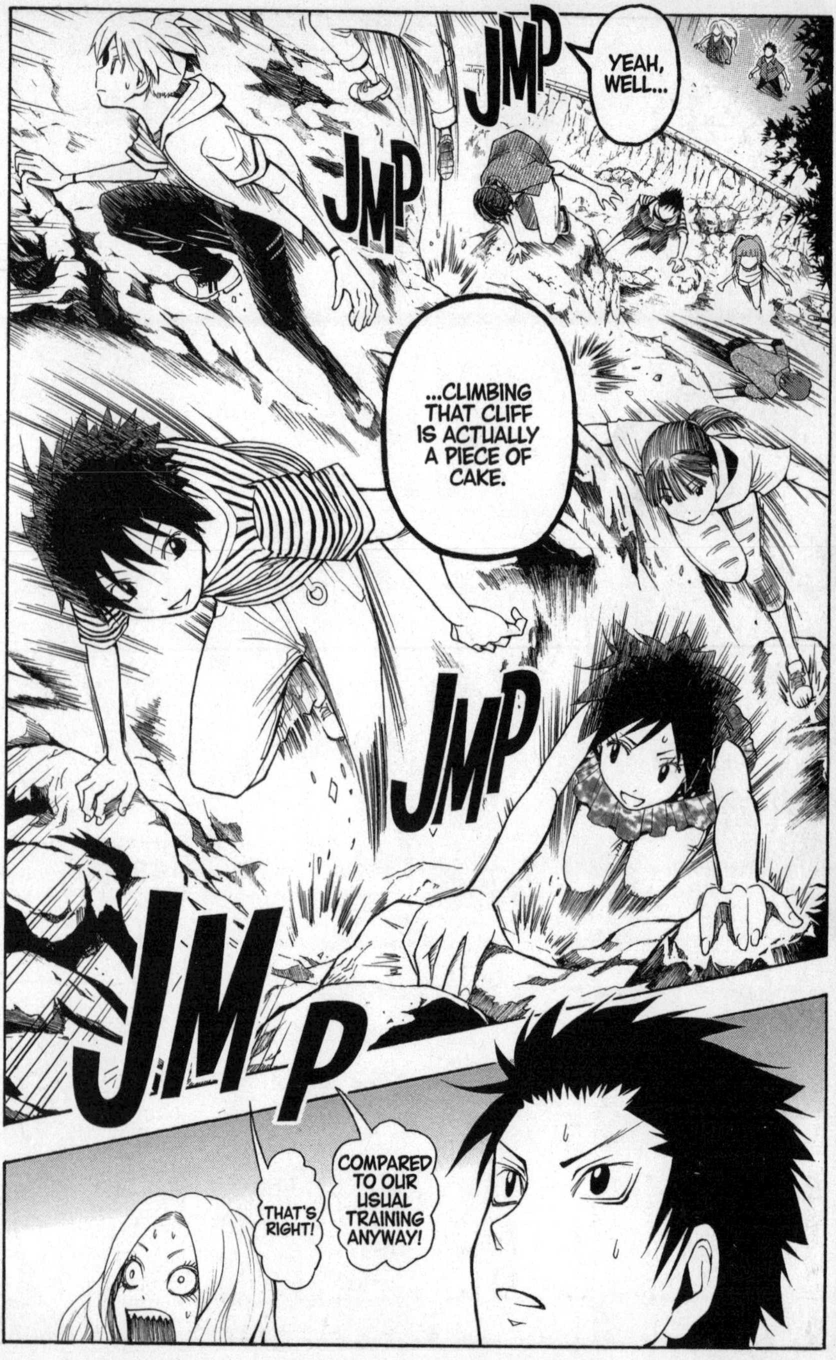
YEAH, WELL...
JMP
JMP
...CLIMBING THAT CLIFF IS ACTUALLY A PIECE OF CAKE.
JMP
JMP
COMPARED TO OUR USUAL TRAINING ANYWAY!
THAT'S RIGHT!

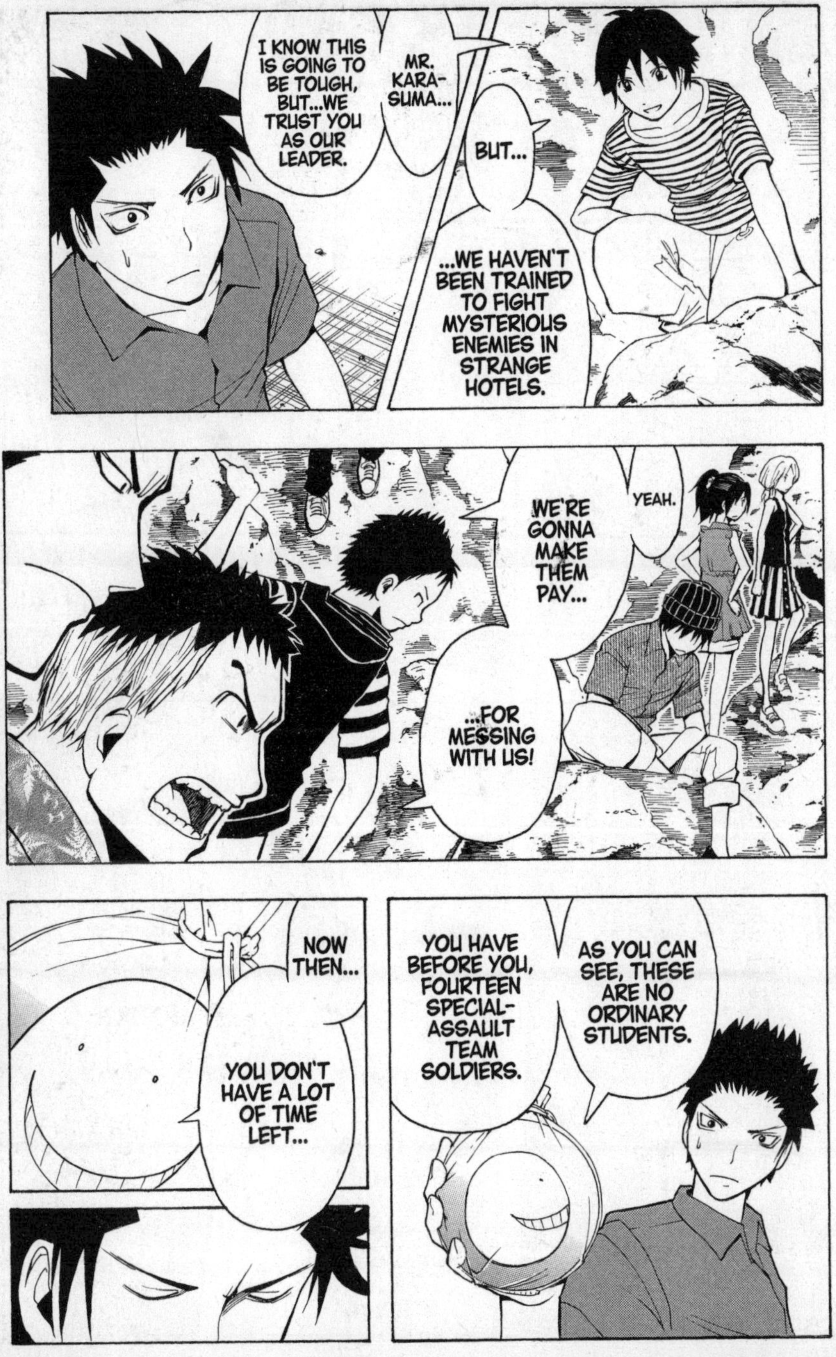
MR. KARA-SUMA...
BUT...
...WE HAVEN'T BEEN TRAINED TO FIGHT MYSTERIOUS ENEMIES IN STRANGE HOTELS.
I KNOW THIS IS GOING TO BE TOUGH, BUT...WE TRUST YOU AS OUR LEADER.
YEAH.
WE'RE GONNA MAKE THEM PAY...
...FOR MESSING WITH US!
AS YOU CAN SEE, THESE ARE NO ORDINARY STUDENTS.
YOU HAVE BEFORE YOU, FOURTEEN SPECIAL-ASSAULT TEAM SOLDIERS.
NOW THEN...
YOU DON'T HAVE A LOT OF TIME LEFT...

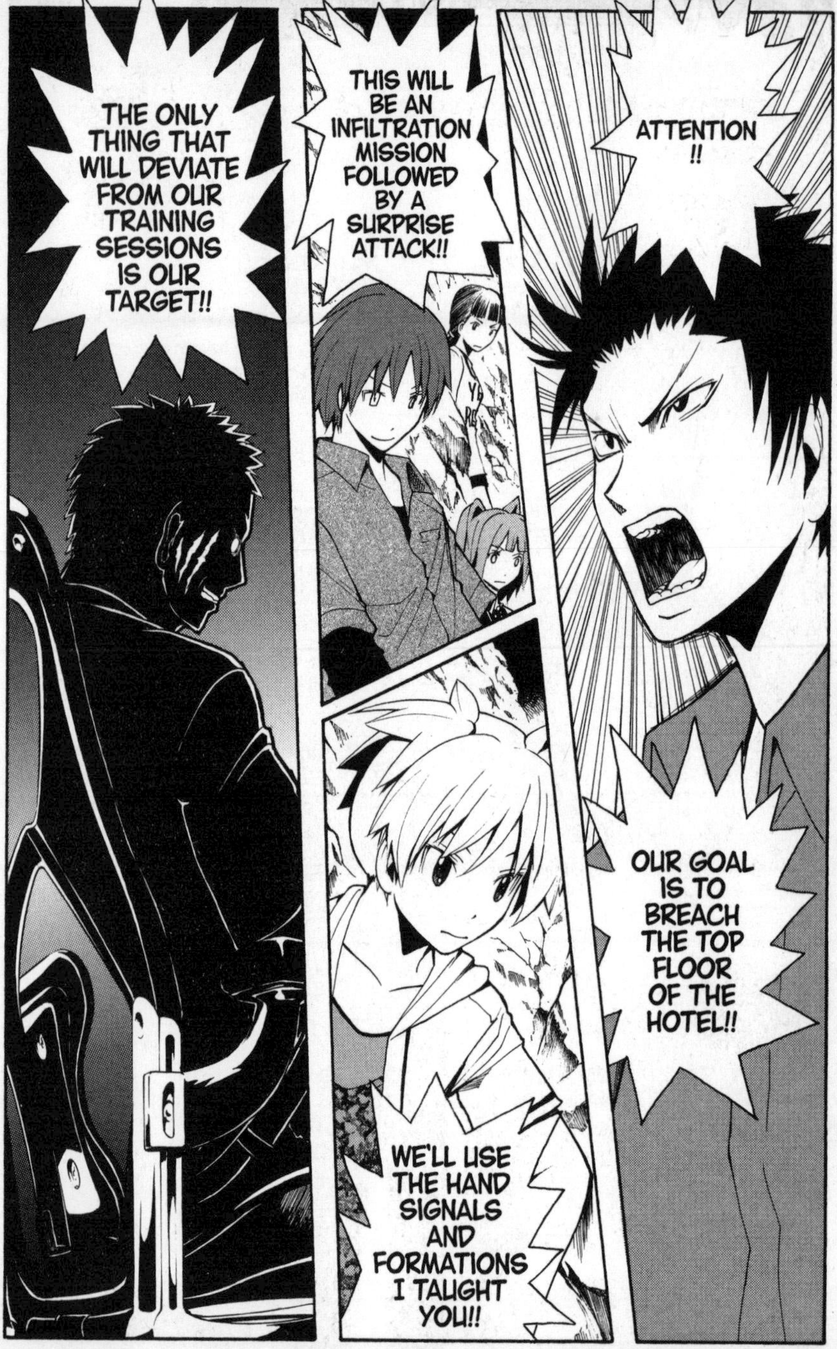
ATTENTION!!
OUR GOAL IS TO BREACH THE TOP FLOOR OF THE HOTEL!!
THIS WILL BE AN INFILTRATION MISSION FOLLOWED BY A SURPRISE ATTACK!!
WE'LL USE THE HAND SIGNALS AND FORMATIONS I TAUGHT YOU!!
THE ONLY THING THAT WILL DEVIATE FROM OUR TRAINING SESSIONS IS OUR TARGET!!

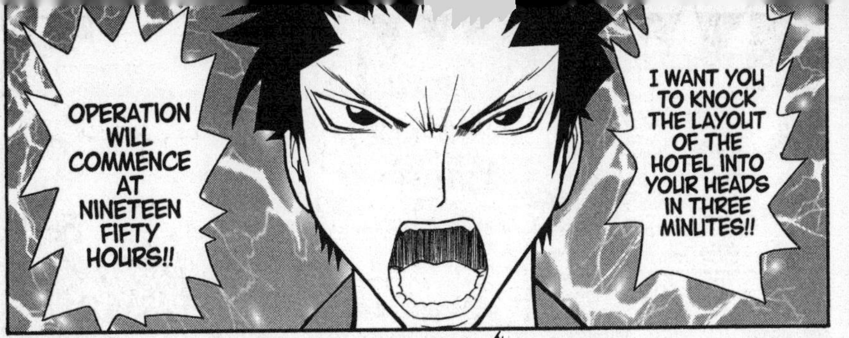
I WANT YOU TO KNOCK THE LAYOUT OF THE HOTEL INTO YOUR HEADS IN THREE MINUTES!!
OPERATION WILL COMMENCE AT NINETEEN FIFTY HOURS!!

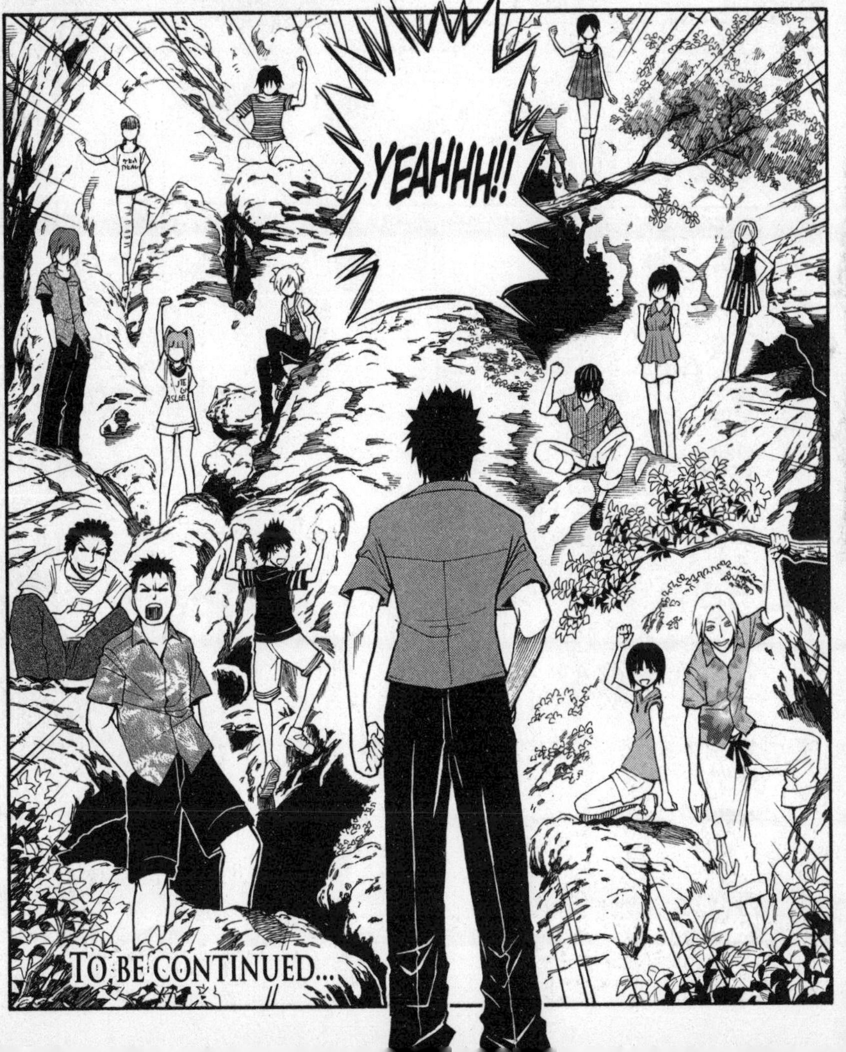
YEAHHH!!
TO BE CONTINUED...

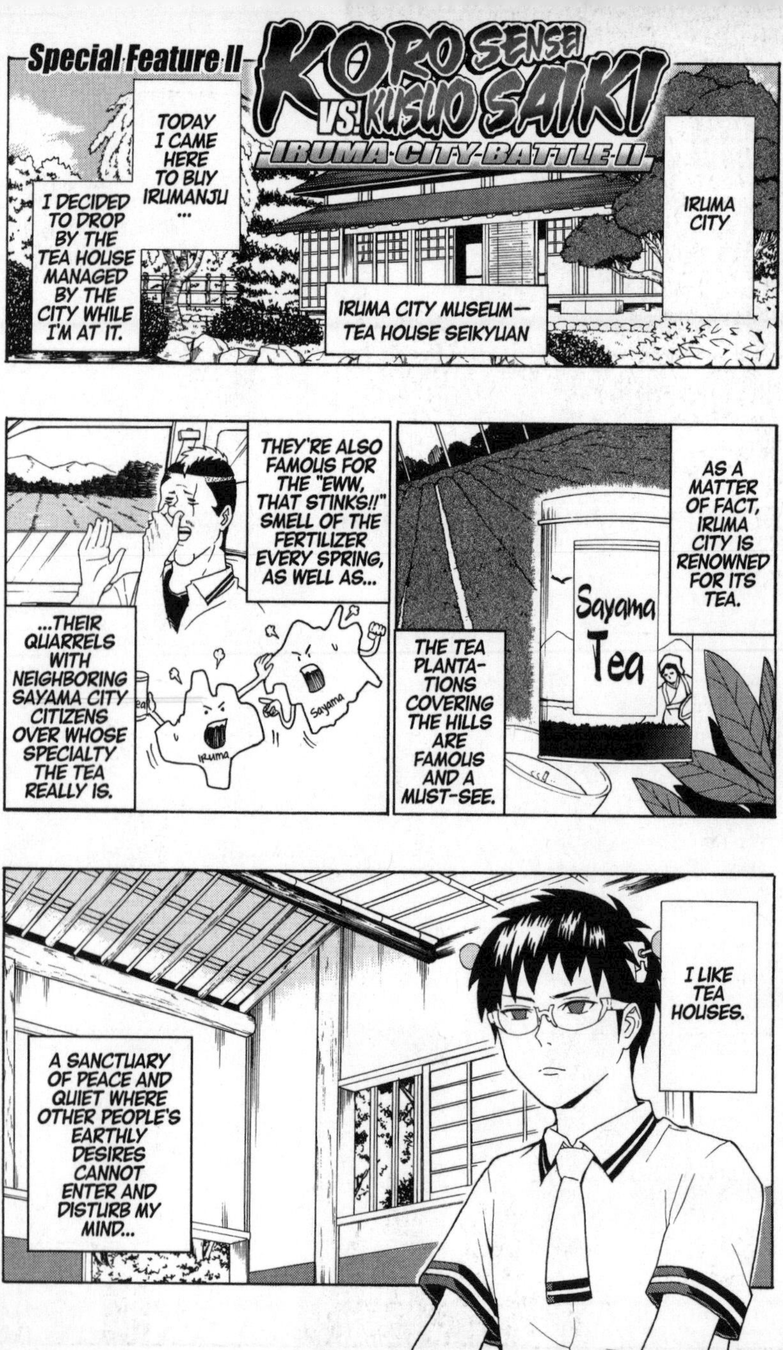
Special Feature II
KORO SENSEI VS. KUSUO SAIKI
-IRUMA CITY BATTLE II-
IRUMA CITY
IRUMA CITY MUSEUM— TEA HOUSE SEIKYUAN
TODAY I CAME HERE TO BUY IRUMANJU...
I DECIDED TO DROP BY THE TEA HOUSE MANAGED BY THE CITY WHILE I'M AT IT.
AS A MATTER OF FACT, IRUMA CITY IS RENOWNED FOR ITS TEA.
Sayama Tea
THE TEA PLANTATIONS COVERING THE HILLS ARE FAMOUS AND A MUST-SEE.
THEY'RE ALSO FAMOUS FOR THE "EWW, THAT STINKS!!" SMELL OF THE FERTILIZER EVERY SPRING, AS WELL AS...
Sayama
Iruma
...THEIR QUARRELS WITH NEIGHBORING SAYAMA CITY CITIZENS OVER WHOSE SPECIALTY THE TEA REALLY IS.
I LIKE TEA HOUSES.
A SANCTUARY OF PEACE AND QUIET WHERE OTHER PEOPLE'S EARTHLY DESIRES CANNOT ENTER AND DISTURB MY MIND...

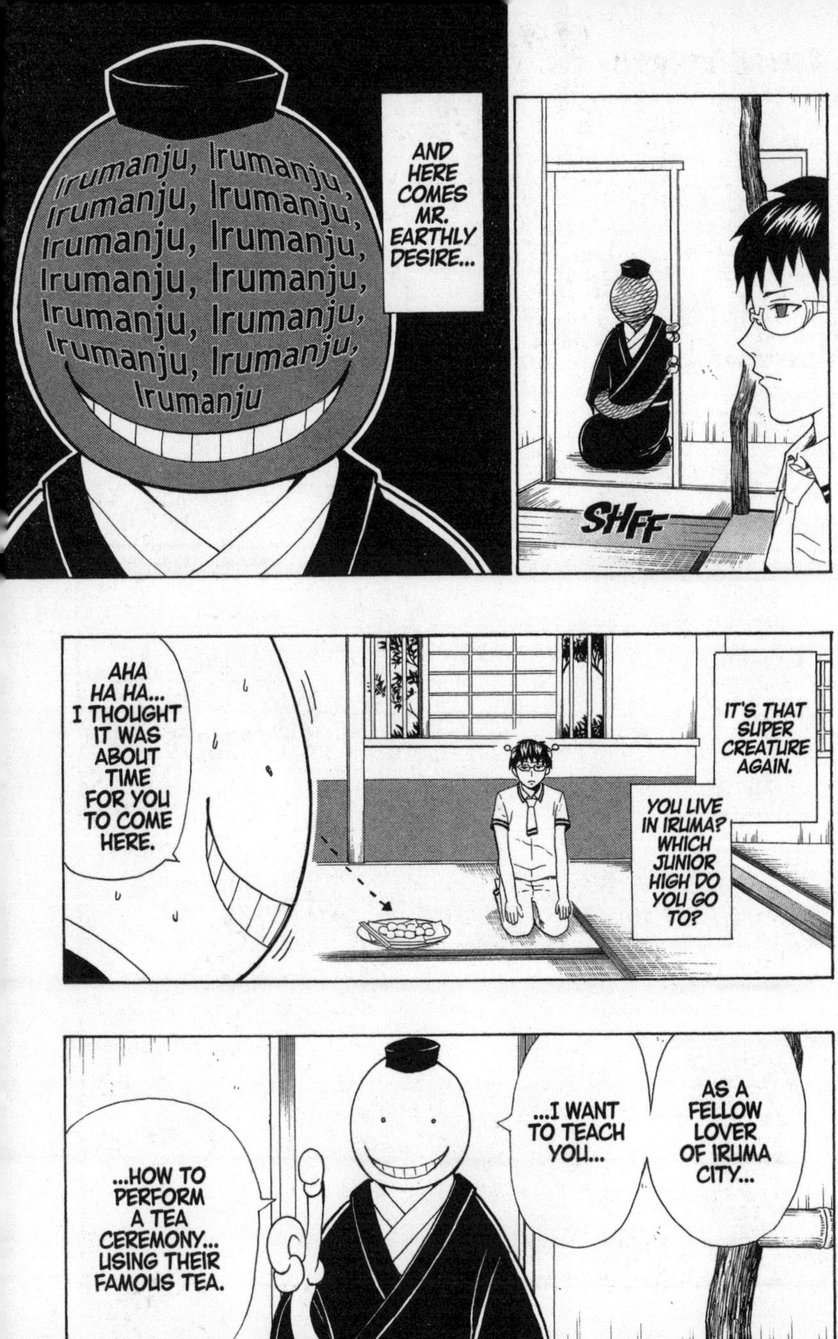
AND HERE COMES MR. EARTHLY DESIRE...
SHFF
Irumanju, Irumanju, Irumanju, Irumanju, Irumanju, Irumanju, Irumanju, Irumanju, Irumanju, Irumanju, Irumanju, Irumanju, Irumanju
IT'S THAT SUPER CREATURE AGAIN.
YOU LIVE IN IRUMA? WHICH JUNIOR HIGH DO YOU GO TO?
AHA HA HA... I THOUGHT IT WAS ABOUT TIME FOR YOU TO COME HERE.
AS A FELLOW LOVER OF IRUMA CITY...
...I WANT TO TEACH YOU...
...HOW TO PERFORM A TEA CEREMONY... USING THEIR FAMOUS TEA.

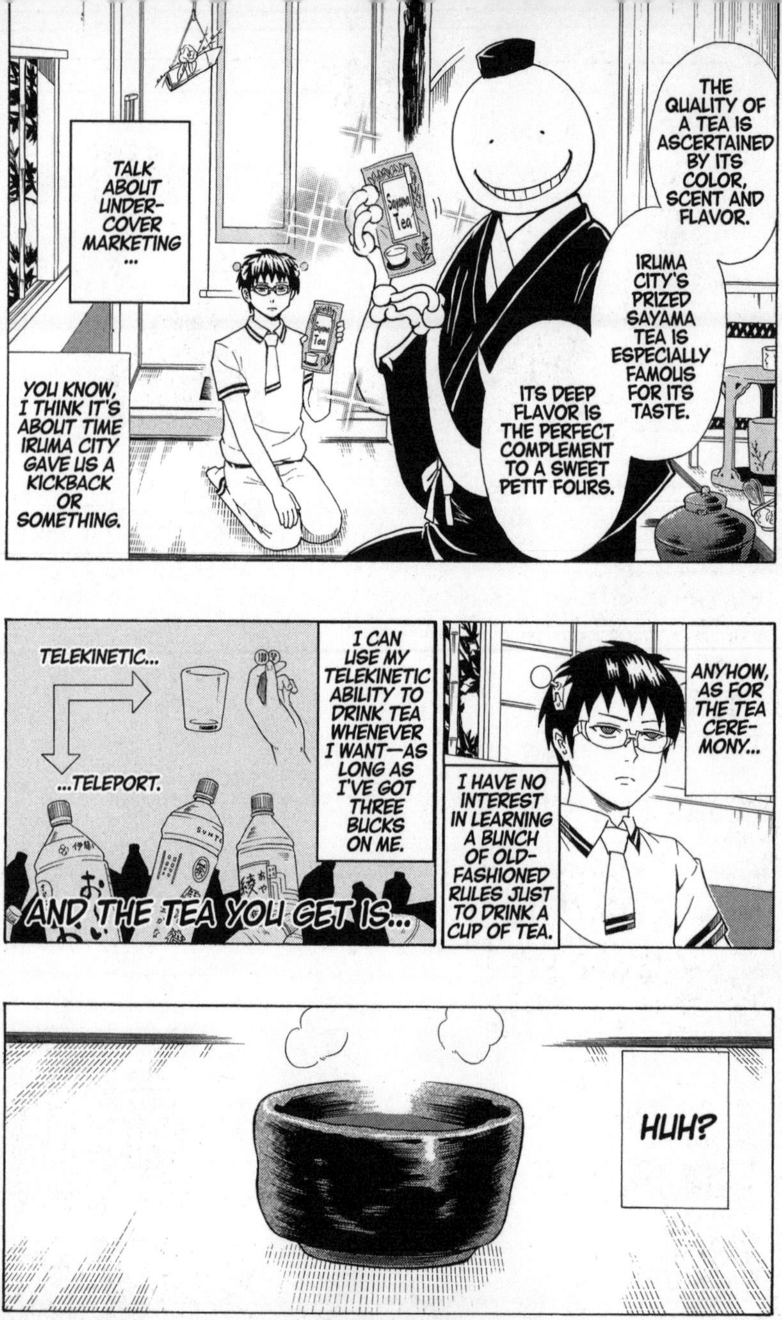
THE QUALITY OF A TEA IS ASCERTAINED BY ITS COLOR, SCENT AND FLAVOR.
IRUMA CITY'S PRIZED SAYAMA TEA IS ESPECIALLY FAMOUS FOR ITS TASTE.
ITS DEEP FLAVOR IS THE PERFECT COMPLEMENT TO A SWEET PETIT FOURS.
Sayama Tea
TALK ABOUT UNDER-COVER MARKETING...
YOU KNOW, I THINK IT'S ABOUT TIME IRUMA CITY GAVE US A KICKBACK OR SOMETHING.
ANYHOW, AS FOR THE TEA CERE-MONY...
I HAVE NO INTEREST IN LEARNING A BUNCH OF OLD-FASHIONED RULES JUST TO DRINK A CUP OF TEA.
I CAN USE MY TELEKINETIC ABILITY TO DRINK TEA WHENEVER I WANT—AS LONG AS I'VE GOT THREE BUCKS ON ME.
TELEKINETIC...
...TELEPORT.
AND THE TEA YOU GET IS...
HUH?

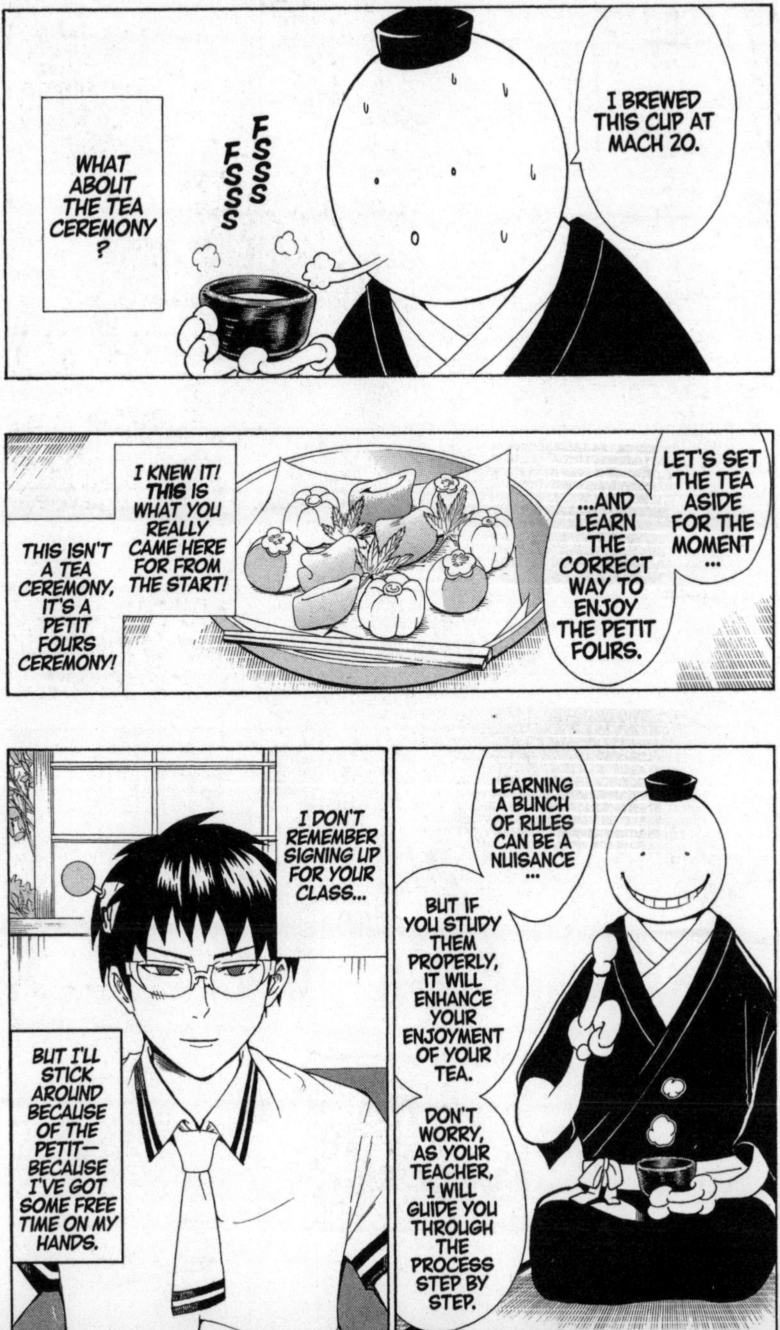
I BREWED THIS CUP AT MACH 20.
FSSS FSSS
WHAT ABOUT THE TEA CEREMONY?
LET'S SET THE TEA ASIDE FOR THE MOMENT...
...AND LEARN THE CORRECT WAY TO ENJOY THE PETIT FOURS.
I KNEW IT! THIS IS WHAT YOU REALLY CAME HERE FOR FROM THE START!
THIS ISN'T A TEA CEREMONY, IT'S A PETIT FOURS CEREMONY!
LEARNING A BUNCH OF RULES CAN BE A NUISANCE...
BUT IF YOU STUDY THEM PROPERLY, IT WILL ENHANCE YOUR ENJOYMENT OF YOUR TEA.
DON'T WORRY, AS YOUR TEACHER, I WILL GUIDE YOU THROUGH THE PROCESS STEP BY STEP.
I DON'T REMEMBER SIGNING UP FOR YOUR CLASS...
BUT I'LL STICK AROUND BECAUSE OF THE PETIT— BECAUSE I'VE GOT SOME FREE TIME ON MY HANDS.

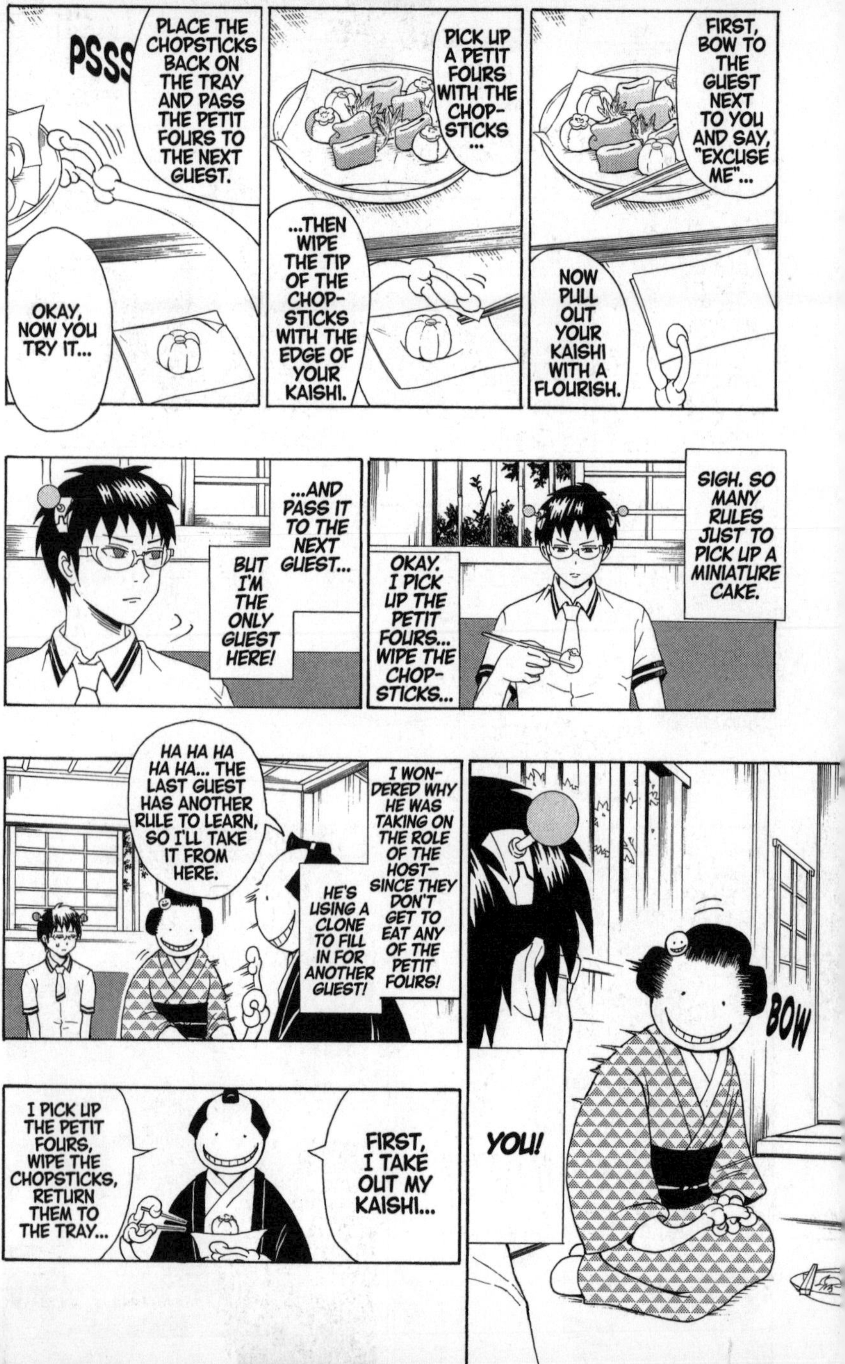
FIRST, BOW TO THE GUEST NEXT TO YOU AND SAY, "EXCUSE ME"...
NOW PULL OUT YOUR KAISHI WITH A FLOURISH.
PICK UP A PETIT FOURS WITH THE CHOP-STICKS ...
...THEN WIPE THE TIP OF THE CHOP-STICKS WITH THE EDGE OF YOUR KAISHI.
PSSS
PLACE THE CHOPSTICKS BACK ON THE TRAY AND PASS THE PETIT FOURS TO THE NEXT GUEST.
OKAY, NOW YOU TRY IT...
SIGH. SO MANY RULES JUST TO PICK UP A MINIATURE CAKE.
OKAY. I PICK UP THE PETIT FOURS... WIPE THE CHOP-STICKS...
...AND PASS IT TO THE NEXT GUEST...
BUT I'M THE ONLY GUEST HERE!
BOW
YOU!
I WONDERED WHY HE WAS TAKING ON THE ROLE OF THE HOST-SINCE THEY DON'T GET TO EAT ANY OF THE PETIT FOURS!
HA HA HA HA HA... THE LAST GUEST HAS ANOTHER RULE TO LEARN, SO I'LL TAKE IT FROM HERE.
HE'S USING A CLONE TO FILL IN FOR ANOTHER GUEST!
FIRST, I TAKE OUT MY KAISHI...
I PICK UP THE PETIT FOURS, WIPE THE CHOPSTICKS, RETURN THEM TO THE TRAY...

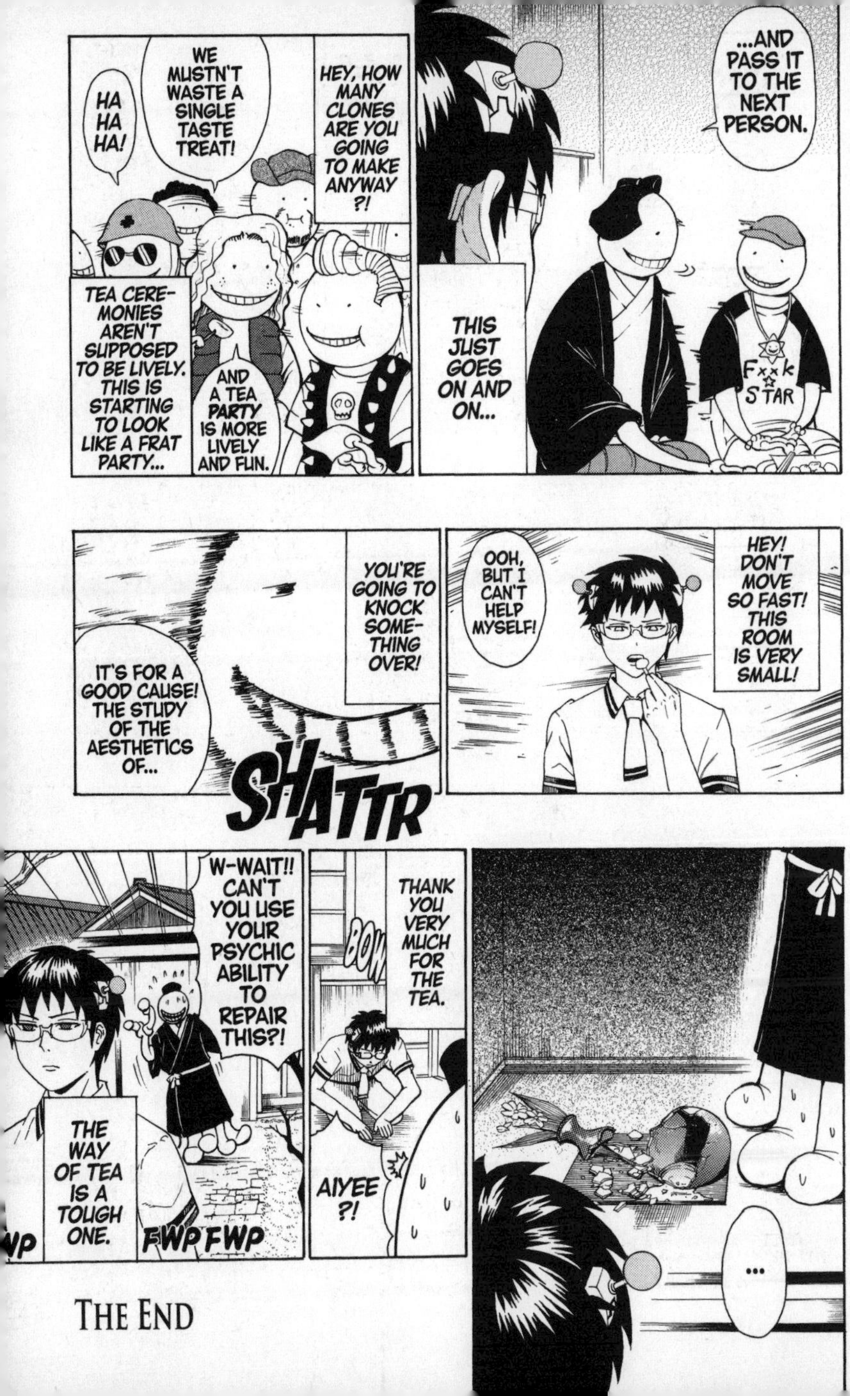
...AND PASS IT TO THE NEXT PERSON.
THIS JUST GOES ON AND ON...
Fxxk ☆ STAR
HEY, HOW MANY CLONES ARE YOU GOING TO MAKE ANYWAY?!
WE MUSTN'T WASTE A SINGLE TASTE TREAT!
HA HA HA!
TEA CERE-MONIES AREN'T SUPPOSED TO BE LIVELY. THIS IS STARTING TO LOOK LIKE A FRAT PARTY...
AND A TEA PARTY IS MORE LIVELY AND FUN.
HEY! DON'T MOVE SO FAST! THIS ROOM IS VERY SMALL!
OOH, BUT I CAN'T HELP MYSELF!
YOU'RE GOING TO KNOCK SOME-THING OVER!
IT'S FOR A GOOD CAUSE! THE STUDY OF THE AESTHETICS OF...
SHATTR
...
THANK YOU VERY MUCH FOR THE TEA.
BOW
AIYEE?!
W-WAIT!! CAN'T YOU USE YOUR PSYCHIC ABILITY TO REPAIR THIS?!
THE WAY OF TEA IS A TOUGH ONE.
FWP FWP

THE END

In Japan, Vol.7 comes in two editions. There's the ordinary edition like the one you're currently holding and the Anime DVD Bundle Edition, which comes with a different cover illustration and some new pages. Since this series began, many people have been supporting it through various projects, collaborations and products. I can't thank them enough.

Because of Koro Sensei's simple design, I start thinking, "Maybe I can ask them to do a collaboration with Koro Sensei!" whenever I see a round shape in town. But...I'll keep working diligently and rein in my greed.

—Yusei Matsui

Yusei Matsui was born on the last day of January in Saitama Prefecture, Japan. He has been drawing manga since elementary school. Some of his favorite manga series are *Bobobo-bo Bo-bobo*, *JoJo's Bizarre Adventure* and *Ultimate Muscle*. Matsui learned his trade working as an assistant to manga artist Yoshio Sawai, creator of *Bobobo-bo Bo-bobo*. In 2005, Matsui debuted his original manga *Neuro: Supernatural Detective* in *Weekly Shonen Jump*. In 2007, *Neuro* was adapted into an anime. In 2012, *Assassination Classroom* began serialization in *Weekly Shonen Jump*.

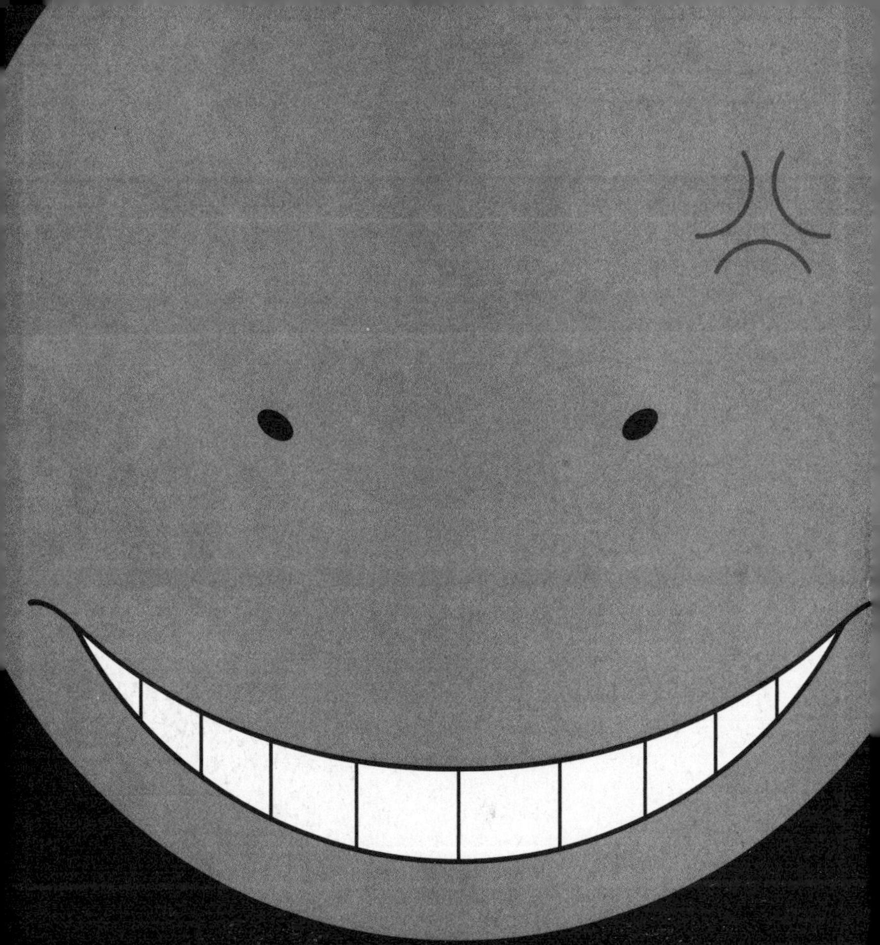

When he's bright red, he's angry. His face turns this color if you interrupt his class or eat the snacks he's been hiding.
Rating: kinda angry

ASSASSINATION CLASSROOM

YUSEI MATSUI

7

ON ISLAND TIME

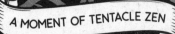

A MOMENT OF TENTACLE ZEN

We won't let him go home
empty–tentacled!

– Olympic Athlete Koro Sensei

ASSASSINATION CLASSROOM

Volume 7
SHONEN JUMP ADVANCED Manga Edition

Story and Art by YUSEI MATSUI

Translation/Tetsuichiro Miyaki
English Adaptation/Bryant Turnage
Touch-up Art & Lettering/Stephen Dutro
Cover & Interior Design/Sam Elzway
Editor/Annette Roman

Printed in the U.S.A.

Published by VIZ Media, LLC
P.O. Box 77010
San Francisco, CA 94107

10 9 8 7 6 5 4 3 2 1
First printing, December 2015

www.viz.com

www.shonenjump.com

RATED T+ FOR OLDER TEEN

PARENTAL ADVISORY
ASSASSINATION CLASSROOM is rated T+ for Older Teen and is recommended for ages 16 and up. It contains realistic violence and suggestive situations.

ratings.viz.com

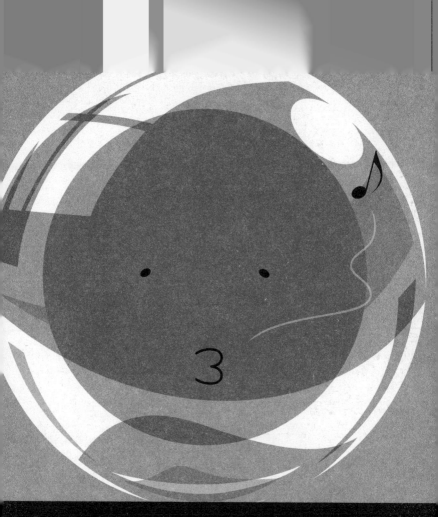

The 3-E students storm the lair of the enemy, who has launched a deadly biological attack. But blocking their path are three master assassins: Smog, Grip and Gastro, who excel, respectively, in the use of poison, brute strength and firearms. With their teacher Karasuma down, Karma and his friends face terrible odds! And then they discover the

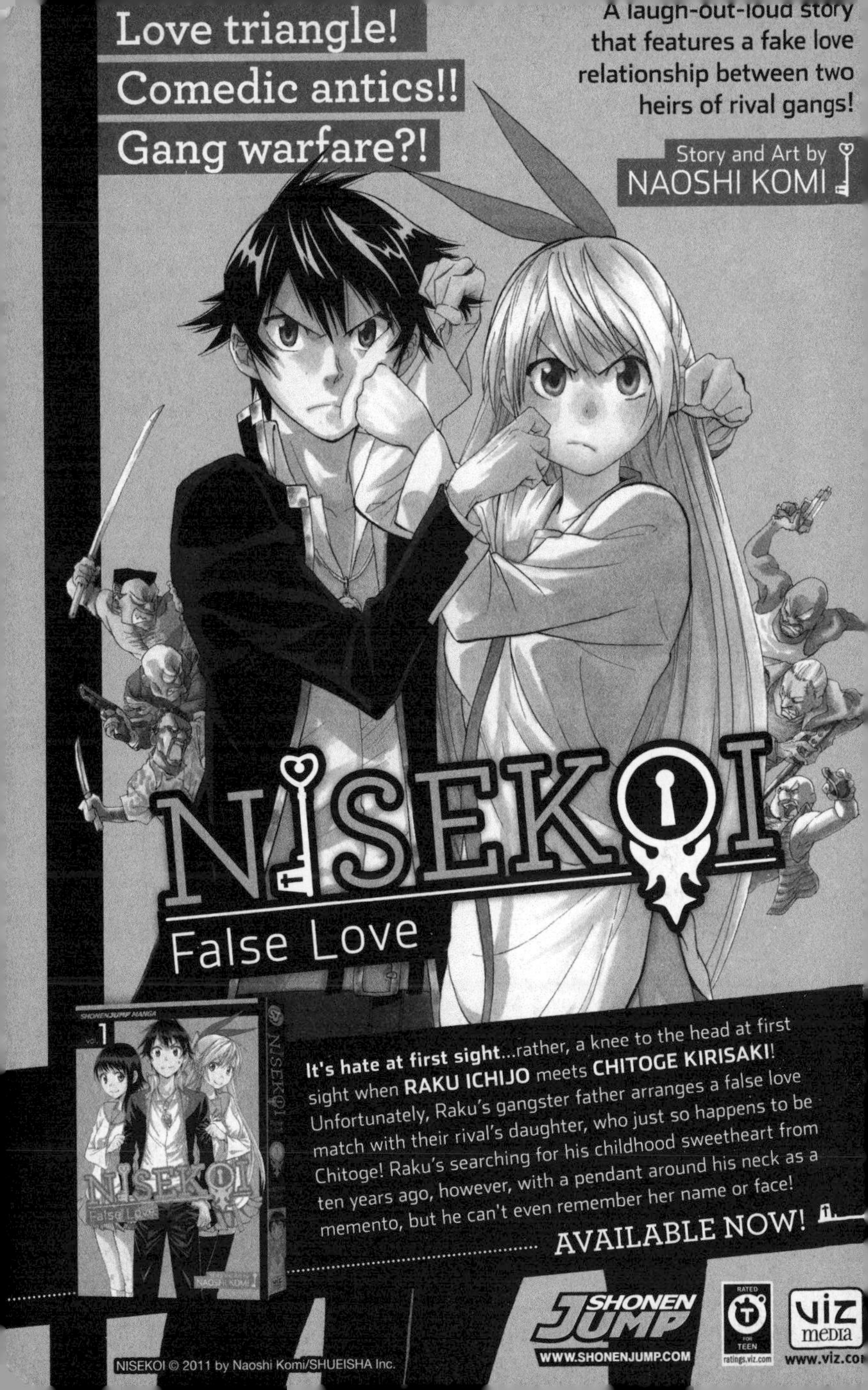
Love triangle!
Comedic antics!!
Gang warfare?!
A laugh-out-loud story that features a fake love relationship between two heirs of rival gangs!
Story and Art by NAOSHI KOMI
NISEKOI
False Love
SHONEN JUMP MANGA
vol. 1
NISEKOI False Love
NAOSHI KOMI
It's hate at first sight...rather, a knee to the head at first sight when RAKU ICHIJO meets CHITOGE KIRISAKI! Unfortunately, Raku's gangster father arranges a false love match with their rival's daughter, who just so happens to be Chitoge! Raku's searching for his childhood sweetheart from ten years ago, however, with a pendant around his neck as a memento, but he can't even remember her name or face!
AVAILABLE NOW!
SHONEN JUMP
WWW.SHONENJUMP.COM
RATED T FOR TEEN
ratings.viz.com
viz media
www.viz.co
NISEKOI © 2011 by Naoshi Komi/SHUEISHA Inc.

You're Reading in the Wrong Direction!!

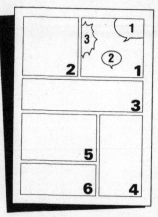

Whoops! Guess what? You're starting at the wrong end of the comic!

…It's true! In keeping with the original Japanese format, **Assassination Classroom** is meant to be read from right to left, starting in the upper-right corner.

Unlike English, which is read from left to right, Japanese is read from right to left, meaning that action, sound effects and word-balloon order are completely reversed… something which can make readers unfamiliar with Japanese feel pretty backwards themselves. For this reason, manga or Japanese comics published in the U.S. in English have sometimes been published "flopped"—that is, printed in exact reverse order, as though seen from the other side of a mirror.

By flopping pages, U.S. publishers can avoid confusing readers, but the compromise is not without its downside. For one thing, a character in a flopped manga series who once wore in the original Japanese version a T-shirt emblazoned with "M A Y" (as in "the merry month of") now wears one which reads "Y A M"! Additionally, many manga creators in Japan are themselves unhappy with the process, as some feel the mirror-imaging of their art skews their original intentions.

We are proud to bring you Yusei Matsui's **Assasssination Classroom** in the original unflopped format.

For now, though, turn to the other side of the book and let the adventure begin…!

—Editor